LEARN, TEACH...

SUCCEED...

With **REA's ICTS** test prep,
you'll be in a class all your own.

WE'D LIKE TO HEAR FROM YOU!
Visit **www.rea.com** to send us your comments
or email us at **info@rea.com**

MEET THE TEAM BEHIND
THE BEST TEST PREP FOR THE ICTS

The best minds to help you get the best ICTS scores

In this book, you'll find our commitment to excellence, an enthusiasm for the subject matter, and an unrivaled ability to help you master the ICTS. REA's dedication to excellence and our passion for education make this book the very best test prep for the ICTS.

Al Davis, M.S., M.A., teaches mathematics in the public schools (grades 1–5) in Champaign, Illinois. He previously taught English and business writing at the University of Illinois at Urbana-Champaign. He has written extensively on education problems, among many other subjects. His most recent book is *101 Things You Didn't Know about Shakespeare*, with Janet Ware. He received his M.S. from the University of Illinois, and he passed the ICTS tests in 2002.

David M. Myton, Ph.D., is Chair, School of Education, and Associate Professor of Chemistry and Education at Lake Superior State University. Dr. Myton received his Ph.D. and M.S.T. from Portland State University. His areas of specialty include teacher education and environmental chemistry.

Renay M. Scott, Ph.D., is Chair, Teacher Education and Professional Development at Central Michigan University. She has served as a social studies teacher in middle and high school. She is currently the President of the Michigan Council for the Social Studies and a former Social Studies Educator of the Year. Dr. Scott has written numerous articles and given numerous presentations on social studies education, methodology and curriculum.

Karen Bondarchuk, M.F.A., teaches in the Foundation Art Program at Western Michigan University. She has been very active in elementary art education. She developed and taught the art program at The Montessori School in Kalamazoo, Michigan, and has taught private and public art lessons to children for many years. She received her M.F.A. from Ohio State University and her B.F.A. from Nova Scotia College of Art and Design in Halifax, Nova Scotia.

John A. Lychner, Ph.D., is Associate Professor of Music Education at Western Michigan University. He has taught in public schools in St. Louis County, Missouri and in Tallahassee, Florida. His Ph.D. is from Florida State University in Music Education. In addition to his work with instrumentalists, he has taught 6th and 7th grade general music and has had numerous articles published in academic music journals.

Janet E. Rubin, Ph.D., is Professor of Theatre and Chair of the Department of Theatre at Saginaw Valley State University. She has served as national president of the American Alliance for Theatre and Education and has received several prestigious research awards from her university. Dr. Rubin has shared her work through numerous publications and national and international presentations.

Ellen R. Van't Hof, M.A., received an M.A. in Communication Arts and Sciences/Dance from Western Michigan University. She did post-master's work in a doctoral dance education program at Temple University. Since 1976 she has been a professor of dance at Calvin College in Grand Rapids, Michigan, and is now the director of Calvin's dance program. She has presented at many state, national, and international dance conferences on the topics of dance education, dance history, integrated arts, Multiple Intelligence Theory, and sacred dance.

Nelson Maylone Ph.D., is Assistant Professor of Educational Psychology at Eastern Michigan University. He has served as a middle grades and high school mathematics teacher, and an elementary and middle school administrator. He is a former NASA NEWMAST fellow. His doctoral dissertation, which examined the relationship between school district socioeconomic status and student achievement, won the Midwest Dissertation of the Year award from Phi Delta Kappa in 2002.

Ginny Muller, Ph.D., is Associate Professor of Teacher Education at Saginaw Valley State University. She has served as a classroom teacher and a curriculum consultant at the preschool, elementary, and middle school levels. Her doctoral dissertation, which examined the relationship between successful language acquisition and reading success in a cleft palate population, won the Robert Fox Award for academic excellence at the University of Michigan.

ICTS

ILLINOIS CERTIFICATION TESTING SYSTEM

BASIC SKILLS TEST (096) & ELEMENTARY/MIDDLE GRADES TEST (110)

TestWare® Edition

Edited By
Al Davis, M.S., M.A.

Research & Education Association
Visit our Educator Support Center: www.rea.com/teacher
Updates to the test and this book: www.rea.com/icts.htm

The ICTS tests were developed and are administered by the Illinois State Board of Education and Pearson Education, Inc.

Research & Education Association
61 Ethel Road West
Piscataway, New Jersey 08854
E-mail: info@rea.com

**The Best Teachers' Test Preparation for the
ICTS Basic Skills and Elementary/Middle Grades Tests
With TestWare® on CD-ROM**

REA® and TestWare® are registered trademarks of Research & Education Association, Inc.

D10-0101

CONTENTS

BASIC SKILLS REVIEW

CHAPTER 1: READING COMPREHENSION   1

CHAPTER 2: LANGUAGE ARTS   33

CHAPTER 3: WRITING ASSIGNMENT   79

Contents

ELEMENTARY/MIDDLE GRADES REVIEW

About Research & Education Association

Founded in 1959, Research & Education Association is dedicated to publishing the finest and most effective educational materials—including software, study guides, and test preps—for students in middle school, high school, college, graduate school, and beyond.

REA's Test Preparation series includes books and software for all academic levels in almost all disciplines. Research & Education Association publishes test preps for students who have not yet entered high school, as well as for high school students preparing to enter college. Students from countries around the world seeking to attend college in the United States will find the assistance they need in REA's publications. For college students seeking advanced degrees, REA publishes test preps for many major graduate school admission examinations in a wide variety of disciplines, including engineering, law, and medicine. Students at every level, in every field, with every ambition can find what they are looking for among REA's publications.

REA's practice tests are always based upon the most recently administered exams and include every type of question that you can expect on the actual exams.

REA's publications and educational materials are highly regarded and continually receive an unprecedented amount of praise from professionals, instructors, librarians, parents, and students. Our authors are as diverse as the fields represented in the books we publish. They are well-known in their respective disciplines and serve on the faculties of prestigious high schools, colleges, and universities throughout the United States and Canada.

Today, REA's wide-ranging catalog is a leading resource for teachers, students, and professionals.

We invite you to visit us at *www.rea.com* to find out how "REA is making the world smarter."

Acknowledgments

We would like to thank REA's Larry B. Kling, Vice President, Editorial, for supervising development; Pam Weston, Vice President, Publishing, for setting the quality standards for production integrity and managing the publication to completion; John Paul Cording, Vice President, Technology, for coordinating the design, development, and testing of REA's TestWare® software; Kathleen Casey, Senior Editor, for preflight editorial review; Diane Goldschmidt, Senior Editor and Alice Leonard, Senior Editor, for post-production quality assurance; Project Manager Heena Patel for her software testing efforts; Rachel DiMatteo, Graphic Artist, for interior page design; and Christine Saul, Senior Graphic Artist, for cover design.

We also gratefully acknowledge Julie O'Connell for editing, Terry Casey Indexing for the index, and Caragraphics for page composition.

ICTS

Illinois Certification Testing System

Introduction

Learn...
Teach...
Succeed...

With this book in hand, you've taken an important step toward becoming a certified teacher in the state of Illinois. REA's all-new **ICTS** test prep for the Basic Skills and Elementary/Middle Grades tests is designed to help you get into an Illinois classroom. The instructive chapters in this book provide complete coverage of the **ICTS** with in-depth reviews of every topic and area you can expect to encounter on exam day. Full-length practice tests carefully modeled after actual ICTS exams will hone your test-taking teacher skills. All practice test questions are explained in thorough detail to provide you with a greater understanding of the exams' content and difficulty. When you finish preparing with this book, you will be well equipped with all the knowledge, practice, and strategies needed to succeed on these important exams.

THE ICTS TESTS AND YOU

Who takes the Basic Skills and Elementary/Middle Grades tests and what are they used for?

While passing the ICTS alone is not sufficient to earn certification to teach in Illinois, it is also true that, except for qualified out-of-state candidates, successful completion of courses of study must include your passing the Basic Skills test and a content-area test such as the Elementary/Middle Grades test.

The Illinois Certification Testing System tests are aligned with the Illinois professional teaching and content-area standards for educators. The ICTS tests are the only tests accepted for certification in Illinois.

The Basic Skills Test (096) consists of 125 multiple choice questions in Reading Comprehension, Language Arts, and Mathematics (which makes up 85% of the test) and a written essay response (which is 15% of the score). The Basic Skills Test is required if you:

- Want to get the **Early Childhood**, **Elementary**, **Secondary**, or **Special Teaching** certificates [alongside the appropriate content-area test(s), and the appropriate Assessment of Professional Teaching (APT) test].

- Want to get a **School Service Personnel or Administrative Certificate** [alongside the appropriate content-area test(s)].

- Are a teacher in an **alternative route program** [alongside the appropriate content-area test, after which you are given a Provisional Alternative Teaching Certificate.

- Seek admission into an **Illinois-approved educator preparation program** [you must successfully complete the Basic Skills test before being admitted to the program]. Each candidate in an Illinois-approved educator preparation program must successfully complete the appropriate content-area test before becoming certified. Universities may require successful completion of the appropriate content-area test prior to student teaching.

The Elementary/Middle Grades Test (110) assesses knowledge and skills required of entry-level educators in Illinois.

This test has 125 multiple-choice questions and it is also scored on a 100 to 300 point scale, with a passing score of 240 or above. The following list details the subareas and approximate numbers of questions per area:

I.	Language Arts and Literacy	21 to 30 questions
II.	Mathematics	11 to 20 questions
III.	Science	11 to 20 questions
IV.	Social Sciences	21 to 30 questions
V.	The Arts, Health, and Physical Education	11 to 20 questions

The test's objectives, which are also included in this book, are listed at *www.icts.nesinc.com*. Also, for more information about who needs to take this test, see the Illinois State Board of Education's Certification website at *http://www.isbe.net/teachers.htm*.

Details on ICTS tests are available in the Illinois Certification Testing System Registration Bulletin, which can be found online at *www.icts.nesinc.com*. The Registration Bulletin and website also contains test dates and information that can assist you in determining which tests must be successfully completed.

How do I achieve "highly qualified" status in accordance with the federal No Child Left Behind Act?

Successful completion of a content test in the area of your teaching assignment is one means of becoming "highly qualified" under the No Child Left Behind (NCLB) Act.

Am I required to take these tests if I hold a teaching certificate from another state?

According to the ICTS website (*http://www.icts.nesinc.com/IL14_whoshouldtest.asp*), an individual who holds a valid, comparable certificate from another state who applies for Illinois certification on or after July 1, 2004, will not be required to pass the ICTS Basic Skills test if the individual has not previously attempted and failed the ICTS Basic Skills test **and**

- the out-of-state certificate was issued before June 30, 2004, **or**

- the individual was required to pass a test of basic skills to obtain the certificate from the other state.

An individual who holds a valid, comparable certificate from another state who applies for Illinois certification on or after July 1, 2004, will not be required to pass an ICTS content-area test if the individual passed an out-of-state test in the same content area in which the individual meets Illinois endorsement requirements **and** the test was required for certification by the other state.

Out-of-state certificate holders are not exempt from taking the APT test that is required of candidates seeking the Illinois Early Childhood, Elementary, Secondary, and Special Teaching Certificates.

Out-of-state certificate holders seeking a Special Pre-School-to-Age-21 Certificate are not exempt from taking the Special Education General Curriculum Test.

Qualification for a testing exemption. Applicants must request that the out-of-state certification authority verify the title of the test that was passed and also that it was required for certification. To do this you must use ISBE Form 73-99, "Confirmation of State Certification Tests Taken," which is available at *www.isbe.net/certification/*. For further information about this exemption, contact your regional office of education. More information on Provisional Certificates may be found at *www.isbe.net/certification*.

How is the test content determined?

Testing has been required of candidates seeking Illinois teaching, school service personnel, and administrative certificates since 1988. Legislation enacted at that time established a testing program as part of the state's certification requirements. Subsequent legislation and the adoption of administrative rules by the Illinois State Board of Education provided addition content requirements and information regarding the specific tests required of certification candidates and by whom and when these tests must be taken.

All tests in the ICTS program are criterion referenced, meaning they are designed to measure candidates' knowledge in relation to an established standard of competence rather than in relation to how other candidates perform. The explicit purpose of the ICTS is to help identify those candidates who have demonstrated the level of knowledge and skills necessary to perform satisfactorily in their fields of educational specialization.

It is important to note that you don't lose points for wrong multiple-choice answers, so you should definitely guess.

Who administers the ICTS?

The ICTS is developed by the state of Illinois and administered by Pearson Education, Inc.

When are the ICTS tests offered?

The ICTS tests are offered up to six times a year. There are two testing sessions on a scheduled test administration date: a morning and an afternoon session. Each test session is five hours in length. The usual testing day is Saturday. If you have a documented disability or if English is not your first language, you may request alternative testing arrangements. To receive more information, consult the Illinois Certification Testing System Registration Bulletin.

The Basic Skills Test (096) and the Elementary/Middle Grades Test (110) are also offered as computer-based tests (see information regarding this as it is explained later in this section).

Additional information is available from the Illinois State Board of Education, to which Pearson Education is under contract. The department can be contacted as follows:

Illinois State Board of Education
100 N. 1st Street
Springfield, IL 62777
Phone: (866) 262-6663
Website: *www.isbe.net/certification*

Is there a registration fee?

Yes. Check with Pearson Education at *www.icts.nesinc.com*.

HOW TO USE THIS BOOK AND TestWare®

What do I study first?

We recommend beginning your study with the comprehensive chapter reviews. It is important to read over each review, noting crucial test-taking suggestions and insights. By studying each review thoroughly, you will reinforce basic skills that are vital to performing well on the ICTS. After reviewing, take the practice tests. This will familiarize you with the actual exam's format, procedures, and level of difficulty. An added bonus to taking these practice tests is knowing what to expect on exam day.

Apart from the book itself, we give you a CD-ROM with two full-length simulated tests. **We strongly recommend that you begin your preparation with the TestWare® practice tests.** The software provides the added benefits of automatic scoring and enforced time conditions.

Wisely scheduling your study time is also a key component to your success on the ICTS. To best utilize your study time, follow our flexible ICTS study schedule found at the end of this chapter. The schedule is based ideally on a seven-week program, but can be condensed if needed.

When should I start studying for the ICTS tests?

It is never too early to start studying for your ICTS test. Time is your ally here. The earlier you begin, the more time you will have to sharpen your skills and focus your efforts. Do not procrastinate! Cramming is not an effective way to study, since it does not allow you enough time to learn what will be required of you. It takes time to learn the tested areas and test format. Make the most of your time while you have it. Use it well to master the essentials necessary to pass.

FORMAT OF THE ICTS TESTS

How were the tests prepared and what are they like?

There are many types of ICTS tests, including: Basic Skills, Assessment of Professional Teaching, Content-Area, Learning Behavior Specialist, English Language Proficiency, and many other specialized fields. This book covers Basic Skills and Elementary/Middle Grades.

The Basic Skills test consists of two sections: multiple-choice questions and a constructed-response section. There are 125 multiple-choice questions covering three primary areas: Reading Comprehension; Language Arts (grammar and writing); and Mathematics. Multiple-choice questions have four answer choices. A single constructed-response writing assignment will require you to provide a written response to an assigned topic. You should allow approximately 60 minutes to complete your written response, thus devoting the remaining 4 hours to the multiple-choice questions.

As a content-area test, the Elementary/Middle Grades test consists of 125 multiple-choice test questions.

Is Computer-based testing available?

Starting in March 2010, computer-based testing is available in addition to the regularly scheduled paper-based administrations for the Basic Skills (096) test and the Elementary/Middle Grades (110) test.

This testing is available at Pearson Professional Centers throughout the United States, its territories, and Canada, including at least six in Illinois. Go to *http://www.icts.nesinc.com/IL14_testdates.asp?pagetype=CBT* for a list of "Test Dates for Computer-Based Testing" and to register. Go to *http://www.icts.nesinc.com/IL14_testdates.asp?pagetype=CBT* "Test Sites for Computer-Based Testing" for a list of the test centers, which include sites in Chicago (Financial District, Wacker Drive), Marion, Peoria, Schaumburg (Chicago NW), and Springfield, as well as in neighboring states (IA, IN, MO, and WI) and at 200 centers outside of Illinois.

You must register online for the computer based test at the ICTS Web site. There is an additional computer-based testing fee of $84 for each test taken on computer, and you must use Visa or Mastercard. The following guidelines apply to computer-based testing registration:

- You should plan to register as early as possible before your desired testing window. Test appointments are scheduled on a first-come, first-served basis and seating is limited.

- Once you have registered for a computer-based test, you must wait until after you have taken the test to register again for the same computer-based test.

- You must wait 120 days after taking a computer-based ICTS test before retaking the same test on computer.

The computer test is involves answering multiple choice questions on a screen and typing your essay response. The ICTS website offers more details regarding what to bring to the test.

Unofficial test results will be posted on the ICTS Web site and official score reports will be mailed on the score report date for each testing administration.

For more information, go to *http://www.icts.nesinc.com/IL14_ictscbt.asp*.

ABOUT THE SUBJECT REVIEWS

The subject reviews in this book are designed purposefully to provide you with critical insight into the content and format of the ICTS. For smarter study, we break down this part of test preparation into more manageable "chunks." Before you begin reviewing, it is important to note that your own schooling experience has taught you most of what is needed to answer the questions on the actual ICTS. Our review is written to help you fit and shape information acquired over the years into a context ideally suited for taking the ICTS.

You may also be taking test preparation classes for the ICTS or have purchased other study guides and textbooks. Reviewing class notes and textbooks along with our subject reviews will provide you with an even better foundation for passing the ICTS.

SCORING THE ICTS

The Basic Skills Test is scored as follows: you are given a status (Pass or Did Not Pass); you are given a score for overall performance on a scale of 100 to 300. Specifically, you need a minimum overall performance score of 240, and you must get 50% of the Reading Comprehension questions right, 50% of the Language Arts questions right, 35% of the mathematics questions right, and a 5 out of 12 on the writing portion. So even if you score above 240, you could dip below these minimum percentiles in just one area and fail. Your score is further subdivided into your performance in the four subareas. These subarea scores are given values on the 100- to 300-scale.

The multiple-choice portion of the test is scored by a computer. For the writing portion, at least two evaluators look at the essay, and it is scored not on expressed opinions but rather on focus (clear main idea), support/elaboration (with examples and details), organization, and grammar/conventions. Since a six point scale is used (six being the highest), each evaluator gives a score and then the two scores are added together. If the scores differ by more than two points, a third reader is introduced to evaluate. Ultimately, the score (out of 12) is converted to a 100- to 300-point score (again with 240 or above being a pass). In a worst-case scenario, an evaluator would issue a score of "U" (which means "unscorable") because the response was illegible, off topic, indecipherable due to second language issues, or too short.

Unofficial scores for the Basic Skills test will be available on the Internet by 5:00 P.M. CT on the score-report date for each test administration. Refer to the test registration schedule on the back cover of the ICTS Registration Bulletin for further information. Unofficial scores are available on the Internet for approximately two weeks. To access your unofficial scores, go to *www.icts.nesinc.com* and follow the score retrieval instructions.

The Elementary/Middle Grades Test (110) is scored on a 100- to 300-point scale, with a 240 or above being the passing requirement. The five subareas are also scored according to the point scale. There is no penalty for guessing on this test. Each score report contains a section titled "How to Read Your Score Report" to help you interpret your results. Examples can be found on the ICTS Web site at *www.icts.nesinc.com*.

Where does my score go?

The score goes to you, to the Illinois Board of Education, and to any institutions you indicate during the registration process.

If you do not achieve a passing score, review the detailed explanations for the questions you answered incorrectly. Note which types of questions you answered wrong, and re-examine the corresponding review. After further review, you may want to retake the practice tests.

And finally, if you do not do well on test day, don't panic! The test can be taken again, so you can work on improving your score on your next ICTS. A score on the ICTS that does not match your expectations does not mean you should change your plans about teaching.

Test-Taking Strategies

Although you may not be familiar with tests like the ICTS, this book will help acquaint you with this type of exam and help alleviate test-taking anxieties. Here are the key ways you can more easily get into an ICTS state of mind:

Become comfortable with the format of the ICTS. Practice tests are the best way to learn the format of the ICTS. When you take a practice test, try to simulate the environmental conditions of the actual testing facility. Remember, you are in training for the ICTS, and simulated testing conditions will only help you perform better. Stay calm and pace yourself. After simulating a test even once, you boost your chances of doing well, and you will be able to sit down for the actual ICTS with much more confidence.

Read all the possible answers. Examine each answer choice to ensure that you are not making a mistake. Jumping to conclusions without considering all the answers is a common test-taking error.

Use the process of elimination. GUESS if you do not know. If you do not know the answer immediately after reading the answer choices, try to eliminate as many of the answers as possible. Eliminating just one or two answer choices gives you a far better chance of selecting the right answer.

Do not leave an answer blank. There is no penalty for wrong answers, and you might even get it right if you had to guess at the answer.

Familiarize yourself with the test's directions and content. Familiarizing yourself with the directions and content of the ICTS not only saves you valuable time, but can also aid in reducing anxiety before the test. Many mistakes are caused by anxiety. It's simply better to go in knowing what you will face.

Answer accurately! Be sure that the answer oval you mark corresponds to the appropriate number in the test booklet. The test is multiple-choice and is graded by machine. Marking just one answer in the wrong place can throw off the rest of the test. Having to correct an error like this can deprive you of precious minutes.

After the Test

When you finish your test, hand in your materials and you will be dismissed. Then, you are free. Go home and relax. Meet with friends. Go out to dinner. Or go shopping. Whatever you do, make it a great day! After all you have done to get this far, you deserve it!

ICTS Study Schedule

The following study schedule allows for thorough preparation to pass the Illinois Certification Testing System (ICTS) tests covered in this book. This is a suggested seven-week course of study. This schedule can, however, be condensed if you have less time available to study or expanded if you have more time. Whatever the length of your available study time, be sure to keep a structured schedule by setting aside ample time each day to study. Depending on your schedule, you may find it easier to study throughout the weekend. No matter which schedule works best for you, the more time you devote to studying for the ICTS, the more prepared and confident you will be on the day of the test.

Week	Activity
1	Study the ICTS test objectives to get a better idea of the content on which you will be tested. You should make a list of the objectives that you know you will have the most trouble mastering so that you can concentrate your study on those areas.
2	Study the subject reviews in this book. Take notes on the sections as you work through them, as writing will aid in your retention of information. Keep a list of the subject areas for which you may need additional aid.
3	Take the full-length practice tests on CD-ROM. Your scores will indicate where your strengths and weaknesses lie. Review the explanations for the questions you answered incorrectly.
4	Identify and review references and sources. The textbooks you used in education courses may be the best source for the Elementary/Middle Grades part of the test, and textbooks for college composition and mathematics courses will help in your preparation for the Basic Skills areas. You may also want to consult the curriculum website at *www.isbe.net.*
5	Condense your notes and findings. You should develop a structured outline detailing specific facts. You may want to use index cards to aid you in memorizing important facts and concepts.
6	Test yourself using the index cards. You may want to have a friend or colleague quiz you on key facts and items. Then, retake the drills and tests. Review the explanations for the questions you answered incorrectly.
7	Study any areas you consider to be your weaknesses by using your study materials, references, and notes. You may want to retake some tests.

INSTALLING REA's TestWare®

SYSTEM REQUIREMENTS

Pentium 75 MHz (300 MHz recommended) or a higher or compatible processor; Microsoft Windows 98 or later; 64 MB Available RAM; Internet Explorer 5.5 or higher.

INSTALLATION

1. Insert the ICTS TestWare® CD-ROM into the CD-ROM drive.

2. If the installation doesn't begin automatically, from the Start Menu choose the Run command. When the Run dialog box appears, type d:\setup (where D is the letter of your CD-ROM drive) at the prompt and click OK.

3. The installation process will begin. A dialog box proposing the directory "Program Files\REA\ ICTS" will appear. If the name and location are suitable, click OK. If you wish to specify a different name or location, type it in and click OK.

4. Start the ICTS TestWare® application by double-clicking on the icon.

REA's ICTS TestWare® is **EASY** to **LEARN AND USE**. To achieve maximum benefits, we recommend that you take a few minutes to go through the on-screen tutorial on your computer. The "screen buttons" are also explained here to familiarize you with the program.

TECHNICAL SUPPORT

REA's TestWare® is backed by customer and technical support. For questions about **installation or operation of your software**, contact us at:

> **Research & Education Association**
> **Phone: (732) 819-8880 (9 a.m. to 5 p.m. ET, Monday–Friday)**
> **Fax: (732) 819-8808**
> **Website: http://www.rea.com**
> **E-mail: info@rea.com**

Note to Windows XP Users: In order for the TestWare® to function properly, please install and run the application under the same computer administrator-level user account. Installing the TestWare® as one user and running it as another could cause file- access path conflicts.

ICTS

Illinois Certification Testing System

Basic Skills Review

Reading Comprehension

I. STRATEGIES FOR THE READING SECTION

II. FOUR-STEP APPROACH

The reading portion of the Basic Skills Test asks the test-taker to utilize critical reading and reading comprehension skills. The objectives for this section of the test are to understand the main ideas of the passage based on the supporting evidence or details and to understand the author's purpose, point of view, and/or intended meaning.

Test-takers will be asked to read a passage and answer questions about the material included in that passage. The reading section is entirely multiple choice. It will be to your benefit to read the questions about the particular passage first. This will give you an idea of what to look for and focus on as you are reading. It is also crucial that you understand the passage as a whole and comprehend the overall intention, meaning, or main idea of the material you have read.

This review was developed to prepare you for the reading section of the Illinois Certification Testing System (ICTS). You will be guided through a step-by-step approach to attacking reading passages and questions. Also included are tips to help you quickly and accurately answer the questions that will appear in this section. By studying this review and practicing questions in the practice test, you will greatly increase your chances of achieving a good score on the reading section of the ICTS.

Fast Facts

The more you know about the skills tested, the better you will perform on the test.

Remember, the more you know about the skills tested, the better you will perform on the test. In this section, the objectives you will be tested on are contained in the following list:

Standard 1   **Determine the meaning of words and phrases in context.**

The following are examples of content that may be covered under this standard.
- Use context clues to determine the meaning of unfamiliar words or words with multiple meanings.
- Recognize the correct use of commonly misused pairs (e.g., affect/effect) in a passage.
- Determine the meaning of figurative or colloquial language in a passage.
- Identify appropriate synonyms or antonyms for words in a passage.

Standard 2   **Understand the main idea and supporting details in written material.**

The following are examples of content that may be covered under this standard.
- Identify the stated main idea of a paragraph or passage.
- Establish the sequence of events or steps presented in a passage.
- Recognize information that supports, illustrates, or elaborates the main idea of a paragraph or a passage.
- Identify the meaning of a figurative expression in a passage.

Standard 3   **Apply skills of inference and interpretation to a variety of written materials.**

The following are examples of content that may be covered under this standard.
- Recognize a writer's implied purpose for writing (e.g., to persuade, to describe).
- Identify the statement that best expresses the implied main idea of a paragraph or passage.
- Recognize implied cause-and-effect relationships in a passage.
- Interpret the content, word choice, and phrasing of a passage to determine a writer's opinions, point of view, or position on an issue.

Standard 4   **Analyze relationships among ideas in written material.**

The following are examples of content that may be covered under this standard.
- Recognize similarities and differences among ideas in a passage.
- Analyze relationships between ideas in opposition (e.g., pro and con).
- Select solutions to problems based on information presented in written material.
- Draw conclusions from information stated or implied in a passage.

Standard 5   **Use critical reasoning skills to evaluate written material.**

The following are examples of content that may be covered under this standard.
- Recognize stated or implied assumptions on which the validity of an argument depends.

- Determine the relevance of specific facts, examples, or graphic data to a writer's argument.
- Recognize fallacies in the logic of a writer's argument.
- Recognize qualifying language and distinguish between fact and opinion in written material.
- Assess the credibility, objectivity, or bias of the author of a passage or the author's sources.

Standard 6   **Apply skills for outlining and summarizing written materials and interpreting information presented in graphs or tables.**

The following are examples of content that may be covered under this standard.
- Organize the main ideas in a passage into an outline or another form of graphic or tabular organization.
- Identify an accurate summary of a passage.
- Interpret information presented in charts, graphs, or tables.

To help you master these skills, we present examples of the types of questions you will encounter and explanations of how to answer them.

THE PASSAGES

The reading passages in the reading section are designed to be on the level of the type of material encountered in college textbooks. They will present you with very diverse subjects. Although you will not be expected to have prior knowledge of the information presented in the passages, you will be expected to know the fundamental reading comprehension techniques presented in this chapter. Only your ability to read and comprehend material will be tested.

THE QUESTIONS

Each passage will be followed by a number of questions. The questions will ask you to make determinations based on what you have read. You will commonly encounter questions that will ask you to:

- Determine which of the given answer choices best expresses the main idea of the passage.

- Determine the author's purpose in writing the passage.

- Determine which fact best supports the writer's main idea.

- Know the difference between fact and opinion in a statement.

- Organize the information in the passage.

- Determine which of the answer choices best summarizes the information presented in the passage.

- Recall information from the passage.

- Analyze cause-and-effect relationships based on information in the passage.

- Determine the definition of a word as it is used in the passage.

- Answer a question based on information presented in graphic form.

I. Strategies for the Reading Section

The following is a recommended plan of attack for answering the questions in the reading section.

When reading the passage,

Step 1: **Read quickly** while keeping in mind that questions will follow.

Step 2: Uncover the **main idea** or theme of the passage. Many times it is contained within the first few lines of the passage.

Step 3: Uncover the main idea of **each paragraph**. Usually it is contained in either the first or last sentence of the paragraph.

Step 4: **Skim** over the detailed points of the passage while **circling key words** or phrases. These are words or phrases such as *but, on the other hand, although, however, yet,* and *except.*

When answering the questions,

Step 1: Approach each question one at a time. **Read it carefully.**

Step 2: Uncover the **main idea** or theme of the passage. Many times it is contained within the first few lines of the passage.

Step 3: If the question is asking for an answer that can only be found in a specific place in the passage, save it for last since this type of question requires you to **go back to the passage** and therefore takes more of your time.

ADDITIONAL TIPS

- **Read over the questions before reading the passage.** This will give you an idea of what you are reading for.

- **Look over all the passages first** and then attack the passages that seem easiest and most interesting.

- **Identify and underline what sentences are the main ideas** of each paragraph.

- If a question asks you **to draw inferences**, your answer should **reflect what is implied** in the passage, rather than what is directly stated.

- **Use the context** of the sentence to find the meaning of an unfamiliar word.

- Identify what sentences are **example sentences** and label them with an "E." Determine whether or not the writer is using facts or opinions.

- **Circle key transitions** and identify dominant patterns of organization.

- Make your final response and move on. **Don't dawdle** or get frustrated by the really troubling passages. If you haven't gotten answers after two attempts, answer as best you can and move on.

- If you have time at the end, go **back to the passages** that were difficult and review them again.

II. A Four-Step Approach

When you take the reading section of the ICTS, you will have two tasks: to read the passage, and to answer the questions.

Of the two, carefully reading the passage is the more important; answering the questions is based on an understanding of the passage. What follows is a four-step approach to reading:

Step 1:   preview
Step 2:   read actively
Step 3:   review the passage
Step 4:   answer the questions

You should study the following exercises and use these four steps when you complete the reading section of the ICTS.

STEP 1: PREVIEW

A preview of the reading passage will give you a purpose and a reason for reading; previewing is a good strategy to use when taking a test. Before beginning to read the passage (usually a four-minute activity if you preview and review), you should take about thirty seconds to look over the passage and questions. An effective way to preview the passage is to quickly read the first sentence of each paragraph, the concluding sentence of the passage, and the questions—but not the answers—following the passage. A passage follows; practice previewing the passage by reading the first sentence of each paragraph and the last line of the passage.

> *Fast Facts*
>
> A preview of the reading passage will give you a purpose and a reason for reading.

Passage

That the area of obscenity and pornography is a difficult one for the Supreme Court is well documented. The Court's numerous attempts to define obscenity have proven unworkable and left the decision to the subjective preferences of the justices. Perhaps Justice Stewart put it best when, after refusing to define obscenity, he declared, but "I know it when I see it." Does the Court literally have to see it to know it? Specifically, what role does the fact-pattern, including the materials' medium, play in the Court's decision?

Several recent studies employ fact-pattern analysis in modeling the Court's decision making. These studies examine the fact-pattern or case characteristics, often with ideological and attitudinal factors, as a determinant of the decision reached by the Court. In broad terms, these studies owe their theoretical underpinnings to attitude theory. As the name suggests, attitude theory views the Court's attitudes as an explanation of its decisions.

These attitudes, however, do not operate in a vacuum. As Spaeth explains, "the activation of an attitude involves both an object and the situation in which that object is encountered." The objects to which the Court directs its attitudes are litigants. The situation—the subject matter of the case—can be defined in broad or narrow terms. One may define the situation as an entire area of the law (e.g., civil liberties issues). On an even broader scale, the situation may be defined as the decision to grant certiorari or whether to defect from a minimum-winning coalition.

Defining the situation with such broad strokes, however, does not allow one to control for case content. In many specific issue areas, the cases present strikingly similar patterns. In examining the Court's search and seizure decisions, Segal found that a relatively small number of situational and case characteristic variables explain a high proportion of the Court's decisions.

Despite Segal's success, efforts to verify the applicability of fact-pattern analysis in other issue areas and using broad-based factors have been slow in forthcoming. Renewed interest in obscenity and pornography by federal and state governments as a result of lobbying campaigns by fundamentalist groups, the academic community, and other antipornography interest groups pro and con indicate the Court's decisions in this area deserve closer examination.

The Court's obscenity and pornography decisions also present an opportunity to study the Court's behavior in an area where the Court has granted significant decision-making authority to the states. In *Miller v. California* (1973) the Court announced the importance of local community standards in obscenity determinations. The Court's subsequent behavior may suggest how the Court will react in other areas where it has chosen to defer to the states (e.g., abortion).

Questions

1. The main idea of the passage is best stated in which of the following?

   A. The Supreme Court has difficulty convicting those who violate obscenity laws.

   B. The current definitions for obscenity and pornography provided by the Supreme Court are unworkable.

   C. Fact-pattern analysis is insufficient for determining the attitude of the Court toward the issues of obscenity and pornography.

   D. Despite the difficulties presented by fact-pattern analysis, Justice Segal found the solution in the patterns of search and seizure decisions.

2. The main purpose of the writer in this passage is to

   A. convince the reader that the Supreme Court is making decisions about obscenity based on their subjective views alone.

   B. explain to the reader how fact-pattern analysis works with respect to cases of obscenity and pornography.

   C. define obscenity and pornography for the layperson.

   D. demonstrate the role fact-pattern analysis plays in determining the Supreme Court's attitude about cases in obscenity and pornography.

3. Of the following, which fact best supports the writer's contention that the Court's decisions in the areas of obscenity and pornography deserve closer scrutiny?

    A.   The fact that a Supreme Court Justice said, "I know it when I see it."

    B.   Recent studies that employ fact-pattern analysis in modeling the Court's decision-making process.

    C.   The fact that attitudes do not operate in a vacuum.

    D.   The fact that federal and state governments, interested groups, and the academic community show renewed interest in the obscenity and pornography decisions by the Supreme Court.

4. Among the following statements, which states an opinion expressed by the writer rather than a fact?

    A.   It is well documented that the area of obscenity and pornography is a difficult one for the Supreme Court.

    B.   The objects to which a court directs its attitudes are the litigants.

    C.   In many specific issue areas, the cases present strikingly similar fact-patterns.

    D.   The Court's subsequent behavior may suggest how the Court will react in other legal areas.

5. The group of topics in the list that follows that best reflects the organization of the topics of the passage is

    A.   I.   The difficulties of the Supreme Court
           II.   Several recent studies
           III.   Spaeth's definition of *attitude*
           IV.   The similar patterns of cases
           V.   Other issue areas
           VI.   The case of *Miller v. California*

    B.   I.   The Supreme Court, obscenity, and fact-pattern analysis
           II.   Fact-pattern analyses and attitude theory
           III.   The definition of *attitude* for the Court
           IV.   The definition of *situation*
           V.   The breakdown in fact-pattern analysis
           VI.   Studying Court behavior

    C.   I.   Justice Stewart's view of pornography
           II.   Theoretical underpinnings
           III.   A minimum-winning coalition
           IV.   Search and seizure decisions
           V.   Renewed interest in obscenity and pornography
           VI.   The importance of local community standards

    D.   I.   The Court's numerous attempts to define obscenity
           II.   Case characteristics
           III.   The subject matter of cases
           IV.   The Court's proportion of decisions
           V.   Broad-based factors
           VI.   Obscenity determination

6. Which paragraph among those that follow is the best summary of the passage?

    A. The Supreme Court's decision-making process with respect to obscenity and pornography has become too subjective. Fact-pattern analyses used to determine the overall attitude of the Court reveal only broad-based attitudes on the part of the Court toward the situations of obscenity cases. But these patterns cannot fully account for the Court's attitudes toward case content. Research is not conclusive on whether fact-pattern analyses work when applied to legal areas. Renewed public and local interest suggests continued study and close examination of how the Court makes decisions. Delegating authority to the states may reflect patterns for Court decisions in other socially sensitive areas.

    B. Though subjective, the Supreme Court decisions are well documented. Fact-pattern analyses reveal the attitude of the Supreme Court toward its decisions in cases. Spaeth explains that an attitude involves both an object and a situation. For the Court, the situation may be defined as the decision to grant certiorari. Cases present strikingly similar patterns, and a small number of variables explain a high proportion of the Court's decisions. Segal has made an effort to verify the applicability of fact-pattern analysis with some success. The Court's decisions on obscenity and pornography suggest weak Court behavior, such as in *Miller v. California*.

    C. To determine what obscenity and pornography mean to the Supreme Court, we must use fact-pattern analysis. Fact-pattern analysis reveals the ideas that the Court uses to operate in a vacuum. The litigants and the subject matter of cases are defined in broad terms (such as an entire area of law) to reveal the Court's decision-making process. Search and seizure cases reveal strikingly similar patterns, leaving the Court open to grant certiorari effectively. Renewed public interest in the Court's decisions proves how the Court will react in the future.

    D. Supreme Court decisions about pornography and obscenity are under examination and are out of control. The Court has to see the case to know it. Fact-pattern analyses reveal that the Court can only define cases in narrow terms, thus revealing individual egotism on the part of the Justices. As a result of strikingly similar patterns in search and seizure cases, the Court should be studied further for its weakness in delegating authority to state courts, as in the case of *Miller v. California*.

7. Based on the passage, the rationale for fact-pattern analyses arises out of what theoretical groundwork?

    A. Subjectivity theory

    B. The study of cultural norms

    C. Attitude theory

    D. Cybernetics

8. Based on data in the passage, what would most likely be the major cause for the difficulty in pinning down the Supreme Court's attitude toward cases of obscenity and pornography?

    A. The personal opinions of the Court Justices

    B. The broad nature of the situations of the cases

    C. The ineffective logistics of certiorari

    D. The inability of the Court to resolve the variables presented by individual case content

9.   In the context of the passage, *subjective* might be most nearly defined as

A.   personal.

B.   wrong.

C.   focused.

D.   objective.

[Answers to these questions are provided beginning on page 19]

By previewing the passage, you should have read the following:

• It is well documented that the areas of obscenity and pornography are difficult ones for the Supreme Court.

• Several recent studies employ fact-pattern analysis in modeling the Court's decision making.

• These attitudes, however, do not operate in a vacuum.

• Defining the situation with such broad strokes, however, does not allow one to control for case content.

• Despite Segal's success, efforts to verify the applicability of fact-pattern analysis in other issue areas and using broad-based factors have been slow in coming.

• The Court's obscenity and pornography decisions also present an opportunity to study the Court's behavior in an area where the Court has granted significant decision-making authority to the states.

• The Court's subsequent behavior may suggest how the Court will react in other areas where it has chosen to defer to the states (e.g., abortion).

These few sentences tell you much about the entire passage. As you begin to examine the passage, you should first determine the main idea of the passage and underline it so you can easily refer to it if a question requires you to do so (see question 1). The main idea should be found in the first paragraph of the passage, and may even be the first sentence. From what you have read thus far, you now know that the main idea of this passage is that the Supreme Court has difficulty in making static decisions about obscenity and pornography.

In addition, you also know that recent studies have used fact-pattern analysis in modeling the Court's decision. You have learned that attitudes do not operate independently and that case content is important. The feasibility of using fact-pattern analysis in other areas and broad-based factors have not been quickly verified. To study the behavior of the Court in an area in which they have granted significant decision-making authority to the states, one has only to consider the obscenity and pornography decisions. In summary, the author suggests that the Court's subsequent behavior may suggest how the Court will react in those other areas in which decision-making authority has previously been ceded to the states. As you can see, having this information will make the reading of the passage much easier.

You should have also looked at the stem of the question in your preview. You do not necessarily need to spend time reading the answers to each question in your preview. The stem alone can help to guide you as you read.

The stems in this case are:

1. The main idea of the passage is best stated in which of the following?

2. The main purpose of the writer in this passage is to _____?

3. Of the following, which fact best supports the writer's contention that the Court's decisions in the areas of obscenity and pornography deserve closer scrutiny?

4. Among the following statements, which states an opinion expressed by the writer rather than a fact?

5. The group of topics in the list that follows that best reflects the organization of the topics of the passage is _____.

6. Which paragraph among those that follow is the best summary of the passage?

7. Based on the passage, the rationale for fact-pattern analyses arises out of what theoretical groundwork?

8. Based on data in the passage, what would most likely be the major cause for the difficulty in pinning down the Supreme Court's attitude toward cases of obscenity and pornography?

9. In the context of the passage, *subjective* might be most nearly defined as _____.

STEP 2: READ ACTIVELY

After your preview, you are now ready to read actively. This means that, as you read, you will be engaged in such things as underlining important words, topic sentences, main ideas, and words denoting the tone of a passage. If you think underlining can help you save time and help you remember the main ideas, feel free to use your pencil.

Read the first sentence of each paragraph carefully, since this often contains the topic of the paragraph. You may wish to underline each topic sentence.

During this stage, you should also determine the writer's purpose in writing the passage (see question 2), as this will help you focus on the main points and the writer's key points in the organization of a passage.

You can determine the author's purpose by asking yourself whether the relationship between the writer's main idea and evidence the writer uses answer one of the following four questions:

- What is the writer's primary goal or overall objective?

- Is the writer trying to persuade you by proving or using facts to make a case for an idea?

- Is the writer trying only to inform and enlighten you about an idea, object, or event?

- Is the writer attempting to amuse you? To keep you fascinated or laughing?

Read these examples and see whether you can decide what the primary purpose of the statements that follow might be.

(A) Jogging too late in life can cause more health problems than it solves. I will allow that the benefits of jogging are many: lowered blood pressure, increased vitality, better cardiovascular health, and better muscle tone. However, an older person may have a history of injury or chronic ailments that makes jogging counterproductive. For example, the elderly jogger may have hardening of the arteries, emphysema, or undiscovered aneurysms just waiting to burst and cause stroke or death. Chronic arthritis in the joints will only be aggravated by persistent irritation and use. Moreover, for those of us with injuries sustained in our youth—such as torn Achilles tendons or knee cartilage—jogging might just make a painful life more painful, cancelling out the benefits the exercise is intended to produce.

(B) Jogging is a sporting activity that exercises all the main muscle groups of the body. That the arms, legs, buttocks, and torso voluntary muscles are engaged goes without question. Running down a path makes you move your upper body as well as your lower body muscles. People do not often take into account, however, how the involuntary muscle system is also put through its paces. The heart, diaphragm, and even the eye and facial muscles take part as we hurl our bodies through space at speeds up to five miles per hour over distances as long as twenty-six miles and more for some.

(C) It seems to me that jogging styles are as identifiable as fingerprints! People seem to be as individual in the way they run as they are in personality. Here comes the Duck, waddling down the track, little wings going twice as fast as the feet in an effort to stay upright. At about the quarter-mile mark, I see the Penguin, quite natty in the latest jogging suit, body stiff as a board from neck to ankles and the ankles flexing a mile a minute to cover the yards. And down there at the half-mile post—there goes the Giraffe—a tall fellow in a spotted electric yellow outfit, whose long strides cover about a dozen yards each, and whose neck waves around under some old army camouflage hat that may have served its time in a surplus store in the Bronx or in the Arabian desert. If you see the animals in the jogger woods once, you can identify them from miles away just by seeing their gait. And, by the way, be careful whose hoof you're stepping on, it may be mine!

In (A) the writer makes a statement that a number of people would debate and which isn't clearly demonstrated by science or considered common knowledge. In fact, common wisdom usually maintains the opposite thesis. Many would say that jogging improves the health of the aging—even to the point of slowing the aging process. As soon as you see a writer point to or identify *an issue open to debate* that stands in need of proof, he or she is setting out to persuade you that one side or the other is the more justified position. You'll notice, too, that the writer in this case takes a stand here. It's almost as if he or she is saying, "I have concluded that . . ." But a thesis or arguable idea is only a *hypothesis* until evidence is summoned by the writer to prove it. Effective arguments are based on serious, factual, or demonstrable evidence, not merely opinion.

In (B) the writer is just stating a fact. This is not a matter for debate. From here, the writer's evidence is to *explain* and *describe* what is meant by the fact. This is accomplished by *analyzing* (breaking down into its constituent elements) the way the different muscle groups come into play or do work when jogging, thus explaining the fact stated as a main point in the opening sentence. The assertion that jogging exercises all the muscle groups is not in question or a matter of debate. Besides taking the form of explaining how something works or what parts it comprises (for example, the basic parts of a bicycle are . . .), writers may show how the idea, object, or event functions. A writer may use this information to prove something. But if the writer doesn't argue to prove a debatable point one way or the other, then the purpose must be either to inform (as here) or to entertain.

In (C) the writer is taking a stand yet not attempting to prove anything; a lighthearted observation is made instead and nothing more. In addition, all of the examples used to support the statement are fanciful, funny, odd, or peculiar to the writer's particular vision. Joggers aren't *really* animals, after all.

Make sure to examine all the facts that the author uses to support the main idea. This will allow you to decide whether or not the writer has made a case, and what sort of purpose it supports. Look for supporting details—facts, examples, illustrations, the testimony or research of experts—that are relevant to the topic in question and show what the writer says is so. In fact, paragraphs and theses consist of *show* and *tell*. The writer *tells* you something is so or not so and then *shows* you facts, illustrations, expert testimony, or experiences to back up whatever is assertedly the case or is not the case. As you determine where the author's supporting details are, you may want to label them with an "S" so that you can refer back to them easily when answering questions (see question 3).

It is also important for you to be able to recognize the difference between the statements of fact presented versus statements of the author's opinion. You will be tested on this skill in this section of the test (see question 4). Look at the following examples. In each case ask yourself whether you are reading a fact or an opinion.

1.   Some roses are red.

2.   Roses are the most beautiful flowers on Earth.

3.   After humans smell roses, they fall in love.

4.   Roses are the worst plants to grow in your backyard.

Item 1 is a fact. All you have to do is look at the evidence. Go to a florist. You will see that item 1 is true. A fact is anything that can be demonstrated to be objectively true in reality or which has been demonstrated to be true in reality and is documented by others. For example, the moon is orbiting about 250,000 miles from the Earth.

Item 2 is an opinion. The writer claims this as truth, but since it is a subjective quality (beauty), it remains to be seen. Others may hold different opinions. This is a matter of taste, not fact.

Item 3 is an opinion. There is probably some time-related coincidence between these two, but there is no verifiable, repeatable, or observable evidence that this is always true—at least not the way it is true that if you throw a ball into the air, it will come back down to Earth if left on its own without interference. Opinions have a way of sounding absolute; they are held by the writer with confidence, but are not facts that provide evidence.

Item 4, though perhaps sometimes true, is nevertheless a matter of opinion. Many variables contribute to the health of a plant in a garden: soil, temperature range, amount of moisture, and number and kinds of bugs. This is a debatable point for which the writer would have to provide evidence.

As you read, you should note the structure of the passage. There are several common structures for the passages. Some of these structures are described below.

MAIN TYPES OF PARAGRAPH STRUCTURES

1.   The structure is a main idea plus supporting arguments.

2.   The structure is a main idea plus examples.

3.   The structure includes comparisons or contrasts.

4.   There is a pro and a con structure.

5.   The structure is chronological.

6.   The structure has several different aspects of one idea.

For example, a passage on education in the United States in the 1600s and 1700s might first define education, then describe colonial education, then give information about separation of church and state, and then outline the opposing and supporting arguments regarding taxation as a source of educational funding. Being able to recognize these structures will help you recognize how the author has organized the passage.

Examining the structure of the passage will help you answer questions that ask you to organize (see question 5) the information in the passage or to summarize (see question 6) the information presented in that passage.

For example, if you see a writer using a transitional pattern that reflects a sequence moving forward in time, such as "In 1982 . . . Then, in the next five years . . . A decade later, in 1997, the . . .," chances are the writer is telling a story, describing history, or the like. Writers often use transitions of classification to analyze an idea, object, or event. They may say something like, "The first part . . . Secondly . . . Thirdly . . . Finally . . ." You may then ask yourself what the analysis is for. Is it to explain or to persuade you of something? These transitional patterns may also help reveal the relationship of one part of a passage to another. For example, a writer may be writing, "On the one hand . . . . On the other hand . . ." This should alert you to the fact that the writer is comparing two things or contrasting them. What for? Is one better than the other? Worse?

By understanding the *relationship* among the main point, transitions, and supporting information, you may more readily determine the pattern of organization as well as the writer's purpose in a given piece of writing.

As with the paragraph examples above showing the difference among possible purposes, you must look at the relationship between the facts or information presented (that's the "show" part) and what the writer is trying to point out to you (that's the "tell" part) with that data. For example, in the data given earlier, in item 6, the discussion presented about education in the 1600s might be used

- to prove that it was a failure (a form of argument).

- to show that it consisted of these elements (an analysis of the status of education during that time).

- to show that education during that time was silly.

To understand the author's purpose, the main point and the evidence that supports it must be considered together. In item 6, no statement appears that controls these disparate areas of information. To be meaningful, a controlling or main point is needed. You need to know that that main point is missing. You need to be able to distinguish between the writer showing data and the writer making a point.

In the two paragraphs that follow, consider the different relationship between the same data above and the controlling statement, and how that controlling statement changes the discussion from explanation to argument.

(A) Colonial education was different than today's education and consisted of several elements. Education in those days meant primarily studying the three "R's" (Reading, 'Riting, and 'Rithmetic) and the Bible. The church and state were more closely aligned with one another—education was, after all, for the purpose of serving God better, not to make more money.

(B) Colonial "education" was really just a way to create a captive audience for churches. Education in those days meant studying the three "R's" in order to learn God's word—the Bible—not commerce. The churches and the state were closely aligned with one another, and what was good for the church was good for the state—or else you were excommunicated, which kept you out of Heaven for sure.

The same informational areas are brought up in both cases, but in (A) the writer treats it more analytically ("consisted of several elements"), not taking as debatable a stand on the issue. However, the controlling statement in (B) puts forth a more volatile hypothesis, and then uses the same information to support that hypothesis.

STEP 3: REVIEW THE PASSAGE

After you finish reading actively, take ten or twenty seconds to look over the main idea and the topic sentences that you have underlined, and the key words and phrases you have marked. Now you are ready to enter Step 4 and answer the questions.

STEP 4: ANSWER THE QUESTIONS

In Step 2, you gathered enough information from the passage to answer questions dealing with main idea, purpose, support, fact vs. opinion, organization, and summarization. Let's look again at these questions.

MAIN IDEA QUESTIONS

Looking back at the questions that follow the passage, you should see that question 1 is a *main idea* question.

1. The main idea of the passage is best stated in which of the following?

    A. The Supreme Court has difficulty convicting those who violate obscenity laws.

    B. The current definitions for obscenity and pornography provided by the Supreme Court are unworkable.

    C. Fact-pattern analysis is insufficient for determining the attitude of the Court toward the issues of obscenity and pornography.

    D. Despite the difficulties presented by fact-pattern analysis, Justice Segal found the solution in the patterns of search and seizure decisions.

In answering the question, you see that answer choice C is correct. The writer uses the second, third, fourth, and fifth paragraphs to show how fact-pattern analysis is an ineffective determinant of the Supreme Court's attitudes toward obscenity and pornography.

Choice A is incorrect. Nothing is ever said directly about *convicting* persons accused of obscenity, only that the Court has difficulty defining it.

Choice B is also incorrect. Though the writer states it as a fact, it is only used as an effect that leads the writer to examine how fact-pattern analysis does or does not work to reveal the "cause" or attitude of the Court toward obscenity and pornography.

Also, answer choice D is incorrect. The statement is contrary to what Segal found when he examined search and seizure cases.

PURPOSE QUESTIONS

In examining question 2, you see that you must determine the author's purpose in writing the passage:

2.   The main purpose of the writer in this passage is to

   A.   convince the reader that the Supreme Court is making decisions about obscenity based on their subjective views alone.

   B.   explain to the reader how fact-pattern analysis works with respect to cases of obscenity and pornography.

   C.   define obscenity and pornography for the layperson.

   D.   demonstrate the role fact-pattern analysis plays in determining the Supreme Court's attitude about cases in obscenity and pornography.

Looking at the answer choices, you should see that choice D is correct. Though the writer never states it directly, the data is consistently summoned to show that fact-pattern analysis only gives us part of the picture, or "broad strokes" about the Court's attitude, but cannot account for the attitude toward individual cases.

Choice A is incorrect. The writer doesn't try to convince us of this fact, but merely states it as an opinion resulting from the evidence derived from the "well-documented" background of the problem.

B is also incorrect. The writer not only explains the role of fact-pattern analysis but also rather shows how it cannot fully apply.

The passage is about the Court's difficulty in defining these terms, not the man or woman in the street. Nowhere do definitions for these terms appear. Therefore, choice C is incorrect.

SUPPORT QUESTIONS

Question 3 requires you to analyze the author's supporting details.

3.   Of the following, which fact best supports the writer's contention that the Court's decisions in the areas of obscenity and pornography deserve closer scrutiny?

   A.   The fact that a Supreme Court Justice said, "I know it when I see it."

   B.   Recent studies that employ fact-pattern analysis in modeling the Court's decision-making process.

   C.   The fact that attitudes do not operate in a vacuum.

   D.   The fact that federal and state governments, interested groups, and the academic community show renewed interest in the obscenity and pornography decisions by the Supreme Court.

Look at the answer choices to answer this question. Choice D must be correct. In the fifth paragraph, the writer states that the "renewed interest"—a real and observable fact—from these groups "indicates the Court's decisions . . . deserve closer examination," another way of saying scrutiny.

Choice A is incorrect. The writer uses this remark to show how the Court cannot effectively define obscenity and pornography, relying on "subjective preferences" to resolve issues.

In addition, choice B is incorrect because the writer points to the data in D, not fact-pattern analyses, to prove this. C, too, is incorrect. Although it is true, the writer makes this point to show how fact-pattern analysis doesn't help clear up the real-world situations in which the Court must make its decisions.

FACT VS. OPINION QUESTIONS

By examining question 4, you can see that you are required to know the difference between fact and opinion.

4. Among the following statements, which states an opinion expressed by the writer rather than a fact?

    A. It is well documented that the area of obscenity and pornography is a difficult one for the Supreme Court.

    B. The objects to which a court directs its attitudes are the litigants.

    C. In many specific issue areas, the cases present strikingly similar fact-patterns.

    D. The Court's subsequent behavior may suggest how the Court will react in other legal areas.

Keeping in mind that an opinion is something that is yet to be proven to be the case, you can determine that choice D is correct. It is the only statement among the four for which evidence is yet to be gathered. It is the writer's opinion that this may be a way to predict the Court's attitudes.

A, B, and C are all derived from verifiable data or documentation, and are therefore incorrect.

ORGANIZATION QUESTIONS

Question 5 asks you to organize given topics to reflect the organization of the passage.

5.   The group of topics in the list that follows that best reflects the organization of the topics of the passage is

    A.   I. The difficulties of the Supreme Court
        II. Several recent studies
        III. Spaeth's definition of *attitude*
        IV. The similar patterns of cases
        V. Other issue areas
        VI. The case of *Miller v. California*

    B.   I. The Supreme Court, obscenity, and fact-pattern analysis
        II. Fact-pattern analyses and attitude theory
        III. The definition of *attitude* for the Court
        IV. The definition of *situation*
        V. The breakdown in fact-pattern analysis
        VI. Studying Court behavior

    C.   I. Justice Stewart's view of pornography
        II. Theoretical underpinnings
        III. A minimum-winning coalition
        IV. Search and seizure decisions
        V. Renewed interest in obscenity and pornography
        VI. The importance of local community standards

    D.   I. The Court's numerous attempts to define obscenity
        II. Case characteristics
        III. The subject matter of cases
        IV. The Court's proportion of decisions
        V. Broad-based factors
        VI. Obscenity determination

After examining all of the choices, you will determine that choice (B) is the correct response. These topical areas lead directly to the implied thesis that the "role" of fact-pattern analysis is insufficient to determine the attitude of the Supreme Court in the areas of obscenity and pornography.

Choice A is incorrect because the first topic stated in the list is not the topic of the first paragraph. It is too global. The first paragraph is about the difficulties the Court has with defining obscenity and how fact-pattern analysis might be used to determine the Court's attitude and clear up the problem.

C is incorrect because each of the items listed in this topic list represents supporting evidence or data for the real topic of each paragraph. (See the list in B for correct topics.) For example, Justice Stewart's statement about pornography is only cited to indicate the nature of the problem the Court has with obscenity. It is not the focus of the paragraph itself.

Finally, D is incorrect. As with choice C, these are all incidental pieces of information or data used to support broader points.

SUMMARIZATION QUESTIONS

To answer question 6, you must be able to summarize the passage.

6.   Which paragraph among those that follow is the best summary of the passage?

   A.   The Supreme Court's decision-making process with respect to obscenity and pornography has become too subjective. Fact-pattern analyses used to determine the overall attitude of the Court reveal only broad-based attitudes on the part of the Court toward the situations of obscenity cases. But these patterns cannot fully account for the Court's attitudes toward case content. Research is not conclusive on whether fact-pattern analyses work when applied to legal areas. Renewed public and local interest suggests continued study and close examination of how the Court makes decisions. Delegating authority to the states may reflect patterns for Court decisions in other socially sensitive areas.

   B.   Though subjective, the Supreme Court decisions are well documented. Fact-pattern analyses reveal the attitude of the Supreme Court toward its decisions in cases. Spaeth explains that an attitude involves both an object and a situation. For the Court, the situation may be defined as the decision to grant certiorari. Cases present strikingly similar patterns, and a small number of variables explain a high proportion of the Court's decisions. Segal has made an effort to verify the applicability of fact-pattern analysis with some success. The Court's decisions on obscenity and pornography suggest weak Court behavior, such as in *Miller v. California*.

   C.   To determine what obscenity and pornography mean to the Supreme Court, we must use fact-pattern analysis. Fact-pattern analysis reveals the ideas that the Court uses to operate in a vacuum. The litigants and the subject matter of cases are defined in broad terms (such as an entire area of law) to reveal the Court's decision-making process. Search and seizure cases reveal strikingly similar patterns, leaving the Court open to grant certiorari effectively. Renewed public interest in the Court's decisions proves how the Court will react in the future.

   D.   Supreme Court decisions about pornography and obscenity are under examination and are out of control. The Court has to see the case to know it. Fact-pattern analyses reveal that the Court can only define cases in narrow terms, thus revealing individual egotism on the part of the Justices. As a result of strikingly similar patterns in search and seizure cases, the Court should be studied further for its weakness in delegating authority to state courts, as in the case of *Miller v. California*.

The paragraph that best and most accurately reports what the writer demonstrated based on the implied thesis is answer choice C, which is correct.

Choice A is incorrect because, while it reflects some of the evidence presented in the passage, the passage does not imply that all Court decisions are subjective, just the ones about pornography and obscenity. Similarly, the writer does not suggest that ceding authority to the states (as in *Miller v. California*) is a sign of some weakness, but merely that it is worthy of study as a tool for predicting or identifying the Court attitudes.

Response B is also incorrect. The writer summons information over and over to show how fact-pattern analysis cannot pin down the Court's attitude toward case content.

D is incorrect. Nowhere does the writer say or suggest that the justice system is "out of control" or that the justices are "egotists," only that they are liable to be reduced to being "subjective" rather than having a cogent and identifiable shared standard.

At this point, the three remaining question types must be discussed: recall questions (see question 7), cause/effect questions (see question 8), and definition questions (question 9). They are as follows.

RECALL QUESTIONS

To answer question 7, you must be able to recall information from the passage.

7.   Based on the passage, the rationale for fact-pattern analyses arises out of what theoretical groundwork?

   A.   Subjectivity theory

   B.   The study of cultural norms

   C.   Attitude theory

   D.   Cybernetics

The easiest way to answer this question is to refer back to the passage. In the second paragraph, the writer states that recent studies using fact-pattern analyses "owe their theoretical underpinnings to attitude theory." Therefore, we can conclude that response C is correct.

Answer choices A, B, and D are incorrect, as they are never discussed or mentioned by the writer.

CAUSE/EFFECT QUESTIONS

Question 8 requires you to analyze a cause-and-effect relationship.

8. Based on data in the passage, what would most likely be the major cause for the difficulty in pinning down the Supreme Court's attitude toward cases of obscenity and pornography?

    A. The personal opinions of the Court Justices

    B. The broad nature of the situations of the cases

    C. The ineffective logistics of certiorari

    D. The inability of the Court to resolve the variables presented by individual case content

Choice D is correct, as it is precisely what fact-pattern analyses cannot resolve.

Response A is incorrect because no evidence is presented for it; all that is mentioned is that they do make personal decisions. Answer choice B is incorrect because it is one way in which fact-pattern analysis can be helpful. Finally, C is only a statement about certiorari being difficult to administer, and this was never claimed about them by the writer in the first place.

DEFINITION QUESTIONS

Returning to question 9, we can now determine an answer.

9. In the context of the passage, *subjective* might be most nearly defined as

    A. personal.

    B. wrong.

    C. focused.

    D. objective.

Choice A is best. By taking in and noting the example of Justice Stewart provided by the writer, we can see that Justice Stewart's comment is not an example of right or wrong. Most of the time, if we are talking about people's "preferences," they are usually about taste or quality, and they are usually not a result of scientific study or clear reasoning, but arise out of personal taste, idiosyncratic intuitions, et cetera. Thus, A is the most likely choice.

C is incorrect because the Court's focus is already in place: on obscenity and pornography. Choice B is incorrect. Nothing is implied or stated about the tightness or wrongness of the decisions themselves. Rather it is the definition of obscenity that seems "unworkable." D is also incorrect. Objective is an antonym of subjective in this context. To reason based on the object of study is the opposite of reasoning based upon the beliefs, opinions, or ideas of the one viewing the object, rather than the evidence presented by the object itself, independent of the observer.

You may not have been familiar with the word *subjective*, but from your understanding of the writer's intent, you should have been able to figure out what was being sought. Surrounding words and phrases almost always offer you some clues in determining the meaning of a word. In addition, any examples that appear in the text may also provide some hints.

INTERPRETATION OF GRAPHIC INFORMATION QUESTIONS

Graphs, charts, and tables may play a large part on the ICTS, and you should be familiar with them. More than likely, you will encounter at least one passage that is accompanied by some form of graphic information. You will then be required to answer any question(s) based on the interpretation of the information presented in the graph, chart, or table.

Graphs are used to produce visual aids for sets of information. Often, the impact of numbers and statistics is diminished by an overabundance of tedious numbers. A graph helps a reader rapidly visualize or organize irregular information, as well as trace long periods of decline or increase. The following is a guide to reading the three principal graphic forms that you will encounter when taking the ICTS.

LINE GRAPHS

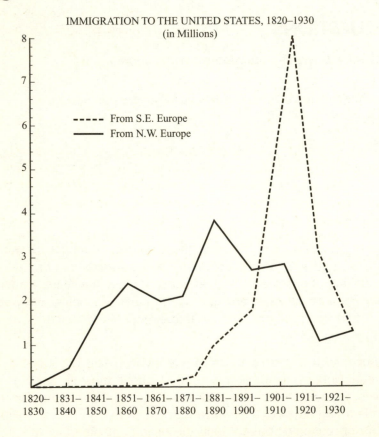

IMMIGRATION TO THE UNITED STATES, 1820–1930
(in Millions)

Source: *Immigration and Naturalization Service of the U.S. Dept. of Justice*

Line graphs are used to track multiple elements of one or more subjects. One element is usually a time factor, over whose span the other element increases, decreases, or remains static. The lines that compose such graphs are connected points that are displayed on the chart through each integral stage. For an example, refer to the preceding immigration graph.

The average number of immigrants from 1820 to 1830 is represented at one point; the average number of immigrants from 1831 to 1840 is represented at the next. The line that connects these points is used only to ease the visual gradation between the points. It is not meant to give a strictly accurate representation for every year between the two decades. If this were so, the line would hardly be straight, even progression from year to year. The sharp directness of the lines reveals otherwise. The purpose of the graph is to plot the average increases or decreases from point to point. When dealing with more than one subject, a line graph must use either differently colored lines (or different types of lines if the graph is black-and-white). In the graph, the dark bold line represents immigration from Northwestern Europe; the broken line represents immigration from Southeastern Europe.

To read a line graph, find the point of change that interests you. For example, if you want to trace immigration from Northwestern Europe from 1861 to 1870, you would find the position of the dark line on that point. Next, trace the position to the vertical information on the chart. In this instance, one would discover that approximately 2 million immigrants arrived from Northwestern Europe in the period of time from 1861 to 1870. If wishing to discover when the number of immigrants reached 4 million you would read across from 4 million on the vertical side of the graph, and see that this number was reached in 1881–1890 from Northwestern Europe, and somewhere over the two decades from 1891 to 1910 from Southeastern Europe.

BAR GRAPHS

Bar graphs are also used to plot two dynamic elements of a subject. However, unlike a line graph, the bar graph usually deals with only one subject. The exception to this is when the graph is three-dimensional, and the bars take on the dimension of depth. However, because we will only be dealing with two-dimensional graphs, we will only be working with a single subject. The other difference between a line and a bar graph is that a bar graph usually calls for a single element to be traced in terms of another, whereas a line graph usually plots either of the two elements with equal interest. For example, in the following bar graph, inflation and deflation are being marked over a span of years.

INFLATION

Inflation is a rise in the general level of prices.
Deflation is a decline in the general level of prices.

Percentage points

   Percentage points are assigned to each year's level of prices, and that percentage decreases (deflation) from 1980 to 1981, and from 1981 to 1982. The price level is static from 1982 to 1983. The price level then increases (inflation) from 1983 to 1984. Therefore, it is obvious that the bar graph is read strictly in terms of the changes exhibited over a period of time or against some other element. Conversely, a line graph is used to plot two dynamic elements of equal interest to the reader (e.g., either number of immigrants or the particular decade in question).

   To read a bar graph, simply begin with the element at the base of a bar and trace the bar to its full length. Once reaching its length, cross-reference the other element of information that match the length of the bar.

PIE CHARTS

   Pie charts differ greatly from line or bar graphs. Pie charts are used to help a reader visualize percentages of information with many elements to the subject. An entire "pie" represents 100 percent of a given quantity of information. The pie is then sliced into measurements that correspond to their respective shares of the 100 percent. For example, in the pie chart that follows, Myrna's rent occupies a slice greater than any other in the pie, because no other element equals or exceeds 25 percent of Myrna's monthly budget.

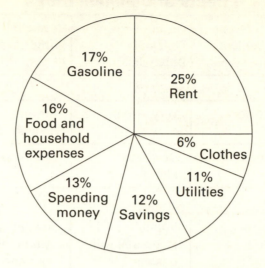

MYRNA'S MONTHLY BUDGET

Another aspect of pie charts is that the smaller-percentage elements are arranged in consecutive order from smallest element to largest element. Therefore, the largest element in the chart will necessarily be adjacent to the smallest element in the chart, and the line that separates them is the beginning or endpoint of the chart.

To read a pie chart, choose the element of the subject that interests you and compare its size to those of the other elements. In cases where the elements are similar in size, do not assume that they are equal. The exact percentage of the element should be listed within that slice of the chart. For example, Myrna's utilities, savings, and spending money are all similar in size, but it is clear when reading the chart that each possesses a different value.

READING TABLES

Tables are useful because they relate to large bodies of information within a confined area. To read a table, cross-reference the column headings that run horizontally across the top of the table with the row headings that run vertically down the left side of the table. Scanning the table for the overall information within is usually done by reading line by line, as if reading regular text, while referring to the appropriate headings of the table to interpret the information listed. Note that some tables possess horizontal subheadings, which further ease the separation of different areas of information.

Effects of Common Drugs

Drug	Psychological Dependence	Physical Dependence	Physical Withdrawal Effects	Development of Tolerance
Depressants				
Alcohol	Mild to very strong	Very strong	Severe/ dangerous	Minimal
Barbiturates	Develops slowly	Develops slowly	Death possible	Minimal
Narcotics				
Opiates (heroin, morphine)	Very strong Develops rapidly	Rapid/ increases with dosage	Frightening symptoms but not dangerous	Very high; Goes down quickly after withdrawal (Danger if user returns to original dose)
Stimulants				
Amphetamines	Strong	Not in formal sense, but body seeks "rush"	Mild	Extremely high
Cocaine	Very strong	None	None (can cause heart spasms and instant death even if healthy)	None
Crack	Strong	Strong	Mild	High
Psychedelics				
LSD	Unpredictable	None	None	Extremely high
Marijuana	Mild to strong	Some, in high doses	None	None (Some to high doses)

To use the preceding table, one should simply choose a particular drug, and then find the appropriate information needed about that drug through the headings listed at the top of the table. For example, the physical withdrawal effects of amphetamines, a stimulant drug, are mild in effect.

HELPFUL HINTS

You should approach any graphic information you encounter as a key to a larger body of information in abbreviated form. Be sure to use the visual aids of the graphics (e.g., the size of slices on pie charts) as aids only; do not ignore the written information listed on the graph, table, et cetera.

Note especially the title and headings so that you know exactly what it is at which you are looking. Also, be aware of the source of the information, where applicable. Know what each element of the graphic information represents; this will help you compare how drastic or subtle any changes are, and over what span of time they take place. Be sure you realize what the actual numbers represent, whether it is dollars, so many thousands of people, millions of shares, and so forth. Finally, note the way in which the graphic information relates to the text it seeks to illustrate; know in what ways the graphic information supports the arguments of the author of the given passage.

Language Arts

The language arts portion of the Basic Skills Test asks the test taker to use skills in the areas of grammar and composition. The objectives for this section of the test are to recognize correct and incorrect grammar and usage and to identify good and bad features of various kinds of writing.

Test takers will be asked to read a passage and answer questions about the words or punctuation included in that passage. You may also be asked to fill in a blank with a sentence or phrase that makes the passage more effective. When taking the test, you should skip ahead to read the questions about the particular passage first. This will give you an idea of what to look for and focus on as you are reading. It is also important that you understand the passage as a whole and comprehend its overall intention, meaning, or main idea.

This review was developed to prepare you for the language arts section of the Illinois Certification Testing System (ICTS). You will be guided through a step-by-step approach to attacking reading passages and questions. Also included are tips to help you quickly and accurately answer the questions. By studying this review, you will greatly increase your chances of achieving a good score on the language arts section of the ICTS.

A. Grammar and Usage

Standard 7   **Demonstrate command of standard usage in edited English in the United States.**

The following are examples of content that may be covered under this standard.
- Understand the standard use of verbs (e.g., subject-verb agreement, verb tense, consistency of tense).
- Identify and apply the standard use of pronouns (e.g., pronoun-antecedent agreement, standard pronoun case, use of possessive pronouns, standard use of relative and demonstrative pronouns).
- Recognize and apply the standard use of modifiers (e.g., adverbs, adjectives, prepositional phrases).

Standard 8   **Understand and apply knowledge of mechanical conventions in edited English in the United States.**

The following are examples of content that may be covered under this standard.
- Recognize instances in which incorrect or extraneous punctuation has been used or necessary punctuation has been omitted.
- Identify standard initial capitalization and standard capitalization with proper words and titles.
- Recognize the standard spelling of words.

B. Writing

Standard 9   **Understand the role of purpose and audience in written communication.**

The following are examples of content that may be covered under this standard.
- Assess the appropriateness of written material for a specific purpose or audience (e.g., a business letter, a communication to parents).
- Determine the likely effect on an audience of a writer's choice of a particular word or words (e.g., to evoke sympathy, to raise questions about an opposing point of view).
- Identify persuasive techniques used by a writer in a passage.
- Demonstrate the ability to adapt forms, organizational strategies, and styles for different audiences and purposes.

Standard 10   **Understand unity, focus, development, and organization in writing.**

The following are examples of content that may be covered under this standard.
- Identify organizational methods used by the author of a passage.
- Distinguish between effective and ineffective thesis statements.
- Recognize unnecessary shifts in point of view (e.g., shifts from first to third person) or distracting details that impair development of the main idea in a passage.

- Select appropriate and effective supporting material.
- Recognize examples of focused, concise, and well-developed writing.

Standard 11   **Understand and apply editing and revision strategies.**

The following are examples of content that may be covered under this standard.
- Apply editing and revision strategies affecting diction, syntax, transitions, organization, clarity, coherence, and point of view.
- Make revisions that improve the unity and focus of a passage or that improve cohesion and the effective sequence of ideas.
- Improve the clarity and effectiveness of a passage through changes in word choice.
- Eliminate or replace unnecessary or imprecise words and phrases.
- Insert appropriate transitional words or phrases (e.g., *however, as a result*) in a passage to convey the structure of the text and to help readers understand the sequence of a writer's ideas.

Standard 12   **Recognize sentences and paragraphs that effectively communicate intended messages.**

The following are examples of content that may be covered under this standard.
- Demonstrate an understanding of unity within paragraphs and apply methods for enhancing paragraph organization and unity.
- Recognize effective topic sentences and distinguish between effective and ineffective development of ideas within a paragraph.
- Identify sentence fragments and run-on sentences.
- Recognize wordiness, redundancy, and ineffective repetition in sentences and paragraphs.
- Recognize inefficiency in sentence and paragraph construction.

To help you master these skills, we present examples of the types of questions you will encounter and explanations of how to answer them. A drill section is also provided for further practice. Even if you are sure you will perform well on this section, be sure to complete the drills, as they will help sharpen your skills.

This chapter contains review material that will cover Standards 7 through 12. Chapter 3, which will help you prepare for the essay you will have to compose for the test's writing assignment, will help you prepare to meet Standard 13 on the Language Arts portion; this chapter contains only a brief review of how to recognize coherence in others' writing.

The Reading Passages

The reading passages in this section are designed for several different audiences. The readings will present you with very diverse subjects. Although you will not be expected to have prior knowledge of the information presented in the passages, you will be expected to know the fundamental writing techniques needed to convey the passage's message to its intended audience. Only your ability to write standard English for a specific audience will be tested. For example, you may get a passage like this one, written for a high-school history textbook:

[1]After the Civil War, raw cotton regained its traditional role as America's largest export good. [2]From 1803 to 1937, the Civil War and two other years excluded, unprocessed cotton was America's largest merchandise export. [3]The United States was also an important exporter of grain and mineral products. [4]What most characterized the growth of American exports in the late nineteenth century, _____, was the rise of manufactured goods exports: refined petroleum, machinery, and other manufactured goods. [5]Most of these goods were mass-produced products made by methods that were not used abroad, such as sewing machines, harvesters, and, later, automobiles). [6]Exports, increased rapidly, as American goods became highly competitive in world markets.

[7]Exports rose even faster than imports, with the consequence that exports always exceeded imports until 1971. [8]When the balance of trade remained consistently positive, Americans gradually recognized that a high tariff policy was no longer necessary or even desirable. [9]In 1913, with traditionally low-tariff Democrats in control of Congress, the Underwood Tariff lowered duties substantially. [10]International commerce expanded faster in the late nineteenth and early twentieth centuries than did worldwide output, with the gold standard aiding in this growth.

The Questions

Each passage will be followed by a number of questions. Some questions may ask you to find mistakes in standard English usage; others may ask you to supply appropriate words or phrases in blanks. You will commonly encounter questions that will ask you to:

- Identify the incorrect use of words.

- Identify the incorrect use of punctuation.

- Determine which sentence best makes the transition from one thought to another.

- Determine which word or phrase would be best for a specific audience.

- Determine the type of organization the author of the passage is using.

For example, questions for the passage above might be like these:

1. Which of the following parts does not use standard punctuation?

    A. Part 2

    B. Part 6

    C. Part 8

    D. Part 9

2. Which of the following words used in the blank in Part 4 would make a good transition from the previous sentence?

    A. consequently

    B. moreover

    C. nevertheless

    D. however

(Note that superscripted numbers in the passage are referred to in the answers as "Part X.")

Sentence Structure

Parallelism

Sentences should use the same kind of grammatical construction for all items in a series—those usually joined by a coordinating conjunction (*and, but, or,* and *nor*). "No smoking, eating, or drinking" is parallel; "No smoking, food, or drinking" is not, because *food* is not a verb form. Making elements parallel also requires knowledge of parallel correlative pairs, that is, the use of appropriate pairs together: *neither* and *nor, either* and *or, both* with *and, whether* with *or,* and *not only* with *but also.*

Parallel structure is used to express matching ideas. It refers to the grammatical balance of a series of any of the following:

Phrases. The squirrel ran *along the fence, up the tree,* and *into his hole* with a mouthful of acorns.

Adjectives. The job market is flooded with *very talented, highly motivated,* and *well-educated* young people.

Nouns. You will need a *notebook, pencil,* and *dictionary* for the test.

Clauses. The children were told to decide *which toy they would keep* and *which toy they would give away.*

Verbs. The farmer *plowed, planted,* and *harvested* his corn in record time.

Verbals. *Reading, writing,* and *calculating* are fundamental skills we should all possess.

Correlative Conjunctions. *Either* you will do your homework *or* you will fail. ***Note:*** Correlative conjunctions must be used as pairs and not mixed with other conjunctions, such as *neither* with *or* or *not only* with *also.*

Near-parallelisms. Sometimes a string of seemingly parallel thoughts are not in fact parallel. Consider this sentence: "I *have quit* my job, *enrolled* in school, and *am looking* for a reliable babysitter." In this sentence the writer has already *quit* and *enrolled* but is still looking for a babysitter; therefore she cannot include all three in a parallel structure. A good revision of this sentence is, "I have quit my job and enrolled in school, and I am looking for a babysitter."

Misplaced and Dangling Modifiers

As the name suggests, a misplaced modifier is one that is in the wrong place in the sentence. Misplaced modifiers come in all forms—words, phrases, and clauses. Sentences containing misplaced modifiers are often very comical: *Mom made me eat the spinach instead of my brother.* Misplaced modifiers, like the one in this sentence, are usually too far away from the word or words they modify. This sentence should read *Mom made me, instead of my brother, eat the spinach.*

Such modifiers as *only, nearly,* and *almost* should be placed next to the word they modify and not in front of some other word, especially a verb, that they are not intended to modify. For example, *I only sang for one reason* is wrong if the writer means to say that there was *only one* reason for singing.

A modifier is misplaced if it appears to modify the wrong part of the sentence or if the reader cannot be certain what part of the sentence the writer intended it to modify. To correct a misplaced modifier, move the modifier next to the word it describes.

UNREVISED: She served hamburgers to the men on paper plates.

REVISED: She served hamburgers on paper plates to the men.

A **squinting modifier** is one that may refer to either a preceding or a following word, leaving the reader uncertain about what it is intended to modify. Correct a squinting modifier by moving it next to the word it is intended to modify.

UNREVISED: Snipers who fired on the soldiers often escaped capture.

REVISED: Snipers who often fired on the soldiers escaped capture. OR Snipers who fired on the soldiers escaped capture often.

A **dangling modifier** is a modifier or verb in search of a subject: the modifying phrase (usually a participle phrase—an *-ing* word group or an *-ed* or an *-en* word group—or an infinitive phrase—a *to* + *verb* word group) has nothing to modify. It is figuratively *dangling* at the beginning or the end of a sentence. The sentences often look and sound correct at first glance: *To be a student government officer, your grades must be above average.* However, the verbal modifier has nothing to describe. You are supposed *to be a student government officer*; *your grades* cannot become an officer.

To correct a dangling modifier, reword the sentence by either (1) changing the modifying phrase to a clause with a subject, or (2) changing the subject of the sentence to the word that should be modified. Here are some other examples of correct revision of dangling modifiers:

UNREVISED: Shortly after leaving home, the accident occurred.

REVISED: Shortly after we left home, the accident occurred.

UNREVISED: To get up on time, a great effort was needed.

REVISED: To get up on time, I made a great effort.

Sentence Fragments

A fragment is an incomplete construction that either (1) lacks a subject or a verb or (2) is preceded by a subordinating conjunction (e.g., *because, which, when, although*). A complete construction, such as a sentence or an independent clause, expresses a complete thought.

UNREVISED: Traffic was stalled for ten miles on the freeway. Because repairs were being made on potholes. (The second "sentence" is a dependent, or subordinate, clause.)

REVISED: Traffic was stalled for ten miles on the freeway because repairs were being made on potholes.

UNREVISED: It was a funny story. One that I had never heard before. (The second "sentence" has no verb for its subject, "One.")

REVISED: It was a funny story, one that I had never heard.

Run-On/Fused Sentences

A run-on, or fused, sentence is not necessarily a long sentence or a sentence that the reader considers too long; in fact, a run-on might consist of two short sentences: *Dry ice does not melt it evaporates.* A run-on results when the writer fuses, or runs together, two separate sentences without any correct mark of punctuation separating them.

UNREVISED: Knowing how to use a dictionary is no problem each dictionary has a section in the front of the book that tells you how.

REVISED: Knowing how to use a dictionary is no problem. Each dictionary has a section in the front of the book that tells you how.

The most common type of run-on sentence is characterized by a comma splice—the incorrect use of only a comma to separate what are really two separate sentences. There are three quick ways to fix a comma splice: (1) replace the comma with a period and start a new sentence; (2) replace the comma with a semicolon; and (3) add a coordinating conjunction, such as *and* or *but,* after the comma.

UNREVISED: Bob bought dress shoes, a suit, and a nice shirt, he needed them for his sister's wedding.

REVISED: Bob bought dress shoes, a suit, and a nice shirt. He needed them for his sister's wedding.

UNREVISED: One common error in writing is incorrect spelling, the other is the occasional use of faulty diction.

REVISED: One common error in writing is incorrect spelling; the other is the occasional use of faulty diction.

UNREVISED: We have never won the track championship, we have won the cross-country title.

REVISED: We have never won the track championship, but we have won the cross-country title.

If one of the complete thoughts is subordinate to the other, you may also use a subordinate conjunction to connect the two:

> UNREVISED: Neal won the award, he had the highest score.

> REVISED: Neal won the award because he had the highest score.

Subordination, Coordination, and Predication

Suppose that you wanted to combine the information in these two sentences to create one statement: *I studied a foreign language. I found English quite easy.* How you decide to combine this information should be determined by the relationship you'd like to show between the two facts. *I studied a foreign language, and I found English quite easy* adds little or nothing to the original meaning. The **coordination** of the two ideas (connecting them with the coordinating conjunction *and*) is therefore ineffective. Using **subordination** instead (connecting the sentences with a subordinating conjunction) clearly shows the relationship between the expressed ideas:

> *After I studied a foreign language, I found English quite easy.* OR

> *Because I studied a foreign language, I found English quite easy.*

When using any conjunction—coordinating or subordinating—be sure that the sentence parts you are joining are in agreement:

> UNREVISED: She loved him dearly but not his dog.

> REVISED: She loved him dearly, but she did not love his dog. OR She loved him, but not his dog, dearly.

Another common mistake is to forget that each member of the pair must be followed by the same kind of construction.

> UNREVISED: She complimented her friends both for their bravery and thanked them for their kindness.

> REVISED: She both complimented her friends for their bravery and thanked them for their kindness.

While refers to time and should not be used as a substitute for *though, and,* or *but.*

> UNREVISED: While I'm usually interested in Fellini movies, I'd rather not go tonight.

> REVISED: Although I'm usually interested in Fellini movies, I'd rather not go tonight.

Where refers to a place and should not be used as a substitute for *that.*

> UNREVISED: We read in the paper where they are making strides in DNA research.

> REVISED: We read in the paper that they are making great strides in DNA research.

After words such as *reason* and *explanation,* use *that,* not *because.*

> UNREVISED: His explanation for his tardiness was because his alarm did not go off.

> REVISED: His explanation for his tardiness was that his alarm did not go off.

Punctuation and Capitalization

Commas

Commas should be placed according to standard rules of punctuation for purpose, clarity, and effect. On the test, you will be given choices that require your knowledge of such rules. The proper use of commas is explained in the following rules and examples.

In **a series**:

> When more than one adjective describes a noun, use a comma to separate and emphasize each adjective. The comma takes the place of the word **and** in the series.

the long, dark passageway

another confusing, sleepless night

an elaborate, complex, brilliant plan

Some adjective-noun combinations are thought of as one word. In these cases, the adjective in front of the adjective-noun combination needs no comma. (If you inserted **and** between the adjective-noun combination, it would not make sense.)

a stately oak tree

a superior elementary school

The comma is also used to separate words, phrases, and whole ideas (clauses); it still takes the place of **and** when used this way.

a lovely lady, an elegant dress, and many admirers

She lowered the shade, closed the curtain, turned off the light, and went to bed.

One question that exists about the use of commas in a series is whether one should be used before the final item. It is standard usage to do so, although newspapers and many magazines do not use the final comma. Occasionally, the omission of the comma can be confusing.

With a **long introductory phrase:**

Usually if a phrase of more than five or six words or if a dependent clause precedes the subject at the beginning of a sentence, a comma is used to set it off:

After last night's fiasco at the disco, she couldn't bear the thought of looking at him again.

Whenever I try to talk about politics, my wife leaves the room.

If an introductory phrase includes a verb form that is being used as another part of speech (a **verbal**), it must be followed by a comma:

UNREVISED: When eating Mary never looked up from her plate.

REVISED: When eating, Mary never looked up from her plate.

UNREVISED: Having decided to leave Mary James wrote her a long email.

REVISED: Having decided to leave Mary, James wrote her a long email.

To separate sentences with **two main ideas:**

To understand this use of the comma, you need to be able to recognize compound sentences. When a sentence contains more than two subjects and verbs (clauses), and the two clauses are joined by a coordinating conjunction (**and, but, or, nor, for, yet**), use a comma before the conjunction to show that another independent clause is coming.

I thought I knew the poem by heart, but he showed me some lines I had forgotten.

He is supposed to leave tomorrow, but he is not ready to go.

Jim knows you are disappointed, and he has known it for a long time.

If the two parts of the sentence are short and closely related, it is not necessary to use a comma.

He threw the ball and the dog ran after it.

Be careful not to confuse a sentence that has a compound verb and a single subject with a compound sentence. If the subject is the same for both verbs, there is no need for a comma.

UNREVISED: Charles sent some flowers, and wrote a long note explaining why he had not been able to attend.

REVISED: Charles sent some flowers and wrote a long note explaining why he had not been able to attend.

UNREVISED: Last Thursday we went to the concert with Julia, and afterwards dined at an old Italian restaurant.

REVISED: Last Thursday we went to the concert with Julia and afterwards dined at an old Italian restaurant.

In general, words and phrases that stop the flow of the sentence or are unnecessary for the main idea are set off by commas.

Abbreviations after names

Martha Harris, PhD, will be the speaker tonight.

Interjections (An exclamation without added grammatical connection)

Oh, I'm so glad to see you!

Hey, let us out of here!

Direct address

Roy, won't you open the door for the dog?

Hey, lady, watch out for that car!

Tag questions

Jerry looks like his father, doesn't he?

Geographical names and addresses

The concert will be held in Chicago, Illinois, on August 12. [**Note:** Punctuation must always follow a state name when that name follows a city—except in postal addresses, as illustrated in the next item.]

The letter was addressed to Mrs. Marion Heartwell, 1881 Pine Lane, Palo Alto, California 95824.

Transitional words and phrases

On the other hand, I hope he gets better.

I've always found, however, that the climate is better in the mountains.

Parenthetical words and phrases

In fact, I planted corn last summer.

The Mannes affair was, to put it mildly, a surprise.

With **nonrestrictive elements:**

Parts of a sentence that modify other parts are sometimes essential to the meaning of the sentence and sometimes not. When a modifying word or phrase is not vital to the meaning of the sentence, it is set off by commas. Because it does not restrict the meaning of the words it modifies, it is called **nonrestrictive**. Modifiers that are essential to the meaning of the sentence are **restrictive**; they are not set off by commas.

ESSENTIAL: The girl *who wrote the story* is my sister.

NONESSENTIAL: My sister, *the girl who wrote the story,* has always loved to write.

ESSENTIAL: The man who is wearing the red sweater is the best-dressed person in the class.

NONESSENTIAL: Jorge, who is wearing the red sweater, is the best-dressed person in the class.

To set off **direct quotations:**

Most direct quotes or quoted materials are set off from rest of the sentence by commas.

"Please read your part more loudly," the director insisted.

"I won't know what to do," said Michael, "if you ever leave me alone."

Who was it who said, "Do not ask for whom the bell tolls; it tolls for thee"?

Note: In American English, commas always go inside the closing quotation mark, even if the comma is not part of the material being quoted.

To set off **contrasting elements.**

Her intelligence, not her beauty, got her the job.

It was a reasonable, though not appealing, idea.

In **dates:**

In the month-day-year form, commas follow the day and year.

She will arrive April 6, 2006, on the *Queen Elizabeth*.

If only the month and year are given, no commas are necessary.

The minister's January 1967 resignation was unexpected.

The day-month-year form requires no punctuation.

The events of 14 April 1865 were unprecedented.

Because a specific date makes a descriptive phrase following it nonessential, that phrase will be nonrestrictive and therefore set off by a comma.

He was married on 7 October 1988, which fell five days after his forty-third birthday.

When a subordinate clause is at the end of a sentence, a comma preceding the clause is optional. However, when a subordinate clause introduces a sentence, a comma should be used after the clause. Here are some common subordinating conjunctions:

after	even though	till
although	if	unless
as	inasmuch as	until
as if	since	when
because	so that	whenever
before	though	while

Semicolons

This review section covers the basic uses of the semicolon: to separate independent clauses not joined by a coordinating conjunction, to separate independent clauses separated by a conjunctive adverb, and to separate items in a series with internal commas.

Use the **semicolon** in the following cases:

To separate independent clauses that are not joined by a coordinating conjunction.

I understand how to use commas; the semicolon I have yet to master.

To separate two independent clauses connected by a conjunctive adverb.

He took great care with his work; therefore, he was very successful.

Usually a comma follows the conjunctive adverb. Note also that a period can be used to separate two sentences joined by a conjunctive adverb. Here are some common conjunctive adverbs:

accordingly	indeed	now
besides	in fact	on the other hand
consequently	moreover	otherwise
finally	nevertheless	perhaps
furthermore	next	still
however	nonetheless	therefore

Then is also used as a conjunctive adverb, but it is not usually followed by a comma.

To combine two independent clauses connected by a coordinating conjunction if either or both of the clauses contain other internal punctuation:

Success in college, some maintain, requires intelligence, industry, and perseverance; *but* others, fewer in number, assert that only geniality is important.

To separate items in a series when each item has internal punctuation. It is important to be consistent; if you use a semicolon between *any* of the items in the series, you must use semicolons to separate *all* of the items in the series.

I bought an old, dilapidated chair; an antique table that was in beautiful condition; and a new, ugly, blue and white rug.

Do *not* use the semicolon in any other cases, especially as a substitute for a comma. Here are some examples of nonstandard semicolon use; all of them should be replaced with a comma:

You should never make such statements; even though they are correct.

My roommate also likes sports; particularly football, basketball, and baseball.

Being of a cynical mind; I should ask for a recount of the ballots.

Note: The semicolon is not a terminal mark of punctuation; therefore, it should not be followed by a capital letter unless the first word in the second clause ordinarily requires capitalization.

Colons

The difference between the colon and the semicolon and between the colon and the period is that the colon is an introductory mark, not a terminal mark. The colon signals the reader that a list, explanation, or restatement of the preceding thought will follow. It is like an arrow, indicating that something is to follow.

Here are some examples of colons used to introduce lists. Note that some lists may have only one item.

I hate just one course: English.

Three plays by William Shakespeare will be presented in repertory this summer at Illinois State: *Hamlet*, *Macbeth*, and *Othello*.

The reasons he cited for his success are as follows: honesty, industry, and a pleasant disposition.

A colon should also be used to separate two independent clauses when the second clause is a restatement or explanation of the first:

All of my high school teachers said one thing in particular: college would be difficult.

You should also use a colon to introduce a word or word group that is a restatement, explanation, or summary of the first sentence:

The first week of camping was wonderful: we lived in cabins instead of tents.

In standard English the colon should only be used after statements that are grammatically complete. Do *not*, for example, use a colon after a verb or a preposition.

UNREVISED: My favorite holidays are: Christmas, New Year's Eve, and Halloween.

REVISED: My favorite holidays are Christmas, New Year's Eve, and Halloween.

UNREVISED: I enjoy different ethnic dishes, such as those from: Greece, China, Provence, and Italy.

REVISED: I enjoy different ethnic dishes, such as those from Greece, China, Provence, and Italy.

However, the use of a colon to set off a *displayed* list is becoming more common and may now be considered standard.

Apostrophes

Apostrophes are used to make a noun possessive, not plural. Remember the following rules when considering how to show possession:

Add **'s** to singular nouns and indefinite pronouns:

Tiffany's flowers

at the owner's expense

a dog's bark

Add **'s** to singular nouns ending in s, unless this distorts the pronunciation:

Delores's paper

the boss's pen

Dr. Yots' class or Dr. Yots's class (depending on pronunciation)

for righteousness' sake

Add **an apostrophe** to plural nouns ending in s or es:

two cents' worth

three weeks' pay

ladies' night

Add **'s** to plural nouns not ending in s:

men's room

children's toys

Add **'s** to the last word in compound words or groups:

brother-in-law's car

someone else's paper

Add **'s** to the last name when indicating joint ownership:

> Joe and Edna's home

> Ted and Jane's marriage

Add **'s** to both names if you intend to show ownership by each person:

> Joe's and Edna's trucks

> Ted's and Jane's marriage vows

Possessive pronouns change their forms *without* the addition of an apostrophe:

> hers, his, its, yours, theirs

Quotation Marks and Italics

The most common use of double quotation marks (") is to set off quoted words, phrases, and sentences.

> "If everybody minded their own business," said Mrs. O'Leary in a huff, "the world would be a much nicer place."

Single quotation marks are used to set off quoted material within a quote.

> "Shall I bring 'Rhyme of the Ancient Mariner' along with us?" asked her brother.

> "If she said that to me," Katherine insisted, "I would tell her, 'I never intend to speak to you again! Goodbye, Susan!'"

To set off titles of poems, stories, and book chapters, use quotation marks. Book, motion picture, newspaper, and magazine titles are italicized when printed.

> The article "Moving South in the Southern Rain," by Jergen Smith, appeared in the *Southern News*.

> The assignment is "Childhood Development," which is Chapter 18 of *Abnormal Behavior.*

Remember that commas and periods at the end of quotations are *always* placed inside the quotation marks even if they are not actually part of the quote. Semicolons and colons are always placed outside. Question marks are placed inside or outside, depending on whether the quotation is a question.

UNREVISED: "If my dog could talk", Mary mused, "I'll bet he'd say, 'Take me for a walk right this minute'".

REVISED: "If my dog could talk," Mary mused, "I'll bet he'd say, 'Take me for a walk right this minute.'"

UNREVISED: She called down the stairs, "When are you going"?

REVISED: She called down the stairs, "When are you going?"

UNREVISED: We have to "pull ourselves up by our bootstraps;" we can't just talk about our plans.

REVISED: We have to "pull ourselves up by our bootstraps"; we can't just talk about our plans.

Remember to use only one mark of punctuation at the end of sentence ending with a quotation mark.

UNREVISED: She thought out loud, "Will I ever finish this project in time for that class?".

REVISED: She thought out loud, "Will I ever finish this project in time for that class?"

Capitalization

There are many conventions for beginning words with capital letters; this section will review just a few of the more common ones. In general, capitalize (1) all proper nouns and adjectives, (2) the first word of a sentence, and (3) the first word of a direct quotation. Points (2) and (3) are easy to figure out, but knowing which nouns and adjectives are "proper" is sometimes difficult. Here is a brief list that will help you remember what words to capitalize.

Names of persons, geographical places, and organizations:

Kelvim Escobar is a pitcher for the Anaheim Angels, who play in the American League.

Titles of books, poems, songs, TV shows, newspapers, and the like:

The *Washington Post* ran an interesting review of Frost's *Collected Poems*; its opinions about "Mending Wall" were especially interesting.

Geographical regions, but not compass directions:

Many movies are set in the West.

The Northern Hemisphere is the part of the earth that lies north of the equator.

The cultural division between East and West has persisted throughout modern times.

Titles of persons, if they appear immediately before the person's name:

President George W. Bush held a press conference last week.

George W. Bush, president of the United States, visited our town twice during his first term.

Political parties and philosophy, but not systems of government or individual adherents to a political philosophy:

The problems within the Communist Party foreshadowed the difficulties that communism would have in establishing itself.

The Republicans and Democrats often argue about how best to spread democracy to other countries.

Pronouns

Pronoun Case

One of the most embarrassing mistakes you can make in written English is confusing the spelling of common pronouns: its and it's and your and you're. The words its and your are possessive pronouns, meaning "belonging to it" and "belonging to you," respectively. It's and you're are contractions for it is and you are.

> Watch *your* step; if you don't, you might break *your* neck.

> *It's* not likely that the company will give back *its* windfall profits.

Other commonly asked questions regarding the use of pronouns are about the confusion of nominative case pronouns with objective case pronouns.

Nominative Case	Objective Case
I	me
he	him
she	her
we	us
they	them
who	whom

Use the nominative case (subject of pronouns) in the following:

Subject of a sentence:

> *We* students studied until early morning.

> Alan and *I* "burned the midnight oil" too.

Pronouns in apposition to the subject:

> Only two students, Alex and *I*, were asked to comment.

Predicate nominative/subject complement:

The cast members nominated for the award were *she* and *I*.

The subject of a subordinate clause:

Robert is the driver *who* reported the accident.

The only pronouns that are acceptable in standard English after prepositions are the objective case pronouns. When deciding between *who* and *whom* in the sentence "We're having difficulty deciding *who* we can trust," try substituting *he* for *who* and *him* for *whom*; then follow these transformation steps:

1.   Isolate the *who* or *whom* clause: who we can trust.

2.   Invert the natural word order if necessary, to the normal English subject–verb order: we can trust who

3.   Read the final form with the *he* or *him* inserted: we can trust ~~who~~ *him*.
      The correct pronoun is thus *whom*.

Use the objective case (subject of pronouns) for the following:

Direct object of a verb:

Mary invited *us* to her party.

Object of a preposition:

The torn books belonged to *her*.

Just between you and *me*, I'm bored.

Indirect object of a verb:

Soren gave *her* a dozen roses.

Appositive of an object:

The committee selected two delegates, Barbara and *me*.

Object of an infinitive:

> The young boy wanted to help *us* paint the fence.

Subject of an infinitive:

> The boss told *him* to work late.

Object of a gerund:

> Enlisting *him* was surprisingly easy.

When a conjunction connects two pronouns or a pronoun and a noun, one good way to determine the case of a pronoun is to remove the "and" and the noun or other pronoun:

> Mom gave ~~Tom and~~ myself a piece of cake.

> Mom gave ~~Tom and~~ I a piece of cake.

> Mom gave ~~Tom and~~ me a piece of cake.

Removal of the crossed-out words reveals that the correct pronoun should be *me*.

Pronoun-Antecedent Agreement

Some questions might ask you about *pronoun-antecedent agreement*. These kinds of questions test your knowledge of using an appropriate pronoun to agree with its antecedent in number (singular or plural form) and gender (masculine, feminine, or neuter). An *antecedent* is a noun or pronoun to which another noun or pronoun refers.

Here are the two basic rules for pronoun reference-antecedent agreement:

1. Every pronoun must have a conspicuous antecedent.

2. Every pronoun must agree with its antecedent in number, gender, and person.

When an antecedent is one of dual gender—such as *student, singer, person,* or *citizen*—use **his** or **her.** Some careful writers change the antecedent to a plural noun to avoid using the sexist, singular masculine pronoun.

UNREVISED: Everyone hopes that they will win the lottery.

CORRECT BUT AMBIGUOUS: Everyone hopes that he will win the lottery.

CORRECT BUT AWKWARD: Everyone hopes that he or she will win the lottery.

REVISED: Most people hope that they will win the lottery.

Ordinarily, the relative pronoun **who** is used to refer to people, **which** to refer to things and places, **where** to refer to places, and **that** to refer to places or things. The distinction between **that** and **which** is a grammatical distinction (see the section on Word Choice Skills). Many writers prefer to use **that** to refer to collective nouns, even for people: A family that traces its lineage is usually proud of its roots.

Many writers, especially students, are not sure when to use the *reflexive case* pronoun and when to use the *possessive case* pronoun. The rules governing the usage of the reflexive case and the possessive case are simple.

Use the **possessive case**:

Before a noun in a sentence:

My dog has fleas, but *her* dog doesn't.

Before a gerund in a sentence:

Her running helps to relieve stress.

As a noun in a sentence:

Mine was the last test graded that day.

To indicate possession:

Brad thought the book was *his,* but it was someone else's.

Use the **reflexive** case:

As a direct object to rename the subject:

I kicked *myself*.

As an indirect object to rename the subject:

Henry bought *himself* a tie.

As an object of a prepositional phrase:

Tom and Lillie baked the pie for *themselves.*

As a predicate pronoun:

She hasn't been *herself lately.*

Do not use the reflexive in place of the nominative pronoun:

UNREVISED: Both Randy and *myself* plan to go.

REVISED: Both Randy and *I* plan to go.

UNREVISED: *Yourself* will take on the challenges of college.

REVISED: *You* will take on the challenges of college *yourself.*

Watch out for careless use of the pronoun form:

UNREVISED: George *hisself* told me it was true.

REVISED: George *himself* told me it was true.

UNREVISED: They washed the car *theirselves*.

REVISED: They washed the car *themselves*.

Notice that reflexive pronouns are not set off by commas:

UNREVISED: Mary, *herself*, gave him the diploma.

REVISED: Mary *herself* gave him the diploma.

Pronoun Reference

Pronoun reference questions require you to determine whether the antecedent is conspicuously written in the sentence or whether it is remote, implied, ambiguous, or vague, none of which results in clear writing. In the following, make sure that every italicized pronoun has a conspicuous antecedent and that one pronoun substitutes only for another noun or pronoun, not for an idea or a sentence.

Pronoun reference problems occur in the following instances:

1. When a pronoun refers to either of two antecedents.

    UNREVISED: Joanna told Tina that *she* was getting fat.

    REVISED: Joanna told Tina, "I'm getting fat." OR Joanna told Tina, "You're getting fat."

2. When a pronoun refers to a nonexistent antecedent.

    UNREVISED: A strange car followed us closely, and *he* kept blinking his lights at us.

    REVISED: A strange car followed us closely, and its driver kept blinking his lights at us.

3. When **this, that,** and **which** refer to the general idea of the preceding clause or sentence rather than the preceding word.

    UNREVISED: The students could not understand the pronoun reference handout, *which* annoyed them very much.

    REVISED: The students could not understand the pronoun reference handout, *a fact that* annoyed them very much. OR The students were annoyed because they could not understand the pronoun reference handout.

4.   When a pronoun refers to an unexpressed but implied noun.

UNREVISED: My husband wants me to knit a blanket, but I'm not interested in *it*.

REVISED: My husband wants me to knit a blanket, but I'm not interested in *knitting*.

5.   When **it** is used as something other than an expletive to postpone a subject.

UNREVISED: The football game was canceled because it was bad weather.

REVISED: The football game was canceled because the weather was bad.

6.   When **they** or **it** is used to refer to something or someone indefinitely, and there is no definite antecedent.

UNREVISED: At the job placement office, *they* told me to stop wearing ripped jeans to my interviews.

REVISED: At the job placement office, I was told to stop wearing ripped jeans to my interviews.

7.   When the pronoun does not agree with its antecedent in number, gender, or person.

UNREVISED: Any graduate student, if *they* are interested, may tend the lecture.

REVISED: Any graduate student, if *he or she* is interested, may attend the lecture.

REVISED: All graduate *students*, if *they* are interested, may tend the lecture.

Verbs

This section covers the principal parts of some irregular verbs, including such troublesome verbs as *lie* and *lay*. The use of regular verbs, such as *look* and *receive*, poses little problem for most writers, because the past and past participle forms end in -ed; it is the irregular forms that pose the most serious problems—for example, *seen, written,* and *begun.*

Verb Tenses

Tense sequence indicates a logical time sequence.

Use **present tense:**

> In statements of universal truth:
>
> > I learned that the sun *is* ninety-million miles from the earth.
>
> In statements about the contents of literature and other published work:
>
> > In this book, Sandy *becomes* a nun and *writes* a book about psychology.

Use **past tense:**

> In statements or questions about action that happened in the past and is now finished:
>
> > I *fell* over the limb and *broke* my arm.
>
> > How *did* you break your arm?
>
> In statements concerning writing or publication of a book:
>
> > He *wrote* his first book in 1949, and it *was published* in 1956.

Use **present perfect tense:**

> For an action that began in the past but continues into the future:
>
> > I *have lived* here all my life.

Use **past perfect tense:**

> For an earlier action that is mentioned in relation to a later action:

Cindy ate the apple that she *had picked.*

(First she picked it; then she ate it.)

Use **future perfect tense:**

For an action that will have been completed at a specific future time:

You *will have graduated* by the time we next meet.

Use **a present participle:**

For action that occurs at the same time as the verb:

Speeding down the interstate, I saw a cop's flashing lights.

Use **a perfect participle:**

For action that occurred before the main verb:

Having read the directions, I started the test.

Use the **subjunctive mood:**

To express a wish or state a condition contrary to fact:

If it were not raining, we could have a picnic.

In "that" clauses after such verbs as **request, recommend, suggest, ask, require,** and **insist;** and after such expressions as **it is important** and **it is necessary:**

It is necessary that all papers *be* submitted on time.

Subject-Verb Agreement

Agreement is the grammatical correspondence between the subject and the verb of a sentence or clause: *I do; you do; we do; they do; he, she, it does.* One source of confusion for many students is which verb form is singular and which plural, so this section begins by focusing on making that distinction and then tackles the task of identifying the real subject of a sentence. Finally, this section deals with subjects that are commonly construed as singular and those that are construed as plural.

Every English verb has five forms, two of which are the bare form (plural) and the **-s** form (singular). Simply put, singular verb forms end in **–s**; plural forms do not.

Study these rules governing subject-verb agreement:

A verb must agree with its subject, not with any additional phrase in the sentence such as a prepositional or verbal phrase.

Your *copy* of the rules *is* on the desk.

Ms. Craig's *record* of community service and outstanding teaching *qualifies* her for a promotion.

In an inverted sentence beginning with a prepositional phrase, the verb must still agree with its subject.

At the end of the summer *come* the best *sales.* Under the house *are* some old Mason *jars.*

Prepositional phrases beginning with compound prepositions such as **along with, together with, in addition to, and as well as** should be ignored, for they do not affect subject-verb agreement.

Gladys Knight, along with the Pips, *is* riding the midnight train to Georgia.

A verb must agree with its subject, not its subject complement.

Taxes are a problem.

One *problem is* taxes.

His main *source* of pleasure *is* food and women.

Food and women are his main source of pleasure.

When a sentence begins with an expletive such as **there**, **here**, or **it**, the verb agrees with the subject, not the expletive.

Surely there *are* several *alumni* who would be interested in starting a group.

There *are* 50 *students* in my English class.

There *is* a horrifying *study* on child abuse in *Psychology Today*.

Indefinite pronouns such as **each**, **either**, **one**, **everyone**, **everybody**, and **everything** are singular.

Somebody in Detroit *loves* me.

Does either [one] of you have a pencil?

Neither of my brothers *has* a car.

Indefinite pronouns such as **several**, **few**, **both**, and **many** are considered plural.

Both of my sorority sisters *have* decided to live off campus.

Few seek the enlightenment of transcendental meditation.

Indefinite pronouns such as **all**, **some**, **most**, and **none** may be singular or plural, depending on their referents.

Some of the food *is* cold.

Some of the vegetables *are* cold.

I can think of some retorts, but *none seem* appropriate.

None of the children *is* as sweet as Sally.

Fractions such as **one-half** and **one-third** may be singular or plural, depending on the referent.

Half of the mail *has* been delivered.

Half of the letters *have* been read.

Subjects joined by **and** take a plural verb unless the subjects are commonly thought of as one item or unit.

Jim and *Tammy were* televangelists.

Guns and Roses is my favorite group.

In cases when the subjects are joined by **or**, **nor**, **either . . . or**, or **neither . . . nor**, the verb must agree with the subject closer to it.

Either the teacher or the *students are* responsible.

Neither the students nor the *teacher is* responsible.

Relative pronouns—such as **who**, **which**, or **that**—require plural verbs if they refer to plural antecedents. However, when the relative pronoun refers to a singular subject, the pronoun takes a singular verb.

She is one of the best *cheerleaders who have* ever attended our school.

She is the only *cheerleader who has* a broken leg.

Subjects preceded by **every** and **each** are singular.

Every man, woman, and child *was* given a life preserver.

Each undergraduate *is* required to pass a proficiency exam.

A collective noun, such as **audience**, **faculty**, and **jury**, requires a singular verb when the group is regarded as a whole, and a plural when the members of the group are regarded as individuals.

The *jury has* made its decision.

The *faculty are* preparing their grade rosters.

Subjects preceded by **the number of** or **the percentage of** are singular; subjects preceded by **a number of** or **a percentage of** are plural.

> *The number of* vacationers in Florida *increases* every year.

> *A number of* vacationers *are* young couples.

Certain nouns of Latin and Greek origin have unusual plural forms.

Singular	Plural
criterion	criteria
alumnus	alumni
datum	data
medium	media

> The *data are* available for inspection.

> The only *criterion* for membership *is* a high GPA.

Some nouns, such as *deer*, *shrimp*, and *sheep*, have the same spelling for both their singular and plural forms. In these cases, the meaning of the sentence will determine whether they are singular or plural.

> *Deer are* beautiful animals.

> The spotted *deer is* licking the salt block.

Some nouns ending in *-ics*, such as *economics* and *ethics*, take singular verbs when they refer to principles or a field of study; however, when they refer to individual practices, they usually take plural verbs.

> *Ethics is* being taught in the spring.

> His unusual business *ethics are* what got him into trouble.

Some nouns that end in **-s** may appear to be plural but are not; examples are *measles* and *news.*

> *Measles is* a very contagious disease.

> *News* of her arrival *was* not welcome.

A verbal noun (infinitive or gerund) serving as a subject is treated as singular, even if the object of the verbal phrase is plural.

Hiding your mistakes *does* not make them go away.

A plural subject followed by a singular appositive requires a plural verb; similarly, a singular subject followed by a plural appositive requires a singular verb.

When the girls throw a party, *they* each bring a *gift*.

The *board*, all ten members, *is* meeting today.

Adjectives and Adverbs

Correct Usage

Be careful and *Drive carefully* are sentences that illustrate the differences that this section discusses: the proper use of an adjective or an adverb, including distinctions between *bad* and *badly* and *good* and *well*.

Adjectives are words that modify nouns or pronouns by defining, describing, limiting, or qualifying those nouns or pronouns.

Adverbs are words that modify verbs, adjectives, or other adverbs and that express such ideas as time, place, manner, cause, and degree. In general, use adjectives as subject complements with linking verbs; use adverbs with action verbs.

The old man's speech was *eloquent*.	ADJECTIVE
Mr. Brown speaks *eloquently*.	ADVERB
Please be *careful*.	ADJECTIVE
Please drive *carefully*.	ADVERB

Good and Well

Good is an adjective; its use as an adverb is colloquial and nonstandard.

NONSTANDARD: He plays *good*.

STANDARD: He plays *well.*

STANDARD: He looks *good* for an octogenarian.

Well may be either an adverb or an adjective. As an adjective it means "in good health."

He plays *well.*	ADVERB
My mother is not *well.*	ADJECTIVE

Do not confuse *good* and *well* when used with *feel.* If you say "*I feel good,*" you're referring to your general health or mood, whereas "*I feel well*" refers only to your sense of touch.

Bad or Badly

Bad is an adjective used after sense verbs, such as *look, smell, taste, feel,* or *sound,* or after linking verbs (is, am, are, was, were).

UNREVISED: I feel *badly* about the delay.

REVISED: I feel *bad* about the delay.

Badly is an adverb used after all other verbs.

UNREVISED: It doesn't hurt very *bad.*

REVISED: It doesn't hurt very *badly.*

Real or Really

Real is an adjective; its use as an adverb is colloquial and nonstandard. It means "genuine."

NONSTANDARD: He writes *real* well.

STANDARD: This is *real* leather.

Really is an adverb meaning "very."

NONSTANDARD: This is *really* diamond.

STANDARD: Have a *really* nice day.

This is *real* amethyst.	ADJECTIVE
This is *really* difficult.	ADVERB
This is a *real* crisis	ADJECTIVE
This is *really* important.	ADVERB

Faulty Comparisons

This section covers comparisons that use adjectives and adverbs with certain conjunctions, such as *than* and *as,* to indicate a greater or lesser degree of what is specified in the main part of the sentence. Errors occur when the comparison being made is illogical, redundant, or incomplete. Watch for **-er** and **-est** forms of words meaning *more* and *most,* and correlative pairs like *as . . . as.* Other clues are *than* and *other.* Often, sentences containing a faulty comparison sound correct because their problem is not one of grammar but of logic. Read such sentences closely to make sure that like things are being compared, that the comparisons are complete, and that the comparisons are logical.

When comparing two persons or things, use the comparative (**-er**), not the superlative (**-est**) form, of an adjective or an adverb. Use the superlative form for comparison of more than two persons or things. Use *any, other,* or *else* when comparing one thing or person with a group of which it, he, or she is a part.

Most one- and two-syllable words form their comparative and superlative forms with **-er** and **-est** suffixes. Adjectives and adverbs of more than two syllables form their comparatives and superlatives with the addition of *more* and *most.*

Word	Comparative	Superlative
good	better	best
old	older	oldest
friendly	friendlier	friendliest
lonely	lonelier	loneliest
talented	more talented	most talented
beautiful	more beautiful	most beautiful

When in doubt, consult a dictionary; most of them give the comparative and superlative forms.

Here are examples of some common types of faulty comparison:

Double comparison

UNREVISED: He is the *most nicest* brother.

REVISED: He is the *nicest* brother.

UNREVISED: She is the *more meaner* of the sisters.

REVISED: She is the *meaner* sister.

Illogical comparison

UNREVISED: The interest at a loan company is higher *than* a bank.

CORRECT: The interest at a loan company is higher *than at* a bank.

Ambiguous comparison

UNREVISED: I like Mary *better than* you. (than you *what*?)

REVISED: I like Mary *better than* I like you. OR I like Mary *better than* you do.

Incomplete comparison

UNREVISED: Skywriting is *more* spectacular.

REVISED: Skywriting is *more* spectacular *than* billboard advertising.

Omission of words **other**, **any**, or **else** when comparing one thing or person with a group of which it, he, or she is a part

UNREVISED: Joan writes better *than any* student in her class.

REVISED: Joan writes better *than any other* student in her class.

Omission of the second *as* in an **as . . . as** construction

> UNREVISED: The University of West Florida is *as large* or larger than the University of North Florida.

> REVISED: The University of West Florida is *as large as* or larger than the University of Northern Florida.

Word Choice

Usage

Consider this sentence: The high school *principal* resigned for two *principal* reasons. If you think that the second *principal* is the wrong word (that it should be *principle*), think again. This usage is correct. You may be asked about words that are commonly confused and misused, as well as the use of words based on their grammatical appropriateness in a sentence, such as the distinction between *principal* and *principle*, *fewer* and *less*, and *lie* and *lay*. Here are some commonly confused pairs:

> *principal*—as an adjective, most important; as a noun, the chief authority.

> *principle*—always a noun: a fundamental law. "We hold these principles to be self-evident."

> *affect*—usually a verb, meaning to *influence*; sometimes a noun, with a specific meaning in psychology. "Her performance was adversely affected by the heat."

> *effect*—usually a noun, meaning something that results from something else; occasionally a verb, meaning *to cause to come into being*. "The heat had no effect on his performance." "Her persistence helped to effect the new zoning ordinance."

Connotative and Denotative Meanings

The denotative meaning of a word is its *literal,* dictionary definition: what the word denotes, or "means." The connotative meaning of a word is what the word connotes or "suggests"; it is a meaning apart from what the word literally means. A writer should choose a word based on the tone and context of the sentence; this ensures that a word bears the appropriate connotation while still conveying some exactness in denotation. For example, a gift might be described as "cheap," but the directness of the word has a negative connotation—something cheap is something of little or no value. The word "inexpensive" has a more positive connotation, although "cheap" is a synonym for "inexpensive." You may very well have to make a decision regarding the appropriateness of words and phrases within the context of a sentence.

Wordiness and Conciseness

Some questions will test your ability to detect redundancies (unnecessary repetitions), circumlocution (failure to get to the point), and padding with loose synonyms. These questions require you to select sentences that use as few words as possible to convey a message clearly, economically, and effectively.

Effective writing is concise. Wordiness, on the other hand, decreases the clarity of expression by cluttering sentences with unnecessary words. Of course, not all short sentences are better than long ones simply because they are brief. As long as a word serves a function, it should remain in the sentence. However, repetition of words, sounds, and phrases should be used only for emphasis or other stylistic reasons. Editing your writing will make a difference in its impact. Notice what revision does here:

UNREVISED: The medical exam that he gave me was entirely complete.

REVISED: The medical exam he gave me was complete.

UNREVISED: Larry asked his friend John, who was a good, old friend, if he would join him and go along with him to see the foreign film made in Japan.

REVISED: Larry asked his good, old friend John if he would join him in seeing the Japanese film.

UNREVISED: I was absolutely, totally happy with the present that my parents gave to me at 7 AM on the morning of my birthday.

REVISED: I was happy with the present my parents gave me on the morning of my birthday.

UNREVISED: It seems perfectly clear to me that although he went and got permission from the professor, he still should not have played that awful, terrible joke on the dean.

REVISED: It seems clear that, although he got permission from the professor, he should not have played that terrible joke on the dean.

Drill: Editing Skills

(A)   South of Richmond, the two roads converge together to form a single highway.

(B)   South of Richmond, the two roads converge together to form an interstate highway.

(C)   South of Richmond, the two roads converge to form an interstate highway.

(D)   South of Richmond, the two roads converge to form a single interstate highway.

The correct answer is (C); *together* is not needed after *converge*, and *single* is not needed to modify *highway*.

(A)   Vincent van Gogh and Paul Gauguin were close personal friends and companions who enjoyed each other's company and frequently worked together on their artwork.

(B)   Vincent van Gogh and Paul Gauguin were friends who frequently painted together.

(C)   Vincent van Gogh was a close personal friend of Paul Gauguin, and the two of them often worked together on their artwork because they enjoyed each other's company.

(D)   Vincent van Gogh, a close personal friend of Paul Gauguin, often worked with him on their artwork.

The correct answer is (B). Choices (A) and (C) pad the sentences with loose synonyms that are redundant. Choice (D), although a short sentence, does not convey the meaning as clearly as choice (B).

Transitions and Coherence

On the Language Arts portion of the ICTS, you will be asked tell whether a particular passage develops its ideas well. You will also be asked to supply missing words, phrases, or sentences that would make a particular passage develop more logically. Let's look at the following passage, which is adapted from a similar passage that appeared in Chapter 1.

Passage

[1]That the area of obscenity and pornography is a difficult one for the Supreme Court is well documented. [2]The Court's numerous attempts

to define obscenity have proven unworkable and left the decision to the subjective preferences of the justices. [3]Perhaps Justice Stewart put it best when, after refusing to define obscenity, he declared, but "I know it when I see it." [4]Does the Court literally have to see it to know it? [5]Specifically, what role does the fact-pattern, including the materials' medium, play in the Court's decision?

[6]Several recent studies employ fact-pattern analysis in modeling the Court's decision making. [7]These studies examine the fact-pattern or case characteristics, often with ideological and attitudinal factors, as a determinant of the decision reached by the Court. [8]In broad terms, these studies owe their theoretical underpinnings to attitude theory. [9]As the name suggests, attitude theory views the Court's attitudes as an explanation of its decisions.

[10]These attitudes, however, do not operate in a vacuum. [11]As Spaeth explains, "the activation of an attitude involves both an object and the situation in which that object is encountered." [12]The objects to which the court directs its attitudes are litigants. [13]The situation—the subject matter of the case—can be defined in broad or narrow terms. [14]One may define the situation as an entire area of the law (e.g., civil liberties issues). [15]On an even broader scale, the situation may be defined as the decision to grant certiorari or whether to defect from a minimum-winning coalition.

[16]Defining the situation with such broad strokes, _____, does not allow one to control for case content. [17]In many specific issue areas, the cases present strikingly similar patterns. [18]In examining the Court's search and seizure decisions, Segal found that a relatively small number of situational and case characteristic variables explain a high proportion of the Court's decisions.

[19]Despite Segal's success, efforts to verify the applicability of fact-pattern analysis in other issue areas and using broad-based factors have been slow in forthcoming. [20]Renewed interest in obscenity and pornography by federal and state governments as a result of lobbying campaigns by fundamentalist groups, the academic community, and other antipornography interest groups pro and con indicate the Court's decisions in this area will get closer examination.

[21]The Court's obscenity and pornography decisions _____ present an opportunity to study the Court's behavior in an area where the Court has granted significant decision-making authority to the states. [22]In *Miller v. California* (1973) the Court announced the importance of local community standards in obscenity determinations. [23]The Court's _____ behavior may

suggest how the Court will react in other areas where it has chosen to defer to the states (e.g., abortion).

Questions

1. This passage would be most appropriate in which type of publication?

    A. A popular newsmagazine such as *Time* or *Newsweek*

    B. An editorial about pornography in a newspaper

    C. A chapter on pornography in a sociology textbook

    D. An article in a law journal

2. Which of the following phrases, if inserted in the blank in Part 16, would best help the reader under the author's progression of ideas.

    A. consequently

    B. however

    C. nevertheless

    D. furthermore

3. In the final paragraph, which words or phrases, if inserted in order in the blanks, help the reader understand the author's logical sequence?

    A. in fact; foolish

    B. will; later

    C. also; subsequent

    D. theoretically; firm

4. Which of the following best describes the method of organization used by the author of this passage?

    A. problem and solution

    B. chronological order

    C. order of importance

    D. comparison and contrast

5. Which of the following sentences, if added between Parts 10 and 11, would be most consistent with the writer's purpose and intended audience?

   A. Situations with which the Court is faced are often quite complex.

   B. Supreme Court justices have been known to read newspapers as well as law journals.

   C. Pornography has been a point of public dispute for many decades now.

   D. If they did operate in a vacuum, predicting a justice's vote on a particular issue from his record before his appointment would be somewhat straightforward.

6. Which word would best replace the underlined words in Part 20?

   A. deserve

   B. are garnering

   C. will continue to elude

   D. have avoided

Answers

Keep in mind that the first step to answering these types of questions involves applying the Four-Step Approach discussed in Chapter 1. You cannot answer questions about the purpose, audience, or organization of a passage without first having analyzed it through the four-step approach. You will see that, in the practice test in this book and in the actual examination, passages are generally shorter than this passage; this one has been included so that you can review the Four-Step Approach while answering these questions.

The answer to Question 1 is **D**. The quotes from scholars eliminate A and B from consideration, because newspapers and magazines for general readers do not usually quote experts without identifying why they are worthy of being experts. Choice B is further eliminated by the fact that the passage takes no position that the average newspaper reader might act upon. The tone of the passage might conceivably be appropriate to choice C, but the passage focuses on law rather than pornography.

The correct answer to Question 2 is **B**. The previous paragraph ended with a statement about a "broad scale," and the new paragraph begins by saying that looking at the broad scale is inadequate. This sentence, then, must convey that contrast, so choices A and D are immediately eliminated. Choice C conveys the correct general meaning, but the use of *nevertheless* directly before a negative—*does not*—would be confusing to a reader.

The correct answer to Question 3 is **C**. To find this answer, you will first have to notice that the author is switching topics from obscenity to states' rights; therefore, the choice A is eliminated, because *in fact* is a transition that signals an example of what has just been discussed. (In addition, nothing in the passage indicates that the author regards the Court's behavior as "foolish.")

Choice B is wrong simply because the word "will" is not accurate: the decisions *already do* present an opportunity for further analysis. Choice D's "theoretically" is plausible, but "firm" is definitely wrong because it does not describe the author's opinion of the Court's 1973 decision, which just announces the importance of local standards rather than making firm law regarding them.

Question 4's answer is **D**. Although a problem and solution are implied in the passage, there is no direct statement of the problem followed by a solution. Chronological order and order of importance are clearly not present here, but the writer does compare and contrast analytical methods and attempts to explicate their strengths and weaknesses.

The best answer to Question 5 is **D**. Choices A and C are far from the point of the paragraph, which concerns how justices reach decisions. The choice of D over B depends on the tone of the two sentences as well as the specific content. The content of the two sentences is similar, although the content of D is somewhat more on message. The tone of choice B, however, is a bit flippant and would undoubtedly be out of place in most articles aimed at law scholars.

The best answer to Question 6 is **A**. Choice D contradicts the facts as presented in the paragraph, and choice C is out of line with the entire passage, which does give close examination to the subject. Choice B is technically correct (although not very informative for a final thought in a paragraph), but the word *garner* would be more at home in a newspaper article ("Duncan Garners Another Award") than in an article like this one.

Writing Assignment

This Chapter covers Part C—the Writing assignment—of Subarea II of the ICTS. Parts A and B of Subarea II appear in Chapter 2.

I. STRATEGIES FOR THE ESSAY
II. RECOGNIZING EFFECTIVE WRITING
III. WRITING YOUR ESSAY
IV. POLISHING AND EDITING YOUR ESSAY

Standard 13

Prepare an organized, developed composition in edited English as used in the United States in response to instructions regarding content, purpose, and audience.

The following are examples of content that may be covered under this standard.

- Compose a unified, focused, and sustained piece of writing on a given topic using language and style appropriate to a specified audience, purpose, and occasion.
- Take a position on a contemporary social or political issue and defend that position with reasoned arguments and supporting examples.
- Use effective sentence structure and apply the standards of edited English in the United States.
- Demonstrate the ability to spell, capitalize, and punctuate according to the standards of edited English in the United States.

The Basic Skills portion of the Illinois Certification Testing System contains a writing assignment. The Basic Skills written assignment asks test-takers to compose a composition, or written response, on a given subject. You will be evaluated on your ability to communicate the written message to a specified audience. The compositions are graded on the following criteria: **focus** (the clarity of the main idea), **support/elaboration** (supporting details are specific and clearly understood), **organization** (logical sequence of thoughts and ideas, and overall clarity of the work), and **grammar and conventions** (the extent to which the response has no errors in usage, spelling, capitalization, punctuation, and the precision of word choice). The responses are graded on a scale from "6" to "1." Other possible scores are "U," or "Unscorable," or "B," "Blank."

In an essay earning a score of 6, ideas are presented clearly, arguments are well organized, and there is extensive and specific supporting detail. The writer communicates through effective sentence structure and uses proper spelling, grammar, and punctuation.

In an essay scoring 4 or 5, ideas are well communicated, but supporting details might not be as precise or extensive as in a paper scoring 6. The ideas might be incomplete or generally ineffective. Minor errors in areas such as punctuation, spelling, word choice, or general usage are present.

A score of 2 or 3 is given to essays that do not support the main idea with specific details, and in which the overall organization of the work is unclear. The purpose of the essay might need to be inferred because it is vaguely stated. Errors are found in word choice, usage, sentence structure, spelling, and punctuation.

The response score 1 would be given to an essay that does not communicate the overall message and is lacking logical sequence of ideas. Often the main idea is not clearly stated, and supporting details are confusing. Common errors include incorrect use of language and sentence structure. Spelling and punctuation errors are found throughout the response.

A response given a U is deemed unscorable. A U score would be given if the essay is not on the given topic, is illegible, too short, or not written in English.

A response given a B is self-explanatory (i.e., a blank sheet that contains no answer).

Sample essays from different scoring levels appear at the end of the Basic Skills Practice Test, accompanied by critical commentary.

Carefully read the assignment before you begin to write. Think about your ideas and what you would like to communicate to the reader. You may wish to make an outline for the topic to help organize your thoughts, but be sure to write the final draft of your response in the test booklet. Your score will be based on what is written in the response booklet. When you have finished writing, be sure to review your work and make any changes you believe would enhance your score.

This review will guide you through a step-by-step process of how to write an essay, from writing strategies to budgeting time during the exam. Even if you feel that you are a good writer, you should still study this review, as it will help you become familiar with essay writing. The strategies included are provided to help you write an essay that is to the point, easily understood, properly structured, well supported, and correct according to the rules of grammar. You will not be expected to write a best-selling book in order to pass this test. Remember, the more you practice the strategies provided in this review, the easier it will be for you to write a good essay.

I. Strategies for the Essay

To give yourself the best chance of writing a good essay, you should follow these steps.

Before the test, this is your plan:

Step 1: Study the following review to enhance your ability to write an essay. Remember, the sharper your skills, the more likely you are to receive a passing grade on your writing sample.

Step 2: Practice writing an essay. The best way to do this is to complete the Practice Test.

Step 3: Learn and understand the directions, so that you don't waste valuable time reading them on the test day. This will allow you to quickly review them before writing your essay.

Step 4: Develop your essay from the notes you have made. Present your position clearly and logically, making sure to provide adequate examples and/or support. Write your draft on scratch paper.

Step 5: Proofread your essay! Check every word for errors in spelling. Be sure that your sentences are concise and grammatically correct. Make any necessary revisions.

Step 6: Copy the final version of your essay into the response booklet.

Additional Tips

- Be sure that you have not strayed from your topic or introduced points that you have not explained.

- Vary your types of sentences so that your essay flows smoothly and is easy to read.

Use vocabulary that suits your audience.

Fast Facts

- Use vocabulary that suits your audience. Make sure not to insult your audience by using simple vocabulary, or by explaining things they already know. Likewise, do not alienate your audience by using complicated jargon, or by assuming that your readers are already familiar with the subject on which you are writing.

II. Recognizing Effective Writing

ORGANIZATION AND PURPOSEFUL DEVELOPMENT

For this test you will need to recognize and generate the elements of an excellent essay. In essence, you will be taking the principles covered in this review and utilizing them to create your own original essay. With that in mind, read carefully the standards and explanations below to prepare you for what to look for in your own essay response.

ESSAY WRITING

In academic writing, two purposes dominate essays:

1. Persuasion through argumentation using one, some, or all of the logical patterns described here.

2. Informing and educating through analysis and using one, some, or all of the logical patterns described here.

All of an essay's organizational strategies may be used to argue in writing. The author offers reasons and/or evidence so an audience will be inclined to believe the position that the author presents about the idea under discussion. Writers use seven basic strategies to organize information and ideas in essays to help prove their point (thesis). All of these strategies might be useful in arguing for an idea and persuading a reader to see the issue the writer's way. Your job is to use strategies that are appropriate to demonstrate your thesis. For example, you may wish to use comparison and contrast to demonstrate that one thing or idea is better or worse than another.

The following seven steps can be used to prove a thesis.

SEVEN STEPS TO PROVE A THESIS

1. Show how a *process* or procedure does or should work, step by step, in time.

2.   *Compare or contrast* two or more things or ideas to show important differences or similarities.

3.   *Identify a problem* and then explain how to solve it.

4.   *Analyze* into its components, or *classify* by its types or categories an idea or thing to show how it is put together, how it works, or how it is designed.

5.   *Explain* why something happens to produce a particular result or set of results.

6.   *Describe* the particular individual characteristics, beauty and features of a place, person(s), time, or idea.

7.   *Define* what a thing is or what an idea means.

Depending upon the purpose of the essay, one pattern tends to dominate the discussion question. (For example, the writer might use *description* and *explanation* to define the varied meanings of "love.")

During this test you will be called upon to exercise control over your writing by using the writing process and by knowing the pitfalls of weak writing and correcting them. Using the steps outlined below, compose your essay in the order suggested and note the elements and qualities to correct during each stage of the process of composing your essay test response. Make any corrections you need during the appropriate stage of the writing process; to correct errors at the wrong stage may waste time and interfere with your producing the best essay response.

COMPOSING YOUR ESSAY: USING THE WRITING PROCESS

Some people (erroneously) think that writers just sit down and churn out a wonderful essay or poem in one sitting in a flash of genius and inspiration. This is not true. Writers use the writing process from start to finish to help them to write a clear document. If you do not reflect on your composition in stages and make changes as you develop it, you will not see all the problems or errors in it. Don't try to write an essay just once and leave the room. Stay and look through it. Reflect upon it using the writing process.

The writing process has five steps: (1) Prewriting, or planning time; (2) The rough draft; (3) Organizing and revising the ideas (not the words or sentences themselves); (4) Polishing, or editing (making sure sentences themselves are sentences, that the words you use are the right words, and that the spelling and punctuation are correct); and (5) Proofreading, to make sure no mistakes are left.

Using this process does not mean that you have to write five drafts. Write one draft (stages 1 and 2), leaving space for corrections (e.g., writing on every other line or on one side of a page only) and then working on the existing draft through the rest of the stages (3 through 5). **If time allows**, you may want to do the whole process on scrap paper and then copy the finished product onto the allotted test paper. But if you do copy it, make sure you proofread your copy to see whether, while transcribing it, you left anything out or said a word twice or made any other errors.

III. Writing Your Essay

PREWRITING/PLANNING TIME

Read the essay question and decide on your purpose. Do you want to persuade your reader? Would you rather explain something?

> Sample: "Television is bad for people."

Do you agree or disagree with this statement? Decide. Take a stand. Don't be noncommittal. Write down the statement of your position.

> Sample: "I agree that television is bad for people."
>
> or
>
> "Television is an excellent learning tool and is good for most people."

This is your thesis.

CONSIDER YOUR AUDIENCE

The writer's responsibility is to write clearly, honestly, and cleanly for the reader's sake. Essays would be pointless without an audience. Why write an essay if no one wants or needs to read it? Why add evidence, organize your ideas, or correct bad grammar? The reason to do any of these things is that someone out there needs to understand what you mean to say. What would the audience need to know in order to believe you or to come over to your position? Imagine someone you know (visualize her or him) listening to you declare your position or opinion and then saying, "Oh yeah? Prove it!"

Fast Facts

The writer's responsibility is to write clearly, honestly, and cleanly for the reader's sake.

In writing your essay, make sure to answer the following questions: What evidence do you need to prove your idea to this skeptic? What would she disagree with you about? What does she share with you as common knowledge? What does she need to be told by you?

CONTROL YOUR POINT OF VIEW

We may write essays from one of three points of view, depending upon the essay's audience. The points of view below are discussed from informal to formal.

1.   Subjective/Personal Point of View:
"I think/believe/feel cars are more trouble than they are worth."

2.   Second-Person:
"If you own a car, you soon find out that it is more trouble than it is worth."

3.   Third-Person Point of View (focuses on the idea, not what "I" think of it):
"Cars are more trouble than they are worth."

For now, stick with one or another; don't switch your "point of view" in the middle. Any one that's properly supported is acceptable.

CONSIDER YOUR SUPPORT

Next, during prewriting, jot down a few phrases that show ideas and examples that support your point of view. Do this quickly on a separate piece of paper for about five minutes. Don't try to outline—simply list things that you think might be important to discuss. After you have listed several, pick at least three to five things you want or need to discuss, and number them in the order of importance that is relevant to proving your point.

WRITE YOUR ROUGH DRAFT

Spend about ten to twenty minutes writing your rough draft. Looking over your prewriting list, write down what you think is useful to prove your point in the order you think best to convince the reader. Be sure to use real evidence from your life experience or knowledge to support what you say. You do not have to draw evidence from books; your own life is equally appropriate.

For example, don't write, "Cars are more trouble to fix than bicycles," and then fail to show evidence for your idea. Give examples of what you mean: "For example, my father's Buick needs 200 parts to make one brake work, but my bicycle only has four pieces that make up the brakes, and I can replace those myself." Write naturally and quickly. Don't worry too much at this point about paragraphing, spelling, or punctuation—just write down what you think or want to say in the order determined on your list.

TRANSITIONS

To help the reader follow the flow of your ideas and to help unify the essay, use transitions to show the connections among your ideas. You may use transitions either at the beginnings of paragraphs, or you may use them to show the connections among ideas within a single paragraph.

Here are some typical transitional words and phrases that you should use when writing your essay.

To link similar ideas, use the words:

again	equally important	in addition	of course
also	for example	in like manner	similarly
and	for instance	likewise	too
another	further	moreover	
besides	furthermore	or	

To link dissimilar or contradictory ideas, use words such as:

although	and yet	as if	but
conversely	even if	however	in spite of
instead	nevertheless	on the contrary	on the other hand
otherwise	provided that	still	yet

To indicate cause, purpose, or result, use:

as	consequently	hence	then
as a result	for	since	therefore
because	for this reason	so	thus

To indicate time or position, use words like:

above	at the present time	first	second
across	before	here	thereafter
afterward	beyond	meanwhile	thereupon
around	eventually	next	
at once	finally	presently	

To indicate an example or summary, use phrases such as:

as a result	in any case	in conclusion	in short
as I have said	in any event	in fact	on the whole
for example	in brief	in other words	to sum up
for instance			

PROVIDING EVIDENCE IN YOUR ESSAY

You may employ any one of the seven steps previously listed to prove any thesis that you maintain is true. You may also call on evidence from one or all of the four following kinds of evidence to support the thesis of your essay. Identify which kind(s) of evidence you can use to prove the points of your essay. In test situations, most essayists use anecdotal evidence or analogy to explain, describe, or prove a thesis. But if you know salient facts or statistics, don't hesitate to call upon them.

1. **Hard data** (facts, statistics, scientific evidence, research)—documented evidence that has been verified to be true.

2. **Anecdotal evidence**—stories from the writer's own experience and knowledge that illustrate a particular point or idea.

3. **Expert opinions**—assertions or conclusions, usually by authorities, about the matter under discussion.

4. **Analogies**—show a resemblance between one phenomenon and another.

ORGANIZING AND REVIEWING THE PARAGRAPHS

The unit of work for revising is the paragraph. After you have written what you wanted to say based on your prewriting list, spend about twenty minutes revising your draft by looking to see whether you need to indent for paragraphs anywhere. If you do, make a proofreader's mark to indicate to the reader that you think a paragraph should start here. Check to see whether you want to add anything that would make your point of view more convincing. Be sure to supply useful transitions to keep up the flow and maintain the focus of your ideas. If you don't have room on the paper, or if your new paragraph shows up out of order, add that paragraph and indicate with a number or some other mark where you want it to go. Check to make sure that you gave examples or illustrations for your statements. In the examples below, two paragraphs are offered: one without concrete evidence and one with evidence for its idea. Study each. Note the topic sentence (T) and how that sentence is or is not supported with evidence.

Fast Facts

Be sure to supply useful transitions to keep up the flow and maintain the focus of your ideas.

PARAGRAPHING WITH NO EVIDENCE

Television is bad for people. Programs on television are often stupid and depict crimes that people later copy. Television takes time away from loved ones, and it often becomes addictive. So, television is bad for people because it is no good.

In this example, the author has not given any concrete evidence for any of the good ideas presented. He just declares them to be so. Any one of the sentences above might make a good opening sentence for a whole paragraph. Take the second sentence, for example:

Watching television takes time away from other things. For example, all those hours people spend sitting in front of the tube, they could be working on building a chair or fixing the roof. (*Second piece of evidence*) Maybe the laundry needs to be done, but because people watch television, they may end up not having time to do it. Then Monday comes around again and they have no socks to wear to work—all because they couldn't stand to miss that episode of "Everybody Loves Raymond." (*Third piece of evidence*) Someone could be writing a letter to a friend in Boston who hasn't been heard from or written to for months. (*Fourth piece of evidence*) Or maybe someone misses the opportunity to take in a beautiful day in the park because she had to see "General Hospital." They'll repeat "General Hospital," but this beautiful day only comes around once.

Watching television definitely keeps people from getting things done.

The primary evidence the author uses here is that of probable illustrations taken from life experience that is largely anecdotal. *Always* supply evidence. Three examples or illustrations of your idea per paragraph is a useful number. Don't go on and on about a single point. You don't have time. In order for a typical test essay to be fully developed, it should have about five paragraphs. They ought to be organized in the following manner:

Introduction: A paragraph that shows your point of view (thesis) about an issue and introduces your position with three general ideas that support your thesis.

Development: Three middle paragraphs that prove your position from different angles, using evidence from real life and knowledge. Each supporting paragraph in the middle should in turn support each of the three ideas you started out with in the introductory or thesis paragraph.

Conclusion: The last paragraph, which sums up your position and adds one final reminder of what the issue was, perhaps points to a solution:

So, television takes away from the quality of life and is therefore bad for human beings. We should be watching the sun, the sky, the birds, and each other, not the "boob tube."

Write a paragraph using this sentence as your focus: "Television takes valuable time away from our loved ones."

CHECK FOR LOGIC

Make sure that you present your argument in a logical manner. If you have not, you may not have proven your point. Your conclusion must follow from a logical set of premises, such as:

- Either/Or—The writer assumes that only two opposing possibilities may be attained: "Either _____, or this _____."

- Oversimplification—The writer simplifies the subject: "The rich only want one thing."

- Begging the question—The writer assumes she has proven something (often counterintuitive) that may need to be proven to the reader: "The death penalty actually increases, rather than deters, violent crime."

- Ignoring the issue—The writer argues against the truth of an issue due to its conclusion: "John is a good boy and, therefore, did not rob the store."

- Arguing against a person, not an idea—The writer argues that somebody's idea has no merit because he is immoral or personally stupid: "Eric will fail out of school because he is not doing well in gym class."

- Non Sequitur—The writer leaps to the wrong conclusion: "Jake is from Canada; he must play hockey."

- Drawing the wrong conclusion from a sequence—The author attributes the outcome to the wrong reasons: "Betty married at a young age to an older man and now has three children and is therefore a housewife."

IV. Polishing and Editing Your Essay

If the unit of work for revising is the paragraph, the unit of work for editing is the sentence. Check your paper for mistakes in editing. To help you in this task, use the following checklist.

POLISHING CHECKLIST

- Are all of your sentences *really* sentences, or have you written some fragments or run-on sentences?

- Are you using vocabulary correctly?

- Have you used a word that seems colloquial or too informal?

- Did you leave out punctuation anywhere? Did you capitalize, or not capitalize, correctly? Did you check for commas, periods, and quotation marks?

PROOFREADING

In the last three to five minutes, read your paper word for word, first forward and then backward, reading from the end to the beginning. Doing so can help you find errors that you may have missed by having read forward only.

Mathematics

Standard 14   **Solve problems involving integers, fractions, decimals, and units of measurement.**

The following are examples of content that may be covered under this standard.
- Solve problems involving integers, fractions, and decimals, including percentages.
- Solve problems involving ratios and proportions.
- Solve problems involving units of measurement, including U.S. customary and metric measurements, and conversions, including scientific notation (e.g., 6.05×10^8).
- Use estimation skills to solve problems.

Standard 15   **Apply mathematical reasoning skills to analyze patterns and solve problems.**

The following are examples of content that may be covered under this standard.
- Draw conclusions using inductive reasoning.
- Draw conclusions using deductive reasoning.
- Identify errors in mathematical explanations.

Standard 16   **Solve problems involving algebra and geometry.**

The following are examples of content that may be covered under this standard.
- Graph numbers or number relationships.
- Find the value of the unknown in a given one-variable equation.
- Express one variable in terms of a second variable in two-variable equations.
- Solve problems involving lines and angles.
- Solve problems involving two- and three-dimensional geometric figures (e.g., perimeter and area problems, volume and surface area problems).

Standard 17   **Understand concepts and procedures related to data analysis and statistics.**

The following are examples of content that may be covered under this standard.
- Interpret information from tables, line graphs, bar graphs, histograms, pictographs, and pie charts.
- Recognize appropriate representations of various data in graphic form (discrete and continuous).
- Demonstrate an understanding of fundamental statistical concepts (e.g., mean, correlation, standard deviation).
- Interpret graphic and nongraphic representations of frequency distributions, percentiles, central tendency, variability, and correlation.

Standard 18   **Solve applied problems using a combination of mathematical skills (including word problems involving one and two variables).**

The following are examples of content that may be covered under this standard.
- Apply combinations of mathematical skills to solve a series of related problems.
- Identify an equation to solve word problems involving one and two variables.
- Apply number concepts and geometric principles to solve practical problems.
- Apply statistical principles to analyze patterns and trends in data.

Basic Number Skills

Fractions need to have common denominators before adding. Thus, to add, say, $\frac{1}{2}$ and $\frac{2}{3}$, change both fractions to equivalent fractions. These new equivalent fractions will have the same *value* as $\frac{1}{2}$ and $\frac{2}{3}$ and will have common (same) denominators, but will look different from the original fractions. The lowest common denominator is 6, because both of the original denominators can be changed into 6; $\frac{1}{2}$ can be written as $\frac{3}{6}$, and $\frac{2}{3}$ can be written as $\frac{4}{6}$.

After changing the "appearance" of $\frac{1}{2} + \frac{2}{3}$ to $\frac{3}{6} + \frac{4}{6}$, we can then simply add the numerators together, giving $\frac{7}{6}$, or $1\frac{1}{6}$.

When adding mixed fractions (those made up of a whole number and a fraction), add the fractions first, then—separately—the whole numbers. If the fractions add up to more than 1, add 1 to the whole number sum. For example, if after adding we have 3 and $1\frac{3}{4}$, the final sum is $4\frac{3}{4}$.

The algorithm for subtracting fractions is generally the same as that for adding: Common denominators are required. A problem, however, may be encountered when attempting to subtract mixed fractions such as $3\frac{2}{5}$ and $1\frac{4}{5}$. Note that $\frac{4}{5}$ can't be subtracted from $\frac{2}{5}$ (without involving negative numbers.) The solution is to rename $3\frac{2}{5}$ as $2\frac{7}{5}$. (This is accomplished by "borrowing" 1, or $\frac{5}{5}$, from the 3.) The new problem—still equivalent to the original—is $2\frac{7}{5}$ minus $1\frac{4}{5}$, or $1\frac{3}{5}$.

One approach to multiplying fractions is to multiply the numerators together and the denominators together, then simplify the resulting product. $\frac{2}{3} \times \frac{3}{4}$, for instance, equals $\frac{6}{12}$, or $\frac{1}{2}$. There is no need to use common denominators (as with fraction addition and subtraction.)

If the numbers to be multiplied are mixed fractions, first rewrite them as "improper" fractions, such as $\frac{14}{3}$, then use the procedure described earlier.

To divide fractions, invert the divisor (or the "second" number; the one "doing the dividing") and multiply instead. In the case of $\frac{1}{5}$ divided by $\frac{3}{8}$, change the original problem to the equivalent problem $\frac{1}{5} \times \frac{8}{3}$. Using the algorithm for multiplying fractions, we get $\frac{8}{15}$ as the quotient.

Decimal notation provides a different way of representing fractions whose denominators are powers of 10. $\frac{13}{100}$, for instance, is written as 0.13, $\frac{1}{1000}$ as 0.001, and so forth.

To add or subtract decimal numbers, arrange them vertically, aligning decimal points, then add or subtract as one would whole numbers. (A whole number can be written as a decimal numeral by placing a decimal point to its right, with as many zeros added as needed. Thus, 7 becomes 7.0, or 7.00, etc.) The decimal point then "drops down" directly into the sum or difference; its position is not shifted.

Using the traditional algorithm for multiplying decimal numbers does *not* require aligning decimal points; the numbers to be multiplied can simply be arranged vertically, with right "justification." The numbers can then be multiplied as if they were whole numbers. The number of digits to the right of the decimal point in the product should equal the total number of digits to the right of the two factors. Here is an example:

$$\begin{array}{r} 1.64 \\ \times \quad 0.3 \\ \hline = 0.492 \end{array}$$

One method for dividing decimal numbers is to use the traditional whole number division algorithm, placing the decimal point properly in the answer. The number of digits to the right of the decimal point in the divisor is how far the decimal point in the quotient (the answer) should be moved to the right, with the decimal point in the dividend as our starting position. Here is an example:

$$0.3\overline{)1.44} = 4.8$$

Note that careful placement of digits when writing both the problem and the quotient help insure a correct answer.

The rules for performing operations on integers (whole numbers and their negative counterparts) and on fractions and decimal numbers where at least one is negative are generally the same as the rules for performing operations on non-negative numbers. The trick is to pay attention to the sign (the positive or negative value) of each answer. The rules for multiplication and division when at least one negative number is involved are the same: two positives or two negatives give a positive, whereas "mixing" a positive and a negative gives a negative ($-5 \times 3 = -15$, for instance). When adding or subtracting and at least one negative number is involved, it may be useful to think of the values as money, with "adding" being thought of as "gaining," "subtracting" being thought of as "losing," positive numbers being seen as "credits" and negative numbers, "debts." (Careful: Adding or "gaining" -8 is like *losing* 8.)

Sometimes, mathematical expressions indicate several operations. When simplifying such expressions, there is a universally agreed-upon order for "doing" each operation. First we compute any multiplication or division, left to right. Then, compute any addition or subtraction, also left to right. (If an expression contains any parentheses, all computation within the parentheses must be completed first.) Think "Please excuse my dear aunt Sally." Treat exponential expressions ("powers") as multiplication. Thus, the expression $3 + 7 \times 4 - 2$ equals 29. (Multiply 7 by 4 *before* doing the addition and subtraction.)

Exponential notation is a way to show repeated multiplication more simply. $2 \times 2 \times 2$, for instance, can be shown as 2^3, and is equal to 8. (Note: 2^3 does *not* mean 2×3.)

Scientific notation provides a method for showing any numbers using exponents (although it is most useful for very large and very small numbers). A number is in scientific notation when it is shown as a number between 1 and 10 times a power of 10. Thus, the number 75,000 in scientific notation is shown as 7.5×10^4.

Other common mathematical notation symbols include the following.

< means "less than"
> means "greater than"
$\neq$ means "not equal to"
$\leq$ means "less than or equal to"
$\geq$ means "greater than or equal to"

Word Problems

When converting word problems into mathematical problems the choice of operations is crucial to success. Often, individual words and phrases translate into numbers and operations symbols, and making sure that the translations are reasonable is important. Consider this word problem:

> Roberto babysat for the Yagers one evening. They paid him $5 just for coming over to their house, plus $7 for every hour of sitting. How much was he paid if he babysat for 4 hours?

"Plus" indicates addition, and "for every hour" suggests multiplication. Thus, the computational work can be set up like this: $5 + (7 \times 4)$ = Roberto's earnings. It would have been unreasonable to use a multiplication symbol in place of the addition sign. He earned $5 *plus* $7 for each of 4 hours.

Each word problem requires an individual approach, but keeping in mind the reasonableness of the computational setup should be helpful. (See more on this topic in Part II of this review, "Solve word problems involving one and two variables.")

Data Analysis

Interpret Information from Graphs, Tables, or Charts

Graphs, tables and charts come in many different forms; most simply represent numerical data in neat visual formats. A bar graph, like the one below, typically shows "how much" for each of many categories (or persons, or time periods, or whatever).

Number of Books Read in April

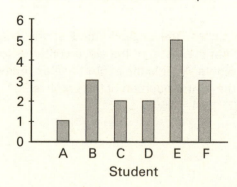

Broken line graphs, like the one below, are reserved for indicating *change over time*. Do not use broken line graphs unless one of the axes (usually the bottom or horizontal axis) indicates time. *Trends* are often revealed by broken line graphs.

Average monthly temperature, January–June 1996, Chicago

Pie graphs (also known as circle graphs or pie charts) often show how finite quantities are "split up." As with the example below, pie graphs may not necessarily be accompanied by specific numeric values. They are especially good for showing relative amounts or allotments at a glance.

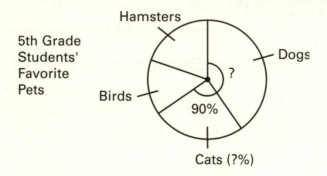

5th Grade Students' Favorite Pets

Because pie graphs are circles, the angle formed at the center by the boundaries of each catagory can be determined from the fact that the circle contains 360°. For example, if dogs are the favorite pets of 40% of fifth graders, what is the central angle? (**Answer:** 40% × 360° = .4 × 360° = 144°.) If the central angle of the "Cats" poprtion of the graph is 90°, what percentage of fifth graders prefer cats? (**Answer:** 90/360 = 1/4 = 25%.)

The graphs of *functions* can be shown on the coordinate plane. Such graphs always indicate a continuous (although not necessarily consistent) "movement" from left to right. Below left is the graph of a function; the graph on the right is *not* a function.

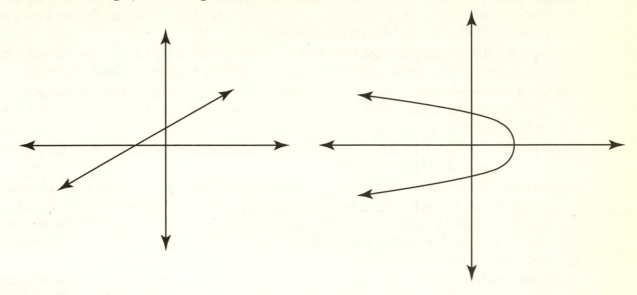

A key to interpretation of graphs, tables, and charts is to pay close attention to labels. Specific axes labels are also important. Don't assume anything about what a graph, table, or chart might be saying without carefully reading all labeled elements.

Statistical Concepts

The term *data* refers to numerical information acquired by counting or measuring. The number of students in a class, their test scores on the Illinois ISAT, and their individual heights are all examples of data.

Data can be represented in *discrete* or *continuous* form, depending on what they represent. If data are discrete, there are gaps between them. The bar graph is a common way to depict discrete data. For example, the bar graph on page 95 represents the number of books read by each of six separate students. Discrete data are generally obtained from counting rather than measuring. Continuous data are usually represented by an unbroken line on a graph, and they are usually obtained by measuring rather than counting. The data shown in the broken line graph on page 96 are continuous because there are no gaps between the months.

Here is a list of other statistical concepts that you might have to know for the test:

mean   The mean is the sum of a set of numbers divided by the quantity of numbers *n* in the set. It gives the *average value* of a data set.

range   The range is the measure of spread (*variation*) that is the difference between the largest value and the smallest value in a set of data.

sample survey   This is a survey of a population, usually human, made by taking a sample judged to be representative of the population. Use of a random mechanism for choosing the sample is essential for validity and believability.

spread of data   Spread, or **variation**, describes the degree to which data are spread out around their center. Useful measures of spread include the standard deviation and range.

standard deviation   This is the most commonly used expression of spread, or variation, of data. The higher the standard deviation, the higher is the degree of spread around the center of the data (that is, the data are more inconsistent with each other).

median   The median is the center value in a set of numbers: there are an equal number of values above and below it.

percentiles   These are the measures of where a piece of data stands in relation to the other data in its set. Perhaps best known from standardized tests, percentiles tell how many other data are lower in value. For instance, a test taker might have a raw score of 82% (that is, 82% of the answers correct) but rank in the 91st percentile, meaning that 90% of all test takers received lower raw scores. The median occurs at the 50th percentile.

frequency distributions   These represent the probability that a statistic of interest will fall in a certain interval; for example, the height of a person chosen at random may follow the *normal distribution*. Following are some samples of kinds of distributions, with location of the means and medians indicated:

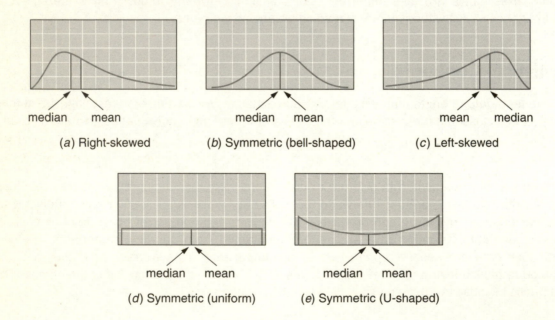

(a) Right-skewed   (b) Symmetric (bell-shaped)   (c) Left-skewed

(d) Symmetric (uniform)   (e) Symmetric (U-shaped)

Distribution (b) in the figure is the famous normal, or bell-shaped, curve on which tests are often said to be graded. Notice that more scores fall in the middle here than on the high or low ends. In the right-skewed distribution, shown in (a), more of the scores are low, and in (c) more of the scores are high (assuming that all of these graphs represent test scores). The distribution in (d) shows that the scores all scores are distributed equally from high to low, and (e) shows a distribution in which most scores were either high or low, with very few being average. Notice that in (a), the right-skewed distribution, the mean is higher than the median, and in (c) the median is higher than the mean.

correlation   Correlation is the relationship between two variables. For example, a graph of tar and nicotine in cigarettes might look like this:

Each dot represents a particular cigarette, and the placement of the dot depends on the amounts of its tar (x-axis) and nicotine (y-axis). Drawings like this are called *scatterplots*. You could draw a straight line through this scatterplot, and it would go up and to the right, because, in general, the higher the amount of tar, the higher the amount of nicotine. The amounts of tar and nicotine are thus *positively correlated*. Some variables are *negatively correlated*; for instance, the weight of a vehicle would be negatively correlated with gas mileage if several models of vehicle were plotted in a scatterplot.

Here are some other scatterplots with varying kinds of correlation:

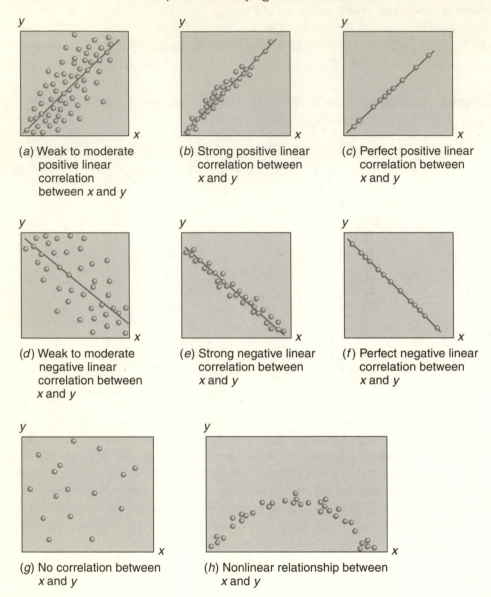

(a) Weak to moderate positive linear correlation between x and y

(b) Strong positive linear correlation between x and y

(c) Perfect positive linear correlation between x and y

(d) Weak to moderate negative linear correlation between x and y

(e) Strong negative linear correlation between x and y

(f) Perfect negative linear correlation between x and y

(g) No correlation between x and y

(h) Nonlinear relationship between x and y

When a correlation is linear or almost linear, you can use the graph to make predictions. For example, in the graph of tar and nicotine above, you could predict with a fair amount of certainty that a cigarette with 10 mg of tar would have between 0.7 and 0.8 mg of nicotine. In scatterplots without a linear correlation (g and h above), it's much harder to predict what y would be given x; in fact, in graph (g) it's nearly impossible.

Algebraic Graphing, Equations, and Operations

Two-Dimensional Graphing

The coordinate plane is useful for graphing individual ordered pairs and relationships. The coordinate plane is divided into four quadrants by an x-axis (horizontal) and a y-axis (vertical). The upper right quadrant is quadrant I, and the others (moving counterclockwise from quadrant I) are II, III, and IV.

Ordered pairs indicate the locations of points on the plane. For instance, (–3, 4) describes a point that's three units *left* from the center of the plane (the "origin") and four units *up*, as shown below.

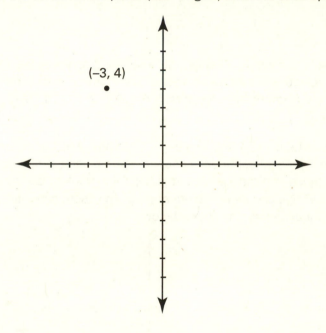

Sets of data can be paired to form many ordered pairs, which in turn can be graphed on the coordinate plane. Consider the following sets of data, which have been paired:

x	y
3	5
4	6
5	7
6	8

Considering each pairing individually, the following ordered pairs are produced: (3, 5), (4, 6), (5, 7), (6, 8). *Plotting* each pair on the coordinate plane produces the following graph:

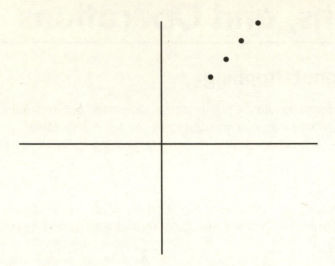

If the sets represent continuous change, the resulting graph may be a line (straight or curved in various ways). Often, relationships between sets of data can be shown as two variable equations or inequalities. Consider the following ordered pairs: (–4, –2), (–2, –1), (0, 0), (2, 1), (4, 2).

Note that the first value in each (the *x* value) is twice as big as the second (the *y* value). Assuming that the ordered pairs represent continuous change, the equation $x = 2y$ can be used to describe the relationship of the *x* values and the *y* values. It is helpful to think of the equation as stating that "*x* is always twice as big as *y*". We can show the equation on the coordinate plane by graphing at least two of the points, then connecting them as shown below.

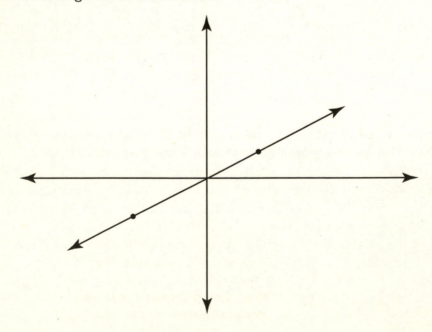

The generic equation $y = mx + b$ is a template for graphs on the plane that are straight lines. That form (sometimes called the "y-intercept form" of an equation) is especially useful because it tells two important characteristics of lines at a glance. The coefficient of x in the equation (or m) indicates the steepness, or *slope* of the line on the plane. The larger the absolute value of m, the steeper the slope of the line. (A number's absolute value is its distance from zero, giving no regard to negative signs.) Consider the two equations that follow and their accompanying graphs.

y = 1/4x + 2   y = 5x − 1

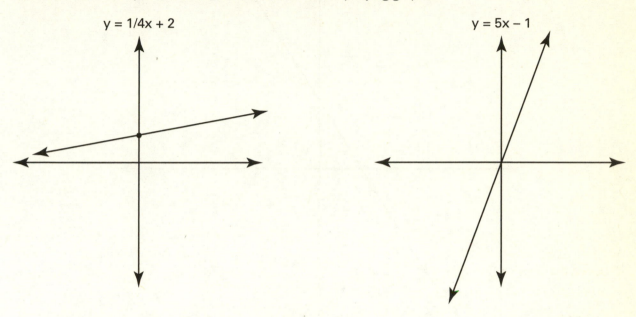

Note that the equation on the left has a small slope ($\frac{1}{4}$), so its graph is nearly horizontal. The other equation has a comparatively large slope (5), so it is steep.

If the coordinates of any two points of a straight line are known, the numerical slope of that line can easily be computed by finding the difference between the points' y values and dividing by the difference of the points' x values. For example, if (2, 5) and (4, 10) are points on a line, the slope of the line is $\frac{5}{2}$ [(5 − 10) ÷ (2 − 4)]. Note that slopes are generally shown as fractions or whole numbers, but not as mixed fractions.

The equation of a straight line in the form $y = mx + b$ tells something else about the line at a glance. The b value indicates where the line will cross or *intercept* the y (vertical) axis. Consider the graph of $y = 2x + 3$ that follows.

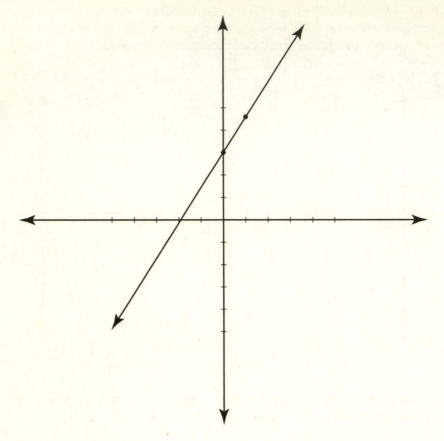

Note that the graph crosses the y-axis at a point that is 3 units above the origin. As long as the equation of a straight line is in the form $y = mx + b$, m gives the slope and b gives the y-intercept. (Note: If $b = 0$, the graph will pass through the origin. In that case, both the equation and the graph are referred to as *direct variations*.)

Other equations may produce curved graphs. For instance, $y = x^2$ produces the following graph, known as a *parabola*.

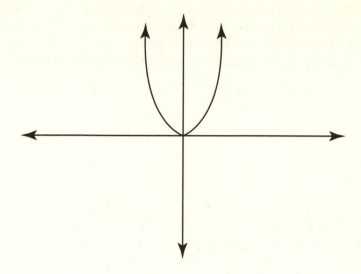

The equation $xy = 4$ is an *inverse variation*; it produces a graph known as a *hyperbola*, as shown below.

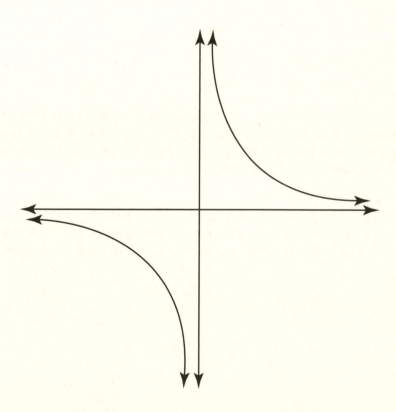

Solving One- and Two-Variable Equations

When attempting to solve one-variable equations, it is helpful to think of the task as that of producing a series of equivalent equations until, in the last equation, the variable has been *isolated* on one side. There are several ways to produce equivalent equations, but chiefly they are produced by performing identical operations on the two expressions making up the sides of equations. The equation $2x = 12$, for instance, can be solved by dividing both sides of the equation by 2, as follows:

$$\frac{2x}{2} = \frac{12}{2}$$

This then gives an equivalent equation of $x = 6$. Therefore, 6 is the solution to the original equation.

There are several caveats to observe when solving one-variable equations in that manner. One is that care must be taken to perform operations on *entire* expressions, and not simply on "parts" of expressions. In the example below, the last equation fails to give a solution to the original equation because, in the second step, only *part* of the expression $2x + 8$ has been divided by 2.

$$2x + 8 = 14$$
$$\frac{2x}{2} + 8 = \frac{14}{2}$$
$$x + 8 = 7$$
$$x = -1$$

Avoid dividing by zero. That operation is considered meaningless and will not provide a solution. Also, not all single-variable equations have solutions. $0x + 3 = 9$, for instance, has no real number solutions. If the variable carries an exponent, as in $x^2 = 16$, taking the square root of each side of the equation produces the solutions. (Note that *both* 4 and –4 work.)

"Solving one variable in terms of a second" simply means rewriting multivariable equations such that the desired variable is isolated on one side of the equation. For instance, the equation $x - 3y = 5$ can be rewritten as $x = 3y + 5$. The variable *x* has been solved in terms of the second variable *y*.

Solving a *system* of two-variable linear equations (such as $y = x + 6$ and $2y = 4x$) means finding the ordered pair (or pairs) of numbers that solves both equations simultaneously. Using trial and error, we can see that (6, 12) works in both of the equations above. There are also more formal methods for solving systems of two-variable equations. If we graph each equation on the coordinate plane, the point of intersection (if any) will give the solution to the system. Another method is to literally add or subtract one equation from the other, with the intention of eliminating one variable in the process, enabling us to solve for one variable, then the other. (One or both equations may first require multiplication in order to "line up" variables with opposite coefficients.) In the example that follows, the system of $y = x + 6$ and $2y = 4x$ has been solved using multiplication and addition.

$$y = x + 6$$
$$2y = 4x$$
$$-2y = -2x - 12$$
$$2y = 4x$$
$$0 = 2x - 12$$
$$x = 6$$

If $x = 6$, y must equal 12, so the solution to the system is (6, 12).

Solving Word Problems Involving One and Two Variables

One helpful approach when attempting to solve algebraic word problems is to *translate* the word problem into an equation (or, sometimes, an inequality), then solve the equation. Consider the word problem: "The Acme Taxicab Company charges riders 3 dollars just for getting into the cab, plus 2 dollars for every mile or fraction of a mile driven. What would be the fare for a 10-mile ride?" "Translating into math" we get $x = 3 + (2 \times 10)$. The equation can be read as "the unknown fare (x) is equal to 3 dollars *plus* 2 dollars for each of the 10 miles driven." Solving the equation gives 23 for x, so $23 is the solution to the word problem.

There are several common translations to keep in mind: The word *is* often suggests an equal sign; *of* may suggest multiplication, as does *product*. *Sum* refers to addition; *difference* suggests subtraction; and a *quotient* is obtained after dividing. The key when translating is to make sure that the equation accurately matches the information and relationships given in the word problem.

Understanding Operations with Algebraic Expressions

Only like (or similar) algebraic terms can be added or subtracted to produce simpler expressions. For instance, $3x^2$ and $5x^2$ can be added together to get $8x^2$, because the terms are like terms; they both have a base of x^2. We *cannot* add $8m^3$ and $6m^2$; m^3 and m^2 are unlike bases.

When multiplying exponential terms together, the constant terms are multiplied, but the exponents of terms with the same variable bases are *added* together, which is somewhat counterintuitive. For example, $5w^2$ times $2w^3$ gives $10w^5$ (*not* $10w^6$, as one might guess).

When like algebraic terms are divided, exponents are subtracted. For example,

$$\frac{7w^5}{2w^2}$$

becomes

$$\frac{7w^3}{2}$$

In algebra, we frequently need to multiply two binomials together. (*Binomials* are algebraic expressions of two terms.) The FOIL method is one way to multiply binomials. FOIL stands for "first, outer, inner, last." Multiply the first terms in the parentheses, then the "outermost" terms, followed by the "innermost terms," and finally the last terms, then add the products together. For example, to multiply $(x + 2)$ and $(3x - 1)$, we multiply x by $3x$ (the "firsts"), x by -1 ("outers"), 2 by $3x$ ("inners"), and 2 by -1 ("lasts"). The four products ($3x^2$, $-x$, $6x$ and -2) add up to $3x^2 + 5x - 2$. If the polynomials to be multiplied have more than two terms (*trinomials*, for instance), make sure that *each* term of the first polynomial is multiplied by *each* term of the second.

The opposite of polynomial multiplication is factoring. Factoring a polynomial means rewriting it as the product of factors (often two binomials). The trinomial $x^2 - 4x - 21$, for instance, can be factored into $(x + 3)(x - 7)$. (You can check this by "FOILing" the binomials.)

When attempting to factor polynomials, it is sometimes necessary to first "factor out" any factor that might be common to all terms. The two terms in $3x^2 - 12$, for example, both contain the factor 3. This means that the expression can be rewritten as $3(x^2 - 4)$, and then, $3(x - 2)(x + 2)$.

The task of factoring a polynomial is often aided by first setting up a pair of "empty" parentheses, like this: $2x^2 - 9x - 5 = (\quad)(\quad)$. The task is then to fill in the four spaces with values which, when multiplied (FOILed), will "give back" $2x^2 - 9x - 5$.

Factoring is useful when solving some equations, especially if one side of the equation is set equal to zero. Consider $x^2 + 3x - 8 = 2$. It can be rewritten as $x^2 + 3x - 10 = 0$. This allows the left side to be factored into $(x - 2)(x + 5)$, giving equation solutions of 2 and -5.

Geometry and Reasoning

Solving Problems Involving Geometric Figures

The following are formulas for finding the areas of basic polygons (informally defined as closed, coplanar geometric figures with three or more straight sides). Abbreviations used are as follows: *A* stands for *area*, *l* stands for *length*, *w* stands for *width*, *h* stands for *height*, and *b* stands for *length of the base*.

Triangle (a three-sided polygon): $A = \frac{b \times h}{2}$. (Note that, as shown in the figure that follows, the height of a triangle is not necessarily the same as the length of any of its sides.)

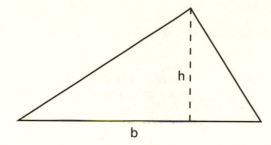

Rectangle (a four-sided polygon with four right angles): $A = l \times w$

Parallelogram (a four-sided polygon with two pairs of parallel sides): $A = l \times w$. (Note that, as with triangles, and as shown in the figure below, the height of a parallelogram is not necessarily the same as the length of its sides.)

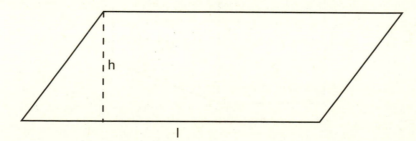

The area of a circle can be found by squaring the length of its radius, then multiplying that product by π. The formula is given as $A = \pi r^2$. (π, or pi, is the ratio of a circle's circumference to its diameter. The value of π is the same for all circles; approximately 3.14159. The approximation 3.14 is adequate for many calculations.) The approximate area of the circle shown below can be found by squaring 6 (giving 36), then multiplying 36 by 3.14, giving an area of about 113 square units.

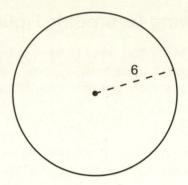

Here are several commonly used volume formulas:

The volume of a rectangular solid is equal to the product of its length, width, and height; $A = l \times w \times h$. (A rectangular solid can be thought of as a box, wherein all intersecting edges form right angles.)

A prism is a polyhedron with two congruent, parallel faces (called bases) and whose lateral (side) faces are parallelograms. The volume of a prism can be found by multiplying the area of the prism's base by its height. The volume of the triangular prism shown hereafter is 60 cubic units. (The area of the triangular base is 10 square units, and the height is 6 units.)

A cylinder is like a prism in that it has parallel faces, but its rounded "side" is smooth. The formula for finding the volume of a cylinder is the same as the formula for finding the volume of a prism: The area of the cylinder's base is multiplied by the height. The volume of the cylinder in the following figure is approximately 628 cubic units. ($5 \times 5 \times \pi \times 8$).

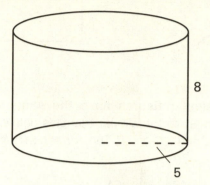

A property of all triangles is that the sum of the measures of the three angles is $180°$. If, therefore, the measures of two angles are known, the third can be deduced using addition, then subtraction.

Right triangles (those with a right angle) have several special properties. A chief property is described by the Pythagorean Theorem, which states that in any right triangle with legs (shorter sides) a and b, and hypotenuse (the longest side) c, the sum of the squares of the sides will be equal to the square of the hypotenuse ($a^2 + b^2 = c^2$). Note that in the right triangle shown hereafter, $3^2 + 4^2 = 5^2$.

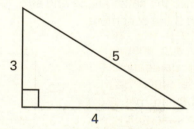

Applying Reasoning Skills

Geometric figures are *similar* if they have the exact same shapes, even if they do not have the same sizes. In transformational geometry, two figures are said to be similar if and only if a similarity transformation maps one figure onto the other. In the figure that follows, triangles A and B are similar.

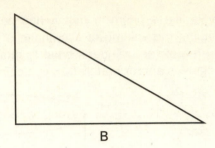

A   B

Corresponding angles of similar figures have the same measure, and the lengths of corresponding sides are proportional. In the similar triangles below, $\angle A \cong \angle D$ (meaning "angle A is congruent to angle D"), $\angle B \cong \angle E$, and $\angle C \cong \angle F$. The corresponding sides of the triangles below are proportional, meaning that:

$$\frac{AB}{DE} = \frac{BC}{EF} = \frac{CA}{FD}$$

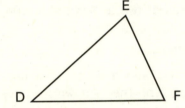

Figures are *congruent* if they have the same shape *and* size. (Congruent figures are also similar.) In the figure below, rectangles A and B are congruent.

A   B

Straight lines within the same plane that have no points in common (that is, they never cross) are parallel lines. Note that the term *parallel* is used to describe the relationship between two coplanar lines that do not intersect. Lines that are not coplanar—although they never cross—are not considered to be parallel. Coplanar lines crossing at right angles (90°) are perpendicular.

When presented with math or logic problems, including geometry problems, *deductive reasoning* may be helpful. Deductive reasoning is reasoning from the general to the specific, and is supported by deductive logic. Here is an example of deductive reasoning:

> All humans who have walked on the moon are males (a general proposition). Neil Armstrong walked on the moon, therefore he is a male (a specific proposition).

Note that conclusions reached via deductive reasoning are only sound if the original assumptions are actually true.

With *inductive* reasoning, a general rule is inferred from specific observations (which may be limited). Moving from the statement "All fish I have ever seen have fins" (specific but limited observations) to "All fish have fins." (a general proposition) is an example of inductive reasoning. Conclusions arrived at via inductive reasoning are not necessarily true.

An example of how logical reasoning can be used to solve a geometry problem is given hereafter. (In this case *deductive* reasoning is used to find the measure of ∠J.)

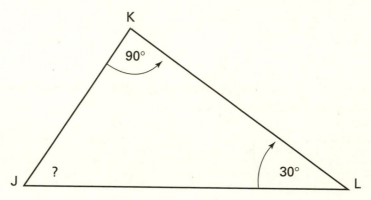

The sum of the measures of the three angles of any triangle is 180° (a general proposition). The sum of the measures of ∠K and ∠L is 120°, therefore the measure of ∠L is 60° (a specific proposition).

ICTS

Illinois Certification Testing System
Basic Skills

Practice Test

This test is also on CD-ROM in our special interactive ICTS TestWare®. It is highly recommended that you first take this exam on computer. You will then have the additional study features and benefits of enforced timed conditions and instant scoring. See page xiii for guidance on how to get the most out of our ICTS book and software.

Answer Sheet

1. Ⓐ Ⓑ Ⓒ Ⓓ	34. Ⓐ Ⓑ Ⓒ Ⓓ	67. Ⓐ Ⓑ Ⓒ Ⓓ	100. Ⓐ Ⓑ Ⓒ Ⓓ
2. Ⓐ Ⓑ Ⓒ Ⓓ	35. Ⓐ Ⓑ Ⓒ Ⓓ	68. Ⓐ Ⓑ Ⓒ Ⓓ	101. Ⓐ Ⓑ Ⓒ Ⓓ
3. Ⓐ Ⓑ Ⓒ Ⓓ	36. Ⓐ Ⓑ Ⓒ Ⓓ	69. Ⓐ Ⓑ Ⓒ Ⓓ	102. Ⓐ Ⓑ Ⓒ Ⓓ
4. Ⓐ Ⓑ Ⓒ Ⓓ	37. Ⓐ Ⓑ Ⓒ Ⓓ	70. Ⓐ Ⓑ Ⓒ Ⓓ	103. Ⓐ Ⓑ Ⓒ Ⓓ
5. Ⓐ Ⓑ Ⓒ Ⓓ	38. Ⓐ Ⓑ Ⓒ Ⓓ	71. Ⓐ Ⓑ Ⓒ Ⓓ	104. Ⓐ Ⓑ Ⓒ Ⓓ
6. Ⓐ Ⓑ Ⓒ Ⓓ	39. Ⓐ Ⓑ Ⓒ Ⓓ	72. Ⓐ Ⓑ Ⓒ Ⓓ	105. Ⓐ Ⓑ Ⓒ Ⓓ
7. Ⓐ Ⓑ Ⓒ Ⓓ	40. Ⓐ Ⓑ Ⓒ Ⓓ	73. Ⓐ Ⓑ Ⓒ Ⓓ	106. Ⓐ Ⓑ Ⓒ Ⓓ
8. Ⓐ Ⓑ Ⓒ Ⓓ	41. Ⓐ Ⓑ Ⓒ Ⓓ	74. Ⓐ Ⓑ Ⓒ Ⓓ	107. Ⓐ Ⓑ Ⓒ Ⓓ
9. Ⓐ Ⓑ Ⓒ Ⓓ	42. Ⓐ Ⓑ Ⓒ Ⓓ	75. Ⓐ Ⓑ Ⓒ Ⓓ	108. Ⓐ Ⓑ Ⓒ Ⓓ
10. Ⓐ Ⓑ Ⓒ Ⓓ	43. Ⓐ Ⓑ Ⓒ Ⓓ	76. Ⓐ Ⓑ Ⓒ Ⓓ	109. Ⓐ Ⓑ Ⓒ Ⓓ
11. Ⓐ Ⓑ Ⓒ Ⓓ	44. Ⓐ Ⓑ Ⓒ Ⓓ	77. Ⓐ Ⓑ Ⓒ Ⓓ	110. Ⓐ Ⓑ Ⓒ Ⓓ
12. Ⓐ Ⓑ Ⓒ Ⓓ	45. Ⓐ Ⓑ Ⓒ Ⓓ	78. Ⓐ Ⓑ Ⓒ Ⓓ	111. Ⓐ Ⓑ Ⓒ Ⓓ
13. Ⓐ Ⓑ Ⓒ Ⓓ	46. Ⓐ Ⓑ Ⓒ Ⓓ	79. Ⓐ Ⓑ Ⓒ Ⓓ	112. Ⓐ Ⓑ Ⓒ Ⓓ
14. Ⓐ Ⓑ Ⓒ Ⓓ	47. Ⓐ Ⓑ Ⓒ Ⓓ	80. Ⓐ Ⓑ Ⓒ Ⓓ	113. Ⓐ Ⓑ Ⓒ Ⓓ
15. Ⓐ Ⓑ Ⓒ Ⓓ	48. Ⓐ Ⓑ Ⓒ Ⓓ	81. Ⓐ Ⓑ Ⓒ Ⓓ	114. Ⓐ Ⓑ Ⓒ Ⓓ
16. Ⓐ Ⓑ Ⓒ Ⓓ	49. Ⓐ Ⓑ Ⓒ Ⓓ	82. Ⓐ Ⓑ Ⓒ Ⓓ	115. Ⓐ Ⓑ Ⓒ Ⓓ
17. Ⓐ Ⓑ Ⓒ Ⓓ	50. Ⓐ Ⓑ Ⓒ Ⓓ	83. Ⓐ Ⓑ Ⓒ Ⓓ	116. Ⓐ Ⓑ Ⓒ Ⓓ
18. Ⓐ Ⓑ Ⓒ Ⓓ	51. Ⓐ Ⓑ Ⓒ Ⓓ	84. Ⓐ Ⓑ Ⓒ Ⓓ	117. Ⓐ Ⓑ Ⓒ Ⓓ
19. Ⓐ Ⓑ Ⓒ Ⓓ	52. Ⓐ Ⓑ Ⓒ Ⓓ	85. Ⓐ Ⓑ Ⓒ Ⓓ	118. Ⓐ Ⓑ Ⓒ Ⓓ
20. Ⓐ Ⓑ Ⓒ Ⓓ	53. Ⓐ Ⓑ Ⓒ Ⓓ	86. Ⓐ Ⓑ Ⓒ Ⓓ	119. Ⓐ Ⓑ Ⓒ Ⓓ
21. Ⓐ Ⓑ Ⓒ Ⓓ	54. Ⓐ Ⓑ Ⓒ Ⓓ	87. Ⓐ Ⓑ Ⓒ Ⓓ	120. Ⓐ Ⓑ Ⓒ Ⓓ
22. Ⓐ Ⓑ Ⓒ Ⓓ	55. Ⓐ Ⓑ Ⓒ Ⓓ	88. Ⓐ Ⓑ Ⓒ Ⓓ	121. Ⓐ Ⓑ Ⓒ Ⓓ
23. Ⓐ Ⓑ Ⓒ Ⓓ	56. Ⓐ Ⓑ Ⓒ Ⓓ	89. Ⓐ Ⓑ Ⓒ Ⓓ	122. Ⓐ Ⓑ Ⓒ Ⓓ
24. Ⓐ Ⓑ Ⓒ Ⓓ	57. Ⓐ Ⓑ Ⓒ Ⓓ	90. Ⓐ Ⓑ Ⓒ Ⓓ	123. Ⓐ Ⓑ Ⓒ Ⓓ
25. Ⓐ Ⓑ Ⓒ Ⓓ	58. Ⓐ Ⓑ Ⓒ Ⓓ	91. Ⓐ Ⓑ Ⓒ Ⓓ	124. Ⓐ Ⓑ Ⓒ Ⓓ
26. Ⓐ Ⓑ Ⓒ Ⓓ	59. Ⓐ Ⓑ Ⓒ Ⓓ	92. Ⓐ Ⓑ Ⓒ Ⓓ	125. Ⓐ Ⓑ Ⓒ Ⓓ
27. Ⓐ Ⓑ Ⓒ Ⓓ	60. Ⓐ Ⓑ Ⓒ Ⓓ	93. Ⓐ Ⓑ Ⓒ Ⓓ	126. Ⓐ Ⓑ Ⓒ Ⓓ
28. Ⓐ Ⓑ Ⓒ Ⓓ	61. Ⓐ Ⓑ Ⓒ Ⓓ	94. Ⓐ Ⓑ Ⓒ Ⓓ	127. Ⓐ Ⓑ Ⓒ Ⓓ
29. Ⓐ Ⓑ Ⓒ Ⓓ	62. Ⓐ Ⓑ Ⓒ Ⓓ	95. Ⓐ Ⓑ Ⓒ Ⓓ	128. Ⓐ Ⓑ Ⓒ Ⓓ
30. Ⓐ Ⓑ Ⓒ Ⓓ	63. Ⓐ Ⓑ Ⓒ Ⓓ	96. Ⓐ Ⓑ Ⓒ Ⓓ	129. Ⓐ Ⓑ Ⓒ Ⓓ
31. Ⓐ Ⓑ Ⓒ Ⓓ	64. Ⓐ Ⓑ Ⓒ Ⓓ	97. Ⓐ Ⓑ Ⓒ Ⓓ	130. Ⓐ Ⓑ Ⓒ Ⓓ
32. Ⓐ Ⓑ Ⓒ Ⓓ	65. Ⓐ Ⓑ Ⓒ Ⓓ	98. Ⓐ Ⓑ Ⓒ Ⓓ	131. Ⓐ Ⓑ Ⓒ Ⓓ
33. Ⓐ Ⓑ Ⓒ Ⓓ	66. Ⓐ Ⓑ Ⓒ Ⓓ	99. Ⓐ Ⓑ Ⓒ Ⓓ	132. Ⓐ Ⓑ Ⓒ Ⓓ

Practice Test: Basic Skills

Time: 5 hours

Read the passage below; then answer the five questions that follow.

WATER

The most important source of sediment is earth and rock material carried to the sea by rivers and streams; glaciers and winds may also have transported the same materials. Other sources are volcanic ash and lava, shells and skeletons of organisms, chemical precipitates formed in seawater, and particles from outer space.

Water is a most unusual substance because it exists on the surface of the Earth in its three physical states: ice, water, and water vapor. There are other substances that exist in a solid and liquid or gaseous state at temperatures normally found at the Earth's surface, but there are fewer substances that occur in all three states.

Water is odorless, tasteless, and colorless. It is the only substance known to exist in a natural state as a solid, liquid, or gas on the surface of the Earth. It is a universal solvent. Water does not corrode, rust, burn, or separate into its components easily. It is chemically indestructible. It can corrode almost any metal and erode the most solid rock. A unique property of water is that, when frozen in its solid state, it expands and floats on water. Water has a freezing point of 0°C and a boiling point of 100°C. Water has the capacity to absorb great quantities of heat with relatively little increase in temperature. When *distilled*, water is a poor conductor of electricity but when salt is added, it is a good conductor of electricity.

Sunlight is the source of energy for temperature change, evaporation, and currents for water movement through the atmosphere. Sunlight controls the rate of photosynthesis for all marine plants, which are directly or indirectly the source of food for all marine animals. Migration, breeding, and other behaviors of marine animals are affected by light.

Water, as the ocean or sea, is blue because of the molecular scattering of the sunlight. Blue light, being of short wavelength, is scattered more effectively than light of longer wavelengths. Variations in color may be caused by particles suspended in the water, water depth, cloud cover, temperature, and other variable factors. Heavy concentrations of dissolved materials cause a yellowish hue, while algae will cause the water to look green. Heavy populations of plant and animal materials will cause the water to look brown.

1. Which of the following lists of topics best organizes the information in the selection?

    A.   I.   Water as vapor
          II.   Water as ice
          III. Water as solid

    B.   I.   Properties of seawater
          II.   Freezing and boiling points of water
          III. Photosynthesis
          IV. Oceans and seas

    C.   I.   Water as substance
          II.   Water's corrosion
          III. Water and plants
          IV. Water and algae coloration

    D.   I.   Water's physical states
          II.   Properties of water
          III. Effects of the sun on water
          IV. Reasons for color variation in water

2. According to the passage, what is the most unique property of water?

    A.   Water is odorless, tasteless, and colorless.

    B.   Water exists on the surface of the Earth in three physical states.

    C.   Water is chemically indestructible.

    D.   Water is a poor conductor of electricity.

3. Which of the following best defines the word *distilled* as it is used in the last sentence of the third paragraph?

    A.   Free of salt content

    B.   Free of electrical energy

    C.   Dehydrated

    D.   Containing wine

4. The writer's main purpose in this selection is to

    A.   explain the colors of water.

    B.   examine the effects of the sun on water.

    C.   define the properties of water.

    D.   describe the three physical states of all liquids.

5. The writer of this selection would most likely agree with which of the following statements?

    A. The properties of water are found in most other liquids on this planet.

    B. Water should not be consumed in its most natural state.

    C. Water might be used to serve many different functions.

    D. Water is too unpredictable for most scientists.

> **Read the passage below, written in the style of a newspaper editorial;
> then answer the four questions that follow.**

¹The zoning regulations of Westown have long been a thorn in the side of local real estate developers. ²The authors of those regulations apparently believed that their regulations would be appropriate in perpetuity, because they _____ to amend. ³The result is a growing area of blight bounded on the north by Bradley Avenue and on the east by Randolph Street.

⁴This coming Wednesday the Westown's city council has a chance to bring its zoning practices into the twenty-first century. ⁵The decisive votes will come from Council members Putman, Beckett, and Reis. ⁶The votes of Putman and Beckett in particular will be of interest to their constituents, because the residents of their wards would stand to gain a great deal from rezoning. ⁷The proposed changes would bring the Fourth Ward some much-needed commerce in the currently run-down Randolph-MacKenzie area and would help _____ the Fifth Ward's steady population loss. ⁸Although each of these self-styled "progressives" have displayed reluctance to vote for anything that would spur development in the recent past, both have strong opposition in the upcoming election and would do well to consider how their votes on this issue will impact the results of that election.

6. Which of the following changes is needed in the passage above?

    A. Part 1: Change "have" to "has"

    B. Part 4: Change "Westown's" to "Westown"

    C. Part 8: Change the comma after "past" to a semicolon

    D. Part 8: Change "how" to "that"

7. Which of the following words would be the best to insert into the blank in Part 7?

    A. alleviate

    B. accelerate

    C. excoriate

    D. exonerate

8. Which of the numbered parts should be revised to correct an error in verb form?

    A. Part 3

    B. Part 5

    C. Part 6

    D. Part 8

9. Which of the following phrases, inserted into the blank in Part 2, would make sense and would be free of errors?

    A   made the regulations very easy

    B.   ensured that the provisions would be difficult

    C.   made them almost impossible

    D.   said the zoning ordinances will be hard

10. Multiply $\frac{3}{4}$ by $\frac{2}{3}$. Show your answer in simplified (reduced) form.

    A. $\frac{5}{7}$

    B. $\frac{5}{12}$

    C. $\frac{1}{2}$

    D. $\frac{6}{12}$

11. Divide 6.2 by 0.05.

    A. 124

    B. 1.24

    C. 12.4

    D. 0.124

12. Perform the indicated operation.

    $(-36) - 11$

    A. 47

    B. 25

    C. −47

    D. −25

13. Simplify: $6 \times 2 + \frac{3}{3}$

    A. 18

    B. 5

    C. 10

    D. 13

14. The number 14 is approximately 22% of which of the following numbers?

    A. 64

    B. 1.6

    C. 308

    D. 636

> **Read the passage below, written in the style of a case study for a college education textbook; then answer the five questions that follow.**

[1]DeMarco was asked if he had read any of the books that were on display in Mrs. W's classroom. [2]He answered that he had read none of them yet, although he usually keeps one or more in his desk.

[3]Nevertheless, the researcher did see him respond positively to the first classroom reading experience of the year. [4]Mrs. W was reading Louis Sachar's *Sideways Stories from Wayside School* while the children, each of whom had a copy of the book, were silently reading along. [5]Like nearly all of the class, DeMarco was laughing in all the right places. [6]The researcher has since noticed that he grasps and comprehends just about anything well when it is read by a competent reader, whether a teacher or an advanced fellow student.

[7]_____ [8]The class writes almost daily in a "Small Moments Journal," in which they are to record, in a few sentences and perhaps a picture, memorable events in their lives. [9]Mrs. W has spent considerable time prompting the

students to write down topics, with the result that some students have well over 100 topics listed so far. [10]DeMarco, through the last day he was observed, had seven. [11]He had written only two entries in his journal, both about a visit two years ago to his relatives in Mississippi. [12]Like many of his classmate's accounts of their <u>comings and goings</u>, his writing lacks detail and personality, but most others have written <u>appreciably</u> more. [13]Asked follow-up questions about the events he has written about, his answers were evasive.

15. Which of the following sentences, used in place of the blank labeled Part 7, would best make a transition to the new paragraph?

    A.   Another topic of interest was the study was DeMarco's writing ability.

    B.   Moreover, DeMarco's writing shows no enthusiasm.

    C.   DeMarco's writing, however, shows no spark at all.

    D.   Consequently, it is advisable that we look at DeMarco's writing.

16. Which of the numbered parts should be revised to reduce its unnecessary repetition?

    A.   Part 3

    B.   Part 5

    C.   Part 6

    D.   Part 8

17. Which of the numbered parts should be revised to correct an error in sentence structure?

    A.   Part 2

    B.   Part 9

    C.   Part 10

    D.   Part 13

18. Which of the following changes is needed in the passage?

    A.   Part 4: Change *Sideways Stories from Wayside School* to "Sideways Stories from Wayside School"

    B.   Part 11: Change "had" to "has"

    C.   Part 11: Change "journal" to "Journal"

    D.   Part 12: Change "classmate's" to "classmates'"

19. Which of the underlined words or phrases in the third paragraph should be replaced by more precise or appropriate words?

   A. record

   B. considerable

   C. comings and goings

   D. appreciably

Read the passage below; then answer the five questions that follow.

THE BEGINNINGS OF THE SUBMARINE

A submarine was first used as a military weapon during the American Revolutionary War. The *Turtle*, a one-man submersible designed by an American named David Bushnell and hand-operated by a screw propeller, attempted to sink a British warship in New York Harbor. The plan was to attach a charge of gunpowder to the ship's bottom with screws and explode it with a time fuse. After repeated failures to force the screws through the copper sheathing of the hull of the H.M.S. *Eagle*, the submarine gave up and withdrew, exploding its powder a short distance from the *Eagle*. Although the attack was unsuccessful, it caused the British to move their blockading ships from the harbor to the outer bay.

On February 17, 1864, a Confederate craft, a hand-propelled submersible carrying a crew of eight men, sank a Federal corvette that was blockading Charleston Harbor. The hit was accomplished by a torpedo suspended ahead of the Confederate *Hunley* as she rammed the Union frigate *Housatonic*, and is the first recorded instance of a submarine sinking a warship.

The submarine first became a major component in naval warfare during World War I, when Germany demonstrated its full potential. The wholesale sinking of Allied supply ships by the German U-boats almost swung the war in favor of the Central Powers. Then, as now, the submarine's greatest advantage was that it could operate beneath the ocean's surface where detection was difficult. Sinking a submarine was comparatively easy, once it was found—but finding it before it could attack was another matter.

During the closing months of World War I, the Allied Submarine Devices Investigation Committee was formed to obtain from science and technology more effective underwater detection equipment. The committee developed a reasonably accurate device for locating a submerged submarine. This device was a trainable hydrophone, which was attached to the bottom of the ASW ship, and used to detect screw noises and other sounds that came from a submarine. Although the committee disbanded after World War I, the British made improvements on the locating device during the interval between the World Wars, and named it ASDIC after the committee.

American scientists further improved on the device, calling it SONAR, a name derived from letters in the words *sound navigation ranging*.

At the end of World War II, the United States improved the snorkel (a device for bringing air to the crew and engines when operating submerged on diesels) and developed the Guppy (short for greater underwater propulsion power), a conversion of the fleet-type submarine of World War II fame. Reducing the surface area, streamlining every protruding object, and enclosing the periscope shears in a streamlined metal fairing changed the superstructure. Performance increased greatly with improved electronic equipment, additional battery capacity, and the addition of the snorkel.

20. The passage implies that one of the most pressing modifications needed for the submarine was to

    A. streamline its shape.

    B. enlarge the submarine for accommodating more torpedoes and men.

    C. reduce the noise caused by the submarine.

    D. add a snorkel.

21. It is inferred that

    A. ASDIC was formed to obtain technology for underwater detection.

    B. ASDIC developed an accurate device for locating submarines.

    C. the hydrophone was attached to the bottom of the ship.

    D. ASDIC was formed to develop technology to defend U.S. shipping.

22. SONAR not only picked up the sound of submarines moving through the water but also

    A. indicated the speed at which the sub was moving.

    B. gave the location of the submarine.

    C. indicated the speed of the torpedo.

    D. placed the submarine within a specified range.

23. According to the passage, the submarine's success was due in part to its ability to

    A. strike and escape undetected.

    B. move more swiftly than other vessels.

    C. submerge to great depths while being hunted.

    D. run silently.

24. From the passage, one can infer that

   A. David Bushnell was indirectly responsible for the sinking of the Federal corvette in Charlestown Harbor.

   B. David Bushnell invented the *Turtle*.

   C. the *Turtle* was a one-man submarine.

   D. the *Turtle* sank the USS *Housatonic* on February 18, 1864.

25. Simplify to a single term in scientific notation:

   $(2 \times 10^3) \times (6 \times 10^4)$

   A. 12×10^7

   B. 1.2×10^{12}

   C. 1.2×10^8

   D. 12×10^{12}

26. Bob gets $6 an hour for babysitting. His sister Keyva gets $7 an hour. One evening Bob babysat for three hours, while Keyva sat for twice that long. How much money did they take in altogether for the evening?

   A. $60

   B. $54

   C. $39

   D. $108

27. The daily high temperatures in Frostbite, Minnesota, for one week in January were as follows:
   Sunday: –2°F
   Monday: 3°F
   Tuesday: 0°F
   Wednesday: –4°F
   Thursday: –5°F
   Friday: –1°F
   Saturday: 2°F

   What was the mean daily high temperature for that week?

   A. 7

   B. –7

   C. –1

   D. 1

28. Nelson's Menswear Shop was selling sweaters for $40 at the beginning of the year. In March, the price of the sweaters was raised by 10%. In September, the price was again raised by an additional 15%. Ignoring tax, what was the price of the sweaters in September?

    A. $50.00

    B. $65.40

    C. $59.00

    D. $50.60

Read the passage below; then answer the five questions that follow.

IMMIGRATION

The influx of immigrants that America had been experiencing slowed during the conflicts with France and England, but the flow increased between 1820 and 1840. Thus, the overall rise in population during these years was due more to incoming foreigners than to a natural, domestically derived increase. Most of the newcomers were from Britain, Germany, and southern Ireland. The Germans usually fared best, since they brought more money and more skills. Discrimination was common in the job market, primarily directed against the Catholics. "Irish Need Not Apply" signs were common. However, the persistent labor shortage prevented the natives from totally excluding the foreign elements. These newcomers huddled in ethnic neighborhoods in the cities, or those who could move on Westward to try their hand at farming.

In 1790, five percent of the U.S. population lived in cities of 2,500 or more. By 1860, that figure had risen to 25%. This rapid urbanization created an array of problems.

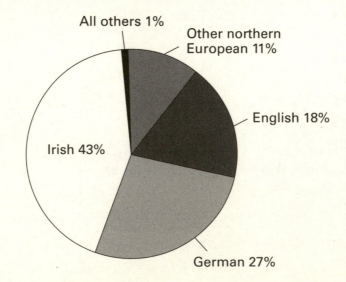

SOURCES OF IMMIGRATION, 1820–1840

All others 1%

Other northern European 11%

English 18%

German 27%

Irish 43%

The rapid growth in urban areas was not matched by the growth of services, however. Clean water, trash removal, housing, and public transportation all lagged behind, and the wealthy got them first. Bad water and poor sanitation produced poor health, and epidemics of typhoid fever, typhus, and cholera were common. Police and fire protection were usually inadequate and the development of professional police and fire forces was delayed until 1894 when the departments adapted a civil service system to fight corruption.

Rapid growth helped to produce a wave of violence in the cities. In New York City in 1834, the Democrats fought the Whigs with such vigor that the state militia had to be called in. New York and Philadelphia witnessed race riots in the mid-1830s, and a New York mob sacked a Catholic convent in 1834. In the 1830s, 115 major incidents of mob violence were recorded. Street crime was common in all major cities.

29. The author's purpose in writing this essay is

    A.   to bring to light the poor treatment of immigrants.

    B.   to show the violent effects of overpopulation.

    C.   to trace the relationship of immigration to the problems of rapid urban growth.

    D.   to dissuade an active life in big cities.

30. Which of the following best defines the word *sacked* as it is used in the last paragraph?

    A.   robbed

    B.   carried

    C.   trespassed on

    D.   vandalized

31. Which of the following statements best summarizes the main idea of the fourth paragraph?

    A.   Racial tensions caused riots in New York City and Philadelphia.

    B.   The rapid growth in urban population sowed the seeds of violence in U.S. cities.

    C.   Street crimes were far worse in urban areas than race riots and political fights.

    D.   The state militia was responsible for curbing urban violence.

32. Ideas presented in the selection are most influenced by which of the following assumptions?

    A.   Urban life was more or less controllable before the flow of immigration in 1820.

    B.   The British had more skills than the Irish.

    C.   Ethnic neighborhoods had always been a part of American society.

    D.   France and England often had conflicts.

33. According to the graph, from 1820 to 1840

    A. there were more Irish immigrants than all other nationalities combined.

    B. the combined number of immigrants from England and Germany exceeded those from Ireland.

    C. one percent of American immigrants were from Italy.

    D. there were an equal number of English and German immigrants.

> **Read the passage below, written in the style of a history of science college textbook; then answer the five questions that follow.**

[1]The Tuskegee Experiment's true nature had to be hidden from the subjects to ensure their cooperation. [2]The sharecroppers' grossly disadvantaged lot in life made them easy to manipulate. [3]Pleased at the prospect of free medical care—almost none of them had ever seen a doctor before—these unsophisticated and trusting men became the dupes in what James Jones, author of the excellent history on the subject, *Bad Blood*, identified as "the longest nontherapeutic experiment on human beings in medical history".

[4]The study was meant to discover how syphilis <u>effected</u> African Americans as opposed to whites—the theory being that whites experienced more neurological complications from syphilis <u>whereas</u> African Americans were more <u>susceptible</u> to cardiovascular damage. [5]_ _____ [6]Although the scientists touted the study as one of great scientific merit, from the <u>outset</u> its actual benefits were hazy. [7]It took almost forty years before someone involved in the study took a hard and honest look at the end results, he reported that "nothing learned will prevent, find, or cure a single case of infectious syphilis or bring us closer to our basic mission of controlling venereal disease in the United States." [8]When the media learns of the experiment in 1972, the CBS news anchor Harry Reasoner called it a project that "used human beings as laboratory animals in a long and inefficient study of how long it takes syphilis to kill someone."

34. Which of the following sentences, used in place of the blank labeled Part 5, would be most consistent with the writer's purpose and intended audience?

    A. If the theory had been proven, much would have changed in the clinical treatment of syphilis.

    B. How this knowledge would have changed the clinical treatment of syphilis is uncertain.

    C. On the other hand, neurological complications were much more important to the scientists.

    D. We will never know what the racist scientists of the 1920s were thinking when they devised this theory.

35. Which of the underlined words or phrases in the second paragraph should be replaced by more precise or appropriate words?

   A.   effected

   B.   whereas

   C.   susceptible

   D.   outset

36. Which of the numbered parts should be revised to correct a nonstandard use of a comma?

   A.   Part 2

   B.   Part 3

   C.   Part 7

   D.   Part 8

37. Which of the following changes is needed in the first paragraph?

   A.   Part 1: Change "experiment's" to "experiments"

   B.   Part 2: Change "easy to manipulate" to "easily manipulated"

   C.   Part 3: Change "had" to "has"

   D.   Part 3: Move the period at the end inside the quotation mark

38. Which of the numbered sentences contains nonstandard use of a verb form?

   A. Part 2

   B. Part 3

   C. Part 6

   D. Part 8

39. Three pounds of cherries cost $4.65. What would five pounds cost (at the same price per pound)?

   A. $7.75

   B. $7.50

   C. $23.00

   D. $23.25

40. The population of the city of Burnsville increased by approximately 0.2% last year. If the population at the beginning of the year was 1,620, what was the approximate population at the end of the year?

    A. 1632

    B. 1623

    C. 1652

    D. 1640

41. Use the pie chart below to answer the question that follows.

VOTES FOR CITY COUNCIL

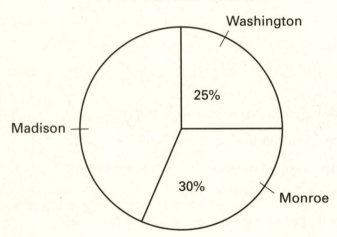

If the total number of people voting was 600, which of the following statements are true?
    I.   Madison received more votes than Monroe and Washington combined.
    II. Madison received 45% of the votes.
    III. Monroe received 180 votes.
    IV. Madison received 330 votes.

    A. I and III only

    B. I and IV only

    C. II and III only

    D. II and IV only

42.   Use the graph to answer the question that follows.

Which of the following scenarios could be represented by the graph above?

A.   Mr. Cain mowed grass at a steady rate for a while, then took a short break, and then finished the job at a steady but slower rate.

B.   Mr. Cain mowed grass at a steady rate for a while, and then mowed at a steady slower rate, then he took a break.

C.   Mr. Cain mowed grass at a variable rate for a while, then took a short break, and then finished the job at a variable rate.

D.   Mr. Cain mowed grass at a steady rate for a while, then took a short break, and then finished the job at a steady but faster pace.

43. Use the bar graph that follows to answer the question thereafter.

MS. PATTON'S EARNINGS, 1998–2002

Only one of the statements below is necessarily true. Which one?

A. The range of Ms. Patton's earnings for the years shown is $15,000.

B. Ms. Patton's annual pay increases were consistent over the years shown.

C. Ms. Patton earned $45,000 in 2003.

D. Ms. Patton's average income for the years shown was $38,000.

Read the passage below; then answer the three questions that follow.

To receive an "A" on a paper in this class one must write sophisticated prose. The criteria will be based on the complexity of both content and expression. The grade will require a demonstration of obvious familiarity with primary texts, as well as additional readings of the course and secondary materials and research sources. An effective combination of personal opinion and outside sources will also be required. Proficiency in organizational skills, format, rhetoric, grammar, syntax, and sentence structure is a must. An additional requirement is a thoroughly proofread essay resulting in no distracting mechanical errors with the possible exception of occasional arguable usage.

44. To receive an "A" grade in the above class, the student must

  A.   turn in a proofread paper with no punctuation errors and demonstrate an understanding of the reading material.

  B.   write an effective paper without mistakes and with an abundance of secondary source materials.

  C.   turn in a thoughtful paper with no corrections as well as demonstrate a proficiency of organizational skills, such as format, rhetoric, and grammar.

  D.   write an intelligent paper without regard for grammar, syntax, or rhetorical strategies, with the possible exception of occasional arguable usage.

45. What does the author mean by "sophisticated prose"?

  A.   A readable text that does not make sense.

  B.   A readable text made up of knowledgeable or thoughtful language.

  C.   A readable text consisting of pompous or ostentatious language.

  D.   A readable text made up of poetic metaphor.

46. When the author of the passage refers to the "primary texts," he means

  A.   the reference materials, such as the dictionary, encyclopedia, thesaurus, etc.

  B.   the primary note pages, works cited page, or preliminary rough draft page.

  C.   the source or principal text in the assignment.

  D.   the first text written about a certain subject.

Read the passage below, written in the style of a sociology textbook; then answer the six questions that follow.

---

[1]Before the Europeans arrived, animism and spirit worship was the hallmark of Timorese belief in a superior force. [2]The great Hindu, Buddhist, and Islamic kingdoms that dominated South and Southeast Asia had not taken root in Timor. [3]The island's geographic location, which was far from the major ports of Asia, and its subsequent lack of commercial activity, placed it off the beaten track for traders and proselytizers. [4]The exceptions being sandalwood and later slave trade.

[5]All that changed with the arrival of the Europeans. [6]By the late 1500s Dominican friars from Portugal had established a mission on Timor, _____ they made only modest headway in converting the Timorese to Christianity. [7]Although the Portuguese were in Timor for centuries they had little positive influence on Timorese culture until after World War II. [8]For years the local people consistently resisted Portugal's attempts to take control of their island, and some of the Dominican missionaries who were posted there supported them in this effort. [9]It was not until Portugal considered

granting East Timor its independence that Catholicism began to be accepted among the people, and _____ it was not until the Indonesian invasion in 1975 that large numbers of Timorese embraced the Catholic faith. [10]Indonesian law requires citizens to have a religious affiliation. [11]The Catholic Church was the only organization that the Indonesian government in Timor allowed relative freedom.

[12]Timorese also found the Church a source of support during the guerrilla war against the Indonesians. [13]Timorese fled to the highlands to escape Indonesian rule, and their families were often relocated in camps far from their villages to prevent them from lending assistance to the guerrillas. [14]The Church saw the abject misery of the people and provided support and comfort. [15]Membership in the Catholic Church grew dramatically from 1975 to 1999 as the Timorese people came to rely on it to protect them and to help them locate missing family members. [16]Today 90% of East Timor's population is Catholic, although many Timorese Catholics include some aspects of animism in their beliefs.

47. Read the following sentence:
"The priests and nuns of the church provided health and education to the Timorese during that chaotic period."
In which of the following locations in the third paragraph should this sentence be placed?

   A. Before Part 12

   B. Before Part 13

   C. Before Part 15

   D. Before Part 16

48. The method of organization for the second and third paragraphs, respectively, is

   A. chronological order; problem and solution

   B. chronological order; cause and effect

   C. order of importance; chronological order

   D. comparison and contrast; cause and effect

49. Which of the numbered parts should be revised to correct a nonstandard sentence structure?

   A. Part 2

   B. Part 4

   C. Part 7

   D. Part 8

50. Which of the following changes is needed in the second paragraph?

    A.   Part 7: Insert comma after "centuries"

    B.   Part 8: Change "who" after "missionaries" to "whom"

    C.   Part 9: Change "its" to "their"

    D.   Part 11: Capitalize "government"

51. Which words or phrases would, if inserted *in order* into the blanks in the second paragraph, help the reader understand the logical sequence of the writer's ideas?

    A.   however; therefore

    B.   and so; in those circumstances

    C.   however; even then

    D.   but; even then

52. Which of the numbered parts should be revised to correct a nonstandard verb form?

    A.   Part 1

    B.   Part 3

    C.   Part 10

    D.   Part 16

53. A line passes through points (–6,0) and (0,4) on the coordinate plane. Which of the following statements are true?

    I.   The slope of the line is negative.
    II.   The slope of the line is positive.
    III. The y-intercept of the line is –6.
    IV.   The y-intercept of the line is 4.

    A.   I and III only

    B.   I and IV only

    C.   II and III only

    D.   II and IV only

54. What is the slope of a line passing through points (–2, 6) and (4, –2) on the coordinate plane?

   A. $-\frac{3}{4}$

   B. $\frac{3}{4}$

   C. $-\frac{4}{3}$

   D. $\frac{4}{3}$

55. Use the graph to answer the question.

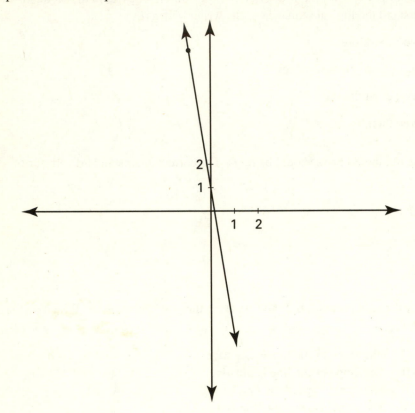

   Which equation best describes the graph above?

   A. $y = 0x$

   B. $y = x + 0$

   C. $y = -8x + 1$

   D. $y = 8x$

56. Which point represents the y-intercept of the equation $2x = 3y - 12$?

   A. (4 ,0)

   B. (0, –6)

   C. (–6, 0)

   D. (0, 4)

57. Use the graph that follows to answer the question.

Which inequality describes the graph?

A. $y < 3$

B. $x < 3$

C. $y > 3$

D. $x > 3$

Read the passage below; then answer the four questions that follow.

Language not only expresses an individual's ideology, it also sets perimeters while it persuades and influences the discourse in the community that hears and interprets its meaning. Therefore, the language of failure should not be present in the learning environment (i.e., the classroom) because it will have a prohibitive impact on the students' desire to learn as well as a negative influence on the students' self-esteem. The *Oxford English Dictionary* defines *failure* as a fault, a shortcoming, a lack of success, a person who turns out unsuccessfully, becoming insolvent, etc. We as educators might well ask ourselves if this is the sort of doctrine that we want to permeate our classrooms. Perhaps our own University axiom, *mens agitat molem* (the mind can move mountains), will help us discover if, indeed, the concepts of failure are really the types of influences we wish to introduce to impressionable new students. Is the mind capable of moving a mountain when it is already convinced it cannot? One must remain aware that individuals acquire knowledge at independent rates of speed. Certainly no one would suggest that one infant "failed" the art of learning to walk because she acquired the skill two months behind her infant counterpart. Would anyone suggest that infant number one *failed* walking? Of course not. What would a mentor project to either toddler were he to suggest that a slower acquisition of walking skills implied failure? Yet we as educators feel the need to suggest student A failed due to the slower procurement of abstract concepts then student B. It is absolutely essential to shift the learning focus from failure to success.

58. Which of the following statements best conveys the meaning of the passage?

    A.   Learning is something that happens at different speeds and is, therefore, natural.

    B.   Instructors need to be sensitive to students' individual needs.

    C.   Instructors need to shift the educational focus from failure to success in learning environments.

    D.   Failure is a potential hazard in the classroom and should be avoided at all costs.

59. As stated in the context of the passage, what does University axiom mean?

    A.   University Latin

    B.   University motto

    C.   University rhetoric

    D.   University sophomore

60. According to the passage, what will have a negative effect on student self-esteem?

    A.   The rhetoric of diction

    B.   The slower procurement of abstract concepts

    C.   The learning focus from failure to success

    D.   The language of failure

61. According to the passage, what does language do besides aid individual expression?

    A.   It establishes individual thought and tells of individual philosophies.

    B.   It paints visual images and articulates individual declaration.

    C.   It suggests individual axioms and community philosophy.

    D.   It persuades and influences the discourse in the community that hears and interprets its meaning.

[1]The Lincoln Cent was first struck in 1909 to celebrate the 100th. Anniversary of the birth of Abraham Lincoln, our 16th President. [2]Designed by Victor D. Brenner, the coin carried the motto "In God We Trust"—the first time it appeared on this denomination coin. [3]It is interesting that the law for the motto was passed during Lincoln's administration as president. [4]Though we might not think so at first glance, the lowly Cent is a fitting memorial for the great man whose profile graces this most common coin of the realm, and a tolerable symbol for the nation whose commerce it serves.

[5]The obverse has the profile of Lincoln as he looked during the trying years of the War Between the States. [6]Faced with the immense problems of a divided nation, the prevention of the split between North and South was difficult. [7]"A house divided against itself cannot stand," he warned the nation. [8]With the outbreak of war at Fort Sumter. Lincoln was saddened to see his beloved country caught up in the senseless war in which father fought against son, brother against brother. [9]Throughout America, war captured the attention of people: the woman who saved the lives of the wounded, the soldier waiting to go into battle, the bewildered child trying hard to understand the sound of guns. [10]Lincoln stood on the broad, silent battlefield at Gettysburg in 1863 to dedicate the site as a national cemetery. [11]Gettysburg had been the scene of some of the most bitter fighting of the war and had ended in a Union victory.

[12]In his special address at Gettysburg, he called upon the American people to end the war. [13]His words boomed out over the large audience before him: [14]"It is rather for us [the living] to be here dedicated to the great task remaining before us—[15]that from these honored dead we take increased devotion to that cause for which they gave the last full measure of devotion; that we here highly resolve that these dead shall not have died in vain; that this nation under God, shall have a new birth of freedom; and that government of the people, by the people and for the people, shall not perish from the earth."

[16]Barely a month before the end of the war, Lincoln took the oath of office a secondly time as President. [17]With the war still raging, his inaugural address took on added meaning: [18] "With malice toward none, with charity for all, with firmness in the right as God gives us to see the right, let us strive on to finish the work we are in, to bind up the nation's wounds, to care for him who shall have borne the battle and for his widow and his orphan, to do all which may achieve and cherish a just and lasting peace among ourselves and with all nations."

62. Which of the following changes is needed in the third paragraph?

A. Part 16: Change "end" to "climax."

B. Part 16: Change "secondly" to "second."

C. Part 17: Change "With" to "Of."

D. Part 17: Change "on" to "in."

63. Which of the following changes is needed in the second paragraph?

A. Part 5: Change "has" to "had."

B. Part 6: Change "the prevention of the split between North and South was difficult" to "Lincoln found it difficult to prevent the split between North and South."

C. Part 9: Change "waiting" to "waited."

D. Part 10: Change "site" to "sight."

64. Which of the following sentences is a nonstandard sentence?

A. Part 2

B. Part 4

C. Part 8

D. Part 11

65. Use the figure to answer the question that follows.

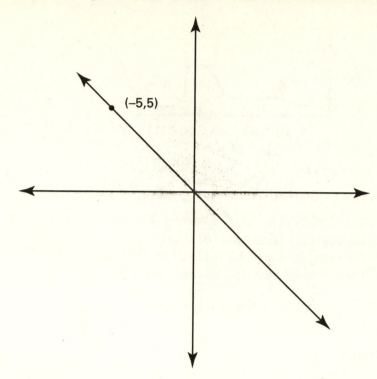

(−5,5)

Which of the following statements about the graph of a linear equation (shown) are true?
- I.   The graph shows an inverse variation.
- II. The graph shows a direct variation.
- III. The slope of the line is −1.
- IV. The slope of the line is 1.

A.   I and III only

B.   I and IV only

C.   II and III only

D.   II and IV only

66. The following graph shows the distribution of test scores in Ms. Alvarez's class.

Which of the following statements do you know to be true?

      I.   The majority of students scored higher than 60.

     II.   The test was a fair measure of ability.

   III.   The mean score is probably higher than the median.

   IV.   The test divided the class into distinct groups.

A.   I and II only

B.   I and IV only

C.   I, III, and IV only

D.   IV only

67. What is the solution to this equation?

$\frac{x}{3} - 9 = 15$

A.   18

B.   8

C.   36

D.   72

> **Read the passage below; then answer the three questions that follow.**

Life in seventeenth-century England was tempestuous indeed. It was a time when religious and secular confrontations resulted in new social abstractions, paradoxes, and ironies. The poet-pastor Robert Herrick (1591–1674) illustrates the ability of lyric poetry to serve not only as an adornment of the era, but as social communiqué, as well. Herrick's Mayday celebration poem "Corinna's Going A-Maying" serves as both an argument against conservative religious dogma and as a response to specific Puritan manifestos. Herrick incorporates abundant Greco-Roman tropes into "Corinna" in order to construct a stylized response to Puritanism based upon traditional structure, symmetry, and thematic representation.

68. The author's attitude toward the subject is one of

    A. lethargy.

    B. apathy.

    C. objectivity.

    D. intensity.

69. The passage fundamentally suggests that

    A. Puritanism is based upon a traditional structure, symmetry, and thematic representation.

    B. lyric poetry has the ability to serve not only as an adornment of an era, but also as social communiqué.

    C. life in seventeenth-century England was tempestuous indeed.

    D. the seventeenth century was a time of religious and secular confrontations, resulting in new social abstractions, paradoxes, and ironies.

70. As used in the passage, the word trope means

    A. a group of people, animals, etc., such as a herd, a flock, a band, and so on.

    B. a style of writing in the Greek or Roman language.

    C. a desire to travel to Greece or Rome.

    D. the use of a word in a figurative sense; a figure of speech; figurative language.

> **Read the passage below; then answer the four questions that follow.**

A Critic can be equivalent to "a person who pronounces judgment; especially a *Censurer.*" Since the late sixteenth century, the title of Critic has embodied implied meanings such as "professionalism" and "a person *skilled* in textual criticism." Thereby, the title insinuates a distinction of hierarchy among laborers, craftsmen, and the "working class" in general. "Censure" has etymological connotations that date back to the late Middle Ages, "critical recension or revision (along with) expression(s) of disapproval, to give opinion, assess critically, find fault, reprove, blame, pronounce sentence," and "condemnatory (especially ecclesiastical) judgement, opinion, correction," which all furthermore suggest a rather antagonistic posture in relationship to the Humanities. The position of critic is tenuous, as they can serve both as censure or social analyst and commentator. Subsequently, the word is loaded with negative innuendoes, but also innuendoes that denote authority, repression, and judicial propriety. In essence, the Critic who chooses to take the point-of-view of the Censure, sits on the mountaintop, not for a better view of literature, but to establish a false sense of superiority over it in relationship to the Author (as well as the reader for that matter).

71. The passage suggests that

    A. critics are good for the social order.

    B. the position of critic is tenuous as they can serve both as censure or social analyst and commentator.

    C. critics attempt to establish a false sense of superiority over the author and the reader as well.

    D. humanitarians do not make good critics as they are too emotional and not callous or impartial enough.

72. The passage indicates that the art of criticism

    A. is a modern phenomenon.

    B. dates back to the Middle Ages.

    C. is a thought-provoking entity.

    D. began at around the same time as the Civil War.

73. Which of the following would make the best title for the passage you just read?

    A. Critical Analysis Ruins Literature for the Rest of Us

    B. Critics Assume a False Superiority Thereby Rendering Critical Judgment Null and Void

    C. The Implications and Connotations of the Critic as Author

    D. Criticism is Synonymous with Censorship

74. What does the term etymological mean as it is used in the passage?

   A.   The history of the Middle Ages

   B.   The history of a word

   C.   The history of critical analysis

   D.   The history of literature

Read the passage below, written in the style of a history of science textbook; then answer the three questions that follow.

[1]Dr. Robert Goddard, at one time a physics professor at Clark University, Worcester, Massachusetts, was largely responsible for the sudden interest in rockets back in the twenties. [2]When Dr. Goddard first started his experiments with rockets, no related technical information was available. [3]He started a new science, industry, and field of engineering. [4]Through his scientific experiments, he pointed the way to the development of rockets as we know them today. [5]The Smithsonian Institute agreed to finance his experiments in 1920. [6]From these experiments he wrote a paper titled "A Method of Reaching Extreme Altitudes," in which he outlined a space rocket of the step (multistage) principle, theoretically capable of reaching the moon.

[7]Goddard discovered that with a properly shaped, smooth, tapered nozzle he could increase the ejection velocity eight times with the same weight of fuel. [8]This would not only drive a rocket eight times faster, but 64 times farther, according to his theory. [9]Early in his experiments he found that solid-fuel rockets would not give him the high power or the duration of power needed for a dependable supersonic motor capable of extreme altitudes. [10]Using liquid fuel, he finally launched a successful rocket in 1926.

[11]It attained an altitude of 184 feet and a speed of 60 m.p.h. [12]This seems small as compared to present-day speeds and heights of missile flights, but instead of trying to achieve speed or altitude at this time, Dr. Goddard was trying to develop a dependable rocket motor.

[13]Dr. Goddard later was the first to fire a rocket that reached a speed faster than the speed of sound. [14]He was first to develop a gyroscopic steering <u>thing</u> for rockets. [15]The first to use vanes in the jet stream for rocket stabilization during <u>the initial phase</u> of a rocket flight. [16]And he was first to patent the idea of step rockets. [17]After proving on paper and in <u>actual</u> tests that a rocket can travel in a vacuum, he developed the mathematical theory of rocket propulsion and rocket flight, including basic designs for long-range rockets. [18]All of his information was available to military men before World War II, but evidently its immediate use did not seem applicable. [19]Near the end of World War II we started intense <u>work </u>on rocket-powered guided missiles, using the experiments and developments of Dr. Goddard and the American Rocket Society.

75. Which of the following should be changed to reflect correct punctuation in the first paragraph?

    A. Part 1: Remove commas after "Goddard" and after "Massachusetts."

    B. Part 2: Remove the comma after "rockets."

    C. Part 4: Put a comma in after "rockets."

    D. Part 6: Remove the comma after "principle."

76. Which of the following parts of the third paragraph is a nonstandard sentence?

    A. Part 14

    B. Part 15

    C. Part 16

    D. Part 17

77. Which of the underlined words in the third paragraph should be replaced by more precise or appropriate words?

    A. thing

    B. the initial phase

    C. actual

    D. work

78. What are the solutions of this equation?

    $3x^2 - 11 = 1$

    A. 2 and –2

    B. 3 and –3

    C. 4 and –4

    D. 1 and –1

79. Solve for y.

    $\frac{y}{3} - \frac{x}{2} = 4$

    A. $y = -\frac{3x}{2} + 12$

    B. $y = \frac{3x}{2} + 12$

    C. $y = \frac{3x}{2} - 12$

    D. $y = -\frac{3x}{2} - 12$

80. Translate this problem into a one-variable equation, then solve the equation. What is the solution?

    "There are ten vehicles parked in a parking lot. Each is either a car with four tires or a motorcycle with two tires. (Do not count any spare tires.) There are 26 wheels in the lot. How many cars are there in the lot?"

    A.   8

    B.   6

    C.   5

    D.   3

81. Which equation could be used to solve the following problem?

    "Three consecutive odd numbers add up to 117. What are they?"

    A. $x + (x + 2) + (x + 4) = 117$

    B. $1x + 3x + 5x = 117$

    C. $x + x + x = 117$

    D. $x + (x + 1) + (x + 3) = 117$

Read the passage below, written in the style of an editorial; then answer the three questions that follow.

[1]We've grown accustomed to seeing this working woman hanging from the subway strap during commuting hours. [2]We may refer disparagingly to her tailored suit and little tie, but we no longer visualize her in a house dress with her hair uncombed. [3]The woman who leaves her children to go to work in the morning is no longer a pariah in her community or her family. [4]Her paycheck is more than pin money; it buys essential family staples and often supports the entire family. [5]But she is the only beneficiary of the increasing presence of women in the workplace.

[6]The situation for men has also changed for the better as a result of women's massive entry into the work force. [7]Men who would once have felt unrelenting pressure to remain with one firm and climb the career ladder are often freed up to change careers in midlife by a second income. [8]They enjoy greatest intimacy and involvement with their children.

[9]The benefits for business are also readily apparent. [10]No senior manager in the country would deny that the huge generation of women who entered management seven or eight years ago has functioned superbly, often outperforming men.

[11]Yet the prevailing message from the media on the subject of women and business is one filled with pessimism. [12]We hear about women leaving their employers in the lurch when they go on maternity leave. [13]Or we hear the flip side, that women are overly

committed to their careers and neglectful of their families. [14]And in fact, it is true that problems arising from women's new work force role do exist, side by side with the benefits.

[15]The problems hurt business as well as individuals and their families. Affordable quality childcare, for one example, is still a distant dream. [16]Some women are distracted at work, and men who would have felt secure about their children when their wives were home are also anxious and distracted. [17]Distraction also impedes the productivity of some high-achieving women with the birth of their first child and causes some to depart with the birth of their second.

82. Which of the following sentences displays a nonstandard placement of a modifying phrase?

A. Part 1

B. Part 3

C. Part 6

D. Part 7

83. Which of the following sentences displays a nonstandard use of a comparative form?

A. Part 4

B. Part 8

C. Part 10

D. Part 13

84. Which of the following sentences is a nonstandard sentence?

A. Part 14

B. Part 15

C. Part 16

D. Part 17

Read the passage below; then answer the five questions that follow.

Frederick Douglass was born Frederick Augustus Washington Bailey in 1817 to a white father and a slave mother. Frederick was raised by his grandmother on a Maryland plantation until he was eight. It was then that he was sent to Baltimore by his owner to be a servant to the Auld family. Mrs. Auld recognized Frederick's intellectual acumen and defied the law of the state by teaching him to read and write. When Mr. Auld warned that education would make the boy unfit for slavery, Frederick sought to continue his education in the streets. When his master died, Frederick, who was only sixteen years of age, was returned to the plantation to work in the fields. Later, he was hired out to work in the shipyards in Baltimore as a ship caulker. He plotted an escape but was discovered before he could get away. It took five years before he made his way to New York City and then to New Bedford, Massachusetts, eluding slave hunters by changing his name to Douglass.

At an 1841 anti-slavery meeting in Massachusetts, Douglass was invited to give a talk about his experiences under slavery. His impromptu speech was so powerful and so eloquent that it thrust him into a career as an agent for the Massachusetts Anti-Slavery Society. Douglass wrote his autobiography in 1845, primarily to counter those who doubted his authenticity as a former slave. This work became a classic in American literature and a primary source about slavery from the point of view of a slave. Douglass went on a two-year speaking tour abroad to avoid recapture by his former owner and to win new friends for the abolition movement.

He returned with funds to purchase his freedom and to start his own anti-slavery newspaper. He became a consultant to Abraham Lincoln and throughout Reconstruction fought doggedly for full civil rights for freedmen; he also supported the women's rights movement.

85. According to the passage, Douglass's writing of his autobiography was motivated by

    A.   the desire to make money for the anti-slavery movement.

    B.   his desire to become a publisher.

    C.   his interest in authenticating his life as a slave.

    D.   his desire to educate people about the horrors of slavery.

86. The central idea of the passage is that Douglass

    A.   was instrumental in changing the laws regarding the education of slaves.

    B.   was one of the most eminent human rights leaders of the nineteenth century.

    C.   was a personal friend and confidant to a president.

    D.   wrote a classic in American literature.

87. According to the author of this passage, Mrs. Auld taught Douglass to read because

    A.   Douglass wanted to go to school like the other children.

    B.   she recognized his natural ability.

    C.   she wanted to comply with the laws of the state.

    D.   he needed to be able to read so that he might work in the home.

88.   The title that best expresses the ideas of this passage is

    A.   The History of the Anti-Slavery Movement in America.

    B.   The Outlaw Frederick Douglass.

    C.   Reading: A Window to the World of Abolition.

    D.   Frederick Douglass's Contributions to Freedom.

89.   In the context of the passage, *impromptu* is the closest in meaning to

    A.   unprepared.

    B.   nervous.

    C.   angry.

    D.   loud.

> **Read the passage below, written in the style of a student essay;
> then answer the three questions that follow.**

[1]In the past 30 years, television has become a very popular pastime for almost everyone. [2]From the time she places the baby in her jumpseat in front of the television until the time the senior citizen in the retirement home watches Vanna White turn the letters on "Wheel of Fortune," Americans spend endless hours in front of the "boob tube." [3]How did we get to be this way?

[4]When my mother was a little girl, what did children do to entertain themselves? [5]They played. [6]Their games usually involved social interaction with other children as well as imaginatively creating entertainment for themselves. [7]They also developed hobbies like woodworking and sewing. [8]Today, few children really know how to play with each other or entertain themselves. [9]Instead, they sit in front of the television, glued to cartoons that are senseless and often violent. [10]Even if they watch educational programs like "Sesame Street," they don't really have to do anything but watch and listen to what the answer to the question is.

[11]Teenagers, also, use television as a way of avoiding doing things that will be helping them mature. [12]How many kids do much homework anymore? [13]Why not? [14]Because they work part-time jobs and come home from work tired and relax in front of the television that's why.

90. Which of the following sentences uses a nonstandard verb form?

    A. Part 4

    B. Part 7

    C. Part 8

    D. Part 12

91. Which of the following sentences in the passage is nonstandard?

    A. Part 2

    B. Part 7

    C. Part 10

    D. Part 14

92. Which of the following changes is needed?

    A. Part 1: Change "has become" to "is."

    B. Part 2: Change "she" to "the mother."

    C. Part 2: Change "watches" to "watched."

    D. Part 4: Change "When" to "Being that."

93. Which equation could be used to solve the following problem?

    "Here is how the Acme Taxicab Company computes fares for riders: People are charged three dollars for just getting into the cab, then they are charged two dollars more for every mile or fraction of a mile of the ride. What would be the fare for a ride of 10.2 miles?"

    A. $3 \times (2 \times 10.2) = y$

    B. $3 + (2 + 11) = y$

    C. $3 \times (2 + 10.2) = y$

    D. $3 + (2 \times 11) = y$

94. Simplify the following expression.

    $\frac{2}{3}x^2 + 7x + 9 + \frac{1}{3}x^2 - 12x + 1$

    A. $x^2 - 5x + 10$

    B. $6x^3 + 10$

    C. $6x^2 + 10$

    D. $x^4 - 5x + 10$

95. Multiply the following binomials.

    $(-2x^2 - 11)(5x^2 + 3)$

    A. $-10x^2 - 8$

    B. $-10x^2 - 14x - 8$

    C. $-10x^4 - 61x^2 - 33$

    D. $-10x^2 - 52x - 33$

Read the passage below; then answer the three questions that follow.

During a class on theories and methods of education, the teaching apprentice initiated the discussion in a clear and well-prepared manner. To _____ the lecture topic, the teaching apprentice utilized overhead transparencies of both lexicon and abstract representation to better _____ the theories behind various pedagogical concepts. The class culminated whereby students established enthymemes extrapolated from the class discussion. The class maintained integrity and continuity.

96. Which of these grouped words, if inserted *in order* into the passage's blank lines, would address the logical sequencing of the narrative?

    A. refute; criticize

    B. conflate; discern

    C. undermine; explain

    D. support; illustrate

97. The definition of the term "pedagogical" as used in the sentence means

    A. academic.

    B. abstract.

    C. meaningless.

    D. obtuse.

98. The passage suggests that the author's classroom experience was

    A. a needless waste of time and energy.

    B. intelligible and pragmatic.

    C. haphazard and disorderly.

    D. too advanced and complicated.

Read the passage below, written in the style of an anthropology textbook;
then answer the two questions that follow.

[1]Actually, the term "Native American" is incorrect. [2]Indians migrated to this continent from other areas, just earlier than Europeans did. [3]The ancestors of the Anasazi—Indians of the four-state area of Colorado, New Mexico, Utah, and Arizona—probably crossed from Asia into Alaska. [4]About 25,000 years ago, while the continental land bridge still existed. [5]This land bridge arched across the Bering Strait in the last Ice Age. [6]About A.D. 500 the ancestors of the Anasazi moved onto the Mesa Verde, a high plateau in the desert country of Colorado. [7]The Wetherills, five brothers who ranched in the area, are generally given credit for the first exploration of the ruins in the 1870s and 1880s. [8]There were some 50,000 Anasazi thriving in the four-corners area by the 1200s A.D. [9]At their zenith, A.D. 700 to 1300, the Anasazi had established widespread communities and built thousands of sophisticated structures—cliff dwellings, pueblos, and kivas. [10]They even engaged in trade with Indians in surrounding regions by exporting pottery and other goods.

99. Which of the following is a nonstandard sentence?

    A. Part 1
    B. Part 2
    C. Part 4
    D. Part 5

100. Which of the following draws attention away from the main idea of the paragraph?

    A. Part 3
    B. Part 4
    C. Part 7
    D. Part 8

101. Factor the following expression into two binomials.

$-8x^2 + 22x - 5$

    A. $(4x - 1)(-2x + 5)$
    B. $(-4x - 1)(-2x - 5)$
    C. $(4x + 1)(-2x + 5)$
    D. $(4x + 1)(2x + 5)$

102. Fully factor this expression.

    $2x^2 - 18$

    A. $(2x - 3)(x + 6)$

    B. $2(x^2 - 9)$

    C. $(2x - 9)(x + 9)$

    D. $2(x + 3)(x - 3)$

103. Simplify the following.

    $3\sqrt{2} \times 5\sqrt{10}$

    A. $30\sqrt{2}$

    B. $15\sqrt{12}$

    C. $30\sqrt{5}$

    D. $15\sqrt{20}$

104. Simplify.

    $\dfrac{\sqrt{75x^7}}{\sqrt{3x}}$

    A. $25x^5$

    B. $5x^5$

    C. $5x^3$

    D. $25x^4$

Read the passage below, written in the style of a student letter to a college newspaper; then answer the three questions that follow.

[1]The dismissal of Dr. Dennis Ruoff is a travesty of justice. [2]It is not a good feeling to know that a tenured professor can be hounded out of his post just because he disagrees with the board of regents. [3]True, his was the only negative vote on the curriculum issue pushed by the university board of regents. [4]However, since when has a dissenting opinion been the catalyst for persecution of faculty members on this campus? [5]_____. [6]English professors, especially, have traditionally had the reputation of fighting courageously against blockhead thinking and against lockstep decision making. [7]They have also historically been the school's champions against injustice.

[8]There cannot be an issue closer to the basis of America's founding principles than this one because the foundation of America is based on freedom of speech.

[9]The students of this university need to know whose to blame for the loss of Dr. Ruoff. [10]He is a stimulating speaker, an engaging person, and one of the finest teachers. "Where will this issue come to a halt? [12]Will other tenured professors now be even more intimidated and hesitate to express any view not consistent with the general consensus of opinion? [13]Will students receive a quality education from a university that infringes on freedom of speech?

105. Which of the following requires revision for unnecessary repetition?

    A.   Part 3

    B.   Part 6

    C.   Part 8

    D.   Part 12

106. Which of the following, if added between Parts 4 and 6, best supports the writer's purpose and audience?

    A.   We should allow teachers to express their own opinions regardless of what we ourselves think.

    B.   This university has always prided itself on teachers who are rather maverick in their thinking, to say the least.

    C.   Don't you think this is a pitiful way to treat a fine teacher?

    D.   One must acknowledge that university professors, as a whole, should support the opinions of fellow faculty members.

107. Which one of the following changes is needed?

    A.   Part 8: Change "closer" to "closest."

    B.   Part 9: Change "whose" to "who's."

    C.   Part 10: Change "finest" to "finer."

    D.   Part 11: Change "Where" to "When."

> **Read the passage below; then answer the three questions that follow.**

The early decades of the fifteenth century were a period in our history when English took a "great (linguistic) vowel shift" by redistributing the vowel pronunciation and configuration. Each vowel changed its sound quality, but the distinction between one vowel and the next was maintained. There was a restructuring of the sounds and patterns of communication, as well. One has to conclude that a concurrent stress and exhilaration was occurring within the perimeters of the literate society as well. Musicians, artists, poets, and authors all must have relished the new freedom and experimentation that was now possible with the new-found linguistic shifts.

108. The passage tells about

    A.   a shift in vowel pronunciation and configuration.

    B.   a fifteenth-century renaissance for musicians, artists, poets, and authors.

    C.   a new-found linguistic freedom from conventional sound and linguistic structure.

    D.   various vowel stresses and their effect on artistic expression.

109. What is the meaning of the word *linguistic* as used in the passage?

    A.   Artistic freedom

    B.   Verbal or rhetorical

    C.   Social or expressive

    D.   Vowel configuration

110. Because "each vowel changed its sound quality,"

    A.   there was a restructuring of the sounds and patterns of communication.

    B.   language could never be spoken in the same way again.

    C.   artists had to develop new means of expression.

    D.   communication went through a divergent change of status and culture.

111. Use the figure below to answer the question.

Which formula can be used to find the area of the triangle?

A. $A = \frac{(l \times h)}{2}$

B. $A = \frac{(l + h)}{2}$

C. $A = 2(l + h)$

D. $A = 2(l \times h)$

112. Use the figure below to answer the question.

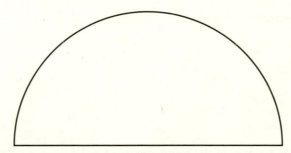

Which formula can be used to find the area of the figure? (Assume the curve is *half* of a circle.)

A. $A = \pi r$

B. $A = 2\pi r^2$

C. $A = \pi r^2$

D. $A = \frac{\pi r^2}{2}$

113. Use the figure below to answer the question that follows. Assume that:

Point *C* is the center of the circle.

Angles *xyz* and *xcz* intercept minor arc *xz*.

The measure of angle *xyz* is 40°.

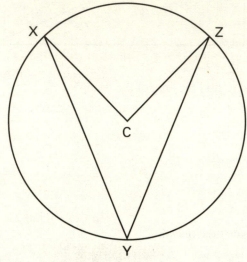

What is the measure of major arc *xyz*?

A.   140°

B.   280°

C.   160°

D.   320°

114. What is the approximate volume of the following cylinder?

A.   904 cm³

B.   301 cm³

C.   151 cm³

D.   452 cm³

Read the passage below, written in the style of a student essay;
then answer the three questions that follow.

[1]A growing number of businesses are providing day care facilities for the children of their employees. [2]Some companies charge a standard fee, but most provide the day care free or at a nominal cost. [3]These care programs provide services that continue through the early teens of the children. [4]Many companies are trying to decide if they should help with day care at all. [5]In the event parents need to work overtime, centers are even open on weekends, and some companies showing special initiative in building company loyalty of each employee <u>makes</u> arrangements for special field trips to zoos and museums. [6]Is this kind of care really necessary? [7]Should businesses really be in the business of day care?

[8]Experts in the field cite many advantages for this system. [9]Therefore, loyalty to the company is built, so morale climbs. [10]Studies show that when a company helps its employees blend parent and worker roles, absenteeism and tardiness drop. [11]In addition, workers feel the company has taken more of a personal interest in them. [12]Turnover becomes a much less significant factor for managers. [13]Human resource managers also estimate that every $1 spent on these programs returns $2 or more in increased productivity.

115. Which of the following improves the first paragraph?

   A.   Change the conjunction from "but" to "and" in Part 2.

   B.   Delete the phrase "in the event parents need to work overtime" from Part 5.

   C.   Delete Part 4.

   D.   Change Part 6 from an interrogative to a declarative sentence, as in "This kind of care is . . ."

116. Which of the following should be substituted for the underlined word in Part 5?

   A.   make

   B.   is making

   C.   should make

   D.   making

117. Which of the following improves the sequence of ideas in the second paragraph?

   A.   Reverse the order of Parts 8 and 9.

   B.   Place Part 12 before Part 9.

   C.   Delete Part 13.

   D.   Place Part 9 after Part 11.

Lead poisoning is considered by health authorities to be the most common and devastating environmental disease of young children. According to studies, it affects 15% to 20% of urban children and from 50% to 75% of inner-city, poor children. As a result of a legal settlement in July 1991, all California MediCal-eligible children, ages one through five, will now be routinely screened annually for lead poisoning. Experts estimate that more than 50,000 cases will be detected in California because of the newly mandated tests. This will halt at an early stage a disease that leads to learning disabilities and life-threatening disorders.

118. Lead poisoning among young children, if not detected early, can lead to

    A.   physical disabilities.

    B.   heart disease.

    C.   liver disease.

    D.   learning disabilities and death.

119. The new mandate to screen all young children for lead poisoning is required of

    A.   all young children in California.

    B.   all children with learning disabilities.

    C.   all MediCal-eligible children, ages one through five, in California.

    D.   all minority children in inner cities.

120. The percentages indicate that more cases of lead poisoning are found among

    A.   children in rural areas.

    B.   inner-city children.

    C.   immigrant children.

    D.   upper-middle class children.

121. The ultimate goal of the newly mandated tests is to

    A.   bring more monies into inner-city medical programs.

    B.   bring more health care professionals into California's inner cities.

    C.   halt at an early stage a disease that leads to learning disabilities and life-threatening disorders.

    D.   screen more test subjects to develop more accurate statistical data.

Read the passage below, written in the style of a sociology textbook; then answer the three questions that follow.

[1]A significant development during the Paleolithic period was the emergence of modern man. [2]During this time, one million years ago to 12,000 B.C., man's brain became much larger. [3]There are two suggested reasons for the rapid evolutionary development of man's brain. [4]First, meat eating led to big-game hunting, an activity that necessitated group planning and cooperation; and second, the use of speech to facilitate planning and coordination of group activities. [5]Tool making was once thought to be a major factor in the development of a large brain for man, but it is now known that many animals use tools and even make tools. [6]Otters will balance a rock on their stomachs as an anvil for breaking open mollusks.

[7]There are two other factors which have greatly influenced the emergence of modern man. [8]Also, food supplies increased significantly after the retreat of the great glaciers about 12,000 years ago. [9]It seems that about 100,000 years ago, genetic evolution became less important than cultural evolution as man developed the ability to pass on accumulated knowledge. [10]This increase in food supplies may have contributed to the ability of man to increase his own numbers, thus ensuring the survival of his species.

122. Which of the following would help the focus of the main idea in the first paragraph?

   A.   Delete Part 1.

   B.   Reverse the order of Parts 1 and 2.

   C.   Add a sentence after Part 2 describing the measurements and configurations of brains.

   D.   Delete Part 6.

123. Which of the following makes the sequence of ideas clearer in the second paragraph?

   A.   Delete Part 7.

   B.   Reverse the order of Parts 7 and 8.

   C.   Reverse the order of Parts 8 and 9.

   D.   Delete Part 10.

124. Which one of the following is needed?

   A.   Part 4: Change "to facilitate" to "facilitated."

   B.   Part 7: Delete "other."

   C.   Part 9: Change "less" to "least."

   D.   Part 10: Change "ensuring" to "ensured."

> **Read the passage below; then answer the two questions that follow.**

America's national bird, the mighty bald eagle, is being threatened by a new menace. Once decimated by hunters and loss of habitat, this newest danger is suspected to be from the intentional poisoning by livestock ranchers. Authorities have found animal carcasses injected with restricted pesticides. These carcasses are suspected to have been placed to attract and kill predators such as the bald eagle in an effort to preserve young grazing animals. It appears that the eagle is being threatened again by the consummate predator, humans.

125. One can conclude from this passage that

    A.   the pesticides used are beneficial to the environment.

    B.   ranchers believe that killing the eagles will protect their ranches.

    C.   ranchers must obtain licenses to use illegal pesticides.

    D.   poisoning eagles is good for livestock.

126. The author's attitude is one of

    A.   uncaring observation.

    B.   concerned interest.

    C.   uniform acceptance.

    D.   suspicion.

127. Use the Pythagorean theorem to answer this question: Which answer comes closest to the actual length of side x in the triangle below?

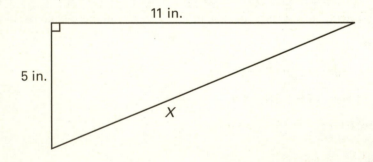

    A.   14 in.

    B.   12 in.

    C.   11 in.

    D.   13 in.

128. Use the figures given to answer the question that follows.

 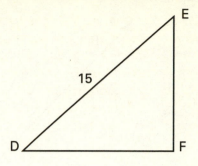

If the two triangles are similar, what is the length of side DF?

A. 12.5 units

B. 13 units

C. 12 units

D. 13.5 units

129. Use the figure given to answer the question that follows.

Given:

    1. Lines *a* and *b* are parallel,
    2. *c* is a line, and
    3. the measure of angle *x* is 50°.

What is the measure of angle *y*?

A. 50°

B. 100°

C. 130°

D. 80°

130. Use the figure given to answer the question that follows. Assume that AD is a line.

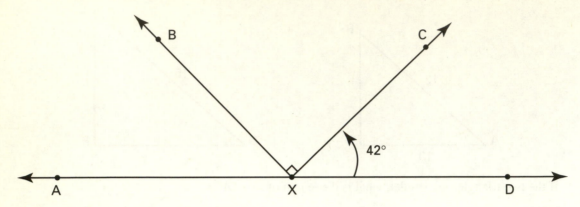

What is the measure of angle AXB?

A.   48°

B.   90°

C.   42°

D.   There is not enough information to answer the question.

131. Use the figures to answer the question that follows.

Which of the following statements about the two triangles are true?
- I.   The triangles are similar.
- II.   The triangles are congruent.
- III.   The measures of angles ABC and XYZ are the same.
- IV.   The lengths of sides BC and YZ are the same.

A.   I and III only

B.   I and IV only

C.   II and III only

D.   II and IV only

132. In a foot race, Fred beat Matt, Curt beat Dwayne, both Pat and Matt beat Ivan, Pat beat Curt, and Dwayne beat Fred. If those were the only boys racing, who came in last?

    A. Don

    B. Matt

    C. Curt

    D. Ivan

WRITING ASSIGNMENT

Read the passage below on studying literature of the past, and then follow the instructions for writing your essay.

Many scholars note the decline of interest in literature written before the twentieth century. A diminishing number of students pursue studies in Classical, Medieval, and even Renaissance literature. Some observers think this trend is acceptable, since the literature of these early periods is not particularly interesting to the general public. Others say that any lessening of study about the past, and especially its artistic expression, is a negative trend.

In an essay written to an English teacher, argue whether you feel that the trend of studying modern versus past literature is commendable or contemptible. Reflect on modern culture and the effects of literature upon it. Discuss the advantages and/or disadvantages of a course of study that excludes or minimizes the literature of earlier periods. Finally, draw upon your own exposure to and attitude toward modern and past literatures, respectively.

You may write in the space provided.

Practice Test Answer Sheets

Begin your essay on this page. If necessary, continue on the next page.

_____

_____

_____

_____

_____

_____

_____

_____

_____

_____

_____

_____

_____

_____

Continue on the next page if necessary.

Continuation of your essay from previous page, if necessary.

ICTS

Illinois Certification Testing System
Basic Skills

Practice Test Answers

Answer Key

1. (D)	34. (B)	67. (D)	100. (C)
2. (B)	35. (A)	68. (C)	101. (A)
3. (A)	36. (C)	69. (B)	102. (D)
4. (C)	37. (D)	70. (D)	103. (C)
5. (C)	38. (D)	71. (B)	104. (C)
6. (B)	39. (A)	72. (B)	105. (C)
7. (A)	40. (B)	73. (C)	106. (B)
8. (D)	41. (C)	74. (B)	107. (B)
9. (B)	42. (A)	75. (A)	108. (A)
10. (C)	43. (B)	76. (B)	109. (B)
11. (A)	44. (A)	77. (A)	110. (A)
12. (C)	45. (B)	78. (A)	111. (A)
13. (D)	46. (C)	79. (B)	112. (D)
14. (A)	47. (A)	80. (D)	113. (B)
15. (C)	48. (B)	81. (A)	114. (A)
16. (C)	49. (B)	82. (C)	115. (C)
17. (D)	50. (A)	83. (C)	116. (A)
18. (D)	51. (D)	84. (B)	117. (D)
19. (C)	52. (A)	85. (C)	118. (D)
20. (A)	53. (D)	86. (B)	119. (C)
21. (D)	54. (C)	87. (B)	120. (B)
22. (D)	55. (C)	88. (D)	121. (C)
23. (A)	56. (D)	89. (A)	122. (D)
24. (A)	57. (A)	90. (D)	123. (C)
25. (C)	58. (C)	91. (D)	124. (A)
26. (A)	59. (B)	92. (B)	125. (B)
27. (C)	60. (D)	93. (D)	126. (B)
28. (D)	61. (D)	94. (A)	127. (B)
29. (C)	62. (B)	95. (C)	128. (A)
30. (D)	63. (B)	96. (D)	129. (C)
31. (B)	64. (C)	97. (A)	130. (A)
32. (A)	65. (C)	98. (B)	131. (A)
33. (B)	66. (B)	99. (C)	132. (D)

Practice Test: Basic Skills

Detailed Explanations of Answers

1. **D**

   D is correct because its precepts are summations of each of the composition's main paragraphs. Choice A only mentions points made in the second paragraph; B and C only mention scattered points made throughout the passage, each of which does not represent a larger body of information within the passage.

2. **B**

   The second paragraph states that this is the reason that water is a most unusual substance. Choices A and C list unusual properties of water, but are not developed in the same manner as the property stated in B. Choice D is not correct under any circumstances.

3. **A**

   The sentence contrasts distilled water to that which contains salt, so A is correct. Choices B, C, and D are not implied by the passage.

4. **C**

   The writer's didactic summary of water's properties is the only perspective found in the passage. Choices A and B are the subjects of individual paragraphs within the passage, but hardly represent the entire passage itself. An in-depth discussion of the physical states of liquids is not offered within the passage.

5. **C**

The correct choice is C because of the many properties of water ascribed to it in the passage, each of which might serve one practical purpose or another. Choices A and D are contradicted within the passage, while B is not implied at all by the passage.

6. **B**

The presence of "the" before "Westown's" means that the reference is to the council, not to a council belonging to Westown. The other choices are all currently correct, and changing them would make them nonstandard.

7. **A**

The editorial is suggesting that the population loss is a bad thing and that proposed changes would be a good thing. Thus, population loss is something the author wants stopped, or at least lessened, so alleviate, which means to lessen, is the only possible choice.

8. **D**

The subject of the first clause is "each," which is singular, so the verb should be "has."

9. **B**

Choice A is wrong because it makes no sense within the sentence; the zoning regulations cannot be easy to change. Choice C makes sense, but its use of "them" is ambiguous—does it refer to the authors or the regulations? Choice D is wrong because, if the authors said the regulations would be hard to change, the word apparently earlier in the sentence would make no sense. Thus Choice B is the best answer.

10. **C**

The useful, traditional approach to multiplying simple fractions (those between 0 and 1) is to first multiply the numerators together and then to multiply the denominators together to find the product. In this case, $\frac{3}{4} \times \frac{2}{3} = \frac{6}{12}$. That fraction is then shown in simplest form, $\frac{1}{2}$.

11. **A**

The traditional whole number division algorithm (method) is helpful when dividing decimals longhand. The work can be set up like this:

$0.05\overline{)6.2}$

Dividing (while temporarily ignoring the zeros and decimal points) gives

$$\begin{array}{r} 124 \\ 0.05\overline{)6.2} \\ \underline{50} \\ 12 \\ \underline{10} \\ 20 \end{array}$$

Next, you count the number of digits to the right of the decimal point in the divisor (two). Two, then, is the number of places that you shift the "inside" decimal point to the right, then "up" into the answer:

$$\begin{array}{r} 124 \\ 0.05\overline{)6.2} \end{array}$$

Because the answer is a whole number, the decimal point does not have to be shown.

12. C

When subtraction involves any negative numbers, a good rule to use is, "Don't subtract the second number. Instead, add its opposite." Using that rule, the original expression,

$(-36) - 11$

becomes

$(-36) + (-11)$.

To be "in debt" by 36, then to be further "in debt" by 11, puts one "in debt" by 47, shown as –47.

13. D

When presented with a simplification problem involving several different operations, the universally accepted order of operations must be used. In this case, working from left-to-right, the multiplication (6×2) and the division $(3 \div 3)$ must be completed first, giving 12 + 1, or 13.

14. A

One way to arrive at the answer is to set up an incomplete proportion, with one corner being x:

$$\frac{14}{x} = \frac{22}{100}$$

To complete the proportion (and to find the answer), you can cross-multiply 14 and 100, equaling 1400, which you then divide by 22, giving approximately 64.

Estimation works well for this problem too. Think of 22% as nearly 20%, or one-fifth. If 14 is one-fifth of something, you can multiply 14 by 5 to get you near the answer. $14 \times 5 = 70$, which is close to 64, or answer A.

15. **C**

This sentence includes a remark about the "lack of spark" in DeMarco's writing, which makes a contrast with the previous sentence, where his potential reading competence is regarded as positive. The rest of the paragraph supports this observation. Choice B is also supported by the rest of the paragraph, but it contains no transition of contrast (moreover rather than however).

16. **C**

The best answer here is Part 6, with its "grasps and comprehends." These two words mean exactly the same thing in this context, so one of them is unnecessary. The phrase "all of the class" in Part 3 is somewhat wordy (it could be "the whole class"), but it is not redundant.

17. **D**

Part 13 contains a **dangling modifier**. The verbal phrase at the beginning of the sentence should modify a person ("answers" cannot be asked a question), but the only choices are "his" and "answers." Thus the phrase modifies nothing and is a dangling modifier.

18. **D**

The sentence in Part 12 refers to journals of all classmates, so the apostrophe should follow the s. Choice A is wrong because Sideways Stories from Wayside School is a book, not a story, a fact which prospective elementary teachers should know. If you didn't, you should get to know some of the more popular authors for elementary school.

19. **C**

The phrase "comings and goings" could possibly fit into this sentence, but it is slightly off, whereas the other choices have little or nothing wrong with them. One problem with "comings and goings" is its informal tone: a case study in a textbook usually does not use slangy terms like this one. In addition, the sentence refers to all the students' accounts, not just their travels.

20. **A**

Choice A is correct because of the importance of streamlining mentioned in the final paragraph. Choices B and C are not suggested in the paragraph, and D is secondary in importance to A.

21. **D**

Since it may be inferred from the general purpose of underwater detection equipment, D is correct. While A and B are true statements, they are not inferences. C is not implied in the passage.

22. **D**

Choice D is correct because the R in SONAR stands for ranging. Choices A, B, and C are neither mentioned nor implied by the passage.

23. **A**

As was mentioned in the third sentence of the third paragraph, A is correct. Choices B, C, and D are not mentioned in the passage.

24. **A**

It may be inferred that Bushnell's invention led to the success of the later version of the submarine. Choices B and C are true, but are not inferences because they are directly stated in the first paragraph. D is not a true statement; the Turtle had no direct link to the 1864 incident.

25. **C**

Because multiplication is commutative (factors can be multiplied in any order), you multiply the 2 and the 6, giving 12; and 10^3 and 10^4, giving 10^7. (Note: To multiply exponential expressions with like bases, you add the exponents.) This gives 12×10^7.

That expression is not in scientific notation (the first number must be between 0 and 10), so you change the 12 into 1.2, and 10^7 into 10^8 to "compensate."

26. **A**

Bob earned $6 an hour for three hours, or $18. Keyva babysat for six hours (twice as long as Bob), earning $7 each hour. That's $42. $18 + $42 = $60.

27. **C**

To find the average (mean) of a set of values, first add them together. In this case, the negative and the positive integers should be added together separately. Those two sums are −12 and 5. (The zero can be ignored; it does not affect either sum.) Then −12 and 5 should be added together for a sum of −7.

To complete the work, the sum of −7 must be divided by the number of values (7), giving −1.

28. **D**

The first price increase is for 10%. That's the same as one-tenth, and one-tenth of $40 is $4. Adding $4 to $40 gives $44 as the March price.

The next increase is 15% of $44. Multiplying 44 by 0.15 (0.15 being another way to represent 15%) gives 6.6, which is read as $6.60. You then increase the March price of $44 by $6.60, giving you $50.60.

Note that you cannot arrive at the answer by adding the individual percent increases (10 + 15 = 25) and then multiplying by 40.

29. **C**

Choice C is correct because it traces the development of the passage with the author's perspective in mind. While A and B are mentioned in the passage, they are not overriding concerns in the passage. D does not directly apply to the passage.

30. **D**

The correct response is D because the incident is situated with other acts of violent aggression. Choices A and C are not implied by the context of the mob riot situation, and B is not implied at all by the paragraph.

31. **B**

The correct answer is B because it represents a theme prevalent in the fourth paragraph. Both A and D represent individual strands within the paragraph, but do not express its main idea; C is not mentioned or implied in the paragraph.

32. **A**

All of the urban difficulties that are mentioned in the passage stem from the rapid growth of immigration. Neither B nor C is implied within the passage. Choice D has no direct bearing on the development of the passage.

33. **B**

The combined percentages of English and German immigrants equal 45 percent (Irish immigrants represent 43 percent of the graph). Choice A is incorrect because the Irish immigrants represent less than half of the graph. Choice C is incorrect because the graph nowhere implies that the "All Others" section of the graph is restricted to Italian immigrants. D is incorrect because the English and German percentages are unequal.

34. **B**

The sentence in Part 7 begins with "Although"—used for mentioning the scientists' public statements—and refers to the "hazy" benefits derived from the study. Thus the sentence has to deal with speculation about the "uncertain" benefits. Choice D fits in with the paragraph's development fairly well, but it not the best answer because the pejorative word "racist" would not generally be used to characterize someone in a textbook. (There is little doubt that the author considers the experiment itself to be racist, but he or she does not otherwise characterize any of the individuals involved in this passage—and should not do so without offering evidence.)

35. **A**

The word should be "affected"; see the discussion of effect and affect in Chapter 2. The other words are used in standard ways and, even though "whereas" may sound out of place, it is not as obviously wrong as "effected" and is therefore not the best answer.

36. **C**

Part 7 contains a comma splice. The sentence has two independent clauses, and they are not joined by a coordinating conjunction. They must therefore be separated by a semicolon, not a comma. Part 3, which contains several commas, is correctly punctuated (except for the period at the end, which will be discussed in Answer 13), but they are all necessary to separate the two nonrestrictive phrases: (a) author of the excellent history on the subject and (b) Bad Blood.

37. **D**

By convention in American English, periods and commas are always placed inside of quotation marks.

38. **D**

The verb learn should clearly be in past tense, not present, because it concerns something that happened in 1972. Incidentally, the word "media" is technically plural, so the verb form should be "learn" rather than "learns" even if present tense were correct.

39. **A**

Finding the answer by setting up a proportion works well here:

$$\frac{3}{4.65} = \frac{5}{x}$$

Proportions often are two fractions set equal to each other, with one "corner" being the unknown value, or x. The equation above can be read as "3 is to 4.65 as 5 is to what?"

One way to solve a proportion (that is; to find the value of x), is to cross-multiply the two corners that have known values (in this case 4.65 and 5.) That gives 23.25, which is then divided by the remaining known value (3), giving 7.75.

40. **B**

The percentage "0.2%" must be seen as "two-tenths of one percent" (and not as "two percent"). Given as a decimal numeral, 0.2% is 0.002. (You move the decimal point two places to the left when converting from a percent to a decimal numeral.)

You then multiply the starting population of 1620 by 0.002, giving 3.24, or approximately 3 people. Adding 3 to 1620 gives 1623.

41. **C**

The chart shows that Madison received less than half of the votes (his slice takes up less than half of the pie), so statement I cannot be true.

Washington and Monroe together received 55% of the votes, and everyone else voted for Madison, so Madison must have received 45% of the votes (all of the candidates' percents must add up to 100%.) Statement II is therefore true.

Monroe received 30% of the 600 votes. 0.30 times 600 is 180, so statement III is true.

Madison received 45% of the vote, and 45% of 600 is 270, so statement IV is false.

42. **A**

The somewhat steep straight line to the left tells you that Mr. Cain worked at a steady rate for awhile. The completely flat line in the middle tells you he stopped for a while—the line doesn't go up because no grass was cut then. Finally the line continues upward (after his break) less steeply (and therefore more flatly), indicating that he was working at a slower rate.

43. **B**

Because Ms. Patton's increases were consistent ($3,000 annually), and because the directions tell you that only one statement is true, answer B must be correct. To be more confident however, you can examine the other statements:

The range of Ms. Patton's earnings is $12,000 (the jump from $30,000 to $42,000), not $15,000, so answer A cannot be correct.

Although Ms. Patton may have earned $45,000 in 2003, you don't know that, so answer C cannot be correct.

Answer D gives the incorrect earnings average; it was $36,000, not $38,000.

44. **A**

The last sentence in these instructions tells the student that the paper must be proofread with no "mechanical" (punctuation) errors. The third sentence states that an understanding of the reading material is required. Answers (B) and (C) contain only a portion of the needed requirements, while (D) is completely inaccurate. Thus, (A) is the correct answer.

45. **B**

As used in the passage, the term "sophisticated prose" means that the student must write a readable paper using thoughtful language, thereby demonstrating a familiarity with the primary text. Answers (A), (C), and (D) all contain language that suggests the opposite of a readable paper.

46. **C**

A primary text is the source material, main, or principal text used in an assignment. The remaining answers (A), (B), and (D) refer to either secondary materials or reference sources.

47. **A**

The last phrase of the sentence—"that chaotic period"—could refer to either the guerilla war mentioned in Part 12 or the period of relocation mentioned in Part 13, meaning that the sentence would have to be inserted after Part 12 or 13 (choices A or B). However, the sentence about the Church's individual members providing support cannot just sit beside a sentence about the church itself providing support: the two thoughts would have to be joined in a logical way. Thus choice B is not as good as choice A. With choice A, Part 12 would be explained by the new sentence, and then Part 13 would describe the circumstances under which the support was provided.

48. **B**

The second paragraph proceeds in from the 1500s to 1975, and the third paragraph describes the cause for the effect mentioned at the end of the second paragraph: the embrace of Catholicism by the Timorese.

49. **B**

Part 4 is a sentence fragment: because "being" is a verbal rather than a standard verb form, it does not act as a verb for "exceptions." (Note: Substituting "were" for "being" would fix the fragment but would not produce an effective sentence—"the exceptions" to what?) Part 7 does contain a punctuation error (discussed in the answer to question 18), but the question specifically asks for nonstandard "sentence structure." Be sure to read each question thoroughly.

50. **A**

Part 7 begins with a subordinate clause, and a comma should separate that clause from the independent clause that follows. The "who" in Part 8 is correct even though it refers to "missionaries," which is the object of a preposition, because it is the subject of its own clause—"who were posted." The "its" following East Timor in Part 9 is correct because the pronoun refers to the country as a whole, not to all the people of the country. The word "government" in Part 11 is not capitalized even though it occurs with the proper adjective "Indonesian."

51. **D**

Because the first blank must show a contrast with the previous thought, choice B is not possible. Because a comma rather than a semicolon precedes the first blank, "however" is not possible, either. If "however" were inserted, the sentence would have a comma splice, because "however" is not a coordinating conjunction ("but" is).

52. **A**

The first sentence has a plural subject—"animism and spirit worship"—so it should have a plural form of verb as well.

53. **D**

It is helpful to make a sketch of the line on the coordinate plane. (To do to that you need to know how to plot individual points.)

The line "travels" from the lower left to the upper right, meaning that it has a positive slope. Statement II is therefore true. The y-intercept of a line is the spot at which the line crosses, or intercepts, the vertical axis. In this case, that's at point (0, 4). (You can simply say that the y-intercept is 4, without mentioning the 0). Statement IV is therefore true as well.

54. **C**

There are several methods for finding the slope of a line if two points are known. The most straightforward method is to use the slope formula:

$$m = \frac{y_2 - y_1}{x_2 - x_1}$$

This can be read as "the slope of a line (m) is equal to the difference of the y coordinates of any two points on the line ($y_2 - y_1$) divided by the difference of the x coordinates.

$(x_2 - x_1)$.

For this problem, you subtract the first y coordinate from the second [(–2) – 6], giving –8. You then do the same for the x coordinates [4 – (–2)], giving 6. Dividing –8 by 6 is the same as showing the fraction $-\frac{8}{6}$ or, in lowest terms, $-\frac{4}{3}$.

55. **C**

There are several ways to determine which equation matches the line. An easy way is to decide first whether the line has a positive or a negative slope. Because the line moves from the upper left to the lower right, you would say it has a negative slope.

In a linear equation of the form y = mx + b (where y is isolated on the left side of the equation), the coefficient of x is the slope of the line. The y-intercept is represented by b, which in this case is 1. The only equation with a negative slope (–8) is response C, so that is the correct answer.

Another clue that C is correct can be found by considering the apparent slope, or steepness/shallowness of the line. The line in problem 17 is fairly steep, and a slope of –8 (or 8) is considered fairly steep too, suggesting that C is correct.

56. **D**

The y-intercept of a linear equation is the point at which its graph passes through, or intercepts, the vertical y-axis. One way to determine the y-intercept is by rewriting the equation in y-intercept form:

$y = mx + b$

If a linear equation is in that form, b tells you where the graph of the line intercepts the y-axis. In this case, you rewrite (or transform) the equation following these steps:

$2x = 3y - 12$

$3y - 12 = 2x$

$3y = 2x + 12$

$y = 2 \div 3\, x + 4$

That final version of the equation is indeed in y-intercept form. The 4 tells you that the graph of the equation intercepts the y-axis at point (0, 4). The answer cannot be C because (–6, 0) is an x-intercept.

57. **A**

Consider various random points in the shaded area: (5, –2), (–1, 2), (12, 2.5) and (–9, 1). Notice that all points in the shaded area have a y-coordinate value less *than 3. The inequality that states this is the one in A ("y is less than 3.")*

58. **C**

The passage suggests that education is primarily based on failure as negative reinforcement and that, in order to create a more productive and positive learning environment, the emphasis must shift to success. While answers A and B may be correct, they are not the main idea of the passage. D is simply a statement that is not based upon any factual evidence whatsoever. Therefore, C is the correct answer.

59. **B**

An axiom in this case is another word for motto. It can also mean an accepted truism or principle, which would also apply here. Answers A, C, and D are erroneous definitions and, therefore B, University motto or principle, is the correct answer.

60. **D**

The passage states that "the language of failure . . . will have a prohibitive impact on the students' self-esteem," and, thus, D is the correct answer. Answers A, B, and C do not apply in this case.

61. **D**

The first paragraph of the passage tells the reader that, in addition to personal expression, language also has the power to "persuade and influence." While answers A, B, and C may indeed be attributes of language, they are not focused upon in the passage.

62. **B**

The adjectival form "second," not the adverbial form "secondly," is appropriate here, since it modifies a noun not a verb.

63. **B**

The opening verbal phrase is a dangling modifier. "Prevention" is not "faced" with anything; Lincoln is. All the other choices are standard English sentences.

64. **C**

"With the outbreak . . ." is a prepositional phrase that is stopped with a period[.]. It has no subject or verb and is not a standard English sentence. All the rest are correct English.

65. **C**

Inverse variations give graphs that are curves. As equations, they take the forms $xy = k$ or $y = \frac{k}{x}$. The graph shown in problem 20 is simpler than that, so statement I is false.

The graphs of direct variations are straight lines that pass through the point (0,0) (the origin.) As equations, they take the form $y = mx + 0$, or simply $y = mx$. The line shown in problem 20 is the graph of a direct variation, so statement II is true.

Because point (–5, 5) is equally distant from both the x- and y-axes, the line "cuts" quadrant II at a 45° angle. Lines that form 45° angles with the x- and y-axes (assuming the same scales on both axes) have slopes of 1 or –1. The line in problem 20 travels from upper left to lower right, meaning that its slope is negative, so statement III is also true.

66. **B**

Just from looking at the graph, it's clear that most of the space under the curve is past the 60 mark on the x-axis, answer D is eliminated because it doesn't include statement I.

Statement II can't be answered by what the graph shows. It appears possible that certain questions were too hard for many in the class and that there weren't enough questions to differentiate B students from C students, but perhaps the class performed exactly as it should have, given the students' ability and Ms. Alvarez's teaching. The distribution can give a teacher many clues about the test and the students and even herself, but by itself tells us nothing about the fairness of the test. Thus, answer A can be eliminated.

Statement III is also false; in left-skewed distributions such as this one, the median is higher than the mean. This is true because the mean is lowered by the lowest scores while the mean is relatively unaffected by them.

Statement IV is true: one fairly large group has scored in the high 80s and 90s and another discernible group in the low to mid-60s, whereas few students fall outside these two groups. Thus, the answer has to be B.

67. **D**

Using the rules for solving one-variable equations, the original equation is transformed as follows:

$$\frac{x}{3} - 9 = 15$$

Adding 9 to each side of the equation gives

$$\frac{x}{3} = 24$$

Multiplying both sides by 3 gives

$x = 72$.

68. **C**

The author remains objective throughout the passage. That is, he remains impartial and factual. Answer A, "lethargy," means sluggish; B, "apathy," means unconcerned. D, "intensity," means vehement or fierce, and thus does not apply.

69. **B**

The third sentence suggests that poetry has the ability to serve both as an adornment or embellishment of an era and as a social commentary. The passage fundamentally suggests that poetry is more than just lyrical fluff, it is a means of social analysis, protest, and interpretation. While A, C, and D are components of the passage, they are not the passage's main topic.

70. **D**

The word *trope* means that a word is used in a figurative sense. That is, it conjures images of Greco-Roman representations. Answer A is a troop; B, and C are types of terminology that do not apply.

71. **B**

The passage suggests that a critic is a viable political force that serves both as a censure and a social commentator. Answers A, C, and D are subjective answers and are, therefore, inappropriate.

72. B

The passage states that the etymology of the word "censure" dates to the Middle Ages, suggesting that it was in use at that time. The passage also states that a critic can also be equivalent to a censurer. It, therefore, could not be A, a modern phenomenon, or D, developed around the time of the Civil War. Answer C is not addressed in the passage, leaving B as the best answer.

73. C

The passage addresses both the implications (indications) and the connotations (meaning) associated with the role of the critic as author. Answers B, and D are only alluded to, while A is a supposition. Thus, C is the correct answer.

74. B

Etymology is the study of the history and/or origin of a word. This definition renders the remaining answers false.

75. A

The phrase "at one time . . ." is a nonrestrictive unit that is not necessary to the basic meaning of the sentence; consequently, both commas are needed. The commas for B and D are necessary to set off introductory or qualifying phrases. No commas are needed in B since the phrase that follows is a direct adjectival qualification of what kind of rockets they are as we know them today. Thus, no comma of separation is needed.

76. B

This is just a long phrase; it has no subject or verb. C is an atypical but rhetorically correct and standard English sentence. Many sentences in English begin with "And." The other choices are standard subject/verb independent sentence units.

77. A

This word is too general for such a specific informational context. B should remain because it is the exact, or first, phrase the writer discusses. C need not be changed because only a synonym such as "real" would be needed, but the meaning would remain the same. D is all right because the writer points not to any specific study, research, or development done, but to all that type of "work" in general.

78. **A**

Again, using the rules for solving one-variable equations produces these transformations:

$3x^2 - 11 = 1$

Adding 11 to each side of the equation gives

$3x^2 = 12$

Dividing both sides by 3 gives

$x^2 = 4$

You next find the square roots of 4; 2 and −2.

The solutions can be checked by substituting them (one at a time) into the original equation to see if they work. In this case, both 2 and −2 indeed do work.

79. **B**

Solving for a particular variable in an equation means to isolate that variable on one side of the equation. In this case, use of the rules for transforming equations allows you to change the original equation into the desired one:

$$\frac{y}{3} - \frac{x}{2} = 4$$

Adding $\frac{x}{2}$ to each side gives

$$\frac{y}{3} = \frac{x}{2} + 4$$

Then, multiplying each side by 3 gives

$$y = \frac{3x}{2} + 12$$

80. **D**

One way to solve the problem is by writing a one-variable equation that matches the information given:

$4x + 2(10 - x) = 26$

The "4x" represents four tires for each car. You use x for the number of cars because at first, you don't know how many cars there are.

(10 − x) represents the number of motorcycle tires in the lot. (If there are ten vehicles total, and x of them are cars, you subtract x from 10 to get the number of "leftover" motorcycles.) Then 2(10 − x) stands for the number of motorcycle tires in the lot.

You know that the sum of the values 4x and 2(10 − x) is 26, and that gives you your equation. Using the standard rules for solving a one-variable equation, you find that x (the number of cars in the lot) equals 3.

Another approach to the problem when given multiple answer choices is to try substituting each answer for the unknown variable in the problem to see which one makes sense.

81. **A**

You know that the correct equation must show three consecutive odd numbers being added to give 117. Odd numbers (just like even numbers) are each two apart. Only the three values given in answer A are each two apart.

Because the numbers being sought are odd, one might be tempted to choose answer D. However, the second value in answer D (x + 1) is not two numbers apart from the first value (x); it's different by only one.

82. **C**

It is not the work force that is "for the better," but the situation for men. This is also supported by the rest of the evidence offered in the paragraph. The other sentences have their modifying phrases directly related to the idea they qualify.

83. **C**

The writer is comparing before and after the appearance of women in management; only two things—therefore the comparative form, not the superlative, is correct: "greater." A, B, and D are all incorrect responses; they have no comparative adjectives, just adverbs used as qualifiers, e.g., "overly." These are used in a standard way.

84. **B**

Part 15 is a run-on sentence, incorrectly punctuated with a comma after "families" instead of a period or a semicolon (i.e., it's a comma splice). The rest of the choices are all standard sentences.

85. **C**

The passage suggests that Douglass was concerned with raising social consciousness about slavery. His interest in refuting those who doubted his claims was for the sake of authenticity.

86. **B**

Douglass was one of the eminent human rights leaders of the nineteenth century. All the other choices, while true, are irrelevant to the question and are not supported by the text.

87. **B**

The passage states "Mrs. Auld recognized Frederick's intellectual acumen." A synonym for "acumen" is intelligence, insight, or natural ability. The other choices are inaccurate.

88. **D**

Choices A, B, and C are too vague or ill-defined. Thus, choice D is correct.

89. **A**

An "impromptu" speech is one given extemporaneously, or off the cuff.

90. **D**

Part 12 has an incorrect agreement between "kids" and "does." Kids [they] do [something] is correct. All the other sentences use standard English syntax.

91. **D**

The sentence is a rhetorical clause that begins with a subordinating conjunction, "because." Consequently, it cannot stand alone as a complete standard sentence. The rest are standard.

92. **B**

The writer never specifies with the correct noun who exactly is placing the baby in her jumpseat. None of the other choices is a required correction.

93. **D**

All riders must pay at least three dollars, so 3 will be added to the cost of the fare. Only answers B and D meet that requirement. The additional fare of two dollars "for every mile or fraction of a mile" tells you that you will need to multiply the number of miles driven (you use 11 because of the extra fraction of a mile) by 2, leading you to answer D.

94. **A**

In the aforementioned expression, $\frac{2}{3}x^2$ and $\frac{1}{3}x^2$ are like terms; their sum is $\frac{3}{3x^2}$, or $1x^2$, or just x^2; $-12x$ and $7x$ are like terms; they add up to $-5x$; 9 and 1 are also like terms, with a sum of 10.

Those three terms; x^2, $-5x$, and 10, are then separated by addition symbols to give the simplified version of the original expression.

95. **C**

Each *term* of each *binomial must be multiplied by* both *terms in the other binomial. That means that four products are generated:*

$(-2x^2) \times (5x^2)$ gives $-10x^4$ (and right here you see that answer C is correct).

$(-2x^2) \times (3) = -6x^2$

$(-11) \times (5x^2) = -55x^2$

$(-11) \times (3) = -33$

The two middle terms are like terms, and can be combined into $-61x^2$. The three terms (which cannot be further combined) give you the answer of $-10x^4 - 61x^2 - 33$.

96. **D**

A teaching assistant would be expected to lay the foundation for her lecture and the present greater detail by way of example, or as the passage puts it, "illustration." Someone in this position, having set this task for herself, would not be prone to refuting her own lecture notes (A), attempting to cause confusion (B), or perhaps least of all, working to subvert the lecture topic she herself had elected to teach (C).

97. **A**

The definition of the term "pedagogical" is A, academic. The answers B, abstract, C, meaningless, and D obtuse are incorrect.

98. **B**

The author's classroom experience was B, intelligible (understandable) and pragmatic (practical or utilitarian). The passage gives credence to this by the author's use of such words as "clear and well prepared." Answers A, and C suggest the opposite of a positive experience, and there is no evidence given that the experience was too advanced or complicated (D).

99. **C**

Choice C is a prepositional phrase, "About 25,000 years ago," which is followed by a subordinate clause. This part should be linked to the previous sentence as it is integral to the migration of the Anasazi. Choices A, B, and D are all complete sentences.

100. **C**

Choice C has to do with the later history of the Mesa Verde area, after the Anasazi had abandoned it. Since this is so far removed chronologically, Part 7 should be deleted or further developed in a third paragraph. Choices A and B discuss the very early history of the Indians. Choice D follows the chronological time order from A.D. 500 and leads into a discussion of the height of the Anasazi civilization.

101. **A**

One approach to factoring the expression is to start with a set of two empty parentheses written as follows: (__ + __) (__ + __). The task is to then fill in the four blanks with values that "multiply back" to the original expression. Educated trial and error works well here. Here's a good place to start: You know that the two blanks at the end of the parentheses must be 1 and 5, because 5 is a prime number; no other whole numbers multiply by anything to give you 5.

A bit more experimentation shows that only $(4x - 1) \times (-2x + 5)$ "multiplies back" to $-8x^2 + 22x - 5$. (Be sure to pay attention to whether values are positive or negative.)

102. **D**

Before attempting to factor the expression into two binomials, you must look for any factors common to both terms. Both $2x^2$ and (-18) are divisible by 2, so you can "factor out" the 2, giving $2(x^2 - 9)$.

$(x^2 - 9)$ should be recognized as the difference of two perfect squares, and can itself be factored into $(x + 3)(x - 3)$. Placing the "factored out" 2 back into the expression as a coefficient, you get $2(x + 3)(x - 3)$.

103. **C**

Multiplication is *commutative*, meaning that the factors being multiplied can be in any order. You can, therefore, rearrange the expression in problem 32 to look like this:

$$3 \times 5 \times \sqrt{2} \times \sqrt{10}$$

which gives

$$15\sqrt{20}$$

The key to completing the task of simplification is to see that the number 20 contains a perfect square (4). You can rewrite $\sqrt{20}$ as $\sqrt{4} \times \sqrt{5}$, or $2\sqrt{5}$.

Multiplying that 2 by 15 gives a coefficient of 30, times the remaining $\sqrt{5}$.

104. **C**

As always when simplifying such expressions, you try to find common factors in the various terms. You see that both 75 and 3 "contain" 3. You can take advantage of this by rewriting the expression this way:

$$\frac{\sqrt{25} \times \sqrt{3} \times \sqrt{x^7}}{\sqrt{3} \times \sqrt{x}}$$

You can further assist the task by rewriting $\sqrt{x^7}$ as $\sqrt{x^6} \times \sqrt{x}$, giving

$$\frac{5 \times \sqrt{3} \times \sqrt{x^6} \times \sqrt{x}}{\sqrt{3} \times \sqrt{x}}$$

You may then cancel equal terms, leaving you with $5x^3$.

105. **C**

*Choice C unnecessarily repeats the words "basis," "based," "founding," and "foundation."
These forms need not be repeated and the sentence should be condensed. Choice A repeats
the phrase "board of regents," found in the previous sentence, but it is needed for transition of
thought. Choice B and choice D are well-worded sentences.*

106. **B**

*Choice B fits between Part 4 and Part 6. Part 4 mentions the topic of dissenting opinion, and
Part 6 elaborates by stating the position that English professors have always been outspoken.
This idea is continued in Part 7. Choice A changes voice to "we," which is out of place in this
letter. Choice C is too casual. Choice D directly contradicts the thesis of the letter.*

107. **B**

*Choice B contains an inappropriate use of words. The contraction for "who is" should be used
to make the sentence correct. The possessive "whose" is not correct in this context. Choice A
correctly uses the comparative degree. Choice C correctly uses the superlative degree. Choice
D does not make a needed change.*

108. **A**

*The passage tells of the "great (linguistic) vowel shift" of the early fifteenth century. While the
passage speaks of B, an artistic renaissance; C, new linguistic freedoms; and D, effects on
artistic expression, these are all results of the shift and not the shift itself. The shift is what the
passage is about. Thus, A is the correct answer.*

109. **B**

*In this case, linguistic refers to speaking, talking, verbiage, and/or the act of oration. A, C, and
D are not acceptable definitions for the word linguistic. Consequently, Choice B, verbal or rhetorical, is the correct answer.*

110. **A**

*Answers B, C, and D are generalized answers resulting from the vowel shift. Choice A is a di-
rect result of the shift and is quoted directly from the passage.*

Therefore, A is the correct answer.

111. **A**

*The area of any rectangle is equal to the measure of its length times the measure of its width (or
to say it differently, the measure of its base times the measure of its height). A right triangle can
be seen as half of a rectangle (sliced diagonally). Answer A represents, in effect, a rectangle's
area cut in half (i.e., divided by 2).*

112. **D**

The formula for finding the area of any circle is A = πr² (about 3.14 times the length of the radius times itself). In this case you need to take half of πr²; hence, answer D.

113. **B**

Angle xyz is an inscribed angle (its vertex is on the circle). Angle xcz is a central angle (its vertex is at the circle's center). When two such angles intercept (or "cut off") the same arc of the circle, there exists a specific size relationship between the two angles. The measure of the central angle will always be double the measure of the inscribed angle. In this case, that means that the measure of angle xcz must be 80°.

That means that minor arc xz also has measure 80°. Every circle (considered as an arc) has measure 360°. That means that major arc xyz has measure 280° (360 – 80).

114. **A**

The formula for finding the volume of a cylinder is:

V = πr²h

This means that the volume is equal to pi (about 3.14) times the measure of the radius squared times the height of the cylinder. In this case, that's

3.14 × 6² × 8

or

3.14 × 36 × 8

or about 904. (Note that the final answer is given in cubic centimeters.)

115. **C**

Choice C, delete Part 4, is the correct choice. The sentence labeled Part 4 introduces a new topic—the fact that some companies are not committed to a day care program. Since the paragraphs are both discussing companies that have already made this decision, and the advantages of having made this decision, Part 4 is out of place. Choice A would make a contradictory statement. Choice B would delete a needed phrase. Choice D would destroy the parallelism created with Parts 6 and 7 that leads naturally as a transition into the next paragraph.

116. A

Choice A is needed for correct subject and verb agreement. The plural subject "companies" should be followed by the plural verb "make." Confusion is caused by an intervening phrase, "showing special initiative in building company loyalty of each employee." Because the phrase ends with a singular noun, it is a common error to make the verb singular also. Choice B, present progressive, and choice C, future, are incorrect tenses for the context of the sentence and the paragraph. Choice D needs a helping verb and cannot stand alone.

117. D

Part 9 begins with the transition word "Therefore," so it is best placed after a sentence that would state a reason for building company loyalty and morale. Part 11 gives a compelling reason—the company's personal interest in each employee. Choice A would remove the topic sentence to a less prominent position, as well as have Part 9 clearly out of order with no idea before it in the paragraph. Choice B does not place a sentence with a clear reason before the transition "therefore." Choice C would weaken the paragraph.

118. D

The passage states that lead poisoning leads to learning disabilities and possibly even death. Choice A is too broad, and B and C are not directly addressed, leaving D as the correct answer.

119. C

The passage states that "all California MediCal-eligible children, ages one through five, will now be routinely screened." Answer choices A, children in California, B, children with learning disabilities, and D, minority children, are generalities not stated in the passage. Only Choice C is clearly stated in the passage.

120. B

The statistics suggest that inner-city children are at the greatest risk from lead poisoning. The statistics do not support answers A, C, and D, leaving B as the only legitimate answer.

121. C

The last sentence of the passage suggests that testing will catch the disease "at an early stage" and prevent serious disorders. Choices A, B, and D do not address this ultimate goal of the testing program. Only Choice C reiterates the program's ultimate purpose.

122. **D**

Choice D discusses the tool-making abilities of an otter, not man, so it should be deleted. Choice A would delete the topic sentence from the paragraph. Choice B is incorrect because Part 2 begins with "During this time," and there would be no antecedent for "this" if the two parts are reversed. Choice C is incorrect because the suggested addition does not pertain to the development of man during this time period.

123. **C**

Parts 8 and 9 need to be reversed. Part 8 begins with the transition word "Also," which clearly introduces a second feature, not a first as the position would indicate. Choice A would delete the topic sentence from the paragraph. Choice B would put the second factor after the topic sentence which introduces it. Choice D is the concluding sentence and should not be eliminated.

124. **A**

Choice A eliminates the fragment in the second half of Part 4. The subject is "the use of speech," so the verb should be "facilitated" and not the infinitive "to facilitate." Choice B would delete the necessary transition word "other," needed to link developments discussed in the first paragraph with developments discussed in the second paragraph. Choice C changes the comparative degree "less," needed to compare two items in Part 9, to the superlative degree needed to compare three or more things. Choice D changes the present participle "ensuring" to the past participle "ensured." This change is incorrect because the present participle is necessary to show that survival is still going on; the past participle would indicate that survival has stopped.

125. **B**

The ranchers believe that killing the eagles will protect their ranches. This is understood by the implication that "attract[ing] and kill[ing] predators . . . in an effort to preserve young grazing animals" will protect their ranches.

126. **B**

The author's use of words such as "mighty bald eagle" and "threatened by a new menace" supports concern for the topic. For the most part, the author appears objective; thus, Choice B, concerned interest, is the correct answer.

127. **B**

You can use the Pythagorean theorem to compute the length of any side of any right triangle, as long as you know the lengths of the other two sides. Here is the theorem:

For any right triangle with side lengths of a, b and c, and where a is the length of the hypotenuse (the longest side, and the one opposite the right angle), $a^2 = b^2 + c^2$.

Substituting the real values for a and b from problem 38, you get

$a^2 = 11^2 + 5^2$

or

$a^2 = 146$

To complete the work, you take the (positive) square root of 146, which is slightly over 12 (12 × 12 = 144).

---

128. A

If two triangles are similar, *that means that they have the exact same shape (although not necessarily the same size). It also means that corresponding angles of the two triangles have the same measure, and that corresponding sides are* proportionate.

One way then to find the solution to this problem is to set up a proportion with one corner the unknown value (x), and then to solve the proportion:

$$\frac{12}{10} = \frac{15}{x}$$

This can be read as "12 is to 10 as 15 is to x." The problem can be solved using cross-multiplication. Thus, 12x = 150, leading to the solution x = 12.5.

---

129. C

When two parallel lines are crossed by another line (called a transversal*), eight angles are formed. There are, however, only two angle measures among the eight angles, and the sum of the two measures will be 180°. All of the smaller angles will have the same measures, and all of the larger angles will have the same measures. In this case, the smaller angles all measure 50°, so the larger angles (including angle y) all measure 130°.*

---

130. A

There are two things one must know in order to answer the question. One is the meaning of the small square at the vertex of angle BXC. That symbol tell you that angle BXC is a right angle (one with 90°.) You must also understand that a straight line can be thought of as an angle that measures 180°. This is a straight angle.

Therefore, the sum of the angles DXC (42°) and BXC (90°) is 132°. This means that the remaining angle on the line must have measure 48° (180° − 132°).

---

131. A

If you know the measures of two angles of any triangle, you can compute the measure of the third angle. (The sum of the three angles is always 180°.) So the measure of the third angle in both of the triangles is 50°, and statement III is correct.

If two triangles have the same degree measures (as established above), then they are similar triangles. (This means that they have the same shape.) Statement I is therefore correct.

Triangles are congruent only if they are exactly the same shape and size. One triangle is larger than the other, so statement II is false.

Because the second triangle is larger than the first, and they're the same shape, there is no way that sides BC and YZ could be the same length. Statement IV is thus false.

132. **D**

This is a problem of deduction. That is, the answer can be deduced from the information given. One solution to this problem is to make a list of the boys' names based on what you know. You could start by taking the very first bit of information, "Fred beat Matt." This allows you to stack those two names like so,

Fred

Matt

with Fred at the top because he was the faster of the two boys.

Then, instead of just taking the next piece of information ("Curt beat Dwayne"), you could instead look for information that tells you more about the boys already listed. You read, for instance, that Dwayne beat Fred. This allows you to add Dwayne to the list:

Dwayne

Fred

Matt

By filling in the other boys' names based on the information given, you should produce the following list:

Pat

Curt

Dwayne

Fred

Matt

Ivan

This shows that Ivan was last in the race.

Writing Sample Examples
WRITING SAMPLE WITH A SCORE OF 6 OR 5
The Literature of the Past

The direction of modern literary scholarship points toward an alarming conclusion. The depreciation of the literary study of bygone periods is a sign of two disturbing trends. First, scholars are avoiding more difficult study in preference to what seems light or facile. Furthermore, the neglect of the literature of former eras is a denial of the contribution that past authors have made toward modern literature. This is not to suggest that all scholars who study modern literature do so because they are either intimidated by past literature or do not appreciate its value. However, the shrinking minority of past literary scholarship is a clear indication that intimidation and awe of past conventions are deterrents to many students of literature.

The dread associated with past literature reflects poorly upon our society. The attempts to simplify literature to accommodate simpler audiences has resulted in a form of literary deflation. The less society taxes its audience's minds, the less comprehensive those unexercised minds become. Information and ideas are now transmitted to the average man through the shallow medium of television programming. Modern students are evolving from this medium, and the gap separating them from the complexity of the classics is continuing to grow.

Once more, it is important to stress that this essay does not seek to diminish students of modern literature. The only demand this argument makes upon modern students is that they supplement their study with significant portions of the classics from which all subsequent literature has been derived, whether consciously or unconsciously. Failure to do so is an act akin to denying the importance of history itself. Like history, literature exists as an evolutionary process; modern literature can only have come into existence through the development of past literature.

Concerning the relative complexity of the classics to modern literature, the gap is not so great as one may think. Surely, one who glances at the works of Shakespeare or Milton without prior exposure will be daunted by them. However, a disciplined mind can overcome the comprehensive barriers erected over the past few centuries through persistence and perseverance.

Unfortunately, the ability to overcome the barriers to past literature may eventually become obsolete. The more frequently students select their courses of study through fear rather than interest, the wider the literary gap will become, until the pampered minds of all future readers will prove unequal to the task of reading the literature of our fathers. The more frequently students deny the usefulness of the literature antedating this century, the more frequently they deny their own literary heritage, the more probable it will become for modern literature's structure to crumble through lack of firm foundation.

FEATURES OF THE WRITING SAMPLE SCORING 6 OR 5

Focus

The essay follows the course presented in the topic paragraph, reemphasizing major points such as the writer's reluctance to condemn all modern scholars. This emphasis is not straight repetition, but carries different viewpoints and evidence for the writer's argument. The digression on television in the second paragraph neatly rounds off the writer's overall concern for cultural consequences of historical literature's depreciation.

Support/Elaboration

The paper's topic and the writer's viewpoint are both well laid out in the first paragraph. The two trends described by the author in the topic paragraph are explored in deeper detail throughout the essay. The language and style fit the writer's audience. The style is formal, but possesses a personalized voice.

The writer follows the suggestions of the writing assignment closely, structuring his essay around the reflections and discussions listed therein. Each paragraph bears an example to lend authority to the writer's argument.

The second paragraph uses the theory of television's vegetative influence. The third paragraph utilizes the evolutionary equality of history. The fourth paragraph evokes names that the reader can relate to in terms of comprehensive difficulty.

Organization

Many transitional conventions are utilized. "Once more . . ."; "Concerning the relative complexity . . ."; "Unfortunately . . ." The examples throughout the paragraphs have a pointed direction. The concluding paragraph completes the argument with a premonition of future calamity should its warning go unheeded.

Grammar and Conventions

The sentences are standardized and vary in form, although some passive constructions ("will be daunted," "the more probable it will become") might have been avoided. The repetition of "the more frequently" in the final paragraph is particularly effective and pointed.

Words are chosen to offer variety. "Past literature" is supplemented by "literary study of bygone days" and "the literature of former eras." Phrasing is consistent and standard, although the third sentence of the second paragraph ("The less society taxes . . . the less comprehensive") is slightly awkward, though the repetition does achieve some effect.

Spelling and punctuation are mostly standard throughout the essay. The sentences in the final paragraph might be divided and shortened, although this may diminish their effect.

WRITING SAMPLE WITH A SCORE OF 4 OR 3

Modern Literature

It doesn't matter whether or not we read past literature. Past literature has been converted into what we now know as "modern literature". The elements of the past are therefore incorporated into the body of what we now have.

When we read a work of modern literature based upon the classics, such as Joyce's *Ulysses*, it doesn't matter whether or not we've read Homer's *Odyssey*. What matters is what Joyce made out of Homer's epic; not what Homer started out with.

When we see *West Side Story* in the movies, it doesn't matter whether or not we've read *Romeo and Juliet*: the end result is the same; therefore, we do not need to know the original source. I don't think it makes a difference whether or not we even recognize Tony and Maria as Romeo and Juliet. Tony and Maria are today's versions of Romeo and Juliet, and they match the culture that they are told in.

It has been said that all of the good plots have been used up by past ages, and that all we create now are variations of those plots. This statement is false. It is rather the case that these plots are universal variables that each age must interpret in its own unique way. I find it rather faseatious to study the interpretation of other cultures. We should be concerned only with our own.

Past literature is not necessary in a modern world that has reformed the mistakes of the past. Anything that hasn't carried over from the past is negligible: what was good for Shakespeare's audience may not be what we need. In conclusion, I would have to strongly conclude that the "trend of studying modern versus past literature" is commendable, and not contemptible.

FEATURES OF THE WRITING SAMPLE SCORING 4 OR 3

Focus

Though the writer knows the point he is trying to promote, his evidence is presented haphazardly and without a logical design. However, his rather abrupt conclusion is somewhat supported by his points.

Support/Elaboration

The main topic is not supplied directly within the work. Though the reader is aware of the conflict between modern and past literature, there is no sense of scholarly consensus as suggested by the writing assignment. The writer's somewhat informal style is unbalanced throughout the work by his uncertainty with his audience.

The essay does not follow a logical pattern; one premise does not meld fluidly into another. Though the premises loosely support the conclusion, they do not support each other.

Organization

Transitions are slight, if any. The repetition of "when we" in the opening two paragraphs is noticeable. Each point should have been further developed. The writer assumes his reader is quite familiar with West Side Story and its characters.

Grammar and Conventions

Most sentences follow standard sentence structure, although some are very irregular. The first sentence of paragraph three expresses two or three independent thoughts and should be separated accordingly. The final sentence of the fourth paragraph contains an unclear modifier: "own" should read either "own interpretation" or "own culture."

Most words are used in their proper context, and an attempt has been made to use some erudite words. "End result" is redundant; "end" should have been excluded. The declaration "this statement is false" in the fourth paragraph is not supported by logical evidence. In this case, the writer should have asserted that this was his own opinion. However, in other cases it is recommended that the writer be bold with assertions. A degree of proof is all that is required to make those assertions. "In conclusion" is redundant with "conclude" in the final sentence of the essay. Contractions such as "we've" and "don't" should be written out in their long forms.

Most words are spelled properly, although "faseatious" should be spelled "facetious." (The period in the second sentence of the first paragraph should lie within the quotation marks.) The comma after "commendable" in the final paragraph should be eliminated because it does not introduce a new clause.

WRITING SAMPLE WITH A SCORE OF 2 OR 1

Literature

Modern literature is no better than past literature, and vice-versa. It is interest that matters. If people aren't interested in the past, then so be it. A famous man once said "To each his own". I agree.

For example, you can see that books are getting easier and easier to understand. This is a good thing, because more knowledge may be comunicated this way. Comunication is what literature is all about: Some people comunicate with the past, and others with the present.

I communicate with the present. I'm not saying we all should. It's all up to your point of view. When a scholer chooses past over present, or vice-versa, that's his perogative. It doesn't make him better or worse than anybody else. We should all learn to accept each other's point of view.

When I read someone like Fitzgerald or Tolkien, I get a different feeling than Shakespeare. Shakespeare can inspire many people, but I just don't get that certain feeling from his plays. "The Hobbit," "The Great Gatsby," "Catcher in the Rye," and "Of Mice and Men." These are all great classics from this century. We should be proud of them. However, some people prefer "The Trojan War" and "Beowulf." Let them have it. Remember: 'To each his own."

FEATURES OF THE WRITING SAMPLE SCORING 2 OR 1

Focus

The writer seems to contradict her own points at times, favoring modern literature rather than treating the subject as objectively as she had proposed. It is clear that the writer's train of thought shifted during the essay. This was covered up by ending with the catch phrase, "to each his own."

Support/Elaboration

The writer attempts to angle her argument in different ways by presenting such concepts as "communication" and "point of view." However, her thought processes are abrupt and underdeveloped.

The writer misconstrues the topic and writes about the relative worth of modern and past literature. The topic does not call for a judgment of period literatures; it calls for a perspective on the way in which they are studied. Her personal style is too familiarized; it is unclear to whom the essay is addressed.

Organization

There is neither direction nor logical flow in the essay. One point follows the next without any transition or connection. All three persons are used to prove his argument: the writer resorts to "I," "you," and "a famous man." There is no clear overall thesis guiding the essay.

Grammar and Conventions

Some sentences follow standard formation. Sentence three of the final paragraph is a fragment. The sentences are short and choppy, as is the thought they convey. Too many sentences are merely brief remarks on the preceding statements (e.g., "I agree," "Let them have it," etc.). These are not appropriate because they do not evoke new thought. The reference to Shakespeare in the first sentence of the final paragraph implies more than the writer intended. It should read: "than when I read Shakespeare."

Many words are repeated without any attempt to supply synonyms (e.g., "communication," "past"). Colloquial expressions are widespread and should be avoided. The Trojan War is evidently an improper reference to Homer's *Iliad*.

There are many mechanical errors. Punctuation and spelling are inconsistent. "Comunication" and "comunicate" are spelled improperly in paragraph two, while "communicate" is spelled correctly in paragraph three. "Scholer" should be spelled "scholar." "Perogative" should be spelled "prerogative." In the fourth sentence of the first paragraph, the period should lie within the quotation marks, as it does in the final sentence of the essay. The book titles in sentences three and six of the final paragraph should be underlined and not quoted.

ICTS

Illinois Certification Testing System

Elementary/Middle Grades Review

Language Arts and Literacy

Vocabulary Skills

Reading Comprehension

The Writing Process

Listening and Speaking Processes

Development of Reading Competence

Research Skills and Strategies

Language is an intensely complex system that allows us to create and express meaning through socially shared conventions. Children generally master their native language within their first four years of life, well before they enter the elementary school, even though their teachers (family members) generally have no special training. Once children enter elementary school, their knowledge of language continues to grow and develop through opportunities to interact with teachers and other children.

When it comes to written language, there are **four cueing systems through which we organize**.

1. The first system is **semantics**, or the meaning system of language. Children, early on, are taught that speech needs to convey meaning. Likewise, texts needs to be meaningful. If some words in a passage are unknown, the child will know that some words make sense in the context of the passage and other words do not.

2. The second cue is **syntax**, or the structural system of language.

3. The third cue, according to this view, is **phonological**, or letter-sound, information. The phonological cue can confirm predictions that are made based on semantics and syntax.

4. The fourth cueing system is the **pragmatic system**, or the social and cultural restraints placed on the use of language, along with differences in pronunciation.

ICTS outlines the following six subareas as being important when it comes to Language and Literacy. They are as follows.

1. Vocabulary Skills

Understand word analysis strategies and vocabulary development and how to use effective, developmentally appropriate approaches to promote students' word analysis and vocabulary skills.

For example:
- Demonstrate knowledge of **phonics and its role in decoding**; of ways to assess students' phonic skills; and of effective instructional strategies, activities, and materials for promoting students' phonetic analysis skills.
- Demonstrate knowledge of **word analysis strategies**, including syllabication, morphology (e.g., use of affixes and roots), and context clues; of ways to assess students' use of word analysis strategies; and of effective instructional strategies, activities, and materials for promoting students' word analysis and contextual analysis skills.
- Demonstrate knowledge of the role of **vocabulary development in reading**; of ways to assess students' vocabulary development; and of effective instructional strategies, activities, and materials for promoting students' vocabulary development.

Vocabulary building is a skill that needs to be worked on daily in the classroom. One of the goals of this type of instruction is to assist children in becoming skillful in **rapid word recognition**. Research suggests that fluent word identification needs to be present before a child can readily comprehend text. If a child needs to painstakingly analyze many of the words in a text, the memory and attention needed for comprehension are absorbed by word analysis, and the pleasure of a good story is lost.

Fast Facts Vocabulary building is a skill that needs to be addressed daily in the classroom.

Typically, children who are just beginning to read **decode** each word as they read it. Through repeated exposure to the same words, instant-recognition vocabulary grows. It is particularly important that developing readers learn to recognize those **words that occur very frequently** in print. A computer analysis of books in print revealed that 100 words make up approximately 50 percent of the words read. Although game-like activities and writing seem to have some impact on developing word recognition, the single best way to develop this necessary, effortless recognition is to encourage children to read, and to provide class time for reading text that is totally the child's choice. Reading and rereading rather easy text seems to be particularly effective.

In addition to working on placing some words into readily available memory, there is sound research suggesting that students can use **context clues** to help identify unknown words. This body of research further suggests that instruction can help improve students' use of such clues. Frequently, **three kinds of context clues** are discussed:

First, **semantic clues** require a child to think about the meanings of words, and what is already known about the topic being read. For example, when reading a story about bats, good teachers help children to activate prior knowledge about bats, and to develop an expectation that the selection may contain words associated with bats, such as *swoop*, *wings*, *mammal*, and *nocturnal*. This discussion might help a child gain a sense of what might be reasonable in a sentence. The word order in a sentence might also provide clues. For example, in the sentence, "Bats can _____," the order of the words in the sentence indicates that the missing word must be a verb. Furthermore, the illustrations in the book can often help with the identification of a word. Still, context clues are often not specific enough to predict the exact word. However, when context clues are combined with other clues such as phonics and word-part clues, accurate word identification is usually possible.

Second, **letter groups** are groups of letters that frequently occur within words. These clusters of letters can be specifically taught. Common prefixes, suffixes, and inflectional endings should be pointed out to students. Being able to rapidly and accurately associate sounds with a cluster of letters leads to more rapid, efficient word identification.

Finally, as young readers build an increasing store of words that they can recognize with little effort, they **use the words they know to help them recognize words that are unfamiliar**. For example, a child who has seen the word *bat* many times and who knows the sound associated with the consonant *r* will probably have little difficulty recognizing the word *rat*.

Vocabulary Development in Reading:

The **best practice** for helping students to gain skill in word-recognition is **real reading and writing activities**. As children read and reread texts of their own choice, they have many opportunities to successfully decode a word, and realize that each time the letter combination b-a-t is in the selection, it's read as *bat*. With each exposure to that word, the child reads the word more easily. A child who writes a sentence with that word as part of the sentence is developing a greater sensitivity to meaning or context clues. The child attempting to spell that word is reviewing and applying what he knows about letter–sound associations.

2. Reading Comprehension

Understand strategies for reading for different purposes and constructing meaning from a variety of reading materials.

For example:
- Demonstrate knowledge of various **reading comprehension strategies and study skills** (e.g., previewing, rereading) for different purposes (e.g., to review facts for

a test, to analyze literature, to conduct research, to respond to social or business correspondence).

- Apply knowledge of strategies for promoting the reading comprehension skills of students who are **at different stages of reading** and for **facilitating comprehension before, during, and after reading** (e.g., prompting students to make predictions).
- Demonstrate knowledge of **literal comprehension skills** (e.g., recognizing facts and opinions, sequence of events, main ideas, or supporting details in a text).
- Demonstrate knowledge of **inferential comprehension skills** (e.g., summarizing, drawing conclusions, or making generalizations from given information; drawing inferences about character, setting, or cause and effect relationships in an excerpt).
- Demonstrate understanding of **interpretive and evaluative comprehension skills** (e.g., analyzing an author's purpose or point of view; evaluating the use of language or illustration to portray characters, develop plot, or create an emotional impact).
- Demonstrate knowledge of **the diverse body of works, authors, and movements** of U.S. and world literature, children's and young adult literature, and other resources that promote students' literary response and analysis skills (e.g., promoting cultural awareness or addressing student issues with young adult literature).
- Analyze major characteristics of **classic and contemporary literature** from the United States and throughout the world, key features of various literary genres (e.g., folk tale, myth, poetry, fiction), and the use of literary elements (e.g., figurative language, dialogue, setting, mood) in various texts.

Helping students read for understanding is the central goal of reading instruction. Comprehension is a complex process involving the text, the reader, the situation, and the purpose for reading. There are a number of factors that come into play as a child attempts to comprehend a passage. First, students cannot understand texts if they cannot read the words. Thus, a teacher who is interested in improving students' comprehension skills needs to teach them to **decode** well. In addition, children need time during the school day to **discuss** what has been read. Most importantly, children need to **read and reread easy texts** often enough that decoding becomes rapid, easy, and accurate.

It has been noted frequently in the literature that children who comprehend well have bigger vocabularies than children who struggle with reading. In part, this is true because their knowledge of vocabulary develops through contact with new words as they read text that is rich in new words. However, it has also been suggested that simply **teaching vocabulary** in isolation does not automatically enhance comprehension.

Strategies for Before, During, and After Reading:

Reading comprehension can be affected by prior knowledge, with many demonstrations that readers who possess rich prior knowledge about the topic of a reading often understand the reading better than classmates with less prior knowledge. Prior knowledge also affects interest. Generally, students like to read about somewhat familiar topics. This is an area in which the skill and interest of the teacher can play a significant role. An able teacher can make a previously unfamiliar topic seem familiar through **pre-reading activities** during which prior knowledge is activated, new prior knowledge is formed, and interest is stirred up. A good teacher will **set a clear purpose for reading**, and ask the students to **gain an overview of the text** before reading, **make predictions** about the upcoming text, and then **read selectively** based on their predictions. Best practice suggests that children should be encouraged to **generate questions** about ideas in text while reading. Successful teachers encourage children to **construct mental images** representing ideas in text, or the actual images from the text. A successful teacher will help readers to process new factual information by helping children to relate new information to their prior knowledge. A potent mechanism for doing this is elaborative interrogation, wherein the teacher poses "why?" questions, encouraging children to question the author and check the answers through text verification. It is through conversation that children are able to compare their predictions and expectations about text content to what was read. It is through these conversations that children see the need to revise their prior knowledge when compelling new ideas that conflict with prior knowledge are encountered. As part of these ongoing conversations, teachers will become alert to students who are applying errant world knowledge as they read and will be able to encourage use of appropriate knowledge. These conversations lead children to figure out the meanings of unfamiliar vocabulary based on context clues, the opinions of others, and sometimes through the use of appropriate source materials such as **glossaries**, **dictionaries**, or an appropriate selection in another text. After reading activities, able teachers encourage children to **revisit the text**—to reread and make notes and paraphrase—to remember important points, interpret the text, evaluate its quality, and review important points. Children should also be encouraged to think about how ideas encountered in the text might be used in the future. As children gain competence, they enjoy showing what they know.

Literal Interpretation:

In reading fictional selections, children should be encouraged to analyze the story using the story-grammar components of setting, characters, problems encountered by characters, attempts at solution to the problem, successful solution, and endings.

Inferential/Evaluative Interpretation:

As children's comprehension grows more sophisticated, they move from merely attempting to comprehend what is in the text to reading more critically. This means that they grow in understanding that any single text provides but one portrayal of the facts. With skillful instruction, children come to read not only what a text says but also how that text portrays the subject matter. They recognize the various ways in which every text is the unique creation of a unique author, and they also learn to compare and contrast the treatment of the same subject matter in a number of texts. Teachers help students grow in comprehension through lessons. At first, teachers are happy if children are able to demonstrate their comprehension of what a text says by being able to engage in some after-reading activity that involves restating what was contained in the text in some authentic way. The next level is to have the children ponder what a text does: to describe an author's purpose, to recognize the elements of the text and how the text was assembled. Finally, some children can attain the skill set needed to successfully engage in text interpretation, to be able to detect and articulate tone and persuasive elements, to discuss point of view, and to recognize bias. Over time, and with good instruction, children learn to infer unstated meanings based on social conventions, shared knowledge, shared experience, or shared values. They recognize implications and draw conclusions, and they move past the point of believing the content of a selection simply because it was in print. In addition, children need to be taught to monitor their own comprehension, and to decide when they need to exert more effort, or to apply a strategy to make sense of a text. The goal of comprehension instruction is for the children to reach a level at which the application of strategies becomes automatic.

Fast Facts — Comprehension is maximized only when readers are fluent in all the processes of skilled reading.

In summary, comprehension is maximized only when readers are fluent in all the processes of skilled reading, from the decoding of words to the articulation and easy, appropriate application of the comprehension strategies used by good readers. Teachers need to teach predicting, questioning, seeking clarification, relating to background knowledge, constructing mental images, and summarizing. The teaching of comprehension strategies has to be conceived as a long-term developmental process, and the teaching of all reading strategies is more successful if they are taught and used by all of the teachers on a staff. In addition, teachers need to allow time for in-school reading and to recognize that good texts are comprehended on a deep level only through rereading and in-depth discussions.

Diverse Body of Works, Authors, and Movements

Teachers today are expected to share a wide range of texts with children by teaching different genres. A genre is a particular type of literature, the classifications of which are based on conventions that apply a basic category to an author's writing. They give the reader a general expectation of what sort of work is being discussed. Charlotte Huck, Susan Hepler, Janet Hickman, and Barbara Kiefer, in their book, *Children's Literature in the Elementary School*, define children's literature as "a book a child is reading." They go on to list picture books, traditional literature, modern fantasy, realistic fiction, historical fiction, nonfiction, biography, and poetry as genres of children's literature. Most genres can be subdivided into a variety of categories, and it is possible that genres could be mixed in a single title.

Picture books are books in which the illustrations and the text work together to communicate the story. There is a huge market for picture books, and they cover many topics. It is a very good idea to share picture books with children in a number of different formats.

Sometimes, able teachers simply read the book to the child without showing any of the pictures. The story is then discussed, and the children are asked if they would like the book to be reread, this time with the pictures being shared. Typically, this technique sparks a lively conversation about why the book with its illustrations is better than hearing the words alone.

Alternatively, teachers may take the children on a picture-walk through of the book, allowing them to speculate about the story before reading it to them. Then, once the book is read, the speculations can be confirmed or reassessed.

Using picture books allows teachers to discuss the elements of higher-level comprehension without the burden of reading lengthy prose, for a picture book can be discussed with an eye on many different factors: design, color, space, media choice, cultural conventions, point of view, showing vs. telling, fairness, realism, or concerns. It is a way to raise issues in a classroom community, and it's a subtle way to affirm classroom members. Nearly any lesson worth teaching is better taught with a picture book in hand. Picture books can be very useful tools in a variety of ways: nearly any concept can be both deepened and expanded by reading the appropriate picture books.

Traditional literature comprises the stories that have their roots in the oral tradition of storytelling. This genre also includes the modern versions of these old stories. It is interesting to read and share multiple versions of old stories, and to compare and contrast each version. It is also interesting to read a number of folktales and keep track of the elements that these old stories have in common. It's also interesting to encourage children to notice where these old stories show up in their day-to-day lives. Children enjoy sharing what they notice. These old stories are woven into ads, comic books, jokes, and other selections.

Modern fantasy is a genre that presents make-believe stories that are the product of the author's imagination. The point of origin for all of these stories is the imagination of the author. Often, they are so beyond the realm of everyday life that they can't possibly be true. Extraordinary events take place within the covers of these books. Fantasy allows a child to move beyond the normal, ho-hum life in the classroom, and speculate about a life that never was, and may never be. But, maybe, just maybe, wouldn't it be grand if an owl were to swoop through an open window and drop a fat letter? What if you dumped some cereal into a bowl, and a lump dropped into the bowl with a thud, and it turned out to be a dragon's egg? What if you could step through a wardrobe and be someplace completely different? Fantasy is a genre that typically sparks rather intense discussions, and provides ample opportunities to illuminate the author's craft for the child.

Historical fiction is set in the past. This type of fiction allows children to live vicariously in times and places they do not normally experience any other way. This type of fiction often has real people and real events depicted, with fiction laced around them. Historical fiction informs the study of social studies. The textbook might say, "and then the tea was dumped in the harbor."

Nonfiction books have the real world as their point of origin. These books help to expand the knowledge of children when they are studying a topic, but they also need to be evaluated for accuracy, authenticity, and inclusion of salient facts. It is a very good idea to include the children in this process, and, when an inaccuracy is detected, it's a good idea to encourage the child (or children) who spotted the flaw to write to the publisher and relate their findings.

Typically, the publisher writes back, thus turning a published flaw into an authentic, empowering writing experience for a child. Again, these books can be the platform for teaching higher-level comprehension skills. Children and their teachers can discuss **fact vs. theory**. For example, the reintroduction of wolves into Yellowstone is a topic that exists in the real world, and reading materials on the subject are readily available. The *fact* is that wolves are carnivorous predators. The *theory* part of the investigation could be a discussion of the impact that reintroducing wolves into the Yellowstone ecosystem might have. This discussion will need to be supported with documentation. The materials read will need to be evaluated in terms of the intended audience, bias, inclusion of enough information, and text structure. These books can also be powerful in creating a community of learners, as they can be used as a means of gathering information about a topic that children are working on together as part of a cooperative learning group. Since nonfiction books are written at a variety of reading levels, all children can find a book to read, and since different titles have different information, the children end up swapping and talking about the books. It makes for some touching and powerful moments in a classroom.

Biography is a genre that deals with the lives of real people. **Autobiography** is a genre that deals with the life of the author. These books enliven the study of social studies because, through careful research, they often include information that transforms a name in a textbook into a person that one may like to get to know better. Did you know that George Washington had false teeth carved from the finest hippopotamus ivory? Did you know that Dolley Madison was stripping wallpaper—very expensive hand-painted silk wallpaper, no less—off the walls in the residence in the White House as British warships were moving up the Potomac River? Again, these books can provide a platform for dynamic lessons about higher-level comprehension skills, especially about bias. Consider the treatment of Helen Keller. Was any information included about how feisty and forward thinking she was?

Poetry is a genre that is difficult to define for children, except as "not-prose." Poetry is the use of words to capture something: a sight, a feeling, or perhaps a sound. Poetry needs to be chosen carefully for a child, as they need to connect with the experience of the poem. All children need poetry in their lives. Poetry needs to be celebrated and enjoyed as part of the classroom experience, and a literacy-rich classroom will always include a collection of poetry to read, reread, savor, and enjoy. Some children enjoy the discipline of writing in a poetic format. Reggie Routman has published a series of slim books about teaching children to write poems on their own.

In summary, today there is an overwhelming variety of children's literature to choose from. When selecting books for use in a classroom, a teacher has a number of issues to consider. Is the book accurate? Aesthetically pleasing? Engaging? Bear in mind the idea that all children deserve to see positive images of children like themselves in the books they read, as illustrations can have a powerful influence on their perceptions of the world. Children also have a need to see positive images of children who are not like themselves, as who is or is not depicted in books can have a powerful influence on their perception of the world as well. Teachers ought to provide children with literature that depicts an affirming, multicultural view, and the selection of books available should show many different kinds of protagonists. Both boys and girls, for example, should be depicted as able.

3. The Writing Process

Understand the process of writing and writing strategies for a variety of purposes and audiences.

For example:

- Recognize **characteristics** of children's development of writing skills, **factors** that influence development of writing skills, **signs** that a student may be experiencing difficulties in written language, and **strategies** for addressing written language needs.
- Demonstrate knowledge of factors to consider when conducting research and writing for **various audiences and purposes** (e.g., expressive, informative, persuasive).
- Apply knowledge of **techniques for generating topics and developing ideas** (e.g., brainstorming, outlining, semantic mapping); methods of organizing written presentations; and strategies for drafting, revising, editing, proofreading, and publishing materials (e.g., peer conferences).
- Analyze and revise written work in relation to **English grammar and mechanics** (i.e., usage, sentence structure, punctuation, capitalization, spelling).
- Analyze and **revise** written work in relation to organization, unity, clarity, and style (e.g., adding topic sentences, reordering sentences, deleting unnecessary information).
- Demonstrate knowledge of activities, instructional resources, and technologies for **promoting students' writing competence** and for **integrating writing with the other language arts**.

Since the early 1970s, Dr. Donald Graves, a professor of education at the University of New Hampshire, has been working in classrooms trying to understand why writing seems to be so difficult to master for so many children. Through conversation with many working teachers, children, their parents, university students, and working writers, and via many keen-eyed observations in classrooms, he developed an approach to writing instruction called *process writing*.

His notion was simple: let's teach children to write the way real writers write. What do writers do? Well, to begin with, they tend to write about what they want to write about. Then they may read about the subject, talk about the subject, take notes, or generally fool around with the topic before they compose. Then they may write a draft, knowing up-front that they are not done at this point. They may share the draft with others, and end up writing all over it. They may also go over every sentence, thinking about word choice, and looking for vague spots, or spots where the piece falls off the subject. They may revise the draft again, share it again, revise it again, and so on, until they are satisfied with the product. Then they publish it. Often, they receive feedback before and after the piece is published, which may lead to a new writing effort. Some writers save scraps of writing in a journal. They may save a turn of phrase, a comment overheard on a bus, a new word, good quotes, or an interesting topic.

Doesn't this sound like a process a child might find helpful? Today, it seems a bit obvious. In the 1970s, 1980s, and even into the 1990s it seemed revolutionary. However, it was well received because teachers were pleased with the way students benefited from this kind of instruction. At the same time, in many schools computers were becoming more readily available to students, and many teachers were finding that writing instruction and computers were a very happy marriage. Also, there were several excellent books available about helping children to write well. Donald Graves wrote *Writing: Teachers and Children at Work* and *A Fresh Look at Writing*. Lucy Calkins wrote *The Art of Teaching Writing*, and Nancy Atwell contributed *In the Middle: Writing, Reading, and Learning with Adolescents*. All of these and others offered support for this new way to augment children's efforts toward learning to write.

Nancy Atwell was particularly skilled in describing how a literacy-rich environment ought to be established and fostered. She argued that children need to be encouraged to read books for enjoyment, but to also look at the craft of the author. Children need to respond to reading in writing. A great deal of research supported the notion that reading informs the writing process, and that the act of writing informs the reading process.

Similarly, Donald Graves advised children to think about events in their lives as a good starting point for discovering topics. He liked to talk about Patricia Polacco books. Almost all of her books are reports of real-life events, things that happened to her and her rotten red-haired brother. For example, *Meteor* was the story of one summer's night when a meteor fell into the yard. It could be told like this: "It was hot. We were outside. A meteor fell, and almost hit us. It didn't." The difference between that account and the published story provides a starting point for a potentially rich discussion about the craft of the writer.

Lucy Calkins, in *The Art of Teaching Writing*, addresses the importance of expecting good writing from children, and then giving them ample time to write, and the needed instruction and encouragement to make it happen. She suggests that children keep a writing notebook where they can keep little scraps of writing that might find their way into a written piece some day. This suggestion also helps with classroom management during a writer's workshop. It gives children something to do instead of wandering around the room or announcing, "I'm done!" and ceasing to write.

Another part of the writing process is to share the writing with a classmate, and allow that peer to edit the piece. Able teachers provide guidance for this process, so that the students do not simply declare the work "good" or leave the classmate in tears because the draft is ruthlessly criticized.

Following an edit for content, the piece is edited for features such as punctuation, capitalization, and spelling. The use of computers has made the entire writing process much easier. Children learn to use a thesaurus, dictionary, and the functions of spelling and grammar. Revisions can be made more easily. One of the best results, however, is that the finished piece *looks* finished. Gone are the days when a child did his or her personal best, only to get the paper back with "messy" scrawled in red across it.

Another aspect of the process is celebration. Children are invited to share their work with the class. After a young author reads their piece, classmates ought to offer affirmations and suggestions. Able teachers ought to have children save each piece of paper generated in the writing process, and store them in a personal portfolio for review.

4. Listening and Speaking Processes

Understand effective communication through the use of listening and speaking skills.

For example:

- Demonstrate understanding of concepts related to **communication theory**, **language development**, **language diversity**, and the **role of language in learning** (e.g., the cultural dimensions of communication, the significance of nonverbal cues in communication).
- Apply knowledge of **listening strategies** for various purposes and contexts (e.g., acquiring or analyzing information, appreciating literature read aloud, social interaction, personal response).
- Recognize factors that affect children's development of **listening skills** and their ability to listen effectively and construct meaning in various situations, and strategies for addressing listening needs.
- Recognize strategies for organizing and presenting ideas and information for **different audiences and purposes** (e.g., to inform, persuade, entertain; to participate in group discussions).
- Recognize factors that affect children's development of **speaking skills**, signs that a child may be experiencing difficulties in language development, and strategies for addressing oral language needs.

Language is an intensely complex system for creating meaning through socially shared conventions. Very young children begin to learn language by listening and responding to to the people in their life. This early listening provides a foundation for acquisition of language. Babies are active listeners. Long before they can respond in speech per se, they encourage the person talking to them to continue by waving their arms, smiling, or wriggling, for example. On the other hand, they are also capable of clear communication when they have had enough by dropping eye contact or turning away, among other examples of body language.

Although listening is used extensively in communication, it does not receive much attention at school. Studies suggest that teachers assume that listening develops naturally. One study from 1986 suggests that teachers are not apt to get much training on teaching listening. His survey of fifteen textbooks used in teacher education programs revealed that out of a total of 3,704 pages of text, only 82 pages mentioned listening.

While there is no well-defined model of listening to guide instruction, there are some suggestions. Some theorists link listening skills to reading skills. They feel that reading and listening make use of similar language comprehension processes. Listening and reading both require the use of skills in phonology, syntax, semantics, and knowledge of text structure, and seem to be controlled by the same set of cognitive processes.

However, there is an additional factor at play in listening: the recipient of the oral message can elect to listen passively, or listen actively, with active listening being the desired goal. A number of studies suggest that the teaching of listening can be efficiently taught by engaging in the kinds of activities that have been successful in developing reading, writing, and speaking proficiencies and skills such as setting a purpose for listening, giving directions, asking questions about the selection heard, and encouraging children to forge links between the new information that was just heard and the knowledge already in place. In addition, children need to be coached in the use appropriate volume and speed when they speak, and in learning how to participate in discussions and follow the rules of polite conversation, such as staying on a topic and taking turns.

5. Development of Reading Competence

Understand literacy development and how to use effective, developmentally appropriate strategies to promote students' literacy skills.

For example:
- Demonstrate knowledge of children's **literacy development**, factors that influence development of reading skills, signs that a child may be experiencing difficulties in reading, and strategies for addressing reading needs.
- Recognize factors that affect a reader's **construction of meaning** through interactions with text (e.g., prior knowledge and experiences, reading rate, characteristics of the text).
- Demonstrate **knowledge of print concepts** (e.g., letter, word, and sentence representation; directionality; tracking); of ways to assess students' understanding of print; and of instructional strategies, activities, and materials for promoting students' interaction with print in varied and meaningful contexts.
- Demonstrate knowledge of **spelling development and its significance for reading**; of ways to assess students' spelling skills; and of effective instructional strategies, activities, and materials for promoting students' spelling skills.
- Relate reading development to the development of skills in **oral and written language**.
- Demonstrate knowledge of the importance of **independent reading** and effective approaches for guiding students to select independent reading materials and for motivating students to read independently.

Literacy can be defined as a child's ability to read and write in order to function adequately in society. A child's literacy skills begin to develop in infancy and continue to expand throughout the school years. An infant's response to a parent's singing, a toddler's ability to choose a book and ask to have it read to her, and a preschooler's interest in attempting to write his name on a birthday card are all examples of **literacy development**. Research has shown that early, frequent exposure to printed words, both in the real world and through being read to on a regular basis, will likely enhance a child's literacy acquisition.

As the child enters school, formal reading instruction begins. How children should be taught to read is a subject that stirs up intense feeling. Basically, it boils down to a discussion about starting points, and how to proceed with instruction. The two approaches are the **skills-based approach**, and the **meaning-based approach**.

In 1967, Jeanne Chall, a Harvard professor, was investigating successful practices in early childhood reading instruction. She wrote a book called *Learning to Read: The Great Debate.* In the book, she stated that the programs that stressed systematic phonics instruction were better at getting young children, and especially poor young children, to read. This pronouncement sparked a great deal of conversation about how small children should be taught, what they should be taught, and where instruction should begin.

The Skills-Based Approach: Phonics

Phonics is a method of teaching beginners to read and pronounce words by teaching them the <u>phonetic</u> value of letters, letter groups, and syllables. Because English has an alphabetical writing system, an understanding of the letter–sound relationship may prove helpful to the beginning reader. However, the suggestion of this view of initial reading instruction is that these relationships should be taught in isolation, in a highly sequenced manner, followed by reading words that represent the regularities of English in print. The children are asked to read decodable texts by sounding out words. Typically, this approach uses reading programs that offer stories with controlled vocabulary made up of letter-sound relationships and words with which children are already familiar. Thus, children might be asked to read a passage such as, "The bug is in the pan. The bug ran and ran." Writing instruction follows in the same vein; children are asked to write decodable words, and fill in the blanks with decodable words in decodable sentences in workbooks, on the assumption that, once the children progress past this initial reading instruction timeframe, meaning will follow. This type of instruction was widely used in the late 1960s and 1970s.

Today, phonics is still being promoted, but the flaw in this kind of unilateral instruction is that many English words, including the highest frequency word of all, *the*, are not phonetically regular. Also, comprehension of text is limited, because there is not a great deal to comprehend if the text is, for example, "The bug is in the pan. The bug ran and ran." The assumption is that textual meaning will become apparent in time. Furthermore, it must be stressed that teaching phonics is not the same as teaching reading. Also, reading and spelling require much more than just phonics; spelling strategies and word-analysis skills are equally important. Nor does asking children to memorize phonics rules ensure application of those rules, and, even if it did, the word the child is attempting to decode is frequently an exception to the stated rule. In summary, the skills-based approach begins reading instruction with a study of single letters, letter sounds, blends and digraphs, blends and digraph sounds, and vowels and vowel sounds in isolation in a highly sequenced manner. The children read and write decodable words, with a great emphasis on reading each word accurately, as opposed to reading to comprehend the text as a whole.

The Meaning-Based Approach: Whole Language

The other side of the great reading debate is the meaning-based approach to reading which grew out of the work of Dr. Kenneth Goodman, a leader in the development of the psycholinguistic perspective, which suggests that, to derive meaning from text, readers rely more on the structure and meaning of language than on the graphic information from text. He and other researchers demonstrated that literacy development parallels language development. One of Goodman's contributions to the field was a process called miscue analysis, which begins with a child reading a selection orally, and an examiner noting variations of the oral reading from the printed text. Each variation is called a miscue and is analyzed for type of variation. Previously, preservice teachers were urged to read and reread texts with young children until the child could read every word in the text perfectly. Goodman suggested, however, that only miscues that altered meaning needed to be corrected, while other, unimportant miscues could be ignored.

Fast Facts — Children are taught to ask themselves, "Does it look right? Does it sound right? Does it make sense?"

Goodman also developed a reading model that became known as the **whole-language approach**, which stands in sharp contrast to phonics. The meaning-based approach to reading emphasizes comprehension and meaning in texts. Children focus on the wholeness of words, sentences, paragraphs, and entire books, seeking meaning through context. Whole-language advocates stress the importance of children's reading high-quality children's literature and extending the meaning of the literature through conversation, projects, and writing. Instead of fill-in-the-blank workbooks, children are encouraged to write journals, letters, and lists, and to participate in writing workshops. Word-recognition skills, including phonics, are taught in the context of reading and writing, and are taught as those things relate to the text in hand. Children are taught the four cueing systems, and are taught to ask themselves, "Does it look right? Does it sound right? Does it make sense?" The children are taught that the reason people read books is to make meaning. Thus, the focus of this approach is on both comprehension and making connections.

The flaw in whole language is that it makes heavy instructional demands on the teacher. With a skilled teacher, it's a joy to watch. Today, many classrooms are places where young children enjoy learning to read and write in a balanced reading instructional program. Research into best practice strongly suggests that the teaching of reading requires solid skill instruction, including several techniques for decoding unknown words, including, but not limited to, phonics instruction embedded in interesting and engaging reading and writing experiences with whole, authentic literature-based texts to facilitate the construction of meaning. In other words, this approach to instruction combines the best skill instruction and the whole-language approach to teach both skills and meaning and to meet the reading needs of individual children.

The following information is also important for students to know when it comes to Language and Literacy.

6. Research Skills and Strategies

Students need to know how to study the information that has been presented to them in texts and other media. **Graphic organizers** help students to review such material, and help them see the relationships between one bit of information and another. A **Venn diagram** helps students see how things are alike and different. It can be used to help students see how a single topic is treated in two readings, or how two books, animals, or ecosystems are alike and different. The student labels the two overlapping circles, and lists items that are unique to each one in each respective circle. In the area in the center where there is an overlap, the student records the elements that the two items have in common.

A **schematic table** strips a story down to the bare bones, and helps students to see the story grammar at work:

Problem	
Who	
What	
Where	
When	
Why	
How	
	↓
Attempted solution	result
Attempted solution	result
	↓
End result	

Another skill students need to master is **note taking**. Unless you want to read passages copied directly out of an encyclopedia or other source material, take the time to actively teach note-taking techniques, and think up an authentic task that requires higher-level manipulation of the located information for the students to accomplish. First, help the children to formulate a researchable question. Next, have them highlight the words that might be used as keywords in searching for information. Then have them brainstorm in groups for other words to be used as keywords. Then ask then to list appropriate sources. Then, as they skim articles, they can fill in the chart with little chunks of information. For example:

Bats of North America

Name	Location	Biome	Endangered?	Diet	Roost	Fact
California leaf-nosed bat	CA, AZ	desert	yes	insects	old mines, caves	
Gray bats	TN,KY, FL	forest	yes	insects	Caves near water	
Big brown bats	All states except Hawaii	varied	no	Beetles insects	Buildings, tunnels, caves, trees	Was seen flying in a snowstorm
Little brown bats	All 50 states	varied	no	mosquitoes		Can eat 500 mosquitoes per hour

The next step here is to think up a task in which the student has to think about all the information and use it in some meaningful way.

Students also need to look closely at the **structure of text** in order to comprehend it. When starting a new unit of study, skillful teachers take the students on a picture, table, and graphic walk-through of the text that will be the object of study, asking questions and pointing out useful text features to the students. Most texts have titles, subtitles, headings, and key words. Where were these placed? What techniques were used to make them stand out? Figuring out the structure of a text helps readers to read more efficiently. Children can anticipate what information will be revealed in a selection when they understand textual structure. Understanding the pattern of the text helps students organize ideas. Authors have a fairly short list of organizational patterns to choose from. The following are the most common patterns:

- Chronological order—relates events in a temporal sequence from beginning to end

- Cause-and-effect relationships between described events, with the causal factors identified or implied

- Problem description, followed by solutions

- Comparisons and/or contrasts to describe ideas to readers

- Sequential materials, presented as a series of directions to be followed in a prescribed order

Overall, when teaching all of the language arts, read to your students daily, and be an encouraging teacher. Notice and celebrate success, no matter how small.

Mathematics

Objectives

Apply a variety of approaches (e.g., estimation, mental mathematics, formal and informal reasoning, modeling, pattern recognition, technology) to solve problems; investigate real-world situations; and analyze, interpret, and communicate mathematical ideas and information.

For example:
- Apply knowledge of appropriate mathematical strategies (e.g., mental computation; working backwards; numerical, geometric, and algebraic pattern recognition) to analyze mathematical ideas, solve problems, and investigate real-world situations.
- Apply knowledge of formal and informal mathematical reasoning processes (e.g., evaluating solutions to problems, judging the validity of arguments, using logical reasoning to draw and justify conclusions from given information).
- Apply knowledge of how to interpret mathematical terminology, symbols, and representations and how to convert among graphic, numeric, symbolic, oral, and written representations of mathematical ideas and relationships.
- Apply knowledge of how to use graphic, numeric, symbolic, oral, and written representations to interpret and communicate mathematical information, reasoning, concepts, applications, and procedures.
- Recognize common uses, benefits, and limitations of calculators and computers as tools for learning, exploration, and problem solving.

Understand concepts and skills related to numbers, number sense, and numeration (including fractions, decimals, ratios, and percents) to support the learning of mathematics.

For example:
- Apply knowledge of strategies for promoting the development of number sense in children and factors that can affect development.
- Recognize and compare properties of whole numbers and the whole number system (e.g., commutative, distributive).
- Apply concepts of the number and numeration systems to compare, order, and round numbers.
- Recognize concepts and skills related to using integers, fractions, decimals, ratios, and percents to solve problems (e.g., finding equivalent forms of fractions, decimals, and percents).
- Demonstrate knowledge of how to select and use a wide range of manipulatives, instructional resources, and technologies to explore concepts and solve real-world problems involving number, number sense, and numeration.

Understand and apply concepts and methods related to algebra and geometry to support the learning of mathematics.

For example:
- Recognize patterns in numbers, shapes, and data and how to use variables, expressions, equations, and inequalities to describe patterns and express relationships algebraically.
- Identify different types of functions (e.g., linear, nonlinear) and uses of patterns and functions to model real-world situations and make predictions.
- Recognize types of geometric figures in one, two, and three dimensions and their properties (e.g., symmetry).
- Solve problems involving perimeter, area, volume, geometric transformations (e.g., reflections, translations), and coordinate systems (e.g., using coordinate systems on lines and planes to solve problems).
- Apply knowledge of how to use various geometric and algebraic concepts (e.g., similarity, congruence, spatial relationships, patterns, functions, variables), models, materials, methods, and technologies to represent and solve real-world problems involving algebra and geometry.

Understand and apply principles, concepts, and procedures related to measurement, statistics, and probability to support the learning of mathematics.

For example:
- Recognize appropriate measurement instruments, units, and procedures for various measurement problems (e.g., involving length, area, angles, volume, mass, temperature).
- Apply knowledge of procedures for estimating and converting measurements within the customary and metric systems and for using measurements to describe and compare phenomena.

- Apply knowledge of basic concepts and principles of statistics and probability (e.g., mean, median, mode, range).
- Identify various methods (e.g., surveys, tables, graphs) of systematically collecting, organizing, describing, and analyzing data.
- Apply knowledge of how to interpret graphic and nongraphic representations of statistical data (e.g., frequency distributions, percentiles).
- Recognize how to use a variety of materials, models, and methods (e.g., combinations, theoretical probability) to represent and solve problems involving probability and mathematical expectations.
- Demonstrate knowledge of how to select and use various age-appropriate simulations, manipulatives, materials, and technologies to explore concepts and solve real-world problems involving measurement, data analysis, statistics, and probability.

Problem Solving

There are several techniques to solve real world problems by converting them into mathematical or logical problems. Here are some strategies you can use:

1. **Guess and check** (not the same as "wild guessing"). With this problem-solving strategy, make your best guess, and then check the answer to see whether it's right. Even if the guess doesn't immediately provide the solution, it may help to get you closer to it so that you can continue to work on it. An example:

   Three persons' ages add up to 72, and each person is one year older than the last person. What are their ages?

   Because the three ages must add up to 72, it is reasonable to take one-third of 72 (24) as your starting point. Of course, even though 24 + 24 + 24 gives a sum of 72, those numbers don't match the information ("Each person is one year older...") So, you might guess that the ages are 24, 25, and 26. You check that guess by addition, and you see that the sum of 75 is too high. Lowering your guesses by one each, you try 23, 24, and 25, which indeed add up to 72, giving you the solution. There are many variations of the guess and check method.

2. **Making a sketch or a picture** can help to clarify a problem. Consider this problem:

Mr. Rosenberg plans to put a four-foot-wide concrete sidewalk around his backyard pool. The pool is rectangular, with dimensions 12' by 24'. The cost of the concrete is $1.28 per square foot. How much concrete is required for the job?

If you have exceptional visualization abilities, no sketch is needed. For most of us, however, a drawing like the one shown below may be helpful in solving this and many other real-life problems.

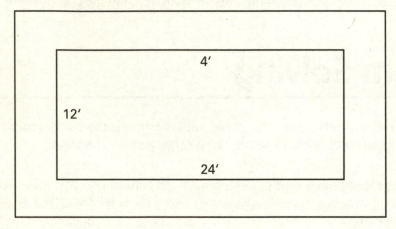

3. **Make a table or a chart.** Sometimes, *organizing* the information from a problem makes it easier to find the solution; tables and charts can be helpful.

4. **Making a list**, like making a table or chart, can help to organize information, and perhaps provide or at least hint at a solution. The strategy would work well for solving this problem: "How many different outcomes are there if you roll two regular six-sided dice?"

5. **Act it out.** Sometimes, literally "doing" a problem, with physical objects, your bodies, and so forth, can help produce a solution. A classic problem that could be solved in this manner is the following: "If five strangers meet, and if everyone shakes everyone else's hand once, how many total handshakes will there be?"

6. **Look for patterns.** This technique encourages you to ask, "What's happening here?" Spotting a pattern would be helpful in solving a problem such as:

Nevin's weekly savings account balance for 5 weeks are as follows: $125, $135, $140, $70, and $80. If the pattern holds, (approximately) what might Nevin's balance be the next week? The answer is 85. The pattern was + 10, + 5, ÷ 2, + 10, so the next move is to add 5.

7. **Estimating by rounding** means finding the solution to a different but simpler problem, hoping that you will spot a way to solve the harder one. *Estimating* can be thought of as working a simpler problem. If you need to know the product of 23 and 184, and no calculator or pencil and paper are handy, you could estimate the product by getting the exact answer to the simpler problem, 20 × 200.

8. **Writing an open math sentence** (an equation with one or more variables, or "unknowns"), then solving it, is often an effective strategy. This is sometimes called "translating" a problem into mathematics. Consider this problem: "Tiana earned grades of 77%, 86%, 90%, and 83% on her first four weekly science quizzes. Assuming all grades are equally weighted, what score will she need on the fifth week's quiz in order to have an average (or mean) score of 88%?" Using the given information, you can set up the following equation, which, when solved, will answer the question:

$$\frac{(77+86+90+83+x)}{5} = 88$$

9. **Work backward.** Consider this problem: "If you add 12 to some number, then multiply the sum by 4, you will get 60. What is the number?" You can find a solution by *starting at the end*, with 60. The problem tells you that the 60 came from multiplying a sum by 4. When multiplied by 4, 15 equals 60, so 15 must be the sum referred to. And if 15 is the sum of 12 and something else, the "something else" can only be 3.

There are of course **hybrid approaches**. You can mix and match problem-solving strategies wherever you think they are appropriate.

Mathematical Communication and Mathematical Terminology, Symbols, and Representations

Here is some basic mathematical terminology and symbolism which you need to know:

Mathematics is, for the most part, a science of precision. When working with math symbols and terminology, you must be very careful. For example, "less than" does not mean the same thing as "not greater than." In the following example, two equations are *not* equivalent (both entire sides of the first equation should be divided by 6).

$$6m + 2 = 18$$

$$\frac{6m}{6} + 2 = \frac{18}{6}$$

Certain mathematical concepts and terms are frequently misunderstood. Here are a few of the "repeat offenders":

Use care with *hundreds* vs. *hundredths*, *thousands* vs. *thousandths*, and so forth. Remember that the "th" at the end of the word indicates a fraction. "Three hundred" means 300, whereas "three hundredths" means 0.03.

Negative numbers are those less than zero. Fractions less than zero are negative numbers, too.

The **absolute value** of a number can be thought of as its distance from zero on a number line.

Counting numbers can be shown by the set (1, 2, 3, 4, . . .). Notice that 0 is not a counting number.

Whole numbers are the counting numbers, plus 0 (0, 1, 2, . . .).

Integers are all of the whole numbers and their negative counterparts (. . . –2, –1, 0, 1, 2, . . .). Note that negative and positive fractions are not considered integers.

Factors are any of the numbers or symbols in mathematics that, when multiplied together, form a product. (The whole number factors of 12 are 1, 2, 3, 4, 6, and 12.) A number with exactly two whole number factors (1 and the number itself) is a *prime number*. The first few primes are 2, 3, 5, 7, 11, 13, and 17. Most other whole numbers are *composite numbers*, because they are *composed* of several whole number factors (1 is neither prime nor composite; it has only one whole number factor).

The *multiples* of any whole number are what are produced when the number is multiplied by counting numbers. The multiples of 7 are 7, 14, 21, 28, and so on. Every whole number has an infinite number of multiples.

Recall that *decimal numbers* are simply fractions written in special notation. All decimal numbers are actually fractions whose denominators are powers of 10 (10, 100, 1000, etc.) 0.033, for instance, can be thought of as the fraction $\frac{33}{1000}$.

There is an agreed-upon order of operations for simplifying complex expressions. First you compute parentheses, then exponents, then any multiplication or division, left to right. Then you compute any addition or subtraction, also left-to-right. "<u>P</u>lease <u>E</u>xcuse <u>M</u>y <u>D</u>ear <u>A</u>unt <u>S</u>ally" is a good way to remember this. Treat exponential expressions ("powers") as multiplication. Thus, the expression $3 + 7 \times 4 - 2$ equals 29. (Multiply 7 by 4 *before* doing the addition and subtraction.)

Exponential notation is a way to show repeated multiplication more simply. $2 \times 2 \times 2$, for instance, can be shown as 2^3, and is equal to 8. (Note: 2^3 does *not* mean 2×3.)

Scientific notation provides a method for showing numbers using exponents (although it is most useful for very large and very small numbers.) A number is in scientific notation when it is shown as a number between 1 and 10 to a power of 10. Thus, the number 75,000 in scientific notation is shown as 7.5×10^4.

Addends (or *addenda*) can be thought of as "parts of addition problems." When addends are combined, they produce *sums*. Likewise, *factors* can be seen as "parts of multiplication problems." When factors are multiplied, they produce *products*. When two numbers are divided, one into the other, the result is a *quotient*.

Equations are not the same as mathematical *expressions*. $12 + 4 = 16$ and $2x + 7 = 12$ are equations. $(144 - 18)$ and $13y^2$ are expressions. Notice that expressions are "lacking a verb," so to speak (you don't say "is equal to" or "equals" when reading expressions). Inequalities are very much like equations, but "greater than" or "less than" replaces "is equal to" or "equals."

A *trend* is a pattern over time.

Careful use of mathematical terms and ideas such as those noted above is essential to communicating mathematically.

The ability to convert among various mathematical and logical representations (graphic, numeric, symbolic, verbal) is an important skill, and, as with problem solving, precision and care are keys to quality conversions. Consider this number line, which might represent ages of students who are eligible for a particular scholarship:

Are 21-year-old students eligible? No, because the conventional notation used on the number line shows a *circle* around the point at 21. That means that 21 is *not* included in the set. Converting the graphic representation to symbolism gives $18 < x < 21$.

Number Skills

Key properties of whole numbers (and some related terms) include the following:

The Commutative Property for Addition and Multiplication states that the order in which addends are added or factors are multiplied does not determine the sum or product. (6×9 gives the same product as 9×6, for instance.) Division and subtraction are not commutative.

The Associative Property for Addition and Multiplication states that "associating" three or more addends or factors in a different fashion will not change the sum or product. For example, $(3 + 7) + 5$ gives the same sum as $3 + (7 + 5)$. Division and subtraction are not associative.

The *Distributive Property of Multiplication over Addition* is shown hereafter in simple notation form:

$$a(b + c) = (a \times b) + (a \times c)$$

An illustration of the Distributive Property is this: multiplying 6 by 47 will give the same result as multiplying 6 by 40, multiplying 6 times 7, then *adding* the products. That is, $6 \times (47) = (6 \times 40) + (6 \times 7)$.

Some pairs of operations are considered to be *inverse*. Addition and subtraction are inverse operations, as are multiplication and division. The operations can be thought of as "undoing" one another: Multiplying 4 by 9 gives 36; dividing 36 by 9 "gives back" 4.

The *Multiplicative Identity Property of One* states that any number multiplied by 1 remains the same. ($34 \times 1 = 34$, for instance.) The number 1 is called the *Multiplicative Identity*.

The *Property of Reciprocals* states that any number (except for zero) multiplied by its reciprocal gives 1. (The *reciprocal* of a number is 1 divided by that number.)

Remember that dividing by zero is considered infinite or to have no meaning; avoid doing it when computing or solving equations and inequalities.

The *Additive Identity Property of Zero* states that adding zero to any number will not change the number ($87 + 0 = 87$, for instance). Zero is called the *Additive Identity*.

Division is *partitive* when you know the total and the number of parts or groups but you don't how many are in each part. Consider: "You have 7 containers of bolts and a total of 98 bolts. How many bolts are in each container (assuming the same number in each)?" Arriving at the answer is an example of partitive division.

With *measurement division*, the number of groups is not known. Using the example above, if you knew that there were 14 bolts per container, and that there were 98 bolts altogether, finding the number of containers would require measurement division.

Rational Numbers, Fractions, and Decimals

A property of real numbers is *The Density Property*. It states that, given any two real numbers, there is always another real number between them. (Think of the number line: No matter how close two points are, there is always a point between them.)

Rational numbers are those that can be written as fractions. (This includes integers; 12, for instance, can be written as $\frac{12}{1}$.)

Decimals (or "decimal fractions"), which come to an end when represented exactly, are *terminating decimals* (2.125, for instance). *Repeating decimals* are those in which the digits repeat a pattern endlessly (3.333333 . . . , for example). To use shorthand notation to show repeating decimals, you can write the "repeating block" just once, putting a bar over it. The example above, for instance, can be shown as 3.$\overline{3}$. (Both terminating and repeating decimals are rational numbers.)

Some numbers are real numbers, but cannot be accurately represented by fractions. The ratio of the length of the diameter of any circle to its circumference, or π, for instance, is irrational. There are useful approximations of π, such as 3.14159, but π is not an exact terminating decimal or an exact fraction.

Fractions, decimal numbers, ratios, and percents can be thought of as different ways of representing values, and any given rational number can be shown any of those ways. It is useful to be able to convert from one to the other. The following are some conversion tips:

The practical method for changing a fraction into a decimal is by dividing the numerator by the denominator. For example, $\frac{1}{4}$ becomes 0.25 when 1 is divided by 4, as follows:

$$
\begin{array}{r}
.25 \\
4\overline{)1.00} \\
\underline{8} \\
20
\end{array}
$$

Naturally, this can be done longhand or with a calculator. (If the decimal number includes a whole number, as with $2\frac{3}{5}$, you can ignore the whole number when doing the division.) The decimal number may terminate or repeat. Converting a simple fraction to a decimal number will never result in an irrational number.

To convert a non-repeating decimal number to a fraction in lowest terms, simply write the decimal as a fraction with the denominator as a power of ten, and then reduce to lowest terms. For example, 0.125 can be written as $\frac{125}{1000}$, which reduces to $\frac{1}{8}$.

Any decimal number can be converted to a percent by shifting the decimal point two places to the right and adding the percent symbol. 0.135, for instance, becomes 13.5%. (If the number before the percent symbol is a whole number, there is no need to show the decimal point.)

A percent can be converted to a decimal number by shifting the decimal point two places to the left and dropping the percent symbol: 98% becomes 0.98 as a decimal.

A percent can be converted to a fraction simply by putting the percent (without the percent symbol) over 100, then reducing. In this way 20% can be shown as $\frac{20}{100}$, which reduces to $\frac{1}{5}$.

Ratio notation is simply an alternative method for showing fractions. For example, $\frac{2}{5}$ can be rewritten as "2 to 5." Ratio notation is commonly used when you want to emphasize the relationship of one number to another. Ratios are often shown as numbers with a colon between them; 2:5 is the same ratio as 2 to 5 and $\frac{2}{5}$.

To illustrate all of the above equivalencies and conversions at once, consider the fraction $\frac{19}{20}$. Shown as a ratio, it's 19 to 20, or 19:20. As a decimal, you have 0.95; as a percent, 95%.

The rules for performing operations on rational numbers (fractions) parallel in many ways the computational rules for integers. Just as adding –3 and –11 gives –14, adding $-\frac{1}{9}$ and $-\frac{5}{9}$ gives $-\frac{6}{9}$ (or $-\frac{2}{3}$ in reduced form.) Note: we added the numerators and not the denominators.

Algebraic Concepts and Methods

An important skill is the ability to represent real problems in algebraic form. A **variable** is simply a symbol that represents an unknown value. Most typically x is the letter used, although any letter can be used. By "translating" real problems to algebraic form containing one or more variables (often as equations or inequalities), solutions to many problems can be found mathematically.

Understanding the relationships among values, and being able to accurately represent those relationships symbolically is another key to algebraic problem solving. Consider the ages of two sisters. If you don't know the age of the younger sister, but know that the older sister is three years older, you can show the information symbolically as follows: The age of the younger sister can be shown as x, and the age of the older sister as x + 3. If you are told that the sum of the sisters' ages is, say, 25, you can represent that information via an equation:

$$x + (x + 3) = 25$$

which can be read as "the age of the younger sister plus the age of the older sister totals 25." This sort of translation skill is crucial for using algebra for problem solving.

Some helpful *translation* tips include the following: The word *is* often suggests an equal sign; *of* may suggest multiplication, as does *product*. *Sum* refers to addition; *difference* suggests subtraction; and a *quotient* is obtained after dividing. The key when translating is to make sure that the equation accurately matches the information and relationships given in the word problem.

Operations with algebraic expressions are governed by various rules and conventions. For instance, only *like* algebraic terms can be added or subtracted to produce simpler expressions. For example, $2x^3$ and $3x^3$ can be added together to get $5x^3$, because the terms are like terms; they both have a base of x3. You cannot add, say, $7m^3$ and $6m^2$; m^3 and m^2 are unlike bases. (Note: To *evaluate* an algebraic expression means to simplify it using conventional rules.)

When multiplying exponential terms together, the constant terms are multiplied, but the exponents of terms with the same variable bases are *added* together, which is somewhat counterintuitive. For example, $4w^2$ multiplied by $8w^3$ gives $32w^5$ (not $32w^6$, as one might guess).

When like algebraic terms are divided, exponents are subtracted. For example,

$$\frac{2x^7}{5x^3}$$

becomes

$$\frac{2x^4}{5}$$

In algebra, you frequently need to multiply two *binomials* together. Binomials are algebraic expressions of two terms. The **FOIL** method is one way to multiply binomials. FOIL stands for "first, outer, inner, last": Multiply the first terms in the parentheses, then the outermost terms, then the innermost terms, then the last terms, and then add the products together. For example, to multiply $(x + 3)$ and $(2x - 5)$, you multiply x by $2x$ (the first terms), x by -5 (outer terms), 3 by $2x$ (inner terms), and 3 by 5 (last terms). The four products ($2x^2$, $-5x$, $6x$, and -15) add up to $2x^2 + x - 15$. If the polynomials to be multiplied have more than two terms (*trinomials*, for instance), make sure that *each* term of the first polynomial is multiplied by *each* term of the second. Note: multiplying a negative times a positive is a negative and a negative times a negative makes a positive.

The opposite of polynomial multiplication is factoring. Factoring a polynomial means rewriting it as the product of factors (often two binomials). The trinomial $x^2 - 11x + 28$, for instance, can be factored into $(x - 4)(x - 7)$. (You can check this by "FOILing" the binomials.)

When attempting to factor polynomials, it is sometimes necessary to factor out any factor that might be common to all terms first. The two terms in $5x^2 - 10$, for example, both contain the factor 5. This means that the expression can be rewritten as $5(x^2 - 2)$.

Factoring is useful when solving some equations, especially if one side of the equation is set equal to zero. Consider $2x^2 - x - 1 = 2$. It can be rewritten as $2x^2 - x - 3 = 0$. This allows the left side to be factored into $(2x - 3)(x + 1)$, giving equation solutions of $\frac{3}{2}$ and -1.

Consider all of the information above as the following problem is first "translated" into an equation, then solved.

Three teachers who are retiring are said to have 78 years of experience among them. You don't know how many years of experience Teacher A has, but you know that Teacher B has twice as many as A, and Teacher C has three more years of experience than B. How many years of experience does each have?

You can start by calling Teacher A's years of experience x. You then consider the relationship to the other two teachers: You can call Teacher B's years of experience $2x$, which allows you to call Teacher C's years of experience $(2x + 3)$. You know that the teachers' years of experience add up to 78, allowing you to write:

$$x + 2x + (2x + 3) = 78$$

Using the rules for solving such an equation, you find that $x = 15$, meaning that the teachers' years of experience are, respectively, 15, 30, and 33 years.

Measurement

Measurement includes estimating and converting measurements within the customary and metric systems; applying procedures for using measurement to describe and compare phenomena; identifying appropriate measurement instruments, units, and procedures for measurement problems involving length, area, angles, volume, mass, time, money, and temperature; and using a variety of materials, models, and methods to explore concepts and solve problems involving measurement.

Here are some key measurement terms and ideas:

Customary units are generally the same as *U.S.* or *English units*. Customary units of length include inches, feet, yards, and miles. Customary units of weight include ounces, pounds, and tons. Customary units of capacity (or volume) include teaspoons, tablespoons, cups, pints, quarts, and gallons.

Metric units of length include millimeters, centimeters, meters, and kilometers. The centimeter is the basic metric unit of length, at least for short distances. There are about 2.5 centimeters to 1 inch. The kilometer is a metric unit of length used for longer distances. It takes more than 1.5 kilometers to make a mile. A very fast adult runner could run a kilometer in about three minutes.

Metric units of weight include grams and kilograms. The gram is the basic metric unit of mass (which for many purposes is the same as *weight*). A large paper clip weighs about 1 gram. It takes about 28 grams to make 1 ounce. Metric units of capacity include milliliters and liters. The liter is the basic metric unit of volume (or capacity). A liter is slightly smaller than a quart, so it takes more than four liters to make a gallon.

Here are some frequently used customary-to-metric ratios. Values are approximate.

1 inch = 2.54 centimeters

1 yard = 0.91 meters

1 mile = 1.61 kilometers

1 ounce = 28.35 grams

1 pound = 2.2 kilograms

1 quart = 0.94 liters

Metric-to-customary conversions can be found by taking the reciprocals of each of the factors noted above. For instance, 1 kilometer = 0.62 mile (computed by dividing 1 by 1.61).

An important step in solving problems involving measurement is to decide which area you are in: Generally, such problems will fall under one of these categories: length, area, angles, volume, mass, time, money, and temperature. Solving measurement problems will likely have you calling on your knowledge in several other areas of mathematics, especially algebra. The following is one example measurement problem that requires knowledge of several math topics:

> Sophie's Carpet Store charges $19.40 per square yard for the type of carpeting you'd like (padding and labor included). How much will you pay to carpet your 9 foot by 12 foot room?

One way to find the solution is to convert the room dimensions to yards (3 yards by 4 yards), then multiply to get 12 square yards. Finally, multiply 12 by the price of $19.40 per square yard, for a total price of $232.80

Geometry

A fundamental concept of geometry is the notion of a *point*. A point is a specific location, taking up no space, having no area, and frequently represented by a dot. A point is considered one dimensional.

Through any two points there is exactly one straight line; straight lines are one-dimensional. Planes (think of flat surfaces without edges) are two-dimensional. From these foundational ideas you can move to some other important geometric terms and ideas.

A segment is any portion of a line between two points on the line. It has a definite start and a definite end. The notation for a segment extending from point *A* to point *B* is $\overline{AB}$. A ray is like a straight segment, except it extends forever in one direction. The notation for a ray originating at point *X* (an *endpoint*) through point *Y* is $\overline{XY}$.

When two rays share their endpoints, an *angle* is formed. A *degree* is a unit of measure of the angle created. If a circle is divided into 360 even slices, each slice has an angle measure of 1 degree. If an angle has exactly 90 degrees it is called a *right* angle. Angles of less than 90 degrees are *acute* angles. Angles greater than 90 degrees are *obtuse* angles. If two angles have the same size (regardless of how long their rays might be drawn) they are *congruent*. Congruence is shown this way: $\angle m = \angle n$ (read "angle *m* is congruent to angle *n*").

A polygon is a closed plane figure bounded by straight lines or a closed figure on a sphere bounded by arcs of great circles. In a plane, three-sided polygons are *triangles*, four-sided polygons are *quadrilaterals*, five sides make *pentagons*, six sides are *hexagons*, and eight-sided polygons are *octagons*. (Note that not all quadrilaterals are squares.) If two polygons (or any figures) have exactly the same size and shape, they are *congruent*. If they are the same shape, but different sizes, they are *similar*.

Polygons may have lines of symmetry, which can be thought of as imaginary fold lines which produce two congruent, mirror-image figures. Squares have four lines of symmetry, and non-square rectangles have two, as shown later. Circles have an infinite number of lines of symmetry; a few are shown on the circle.

The *diameter* of a circle is a straight line segment that goes from one edge of a circle to the other side, passing through the center. The *radius* of a circle is half of its diameter (from the center to an edge). A *chord* is any segment that goes from one spot on a circle to any other spot (all diameters are chords, but not all chords are diameters).

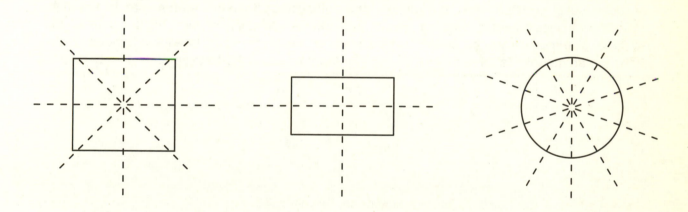

The *perimeter* of a two-dimensional (flat) shape or object is the distance around the object.

Volume refers to how much space is inside of three dimensional, closed containers. It is useful to think of volume as how many cubic units could fit into a solid. If the container is a rectangular solid, multiplying width, length, and height together computes the volume. If all six faces (sides) of a rectangular solid are squares, then the object is a cube.

Parallel and perpendicular are key concepts in geometry. Consider the two parallel lines that follow, and the third line (a *transversal*), which crosses them. Perpindicular lines intersect in a 90° angle. Parallel lines never intersect.

Note that among the many individual angles created, there are only two angle measures: 30° (noted in the figure) and 150° (180° − 30°).

Triangles have various properties. One is that the sum of the measures of the three angles of any triangle is 180°. If, therefore, the measures of two angles are known, the third can be deduced using addition, then subtraction. The Pythagorean theorem states that in any right triangle with legs (shorter sides) a and b, and hypotenuse (longest side) c, the sum of the squares of the sides will be equal to the square of the hypotenuse. In algebraic notation the Pythagorean theorem is given as $a^2 + b^2 = c^2$. An example is a 3,4,5 triangle ($3^2 + 4^2 = 5^2$).

Geometric Figures

Square

Area = s^2
Perimenter = $4s$

Rectangle

Area = ℓw
Perimenter = $2\ell + 2w$

Circle

Area = πr^2
Perimenter = $2\pi r$
Diameter = $2r$

Triangle

Area = $\frac{1}{2}bh$

Right Triangle

Pythagorean formula: $c^2 = a^2 + b^2$

Sphere

Surface area = $4\pi r^2$
Volume = $\frac{4}{3}\pi r^3$

Cube

Surface area = $6s^2$
Volume = s^3

Rectangular Solid

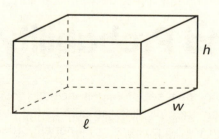

Surface area = $2\ell w + 2\ell h + 2wh$
Volume = ℓwh

Right Circular Cylinder

Surface area = $2\pi rh + 2\pi r^2$
Volume = $\pi r^2 h$

Two important coordinate systems are the number line and the coordinate plane, and both systems can be used to solve certain problems. A particularly useful tool related to the coordinate plane is the Distance Formula, which allows you to compute the distance between any two points on the plane. Consider points C and D in the following figure.

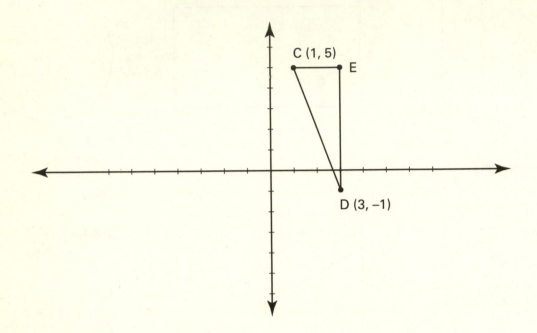

By finding the difference of the points' x coordinates (3 − 1, or 2) and the difference of their y coordinates (−1 − 5, or −6), you have found the lengths of the sides of triangle CED (2 units and 6 units—you can ignore the negative sign on the 6.) You can now use the Pythagorean theorem to find the length of the hypotenuse of triangle CED, which is the same as the length from point C to D ($2^2 + 6^2 = 40$, and the square root of 40 is approximately 6.3). Here is the distance formula in algebraic form:

$$d = \sqrt{(x_2 - x_1)^2 + (y_2 - y_1)^2}$$

Statistics and Probability

Measures of central tendency of a set of values include *mean*, *median*, and *mode*. The mean is found by adding all the values, then dividing the sum by the number of values. The median of a set is the middle number when the values are in numerical order. (If there is an even number of values, and therefore no middle value, the mean of the middle two values gives the median.) The mode of a set is the value occurring most often. (Not all sets of values have a single mode; some sets have more than one.) Consider the following set.

6   8   14   5   6   5   5

The mean, median, and mode of the set are 7, 6, and 5, respectively. (Note: The mean is often referred to as the average, but all three measures are averages of sorts.)

Probability theory provides models for chance variations. The *probability* of any event occurring is equal to the number of desired outcomes divided by the number of all possible events. Thus, the probability of blindly pulling a green ball out of a hat (in this case the desired outcome) if the hat contains two green and five yellow balls, is $\frac{2}{7}$ (about 29%). *Odds* are related to probability, but are different. The odds that any given event *will* occur is the ratio of the probability that the event will occur to the probability that the event *will not* occur (typically expressed as a ratio). In the example above, the odds that a green ball will be drawn are 2:5.

Statistics is the branch of mathematics that involves collecting, analyzing, and interpreting data. Statistics involves organizing data so we can draw conclusions and make decisions. Statistics builds on probability, and typically studies "populations," meaning quantifiable groups of things. Trends and patterns not otherwise noticed may be revealed via statistics.

One key statistical concept is that of *standard deviation*. The standard deviation of a set of values tells how "tightly" all of the values are clustered around the mean of the set. When values are tightly clustered near the mean, the standard deviation is small. If values are widespread the standard deviation is large. Here is one way to find the standard deviation of a set. Consider the set used earlier:

6   8   14   5   6   5   5

First find the mean (7). Next, find the difference of each value in the set and the mean (ignoring negative signs). This gives 1, 1, 7, 2, 1, 2, and 2. Now, you square each of those values, giving 1, 1, 49, 4, 1, 4, and 4. You next take the sum of those squares (64) and divide the sum by the number of values ($\frac{64}{7}$ = 9.14). Finally, you take the square root of 9.14, giving a standard deviation of 3.02. Think of 3.02 as the amount that the values in the set "typically" vary from the center.

Mathematical Reasoning Processes

Mathematical reasoning includes selecting strategies to solve problems; evaluating solutions to problems; constructing arguments and judging the validity or logic of arguments; and using logical reasoning to draw and justify conclusions from given information.

Problem-solvers must rely on both formal and informal *reasoning processes*. A key informal process relies on *reasonableness*. Consider this problem:

Center Town Middle School has an enrollment of 640 students. One day, 28 students were absent. What percent of the total number of students were absent?

Even if someone forgot how to compute percents, some possible answers could be rejected instantly: 28 is a "small-but-not-tiny" chunk of 640, so answers like 1%, 18%, and 25% are *unreasonable*.

There are also formal reasoning processes, such as *deductive reasoning*. Deductive reasoning is reasoning from the general to the specific, and is supported by deductive logic. Here is an example of deductive reasoning:

All ducks have wings (a general assertion). Donald is a duck; therefore Donald has wings (a specific proposition).

With *inductive reasoning*, a general rule is inferred from specific observations (which may be limited). Moving from the statement "All boys in this classroom are wearing jeans" (a specific but limited observation) to "All boys wear jeans" (a general assertion) is an example of inductive reasoning. Note that conclusions arrived at via deductive and inductive reasoning are not necessarily true.

Chapter 7

Science

Scientific knowledge is a body of statements of varying degrees of certainty—some most unsure, some nearly sure, but none absolutely certain . . . Now, we scientists are used to this, and we take it for granted that it is perfectly consistent to be unsure, that it is possible to live and not know.

Richard P. Feynman (1918–1988), Nobel Prize in Physics, 1965

Science education has as its goal the training of a scientifically literate public that fully participates in the economic, political, and cultural functions of our society. Scientifically literate individuals, students and teachers alike, must have knowledge that is connected and useful. The Illinois science curriculum, both for the preparation of preservice teachers and for K-12 instruction, is guided by this principle.

The Illinois curriculum operationally defines the scientifically literate individual as one who uses scientific knowledge, constructs new scientific knowledge, and reflects on scientific knowledge. Such individuals have specific science content knowledge, they build upon that knowledge through their experiences and activities, and they can evaluate objectively and critically the value and limitations of that knowledge.

1. LIFE SCIENCE

I venture to define science as a series of interconnected concepts and conceptual schemes arising from experiment and observation and fruitful of further experiments and observations. The test of a scientific theory is, I suggest, its fruitfulness.

James Bryant Conant (1893–1978), Chemist and Educator

Understand and apply fundamental concepts and principles of life and environmental science to interpret, analyze, and explain phenomena.

For example:

*   Recognize basic processes and concepts related to **cells** and the characteristics, needs, and organization of living things.
*   Recognize the basic structures and functions of the **human body** in comparison to those of other organisms.
*   Recognize the processes by which energy and nutrients cycle through **ecosystems** and are used by organisms (e.g., photosynthesis, respiration).
*   Analyze how organisms interact with one another and with their environment.
*   Apply knowledge of the principles of **genetics and evolutionary theory** to understand how organisms change over time.
*   Apply knowledge of how to use major concepts, processes, and themes of life science (e.g., those related to **heredity**, flow of energy, systems, interactions) and the interconnections of life, physical, environmental, earth, and space sciences to interpret, analyze, and explain everyday phenomena.
*   Recognize relationships among life and **environmental science**, technology, and society in historical and contemporary contexts.
*   Identify a wide range of instructional resources and technologies to support the learning of life and environmental science.

1.1 Cells

The concept of a **cell** is central to our understanding of the life sciences. Cells are the simplest living unit of life, just as atoms are the building blocks of molecules, and molecules of cells. Each cell has a nucleus, cytoplasm, and a cell wall. Cell Theory states that all organisms are composed of cells, that all cells arise from preexisting cells, and that the cell is the basic organizational unit of all organisms. Groups of specialized cells, or tissues, may have highly specialized characteristics and functions within an organism. A single organism may comprise only a single cell, or many billions of cells, and cells themselves range in size from the micron to many centimeters in dimension. Growth in most organisms is associated with cell division and replication, in addition to enlargement of the cells.

1.2 Classification

A dichotomous key is a tool of science that allows us to organize and classify objects by their observable traits and properties. In the life sciences, classification keys are widely used, and the simplest are based on the gross anatomy of all organisms, including plants, animals, fungi, protists, and two kingdoms of bacteria. Through comparison of the number of wings or legs, habitat, and eating habits we begin, at the earliest levels, to understand patterns in nature, constructing our own understanding of the world around us, and practice the basic elements of scientific thought and discovery.

Life Cycles

Scientific knowledge may be classified or organized by grouping similar types of knowledge into thematic concepts. Many concepts are so broad as to find application in multiple disciplines. Cycle, for example, is a powerful concept that has widespread application throughout science, useful for both explanation and prediction. Life cycles are central to the study of biology. The recurring pattern of events in the life cycle links birth, growth, reproduction, and death. The concept of a cycle is also evident in the carbon cycle, nitrogen cycle, Krebs cycle, hydrogeologic cycle, periodic table, and many other processes, including the transformations of energy needed to sustain life. The food chain represents the complex interdependency of all plants and animals on the energy from the Sun, and the recycling of nutrients from simple to complex organisms. An example of a life cycle is **photosynthesis** which takes place when light's energy is changed into food for plants. The human life cycle begins when the egg and sperm unite to form a zygote, which develops into an embryo and (after nine months) an infant. This person proceeds through life stages (toddler, child, adolescent, adult, elder person).

> **Life cycles are central to the study of biology.**
>
> *Fast Facts*

1.3 Heredity

The discussion of life cycles brings forward the concept that the offspring of one generation bears likeness to, but also variation from, the previous generation. Some characteristics of the individual parent are passed along, while others appear not to be. We observe the connections between the visible traits of the parents and children, connections evident in all sexually reproducing organisms. It is clear that the offspring of dogs are other dogs, which generally look much like the parent dogs. Details of how such traits are conveyed through genetics are important to understand; yet instruction in these topics is allocated to the curriculum of higher grades.

1.4 Evolution

The goal of science education is to develop a scientifically literate public. At the elementary level this involves an understanding of how physical traits promote the survival of a species, how environmental changes affect species that are not adapted to those new conditions, and the role of heredity in passing and modifying the traits of successive generations. There are ample examples available to illustrate these concepts to the elementary student. A rabbit whose coat regularly turns white before the snowfall is therefore subject to a lesser degree of predation. Adaptation is how living things adjust. For example, if the fruit grows high in the tree, the animals with longer necks will survive and produce offspring with longer necks. This relates to Darwin's idea of survival of the fittest: basically, when resources are limited, it is the strongest who survive. Technology, the application of knowledge for man's benefit, includes activities that are designed to select those traits that are intended to lead to healthier, stronger, and more productive crops and animals.

Fast Facts A *scientific fact* is an observation that has been repeatedly confirmed.

While the tenets of evolution as scientific theory are widely accepted, particularly as they apply to the short-term changes and adaptations within a species, the subject continues to generate some debate. To place the discussion in its proper context, some discussion of the scientific use of terms is appropriate, because the common usage of a term may differ significantly from its scientific usage. A *scientific fact* is an observation that has been repeatedly confirmed. However, scientific facts change if new observations yield new information. Frequently, the development of new, more sophisticated or precise instruments leads to such new information. A *scientific hypothesis* is a testable statement about the natural world, and as such is the starting point for most scientific experimentation. In an experiment, the scientist tests a hypothesis or educated guess. A hypothesis can generally be proven wrong, but is seldom proven right. *Scientific theories*, like atomic theory and cell theory, are well-substantiated explanations of some aspect of the natural world. A scientific theory provides a unified explanation for many related hypotheses. While a theory is generally widely accepted (e.g., through much of human history people accepted a flat Earth circled by a moving Sun), theories remain open to revision or even replacement should a better, more logical, more comprehensive or compelling explanation be found.

Not all issues of our human experience are subject to the analysis and rigors of scientific experimentation and validation. Our understanding of art, poetry, philosophy, and religion rely on ways of thinking and understanding that are not necessarily subject to repeated validation through the controlled scientific experiment, or which may rely more on personal values or deference to authority. The scientifically literate individual will distinguish the role and value of scientific thought from other ways of knowing, while maintaining respect and appreciation for the ways of thinking and understanding practiced in disciplines outside of science.

1.5 Ecology

Our surroundings are a complex, interconnected system in which the living organisms exist in relationship with the soil, water, and air, linked together through chemical and physical processes, and in states of continual change or dynamic equilibrium. *Ecosystem* is the term for all the living and nonliving things in a given environment and how they interact. Within an ecosystem, there is a food chain in which lower members on the chain are eaten by higher members. Scientifically literate individuals are aware of their surroundings, the interdependence of each part, and the effects that man's activities can have on those surroundings. Mutualistic and competitive relationships also exist between the organisms in an ecosystem, defining how organisms rely upon each other, and exist in competition and conflict with each other.

Energy transformations are the driving force within an ecosystem. Many organisms obtain energy from light. For example, light drives the process of photosynthesis in green plants. Solar energy also provides necessary heat for cold-blooded animals. Organisms may also derive energy from other organisms, including other plants and/or animals. When one source of energy is depleted in an ecosystem, many organisms must shift their attention to other sources of energy. For example, a bear will eat berries, fish, or nuts depending on the season. The energy pyramid for an ecosystem illustrates these relationships and identifies those organisms that are most dependent on the other organisms in the system. Higher order organisms cannot survive for long without the other organisms beneath them in the energy pyramid. The availability of adequate food within an ecosystem can be used to explain the system's functioning, the size of an animal's territory, or the effects of over-predation of a single species upon those organisms above it in the food chain.

Ecosystems change over time, both from natural processes and from the activities of man. The scientifically literate individual will be able to identify how the environment changes, how those changes impact the organisms that live there, and recognize the differences between long-term and short-term variation. Natural succession is observed when one community replaces another, for example the colonies of fungus that grow, thrive, and then are replaced by different colonies on rodent droppings held under ideal conditions.

2. PHYSICAL SCIENCE

All of physics is either impossible or trivial. It is impossible until you understand it, and then it becomes trivial.

Ernest Rutherford (1871–1937) Physicist, Nobel Prize for Chemistry, 1908

Understand and apply fundamental concepts and principles of physical science to interpret, analyze, and explain phenomena.

For example:
*   Apply knowledge of basic concepts related to **matter and energy** (e.g., composition and structure of matter, conservation of energy).
*   Recognize the physical and chemical properties of matter (e.g., mass, boiling point, pH).
*   Apply knowledge of characteristics of different forms of energy (e.g., **sound**, **heat**).
*   Analyze the interactions of matter and energy in a system, including transfers and **transformations of energy** and **changes in matter**.

- Apply knowledge of how to use **major concepts**, processes, and themes of physical science (e.g., those related to motion of objects, waves and vibrations, changes in matter), as well as the interconnections of physical, life, environmental, earth, and space sciences to interpret, analyze, and explain everyday phenomena.
- Recognize relationships among physical science, technology, and society in historical and contemporary contexts.
- Identify a wide range of instructional resources and technologies to support the learning of physical science.

2.1 Matter & Energy

Broadly speaking, our experiences with the world involve interactions with and between matter and energy. The physical sciences give us a clearer understanding and appreciation of our surroundings and the way we interact with and affect those surroundings. **Matter** can be described and distinguished by its chemical and physical properties. Physical properties, such as color and density, are termed *intrinsic* when they do not change as the amount of the matter changes. Properties like mass or volume do vary when matter is added or removed, and these are termed "extrinsic properties." **Mass** is the amount of matter in an object, which is sometimes measured using a lever arm balance. Weight, although sometimes incorrectly used interchangeably with mass, is a measure the force of gravity experienced by an object, often determined using a spring scale. An electronic scale may display an object's mass in grams, but it is dependant on gravity for its operation. Such a device is only accurate after using a calibration mass to adjust the electronics for the unique local gravitational force. While we may say an object is "weightless" as it floats inside the space shuttle, it is still affected by the gravitational forces from both the Earth and Sun, which keep it in orbit around each. The force of gravity is proportional to the product of the masses of the two objects under consideration divided by the square of the distance between them. Earth, being larger and more massive than Mars, has proportionally higher gravitational forces. This is the basis of the observation in H. G. Wells' *The War of the Worlds* that the Martian invaders were "the most sluggish things I ever saw crawl."

Density, the ratio of mass to volume, is an intrinsic property that depends on the matter, but not the amount of matter. **Volume** is defined as the amount of space an object occupies. The density of a 5-ton cube of pure copper is the same as that of a small copper penny. However, the modern penny is a thin shell of copper over a zinc plug, and the density of this coin is significantly lower than that of the older pure copper coin. Density is related to buoyancy. Objects sink, in liquids or gases alike, if they are denser than the material that surrounds them. Density is not the same as **viscosity**, a measure of thickness or flowability.

All matter is composed of **atoms**, or combinations of atoms selected from among the more than one hundred elements. The atom is the smallest particle of an element that retains the properties of the element; similarly, the **molecule** is the smallest particle of a **compound**. Chemical equations consist of adding elements together into a compound (C + O = CO). Molecules cannot be separated into smaller particles (atoms or smaller) without a chemical change disrupting the chemical bonds that bind the molecule together. Physical separations, through the use of filter paper, centrifuge, or magnet for example, do not affect chemical bonds.

The scientific concept of a cycle, in this case without a time dependence, is evident in the fundamental makeup of matter and reflected in the structure of the periodic table. Mendeleev is credited with the development of the modern periodic table, in part for his predicting the existence of then-unknown elements based on the repeating trends in reactivity and physical properties. The concepts associated with atoms and molecules are not found in the elementary benchmarks, but they should be well understood by the elementary teacher nonetheless, as they provide the basis of all our understanding of matter and chemical change.

Energy is loosely scientifically defined as the ability to do work. Kinetic energy is the energy of motion ($KE = 1/2mv^2$), where m is the mass and v the velocity of an object. An example of kinetic energy is a rock tumbling down a mountain. Chemical energy is stored in the bonds of our food, held for later conversion to kinetic energy and heat in our bodies. Potential energy is held in an icicle hanging off the roof ($PE = mgh$) where m is mass, g is the gravitational force constant, and h is the height. When the icicle falls, its potential energy is converted to kinetic energy, and then to sound energy as it hits the pavement, and additional kinetic energy as the fragments skitter off. At the elementary level, students need to be able to identify the types of energy involved in various phenomena and identify the conversions between types. In the popular Rube Goldberg competitions, students use a number of sequential energy conversions to perform a simple task like breaking a balloon or flipping a pancake. Energy is conserved in each of these normal processes, converted to less useful forms (e.g., heat) but not created or destroyed. Similarly, matter is never created or destroyed in a normal chemical reaction. (Nuclear fusion is an obvious exception to both rules.)

Students gain useful experience with energy conversions as they study simple electrical circuits and chemical dry cells. The dry cell produces electrical energy from chemical potential energy. The size of the dry cell is proportional to the available current, but not the voltage, which is an **intrinsic property**. The D cell produces the same 1.5-volt potential as the AAA cell; the difference is in how long they can maintain the flow of current in the circuit. The battery is dead when one or more of the starting materials has been depleted, or when the essential electrolytic fluid leaks or dries out. The measured cell voltage depends on the oxidation and reduction potentials and of the half-reactions involved and on the concentration of each chemical species. When a cell reaches equilibrium, the measured cell potential and free energy of the cell both reach zero.

Seldom do we find chemical reactants present in the precise quantities to match the ideal stoichiometric ratio indicated by the chemical equation defining a reaction. In a battery, or any reaction for that matter, one of the chemicals will be depleted before the others. The concept of a **limiting reactant** is important in chemistry, whereby one reactant is consumed before the other, similar to the summer BBQ where hot dogs are in packages of ten, but the buns are in packages of eight. In this case, the buns are the limiting reactant. Many chemical reactions also involve multiple steps, where one step, the rate-limiting step, controls the rate of the entire process.

Simple dry cells do not pose a serious safety hazard—always an issue in hands-on activities—and are thus good for student experiments. A series connection linking dry cells in a chain increases the overall voltage, and thus the brightness of the bulb, a parallel connection with batteries placed in the circuit (like rungs in a ladder) increases the effective size of the cell but the voltage remains the same.

2.2 Changes in Matter

Scientific theories have their utility in providing a unified explanation for diverse and varied observations. Atomic theory, which views atoms and molecules as the fundamental building blocks of all matter, would be modified or abandoned if it didn't also explain other observations. Snow tracked into the kitchen quickly melts before either evaporating or being absorbed into someone's socks, which then must be hung by the fire to dry. In either of these changes the fundamental particles of water are the same, an assembly of three atoms held by covalent (shared electron) bonds in a bent molecular geometry associated with polar molecules. New attractions are possible between polar water molecules and the ions formed when some compounds are dissolved in solution. The relative strength of the new attractions to the water overcomes the attractions within the pure solid, allowing the solid to dissolve and in some cases dissociate in solution. Insoluble compounds do not dissolve because the strength of the attractions within the solid exceeds those available between the molecules and/or ions and the solvent.

Phase changes are also explained using atomic theory. **Evaporation** from a liquid occurs when individual molecules gain sufficient energy to break free from the intermolecular attractions in the liquid phase. The stronger the intermolecular attractions, the lower the vapor pressure and the higher the boiling point. The boiling point is the temperature at which the vapor pressure of molecules leaving solution equals the atmospheric pressure. Lowering the atmospheric pressure above a liquid makes it easier for the highest energy liquid molecules to escape, thus the boiling point is lower. Cooking while camping at high altitudes requires more time and, thus, more fuel because food cooks slower as a result of the lowered boiling temperature.

All matter has a temperature above the theoretical value of absolute zero because all matter is in continual motion. In a balloon filled with nitrogen gas, some molecules are moving relatively fast, others relatively slowly. The temperature of the gas is a measure of this motion, a measure of the average kinetic energy of the particles. Molecules are very small and fast moving, and there are vast empty spaces between them. The average speed of nitrogen molecules at 25°C is over 500 meters per second, whereas the lighter hydrogen molecules have an average speed in excess of 1,900 meters per second. Gases have significant empty spaces between the molecules and thus can be compressed, whereas liquids and solids have less or no compressibility, respectively.

While the atoms and molecules of all materials are in constant motion (vibrational energy), those in gases and liquids are also free to move about their own axes (rotational energy), and about the container (translational energy). Increasing the temperature of a solid imparts additional energy, which increases the vibrational energy. Once any particular atom or molecule gains sufficient energy to break free of the intermolecular attractions to the bulk solid or liquid it will slip or fly away (melt or evaporate respectively). Hotter atoms require more space in which to vibrate. For this reason wagon wheel rims are heated in the forge to expand the metal before slipping the rim onto the wheel, basketballs left outside on a cold night don't bounce well, and in thermometers the expansion of alcohol or mercury is used to indicate temperature.

2.3 Motion

Motion is when something moves from one place to another. There is a relationship between speed, distance, and time: $D = R \times T$. Newton's Laws of motion expressed his theory of motion: essentially what goes up must come down. The motion of atoms and molecules is essential to our understanding of matter at the molecular level, but we have many examples of motion readily available on the macroscopic level in the world around us. Many an idle moment can be passed with a young child timing small athletic feats, for example "how long will it take you to run to that tree and back," "the time to beat is 8.65 seconds, who can do it faster?" These experiences provide an informal experience with measurements of motion that serve as the basis for more scientific descriptions of speed, direction and changes of speed.

We can use time and motion to evaluate other chemical and physical phenomena. The periodic motion of a pendulum can be timed to determine the period, and experiments devised to explore the effect of pendulum mass, string length or amount of initial deflection. Hook's law can be studied by timing the vibrations of a spring. Chemical kinetics can be studied by timing reactions and observing changes in absorbance, conductivity, or pH. The growth rates of seedlings can be studied as a function of soil, water and light conditions. Such activities provide a natural framework to teach the concepts of scientific exploration, control of variables, collection, and presentation of data.

2.4 Waves and Vibrations

Waves are one mechanism of energy transport from one location to another. We experience waves directly in the forms of light, sound and water, and indirectly through radio and TV, wireless networks, and X-rays. Waves are periodic or cyclical in their nature. Energy is transmitted through a material in a translational wave when in water. For example, particles of water move perpendicular to the direction of energy travel. A wave with greater energy has greater amplitude. AM radio refers to amplitude modulation of the radio signal, where the carrier wave amplitude is modified by adding the amplitudes of the voice or music waves to create a cumulative and more complex wave form. The receiver must subtract from this complex waveform the simple sinusoidal waveform of the carrier to leave the voice or music.

Compressional waves, like sound, are characterized by having the media move along the same axis as the direction of energy travel. The speed of sound waves is dependant on the medium through which it travels, faster in denser materials like railroad track, and faster in water than through air, yet faster in warm air than colder air. Cold air is denser, but the gas molecules in warm air move faster and more quickly convey the sound energy. Sound cannot travel in a vacuum (referring to the absence of all matter in a given space) because, as a compressional wave, it needs to have particles to compress as it travels.

Light is energy, and darkness is simply the absence of that energy. A shadow is not "cast" by an object, but rather the stream of light energy is blocked by the object, leaving an area of darkness. A black light, however, is a light that is at a frequency too high and a wavelength too short for our eyes to see (thus the light appears black to us). Some objects held beneath a black light absorb the energy from the ultraviolet light, and reemit this light at slightly lower wavelengths than our eyes can see, giving them the appearance that they glow in the dark. Laundry soaps with whiteners and brighteners contain additives that convert portions of the invisible UV radiation from the Sun into lower frequency to make your "whites whiter."

White light is light composed of all visible wavelengths. Color is a property of light which depends on the wavelength of the light that strikes it. White light passing through a prism, raindrop, or spectroscope can be separated into its constituent colors. An object appears red because it, or the dye molecules it contains, reflects the red wavelengths constituent in the white light that strike it. If a red shirt is illuminated by a blue light the shirt will appear black because there is no red light for it to reflect. Blue paint reflects blue light from a white source, and yellow paint reflects yellow. Mixing the paints gives a material that reflects blue and yellow light, and our eye sees the mixture as green. A blue filter placed before a white light allows only the blue light to pass, absorbing all other wavelengths. A red shirt, when viewed through a blue filter, will appear black because the shirt can only reflect red light, but the filter can only pass blue light. The phosphors of our TV screen are in sets of red, green, and blue, which when illuminated together release white light.

3. EARTH AND SPACE SCIENCE

One had to be a Newton to notice that the Moon is falling, when everyone sees that it doesn't fall.

Paul Valéry (1871–1945), French poet and philosopher

Understand and apply fundamental concepts and principles of Earth and space science to interpret, analyze, and explain phenomena.

For example:
- Apply knowledge of the geological composition and **history of the earth**.
- Analyze the major features of the earth in terms of the natural processes that shape them (e.g., **plate tectonics, erosion, volcanic activity**).
- Demonstrate understanding of the **water cycle**.
- Recognize fundamental **weather processes** and phenomena (e.g., storms, atmospheric circulation) and factors that influence them.
- Apply knowledge of the basic components and structure of the **solar system**.
- Apply principles and concepts of **Earth and space science** to describe the composition, motions, and interactions of objects in the universe.

- Apply knowledge of how to use major processes and themes of Earth and space science (e.g., those related to weather, the water cycle, patterns of change), as well as the interconnections of Earth, space, physical, life, and environmental sciences to interpret, analyze, and explain everyday phenomena.
- Recognize interrelationships among Earth and space science, technology, and society in historical and contemporary contexts.
- Identify a wide range of instructional resources and technologies to support the learning of physical science.

3.1 Geosphere

Scientifically literate individuals have an understanding and appreciation for the world around them. Rocks hold an early fascination, both for their utility: as objects for throwing, skipping; and also for their beauty, texture, and diversity. Physical landforms vary considerably across the face of the Earth, revealed to the observant and thoughtful eye in road cuts, and the scenic viewpoints everywhere. On a small scale, each puddle, rivulet, and mass of sand and gravel in a yard or parking lot reveals the same actions of erosion, deposition, and graded sorting of material by size and mass that are at work on a global scale to form and reform our physical environment. The scientifically literate individual continually constructs new knowledge by study of the geosphere through direct observation, through photographs, models and samples, and through graphical representations (maps). The geosphere is the source for many natural resources essential for modern life, and the recipient of pollution caused by man's activities.

The major layers of the earth are the crust, mantle, outer, and inner core. Plates are large moving sections of the earth created by faults, earthquakes, volcanoes, and mountains. A volcano is an opening, or rupture, in the earth's surface which allows magma, or molten rock beneath the earth's crust, to escape from deep below the surface. An earthquake or a trembling/shaking of the earth's surface, occurs as a result of plate tectonics (plates moving against each other and causing stress).

Other processes of the earth include weathering (the process of breaking down rocks and soil through wind, water, rain, heat, ice, and snow) and erosion (the wearing away of the surface of the earth through water, rain, and ice.

When we consider the history of the earth, we are talking about the initial formation in the big bang about 13.7 billion years ago, when scientists theorize that matter was concentrated until a huge explosion sent it across the universe. After it cooled, it formed the planets and other heavenly bodies. We measure time on earth in four eras: Cenozoic, Mesozoic, Paleozoic, and Precambrian. We can tell a lot about these periods by examining and dating rocks, which is known as the rock record, or by looking at fossils (the remains of animals in rocks).

Evidence of physical changes to the geosphere is abundant, and frequently newsworthy. Each landslide, earthquake, or volcanic eruption reveals something about the Earth and its structures.

Fossils, preserved remnants of or marks made by plants and animals that were once alive, are one source of evidence about changes in the environment over time. Finding fossils of marine organisms in what is now a desert is an opportunity to discuss scientific ways of knowing, of how science forms and tests hypotheses, and how theories develop to explain the reasons behind observations. The scientifically literate individual understands the concepts of uncertainty in measurement and the basis of scientific theories. Such an understanding may lead the teacher in an elementary classroom to refer to fossils and rocks simply as "very old," to dinosaurs as "living long ago," and to occasionally preface statements of scientific theory with the observation that "many scientists believe. . . ."

3.2 Hydrosphere

With about seventy-five percent of the Earth's surface covered with water, the hydrosphere defines our planet and its environment. Most people live near the ocean, but few people live on, or have even experienced, the vast reaches of the world's oceans. Closer to our daily lives, and important because of the fresh water necessary to sustain life and commerce, are the rivers, and streams that are abundant and familiar to residents of Illinois. The hydrosphere includes not just the surface waters described, but the subsurface waters of aquifers, and the water vapor present in the atmosphere. Man has a significant impact on the hydrosphere through activities that contaminate, divert, and attempt to control the flow of water. These activities can benefit one part of the environment or society while harming another.

The water cycle is made up of evaporation, condensation, and precipitation (rain, snow, ice, etc.). The scientific concept of cycle is also used to describe the movement of water through its various phases, and through each part of the environment. A climate chamber formed from discarded polyethylene soda bottles can easily demonstrate these changes, and when soil, plants, and small frogs are added, a nearly complete ecosystem is formed if we count the food we add for the frog each day. In this chamber the student can observe the water cycle as liquid water evaporates, then condenses again against an ice-filled chamber to fall back to the surface. Only two phases, solid and liquid, can be observed directly, since the individual molecules of water vapor are too small to be seen by the naked eye. The white cloud visible at the tip of the teakettle, like our breath when we exhale on a cold winter day and fog, are examples of condensed water vapor (liquid water). The supply of fresh water on the Earth is limited, and water is a reusable resource that must be carefully managed. With this in mind, we are grateful for the technology to treat and purify water, which has done much to extend the human lifespan and reduce disease by providing clean and reliable sources of water in some parts of the world.

3.3 Atmosphere

The atmosphere is the layer of gases held close to the Earth by gravitational forces. In size, it has been compared with the skin on an apple. The atmosphere is densest close to the surface, where gravity holds the heavier gases and the pressure is greatest. The atmosphere becomes less dense and pressure decreases exponentially as altitude increases. The various gases that make up the atmosphere are, in descending order, nitrogen, oxygyn, carbon dioxide, and trace gases. The atmosphere has several layers: the thermosphere, mesosphere, stratosphere, and troposphere. All weather is contained within the lowest layer of the atmosphere (troposphere) and the temperature decreases as one rises through this layer. We can often observe the top of this layer as clouds form anvil shaped tops when they cannot rise further than the height of the cold boundary between the lowest layer (troposphere) and the overlying layer (stratosphere).

The concept of cycle reappears in the discussion of the recurring patterns of weather, and the progression of the seasons. The basis of the seasons has much more to do with the angle of light striking the Earth, and very little to do with the distance from the Sun. Classroom weather stations and weather charts are useful learning tools, and projects to build thermometers, hygrometers, and barometers are popular in classrooms.

Density variations related to temperature drive the movement of air. Heat energy warms the air and increases water evaporation, warm air expands and rises above cooler surrounding air, rising air cools and water vapor condenses forming clouds and precipitation. Cold, heavy air settles over the polar caps and flows toward the equator, generally leading to weather trends that bring cold northerly winds into Illinois for part of the winter. Temperature gradients and the resulting air movement are readily observed at home where the basement is cool, the upstairs warmer, and a draft is often felt when sitting near the stairway.

3.4 Space Science

The concept of cycle again finds application in the periodic movement of the Sun and planets. The size of objects, and distances between them, are difficult to represent on the same scale. The National Mall in Washington, D.C., contains a 1/10,000,000,000th-scale solar system model in which the Sun is the size of a grapefruit, and Pluto, located some 650 yards away, is the size of a poppy seed. The openness of space is mirrored at a much smaller scale by vast open spaces between atoms and between nuclei and their electrons.

A ball rolling down the aisle of a school bus appears, to observers sitting on the bus, to swerve to the right and hit the wall as the bus makes a left-hand turn. To an observer outside the bus, the ball continued its straight-line motion until acted upon by a force, often resulting from a collision with the wall. For centuries the best science available held that the Sun rose in the east and set in the west. As scientific instruments developed and improved (telescopes for example), scientists collected new information that challenged old theories. New theories are not always well received, a fact to which Galileo would attest. We now understand that the Sun is the gravitational center of the solar system, and that the planet's motions are defined by their path along an elliptical orbit defined by its speed and its continual gravitational attraction to the Sun.

4. PRINCIPLES AND PROCESSES OF SCIENTIFIC INVESTIGATIONS

Happy is he who gets to know the reasons for things.

Virgil (70–19 BCE), Roman poet

Understand the principles and processes of scientific investigation and how to promote students' development of scientific knowledge and skills, including their use of scientific thinking, inquiry, reasoning, and investigation.

For example:
- Determine the type of scientific investigation (e.g., experimentation, systematic observation) that best addresses a given question or hypothesis.
- Demonstrate knowledge of considerations and procedures, including safety practices, related to designing and conducting experiments (e.g., formulation of hypothesis; use of control and experimental groups; recognition of variables being held constant, those being manipulated, and those responding in an experiment).
- Recognize how to use methods, tools, technologies, and measurement units to gather and organize data, compare and evaluate data, and describe and communicate the results of investigations in various formats.
- Recognize the values inherent in science (e.g., reliance on verifiable evidence, reasoning, logic, avoidance of bias) and strategies for helping students discover new knowledge through the use of scientific thinking and reasoning.
- Demonstrate knowledge of strategies to engage students in discovering new knowledge through the use of scientific thinking and reasoning (e.g., exploration labs, learning cycle approach).

4.1 Tools of Science

From the pencil and field notebook to modern instruments in the laboratory, science involves the tools of observation, measurement, and computational analysis. The microscope and telescope each extend the range of human observation beyond human physiology. The spectroscope separates visible light into its component colors, and the spectrophotometer measures the selective absorption of those colors as a function of some property of a solution, solid, or gas. Mathematics is a tool to evaluate the results of our observations, to organize large quantities of data into averages, ranges, and statistical probabilities.

All measurements are limited by the fundamental uncertainty of the measuring device. The concept of significant figures is derived from the simple assumption that calculations on measurements cannot generate results that are more precise than the measurements themselves.

If we divide one pie into three pieces the calculator might report that each piece is 0.33333333 (depending on the number of digits on the calculator display). We know from experience that there will be crumbs left in the pan and that no amount of care in dividing the pieces will result in the level of accuracy the calculation suggests. Every measuring device is presumed to be accurate to the smallest of the subdivisions marked, and every measurement with such a device should include one additional estimated digit. Measurements made with a ruler whose smallest divisions are one centimeter apart should be recorded to the tenth of a centimeter (the smallest measured digit plus one estimated digit). When scientists read the results of measurements made by others they therefore presume that the recorded values include a final digit that is an estimate based on the inherent inaccuracy of the instrument or device.

> **All measurements are limited by the fundamental uncertainty of the measuring device.**
>
> **Fast Facts**

4.2 Technology

Compared to the goose quill, the modern mechanical pencil is a dramatic advancement in the technology of written communication. However, neither replaces the critical, analytical, and creative act of authorship. Many tools are available to assist in the observation, collection of data, analysis, and presentation of scientific information, yet none replace the role of the investigator who must formulate meaningful questions that can be answered using the tools of science. It is through the application of technology that we have the tools upon which all of modern science is based. We make some of these tools available in our classrooms to give students the opportunity to participate firsthand in the process of inquiry and discovery. The technology we employ in this context must facilitate student learning, remove barriers to understanding, and not create new barriers to delay and obscure the scientific concepts that we want to teach.

Scientific process skills, including the proper and accurate use of laboratory equipment, are an important component of science education. Instruction is necessary to guide the effective use of each measurement or observational tool: rulers, microscopes, balances, laboratory glassware, and so forth. As students develop these skills, they move from simple observations and confirmatory activities to using these tools to find answers to questions that they develop themselves.

4.3 Health and Safety

Through active, hands-on activities, science instruction is made a richer and more meaningful experience. From simple observations and activities at early grades, through detailed controlled experiments at higher grades, students who do science to learn science understand science better. While students are engaged in the process of discovery and exploration, the teacher must be engaged in protecting the health and safety of these students. The hazards vary with the discipline, and thoughtful planning and management of the activities will significantly reduce the risks to students. In all cases, students must utilize appropriate personal hygiene (hand washing) and wear personal protective equipment (goggles, gloves) while engaged in laboratory or field activities. Substitution of less hazardous materials whenever possible is a high priority. For example, in the physical sciences, replace mercury thermometers with alcohol or electronic, replace glass beakers and graduated cylinders with durable polyethylene, and eliminate or reduce the use of hazardous chemicals. In the earth sciences, rocks and minerals used in class should not contain inherently hazardous materials, students should not be allowed to taste the minerals, and reagents like HCl used for identification of carbonate minerals should be dispensed from spill-proof plastic containers. In the life sciences, special care should be given to topics such as safe practices for sharps, the safe handling of living organisms, and the care and use of microscopes. Experiments or activities involving the collection or culture of human cells or fluids should be discouraged, and proper sterilization procedures followed to prevent the growth or spread of disease agents. When they are possible, outdoor, museum, and other field activities can bring a valuable enrichment to the science curriculum in all disciplines. They also bring additional responsibilities for the safe planning and implementation of activities that increase student learning while maintaining the health and safety of the students.

4.4 Experimental Design

> *It is a capital mistake to theorise before one has data. Insensibly one begins to twist facts to suit theories instead of theories to suit facts.*
>
> Sherlock Holmes, the fictional creation of Arthur Conan Doyle (1859–1930), British physician and novelist

We trust the results of experiments, both formal and informal, to help us understand our surroundings. Unfortunately, without proper control of the variables and a sound experimental design, our observations may lead us to entirely wrong-headed or incorrect conclusions. Therefore, we must be very careful to plan and document our experiments carefully so they may be reproducible in any lab.

4.5 Scientific Method

The scientific method is not a specific six-step method that is rigorously followed whenever a question arises that can be answered using the knowledge and techniques of science. Rather, it is a process of observation and analysis that is used to develop a reliable, consistent, and nonarbitrary representation and understanding of our world. We can use the scientific method (observation and description, formulation of hypotheses, prediction based on hypotheses, and tests of predictions) for many, but not all questions. The approach is best applied to situations in which the experimenter can control the variables, eliminating or accounting for all extraneous factors, and perform repeated independent tests wherein only one variable is changed at a time.

4.6 Controlling Variables

The science fair project is a common tool for instruction in the scientific method. Many formal and informal sources, often Web based, provide lists of suggested science fair topics, but not all are experiments. For the youngest students it is appropriate and useful for the focus to be upon

models and **demonstrations**, for example the solar system model, volcano, or clay cross section of an egg. Later the students should move to true experiments where the focus is on identifying a **testable hypothesis**, and the control of all experimental variables but the one of interest. Many projects may be elevated from model or demonstration to experiment. A proposal to demonstrate how windmills work can be made an experiment when the student adds quantitative measurements designed to measure one variable while varying only one other and while holding all other variables constant. For example, using an electric fan, the number of rotations per minute can be measured as a function of the fan setting (low, medium, or high). However, while keeping the fan setting constant, several different experiments could vary any one of the following variables: number of fins, size of fins, or shape of fins while in each case measuring the rotational speed.

4.7. Collecting and Presenting Data

The male has more teeth than the female in mankind, and sheep and goats, and swine. This has not been observed in other animals. Those persons which have the greatest number of teeth are the longest lived; those which have them widely separated, smaller, and more scattered, are generally more short lived.

Aristotle (384–322 BCE), Greek philosopher

Scientifically literate individuals have detailed and accurate content knowledge that is the basis of their scientific knowledge. They do not strive to recall every detail of that knowledge, but build conceptual frameworks upon which prior knowledge, as well as new learning, is added. From this framework of facts, concepts, and theories the scientifically literate individual can reconstruct forgotten facts, and use this information to answer new questions not previously considered. The scientifically literate individual is a lifelong learner who asks questions that can be answered using scientific knowledge and techniques.

Science is based upon experimentation and observation. The scientifically literate individual is informed by existing knowledge, and is knowledgeable about the sources, accuracy, and value of each source. Not every source is equally reliable, accurate, or valid. Classroom teachers are advised to use trusted educational sites such as those sponsored by the Illinois State Board of Education (ISBE), which lists links at www.isbe.state.il.us/ils/science/resources.htm.

Scientifically literate individuals must be able to evaluate critically the information and evidence they collect, and the conclusions or theories to which that information and evidence leads. Such analysis incorporates an understanding of the limitations to knowledge in general, and the limitations of all measurements and information based on the quality of the experimental design. The literate individual can evaluate claims for scientific merit, identify conflicting evidence and weigh the value and credibility of conflicting information. They can also recognize that not every question can be answered using scientific knowledge, valuing the contributions of other cultures and other ways of knowing, including art, philosophy, and theology.

Scientific information is communicated to nonscientific audiences in order to inform, guide policy and influence the practices that affect all of society. This information is presented through text, tables, charts, figures, pictures, models, and other representations that require interpretation and analysis. Scientifically literate individuals can read and interpret these representations, and select appropriate tools to present the information they gather.

4.8 Interdiciplinary Science

All theoretical chemistry is really physics; and all theoretical chemists know it.

Richard P. Feynman (1918–1988), Nobel Prize in Physics, 1965

The separation of the natural sciences into life, physical, and earth sciences is relatively arbitrary. Many school curricula, and state-level science standards, are based on the cross-disciplinary integration of science based on key concepts rather than individual disciplines. The science concept of cycle is one of many concepts that find application, and can be used to understand science content, in more than one scientific discipline. This approach to science instruction is viewed as important for several reasons. It is consistent with the goals of scientific literacy and of developing science content knowledge upon which students build and extend their own understanding. Science knowledge is constantly developing and expanding in a continuous process, made more meaningful through the development of an organizing framework. Scientific concepts, which often have application in contexts outside the laboratory, help us see similarities and recognize patterns, which allow us to better function within society.

Science concepts can serve as organizers, often unifying disparate topics in the process of learning science. Examples of key interdisciplinary science concepts include: cause-effect, model, cycle, equilibrium, population, and gradient. As an example, the concept of model is among the most ubiquitous in all of science. **Models** are tentative schemes or structures that relate to real world objects or phenomena. Our explanations of many phenomena rely on models, including descriptions of electricity, atoms, tectonics, and genetics. Like a model airplane, a scientific model will bear a certain resemblance to the real object that is useful at some level to represent, but not fully replicate, the real object. Models are used when the phenomenon or object of interest cannot be used directly. Models may be constructed to scale, but often are not, in order to emphasize some portion of the object. An artistic drawing is a model, as is a three-dimensional, cross-sectional plastic casting, or a computer-rendered animation. Each has its limitations, and its beneficial function, to extend our understanding of the object or phenomenon. Models can limit our understanding when they are treated as statements of descriptive fact or when the limitations of the physical model are confused with the characteristics of the real object or phenomenon.

4.9 Science, Technology, and Society

It is unworthy of excellent men to lose hours like slaves in the labor of calculation which could be relegated to anyone else if machines were used.

Gottfried Wilhelm von Leibniz (1646–1716), German polymath

Science disciplines hold to certain central values that unify them in their philosophy and methodology. Science relies on evidence collected in verifiable experiments, on conclusions validated by replication, and on theories that explain observations and that are capable of making testable predictions. Modern scientific thought traces a significant portion of its development to the work of Western European scientists, but it is important to recognize the contributions made by all peoples and cultures to the development of scientific knowledge. Men and women from all continents and races continue to make meaningful contributions to the advancement of science in all disciplines. Examples are readily available for enrichment and instruction from online resources.

Technology can be loosely defined as the application of science for the benefit of mankind. For both political and economic reasons not all peoples have the same ready access to clean, safe water supplies nor to adequate food supplies, in spite of the technological capabilities that basic science has provided. Science certainly can benefit, but it too, arguably, can harm mankind and our environment. Science gives us the knowledge and tools to understand nature's principles and that knowledge can often be applied for some useful purpose. Few would debate the benefits of the wheel and axle, the electric light, the polio vaccine, or plastic. The benefits of science and technology become more complicated to evaluate when discussing the applications of gene splicing for genetically modified foods, of cloning, of nuclear energy to replace fossil fuels, or the application of atomic energy to weapons of mass destruction. Science can tell us how to do something, not whether we should.

> **Science can tell us how to do something, not whether we should.** *Fast Facts*

Scientific literacy helps us participate in the decision-making process of our society as well-informed and contributing members. Real-world decisions have social, political, and economic dimensions, and scientific information is often used to both support and refute these decisions. Understanding that the inherent nature of scientific information is unbiased, and based on experimental evidence that can be reproduced by any laboratory under the same conditions can help us all make better decisions, recognize false arguments, and participate fully as active and responsible citizens.

Social Sciences

The ICTS Social Sciences section includes five test objectives. These objectives represent a broad range of integrated social sciences concepts from the content areas of government, economics and political principles, history, geography, and development of social science knowledge and skills. Embedded within each broad objective are a number of essential social sciences concepts. A thorough understanding of each objective requires knowledge of the embedded concepts coupled with the ability to analyze concepts in a comparative analysis of Illinois, U.S., and world contemporary and historic society. For each objective, an explanation of the embedded concepts is provided. Following the explanation is a set of practice test questions designed to give you an idea of the nature and type of questions included on the test.

When preparing for this part of the test, you should review each social science objective concept, ascertain how each concept theme would play out in an elementary/middle school classroom, and relate the concept to past and present developments in Illinois, the United States, and the world.

Understand the structures and functions of government; the rights and responsibilities of citizenship in the United States; and the skills, knowledge, and attitudes necessary for successful participation in civic life.

For example:
*   Recognize basic purposes and concepts of government, including the constitutional principles and democratic foundations of U.S. government.

- Demonstrate knowledge of the basic structures and functions of federal, state, and local government in the United States (e.g., the branches of federal government and their roles, key aspects of government in Illinois).
- Demonstrate knowledge of basic democratic principles and rights (e.g., due process, equal protection) and fundamental democratic values and beliefs (e.g., majority rule, individual participation) and their significance for individuals, groups, and society.
- Apply knowledge of the responsibilities of U.S. citizens, including classroom, school, and community applications (e.g., respecting others' rights, obeying laws and rules, voting in class elections) and the skills, knowledge, and attitudes necessary for successful participation in civic life (e.g., compromise, consensus building, cooperation).
- Recognize the role of law in the Illinois and U.S. constitutional systems.
- Identify a wide range of instructional resources and technologies to support the learning of the structures and functions of government.

Understand the interrelationships of economic and political principles, concepts, and systems and their relationship to historical and contemporary developments in Illinois, the United States, and the world.

For example:
- Demonstrate understanding of fundamental concepts and principles of economics (e.g., supply and demand) and key features of different economic systems (e.g., command, market, mixed).
- Recognize major features of the U.S. economic system, including the roles of consumers and producers and types of economic resources and activities in various regions, including Illinois.
- Recognize key features and historical developments associated with different types of political systems; the interrelationships of economic and political systems; and their relationship to historical and contemporary developments in Illinois, the United States, and the world.
- Demonstrate knowledge of the political processes and the role of political parties in the United States.
- Analyze political relationships between the United States and other nations; the role of the United States in world affairs; and global patterns of trade, exchange, and interdependence among individuals, businesses, and governments.
- Identify a wide range of instructional resources and technologies to support learning about economic and political systems.

Understand from multiple perspectives the significant eras, themes, events, and cultural developments in the history of Illinois, the United States, and the world.

For example:
- Demonstrate knowledge of significant eras, themes, events, and people in the history of Illinois, the United States, and the world.

- Analyze ways in which cultural groups have affected and been affected by U.S. society and ways in which cultural heritage and diversity have influenced historical developments in the United States.
- Analyze the influence of science, technology, economic activity, and religious and philosophical ideas on contemporary societies and societies throughout history.
- Recognize how economic, political, cultural, geographic, and social processes interact to shape patterns of human population, cooperation, and conflict.
- Demonstrate knowledge of how to use historical concepts and themes to analyze events, patterns, and relationships in Illinois, the United States, and the world.
- Identify a wide range of instructional resources and technologies to support the learning of history.

Understand major principles, concepts, and phenomena of geography and the interrelationships between people and their environment.

For example:
- Demonstrate understanding of major geographic features of Illinois, the United States, and the world and their historical and contemporary significance.
- Recognize how to use maps, globes, and other geographic tools to locate and derive information about people, places, and environments.
- Apply concepts of geography (e.g., location, movement, population, migration) to analyze contemporary and historical issues and trends.
- Recognize the connections among and common concerns of world societies (e.g., food production and distribution, human rights) and analyze the influence of these global connections and concerns on people, places, and events.
- Recognize basic concepts related to the structure and organization of human societies and processes of socialization and social interaction.
- Analyze the nature and implications of various types of interactions between people and the environment and the effects of human activities (e.g., consumption of natural resources, pollution) on the environment.
- Identify a wide range of instructional resources and technologies to support the learning of geography.

Understand concepts, skills, and processes of inquiry in the social sciences (e.g., locating, gathering, organizing, formulating hypotheses) and how to promote students' development of knowledge and skills in this area.

For example:
- Demonstrate knowledge of common themes and concepts in the social sciences (e.g., continuity, change, culture) and how to apply them in understanding people, places, and events.
- Demonstrate understanding of the basic principles and procedures of inquiry in the social sciences (e.g., modes of inquiry, formulation of research questions and hypotheses, use of historical analysis to make informed decisions).
- Apply principles and procedures for gathering, organizing, comparing, interpreting, analyzing, and summarizing social science information presented in various forms (e.g., tables, maps, graphs, narratives).

- Recognize how to use children's and young adult literature to support learning in the social sciences.
- Demonstrate knowledge of a wide range of instructional resources and technologies to support learning in the social sciences.

Government and the Responsibilities of Citizens

The social sciences portion of the Elementary Education test requires comprehension of the basic issues of governing power, the ideals of American democracy, and the core set of values expressed in America's essential founding documents, the Declaration of Independence, the Articles of Confederation, the U.S Constitution, and the Bill of Rights. Those values include life, liberty, pursuit of happiness, common good, justice, equality, truth, diversity, popular sovereignty, and patriotism.

Furthermore, the ideals of American democracy include the following essential Constitutional principles: the rule of law, separation of powers, representative government, checks and balances, individual rights, freedom of religion, federalism, limited government, and civilian control of the military. Essential democratic principles include those principles fundamental to the American judicial system, including: the right to due process of law; the right to a fair and speedy trial, protection from unlawful search and seizure, the right to decline to self-incriminate, and the rights to equal protection and freedom from racial and other unlawful discrimination.

Fast Facts **It is essential for citizens to be active in order to maintain a democratic society.**

Comprehension of the rights and responsibilities of citizens of the United States involves understanding that it is essential for citizens to be active in order to maintain a democratic society. This activity includes developing an awareness of governance issues, participation in political activities such as voting, providing service to communities, and regulating oneself in accordance with the law.

Diversity

Understanding the role of cultural diversity in shaping Illinois, the United States, and the world begins with knowledge of the commonalities and differences among such groups as African-Americans, Asian-Americans, Hispanic-Americans, and Native Americans. Commonalities and differences can be found when analyzing the role of language, education, religion, culture, and struggles for equality within and among groups. Understanding the role of cultural diversity in shaping Illinois, the United States, and the world should include an understanding of the struggles various groups undertake to gain equality and recognition within society.

A historical perspective of the role of cultural diversity in shaping the development of Illinois and the United States begins by gaining a sense of the types of people who came to Colonial America and their reasons for coming. This understanding can help one gain an appreciation for the diversity of people who eventually won their independence from Great Britain. Following those persons from the east during their various migrations westward can explain how they eventually settled what today is the American West. Studies of Old Immigration (1830–1850) and New Immigration (1900–1920) further explain the settling of America encouraged people of different cultures. Within this historical understanding, one should be able to identify examples of how immigrants were able to assimilate themselves into American culture, the contributions of immigrant groups to our culture, and the ways that immigrants have been exploited during that process.

Diverse cultural groups have shaped world history. Diversity has both positive and negative results—from contributing to disputes over territories, creating alliances that eventually lead to world and regional conflicts, outsourcing of jobs, and relocation of companies from the United States to foreign countries, to more positive examples such as the economic specialization that enhances choice and the modern globalization that results in economic interdependence. The impact of cultural diversity on world history can be explored by careful analysis of the following events, among others: the origin and spread of Christianity and Islam; colonialism and exploration; the beginning of World War I; and contemporary conflict in the Middle East.

Economic and Political Principles

An understanding of economics involves exploring the implications of scarcity (the concept that wants are unlimited while resources are limited). Exploration of scarcity involves an understanding of economic principles ranging from personal finance to international trade. Economic understanding means exploring principles of choice, opportunity costs, incentives, trade, and economic systems. (For a definition of each of the economic principles see the Handy Dandy Guide (HDG) development by the National Council on Economic Education (1989). For brief definitions based upon this guide see the Web site: *http://ecedweb.unomaha.edu/lessons/handydandy.htm*). This exploration includes analysis of how those principles operate within the economic choices of individuals, households, businesses, and governments.

An understanding of economics involves exploring the implications of scarcity. *Fast Facts*

In addition, economic understanding includes knowledge of the role that price, competition, profit, inflation, economic institutions, money, and interest rates play within a market system. A complete understanding of markets includes knowledge of the role of government within an economic system, including how monetary and fiscal policy impacts the market. (These economic concepts are based upon the *Content Standards for Economics* published by the National Council on Economic Education. A brief overview and complete list of standards can be found at: *http://ncee.net/ea/standards/*). This list includes concepts like choice, cost, incentives, systems, trade, and the consequences of economic decisions.

An understanding of political systems involves the ability to compare their different ideologies, structures, institutions, processes, and political cultures. This requires knowledge of alternative ways of organizing constitutional governments from systems of shared power from parliamentarian systems. Systems of shared power include federal systems, where sovereign states delegate powers to a central government; a federal system, where a national government shares power with state and local governments; and Unitarian systems where all power is concentrated in a centralized government.

Understanding local and state governments results from knowledge of the role federal and state constitutions play in defining the power and scope of state and local government. That knowledge should include comprehension of reserved and concurrent powers. Furthermore, an understanding of state and local government results from knowledge of the organization and responsibilities of such governments.

Understanding of the role of law in a democratic society results from a knowledge of the nature of civil, criminal, and constitutional law and how the organization of the judicial system serves to interpret and apply such laws. Essential principles of federal judicial procedure include the right of due process, the right to a fair and speedy trial, and the right to a hearing before a jury of one's peers. Additional judicial principles include an understanding of the protections granted in the Constitution, which include protection from self-incrimination and unlawful searches and seizures.

Understanding global interdependence begins with recognition that world regions include economic, political, historical, ecological, linguistic, and cultural regions. This understanding should include knowledge of military and economic alliances such as NATO, the G8 members, or cartels such as OPEC, and how their existence affects political and economic policies within regions. Knowledge of world regions and alliances leads to identification of issues that affect people in these areas. Common issues that affect people around the world include food production, human rights, resource use, prejudice, poverty, and trade.

A true sense of global interdependence results from an understanding of the relationship between local decisions and global issues. For example, how individual or community actions regarding waste disposal or recycling may affect worldwide resource availability. Or how fuel emissions standards affect air pollution or how fuel standards affect oil supply and gas prices.

History

Developing historical perspective includes knowledge of events, ideas, and people from the past. That knowledge encompasses an understanding of the diversity of race, ethnicity, social and economic status, gender, region, politics, and religion within history. Historic understanding includes the use of historical reasoning, resulting in a thorough exploration of cause-effect relationships to reach defensible historical interpretations through inquiry.

Significant knowledge of events, ideas, and people from the past results from careful analysis of cause and effect relationships in the following chronological eras: beginnings of civilization to 1620; colonization and settlement (1585–1763); revolution and the new nation (1754–1815); expansion and reform (1801–1861); Civil War and Reconstruction (1850–1877); the development of the industrial United States (1870–1900); the emergence of modern America (1890–1930); the Great Depression and World War II (1929–1945); postwar United States (1945–1970); and contemporary United States (1968–present).

Significant knowledge of historical events, ideas, and people from Illinois' past would result from careful analysis of cause and effect relationships in the chronological eras listed above for the United States. Included in this knowledge is an understanding of the evolution of political ideas, institutions, and practices in Illinois and the influence of technology, agriculture, urbanization, industry, and labor on the development of the Illinois economy. It is also necessary to understand the importance of family and local history.

This objective involves the ability to analyze and interpret the past lest we be forced to relive our mistakes. The basic primary and secondary sources for hisorical analysis are based upon conclusions resulting from careful review of documents, eyewitness accounts, letters, diaries, artifacts, photos, and historical sites.

Geography

Understanding major geographic concepts involves comprehending both physical features and the cultural aspects of geography. This would include knowledge of the fundamental themes of geography: comprehension of the relationships within and between places, understanding interdependence within the local, natural, and global communities, and familiarity with global issues and events.

The five themes of geography are: place; human-environmental interaction; location; movement and connections; and regions, patterns, and processes. An understanding of these themes would include the ability to use them to analyze regions within Illinois, the United States, and the world to gain a perspective about interrelationships among those regions. The use of the five themes should also result in the ability to compare regions.

An understanding of the theme of location requires knowledge of both absolute and relative location. Absolute location is determined by longitude and latitude. Relative location deals with the interactions that occur between and among places. Relative location involves the interconnectedness among people because of land, water, and technology. For example, knowledge of the history of Chicago includes an understanding of how its location at the base of Lake Michigan and its relationship to rivers has contributed to its economic development and vitality.

An understanding of the theme of human-environmental interaction involves consideration of how people rely on the environment, how we alter it, and how the environment may limit what people are able to do. For example, knowledge of the meat and grain industries in Illinois' history includes an understanding of how the people of Illinois utilized the Great Lakes and Ohio and Mississippi rivers to transport their products to regional markets. For example, an adaptation of the environment that aided Illinois' shipping industry was the development of the lock and dam system on the Mississippi.

An understanding of the theme of location, movement, and connections involves identifying how people are connected through different forms of transportation and communication networks and how those networks have changed over time. This would include identifying channels of the movement of people, goods, and information. For example, the steel industry in Chicago had a profound impact on the movement patterns of ideas and people of both the Chicago area and downstate.

An understanding of the theme of regions, patterns, and processes include identifying climatic, economic, political, and cultural patterns within regions. Understanding why these patterns were created includes understanding how climatic systems, communication networks, international trade, political systems, and population changes contributed to a region's development. An understanding of regions enables a social scientist to study their uniqueness and relationship to other regions.

Understanding global issues and events includes comprehending the interconnectedness of peoples throughout the world. For example, knowledge of the relationship between world oil consumption and oil production would result in an understanding of the impact that increased demand for oil in China would have on the price of a barrel of oil, which in turn could affect the decisions of consumers of new vehicles in the United States.

Locating, Organizing, and Interpreting Social Sciences Information

The ability to understand and apply skills and procedures related to the study of social sciences involves knowledge of the use of systematic inquiry. Inquiry is essential for use in examining single social sciences topics or integrated social sciences. Being able to engage in inquiry involves the ability to acquire information from a variety of resources, and organize that information, which leads to the interpretation of that information. Inquiry involves the ability to design and conduct investigations, which in turn leads to the identification and analysis of social sciences issues.

In addition, this understanding includes knowledge about and the use of the various resources used in systematic social science inquiry. Those resources include primary and secondary sources, encyclopedias, almanacs, atlases, government documents, artifacts, and oral histories.

The Arts, Health, and Physical Education

The Arts

Understand historical, cultural, and societal contexts for the arts (visual arts, music, drama, dance) and the interrelationships among the arts.

For example:
- Demonstrate knowledge of characteristic features of various artistic traditions and the role of art in various contexts.
- Recognize the role and functions of the arts in various cultures and historical periods and ways in which the arts can be used to explore various cultures and historical periods.
- Demonstrate understanding of how music, visual art, creative drama, and dance can be used as forms of communication, self-expression, and social expression (e.g., to express ideas and values, share life experiences, explore feelings).
- Recognize and evaluate strategies and activities intended to foster skills in creating, producing, viewing, responding to, analyzing, and appreciating music, visual art, drama, and dance.
- Demonstrate knowledge of the interrelationships among the arts and the connections between the arts and other subject areas.

Understand concepts, techniques, and materials related to visual art, music, and dramatic activities and how to provide students with learning opportunities that encourage them to express themselves through the arts.

For example:
- Demonstrate knowledge of basic terms and concepts of visual art (e.g., elements of art and principles of design) and types and characteristics of materials, tools (including technology), techniques, and processes (e.g., drawing, painting, printmaking, desktop publishing) used to create and evaluate works of visual art.
- Demonstrate knowledge of common musical terms and concepts (e.g., harmony, melody, rhythm); types and characteristics of instrumental and vocal music; and techniques, activities, technology, and materials for producing, listening to, analyzing, and responding to music.
- Demonstrate knowledge of basic types of dramatic activities (e.g., creative drama, puppet theater, pantomime, improvisation); of ways in which creative drama can be used across the curriculum; and of techniques, activities, technology, and materials for creating, producing, viewing, evaluating, and responding to drama.
- Demonstrate knowledge of basic types of creative movement and dance; of ways in which creative movement and dance can be used across the curriculum; and of techniques, activities, technology, and materials for performing, viewing, evaluating, and responding to creative movement and dance.

The arts are a part of the core curriculum, both in terms of Illinois standards and the No Child Left Behind federal mandate. Dance, music, drama, and the visual arts are essential parts of a complete education. Study of one or more art forms develops the intellect, provides unique access to meaning, and connects individuals with works of genius, multiple cultures, and contributions to history.

Visual Arts

Why We Create Visual Art

Visual Communication

At its most fundamental level, art—be it opera, ballet, painting, or pantomime—is a form of communication. Visual art encompasses many forms of communication, including sculpture, painting and drawing, ceramics, performance art, printmaking, jewelry, fiber art, photography, and film and video. Each medium or field of specialization communicates differently than the others. Take, for instance, the difference between viewing a sculpture and a tapestry. Sculpture requires the viewer to physically move around in space to comprehend the work, whereas a tapestry can generally be viewed from a stationary position. Sculpture is three-dimensional, encompassing height, width, and depth, whereas a tapestry is two-dimensional, encompassing only height and width. While both forms of art can have a strong visual presence, sculpture is unique in that it has the capacity to be fully physically engaging in actual space. Artists choose different disciplines and media because each method and medium has its own communicative potential.

Aesthetics

As viewers, we can be affected by visual art in ways that are difficult to define. The powerful experience of encountering, for example, a huge carved Olmec head sculpture in an outdoor garden in Villahermosa, Mexico, or contemplating a quiet, delicate Vermeer painting in The Hague, Netherlands, is sometimes termed an aesthetic moment or experience. We may try to put into words the experience of these moments—beautiful, colossal, overwhelming, transcendental—but the words often seem inadequate. What the art is communicating is perhaps hard to verbalize, but the feeling is undeniable. As viewers, we are momentarily transported so that we are no longer aware of our surroundings or ourselves. When art communicates to us in such a direct and forceful way, we consider this an aesthetic experience.

Although aesthetics has long been recognized as the branch of philosophy pertaining to beauty, it is impossible to find agreement on what is beautiful. In keeping with the root of the word, aesthetics can be understood as a study of sensation or feeling. This broader understanding of aesthetics has the ability to encompass the range of sensations that one can experience in viewing a work of art. Art is not always beautiful in the traditional sense of the word, and our aesthetic philosophies must be able to encompass this reality.

Current Tendencies in Visual Art

Visual art, like other forms of communication, has the capacity to convey the complexity of issues, ideas, and feelings. What generally (and traditionally) distinguishes visual art from the other disciplines in the arts is the emphasis on the visual. However, there are numerous visual artists who work entirely in sound, for example. What, then, is the factor that distinguishes visual artists from experimental sound artists, video artists from cinematographers, and performance artists from actors or dancers? The categories that distinguish one discipline from another are becoming increasingly blurred. While the traditional areas of fine art (namely music, theatre, dance, and visual art) still exist, many artists today are *interdisciplinary*: they are often conversant with different art disciplines while maintaining an identity in their primary field of study. The interdisciplinary crossover of art forms has opened up many exciting possibilities for music, theatre, dance, and visual art. Indeed, interdisciplinary art has the potential to capture the complexities of our present world differently than was previously possible.

Understanding Art

The Role of Visual Art in Society

From the earliest cave paintings to the most recent art installations, visual art has functioned as a form of commentary on the society from which it springs; consequently, visual art is continually changing. Over the millennia, visual art has played (and continues to play) a key role in the dissemination of aesthetic tendencies, political ideas, religious and spiritual doctrines, cultural beliefs and critiques, and societal norms and trends. Conversely, visual art has adapted to these same influences. In essence, visual art has the capacity to both shape and be shaped by the society in which it exists.

Visual art has also served the vital role of empowering the artist in his or her subject matter. For example, there has been broad speculation about the functions of the animal imagery that adorns the caves of France and Spain: Some suggest that the act of representing the animals gave the creator power over the creature or the creature's soul, while others have postulated that these artistic gestures were an early form of inventory—a means to count, organize, and track the myriad animals that existed in the outside world.

The function of art as an empowering tool is as vital today as it was in past millennia. Much like the cave painters of the past, contemporary artists often use their art as a means to chart and order the complexities, wonders, and inspirations of the present-day world.

Anonymous Artist

The earliest examples of art known to us date back to about 40,000 BCE, and the majority of this art remains anonymous to us. For example, all of the extant art from Egypt, of which thousands of examples survive, was created anonymously, in service to the pharaohs, gods, and society of the artists. There are instances of work crews having inscribed their names on the pyramids; however, since the form, subject matter, and imagery were determined by the dictates of that society, this seems to be more about individuals taking pride in their work than a desire for individual recognition. While this began to change during the Greek and Roman eras (wherein we begin to recognize individual artists' styles and artists more commonly signed their names), the role of the artist as an individual creator (and the subject, form, and content of art being determined by the individual artist) is a relatively recent phenomenon.

Fast Facts The earliest examples of art known to us date back to about 40,000 BCE, and the majority of this art remains anonymous to us.

It is also important to recognize that what remains of a past society like Egypt is always incomplete. We do not have the benefit of knowing what did not survive (e.g., homes, art, and utilitarian objects of everyday life).

How We View Art

A critical aspect of understanding art requires consideration of the context in which the art has been created; indeed, by examining the specifics of an artist's milieu—geographical, political, racial, social, religious, economic, and so forth—it is possible to truly appreciate and comprehend the profound differences that occur among works of art. Moreover, the way we view art is always mitigated by all of these same factors. Throughout history, art has readily been categorized based on some of the above factors, particularly temporal, geographic, and cultural ones. For instance, we tend to distinguish pre-Colombian artifacts by time periods (classical, postclassical), regional stylistic variations (Puuc, Zapotec), and tribal or geographical distinctions (Incan, Mayan, Aztec). These categories exist as a means of organizing and distinguishing the myriad groups of people, objects, styles, and places from which visual art arises. In today's visual art world, these same categories are often incomplete or inappropriate in illuminating the distinctions between art forms. Moreover, there is a long-standing tradition of Western scholars using a Eurocentric, comparative value system when examining the differences between visual arts of various cultures. This system is often biased and generally lacking in that it does not account for the contextual specifics of each culture, Some scholars have relegated or dismissed works of art as "primitive," "naïve," or simply "crude," based upon comparisons with art that is created under the aesthetic traditions of Europe. Comparing visual art from one culture to another is a rich, valuable, and worthwhile form of study, but only if cultural biases are not informing the process.

Consider the world we live in: In less than a day, one can travel to Micronesia, sub-Saharan Africa, or New Zealand. Furthermore, the Internet allows us immediate access to any person, group, country, company, or interest. Our understanding of influences in visual art has to encompass the understanding that the global network that reaches every part of the planet now influences every region of the world. In this global climate, it is not always possible to neatly categorize or even identify the influences that occur in visual art. It is possible, however, to recognize, distinguish and appreciate certain tendencies in visual art.

Concepts And Skills

Principles and Elements

In viewing and creating visual art, there are endless considerations in how to convey ideas, thoughts, and feelings in the visual realm. The elements—point, line, plane, shape, value, texture, color—and principles—balance, harmony, variety, directional thrust, focal area, and so forth—of art play an integral role in creating, viewing, and analyzing visual art. For instance, the choice of a particular color in a painting can change the whole mood of the work. Additionally, the meaning of a certain color in a work of art can change dramatically depending on the period or culture in which the work of art was created.

The color red, for instance, can simultaneously signify love, war, anger, passion, danger, warmth, death, life, and many other things depending on the cultural significance of the color, the context of the color in the work of art, and the intention of the artist.

Form and Meaning

As discussed previously, visual art functions as a reflection of the values, beliefs, and tendencies of an individual or society. Naturally, the *form* of art changes in relation to its function or meaning. For instance, the native carvers of Africa's Ivory Coast ascribe specific meaning to forms in the carving of their ceremonial masks. Each formal element on the mask—bulging eyes, elongated nose, perforated cheeks, and so on—serves a spiritual, cultural, and symbolic function during a ceremony, in that the mask creates a connection to the spirit world for both the performer and the tribe.

Figure 1.1   Ivory Coast Ceremonial Mask. Date unknown.

The forms on the mask, therefore, were created for a specific and culturally-recognizable purpose. This is very different from the view of visual art that emerged during the nineteenth century in Europe: namely, the role of form in a work of visual art was elevated to a primary level, while subject and content took an increasingly secondary role. The result of this elevation of form in visual art is what was eventually termed *formalist* art in the twentieth century in North America.

Formalism, at its peak with Post-Painterly Abstraction in the 1950s and 1960s, prided itself on its lack of meaning, symbolism, and subject matter: Simply put, it was about form or material and nothing more. It is astounding that one culture can ascribe deep, symbolic meaning to form or material while another culture can revel in its relative meaninglessness. The stark contrast between the beliefs of the Baule and the Post-Painterly Abstractionists indicates the vast differences that occur between art forms from different cultures and the importance of understanding how material associations can affect meaning in a work of art.

Figure 1.2   Student work by Regina Chandler

Deciphering Clues

Sometimes when viewing a work of art, we are unable to obtain information about the artist or the artist's intentions. In these instances, our role as viewer is akin to being a detective: We must collect as much information about the work of art as possible in order to make an educated guess about its meaning. The following mixed media drawing can be analyzed and understood based solely upon the clues we are given in the artwork.

By considering aspects of the art principles and elements in the drawing, we are often able to learn about the artist's intentions. The first thing we may notice in the drawing is the chair, which for many reasons draws the attention of a viewer. It appears to be the closest object to the viewer; it is the largest object (relatively speaking) in the drawing, and it can lead one's eyes into the space behind it. Another noticeable feature is the viewer's relationship to the chair. The chair is drawn in extreme, slightly distorted three-point perspective. The initial point of view that the viewer confronts is one of ambiguity. In one way, the viewer is looking down the stairs and the chair appears to be falling away; in another way, the viewer is looking up the stairs and the chair is falling toward the viewer. Adding to the ambiguity in this drawing are the light source and shadows; indeed, the viewer is given at least two light sources that create shadows on the stairs and on the underside of the chair. Lastly, the viewer of this piece is confronted with the randomly collaged atmosphere of road maps. The predominant theme that seems to emerge from the drawing is one of confusion and ambiguity. One might assume that, based on these observations, the student's intention here was to play with the rules of perspective in order to create an indeterminate space and feeling. The drawing holds one's attention by virtue of its changeability. It is possible that the student had specific intentions about the choice of maps and the illusion of the chair (perhaps a memory or a symbolic reference to somewhere specific), and sometimes we are fortunate enough to learn the inspiration of an artist's work. Yet, in this particular example, one is able to piece together enough clues from the drawing to enjoy and appreciate the work without knowing all of the specifics of the artist's motivation.

Material Factors

Understanding the differences between works of art happens on many levels. As previously discussed, the aesthetic standards by which one assesses a work of art must take into account the many cultural factors that influence visual art. Equally important to aesthetic consideration is knowledge of the many tools, techniques, and materials that artists employ in their art. The number of potential materials for creating works of art has increased exponentially over the past 150 years or so. This situation can be attributed both to industrial innovations and to artists' broadening their scope to include found materials and unusual non-art objects and media. The foregrounding of materiality that occurred with the formalist artists in the twentieth century has further contributed to the recent expanse of materials for art making. The inclusion of uncommon materials in visual art has dramatically changed the criteria by which one assesses visual art; in fact, it is no longer unusual to be confronted with traditionally carved marble sculptures (Louise Bourgeois) and cast and licked chocolate sculptures (Janine Antoni) in the same gallery space. What becomes important in analyzing these diverse works is an understanding of the motivation behind the artwork. Ultimately, it is critical for us to respect the diversity that contributes to the variety, richness and complexity of the art world.

Music

When preparing for this part of the exam, it is important to focus on the objectives to which music is primarily related. They include contexts for the music, concepts and skills involved in experiencing music, and the aesthetic and personal dimensions of music.

One objective is to "understand historical, cultural, and societal contexts for the arts (visual arts, music, drama, dance) and the interrelationships among the arts." This suggests an integration of subject matter that is an opportunity for teachers and students to make connections between social studies, reading or language arts, and the fine arts. For example, when students are reading stories about the American Revolution, they should be aware that it occurred during the period known as the Classical Period in music history. Listening to a work by Haydn or Mozart and talking about how they reflected the "old world" and then comparing the work to a Colonial American tune of the time like "Chester" by William Billings is a great exercise. Similarly, the visual art of Andy Warhol, the music of the Beatles, the assassination of John F. Kennedy, and the war in Vietnam all share the same approximate time frame. In these and the virtually infinite number of other cases or combinations, the students can be asked to find contrasts and similarities or they can attempt to find ways that historical context affected art and ways that art affected and reflected history.

These examples from American History are easy for most to grasp quickly. However, the objective seeks to have teachers and students consider the role of the Arts, to include music, in history and culture beyond the American experience. Listening to music from China, Japan, Germany, Australia, or Africa when studying those cultures can enrich the experience and make it more memorable for students. It is even more valuable to experience live or videotaped performances of the music and dance of these cultures because often the music is performed in traditional costume with traditional instruments (sometimes very different from modern instruments) and seeing the costumes and the movement are an important part of understanding the culture.

According to the objective, merely experiencing the music is not enough. The students must be able to recognize the music or art as part of its historical context and then, through discussion or written exercises that emphasize higher order thinking, they must demonstrate an understanding of the music's place in the historical context and be able to note things that are common and things that are different from context to context—period to period, culture to culture, and so forth—appropriate to their age and level of development. For example, Haydn, Mozart, and Billings used simple melodies in their compositions, but Haydn and Mozart wrote mostly large works like symphonies and operas, whereas Billings wrote mostly psalms and songs. Students must be aware of these facts and then consider why more highly developed forms were preferred in the "old world" while basic psalms and songs were more common in the Colonies. The obvious answer is that colonists did not have the time or the resources to encourage or produce larger musical works. However, the discussion could go beyond that basic step depending on the sophistication of the students.

Another objective is to "understand concepts, techniques, and materials" for producing, listening to, and responding to music. Understanding concepts and techniques suggests more than an appreciation of these concepts and skills. The students ought to experience music making and be taught to listen as musicians listen. They should learn how to put their response to music into accepted music terminology.

Music is an important part of culture, religious practice, and personal experience for all people. It is important that students have the opportunity to experience as many forms of music making as possible. It is through the acquisition of basic skills in singing and playing instruments that people can grow in their ability to express themselves through music. As students develop skills, they are also exposed to basic musical concepts such as melody, harmony, rhythm, pitch, and timbre. Then, with experience, they come to make decisions about what is acceptable or not acceptable within a given cultural or historical context and thereby develop their own aesthetic awareness.

Listening is a skill that is often taken for granted. There is not a "right" way to listen. However, listening can be much more than allowing the sound to flow past the ears. It can be as basic as listening for melodies and analyzing for form and chord structure or as advanced as critiquing the interpretation on its musical and aesthetic merits. Listening with knowledge and understanding can make the experience of a musical performance much deeper and more meaningful. While music can be experienced and found satisfying, challenging, or beautiful without prior knowledge of a piece or an understanding of its form, cultural significance, and so forth, these things can enrich the experience.

In order to share their responses to music, people must learn how to put their responses to it into musical terminology. Some people call music a language, but it does not function as a spoken language. It does not provide specific information, instructions, or reactions. Rather, it sparks thoughts, feelings and emotions. In order to try to put the experience into words, musicians and artists have developed vocabulary and approaches to discussing music and art. This includes things as basic as melody and harmony and as profound as the aesthetic experience.

Fast Facts *Music does not provide specific information, instructions, or reactions. People respond to it naturally.*

The type of music or the period or the performer does not necessarily limit the aesthetic experience. It is equally possible to have an aesthetic experience when listening to a child sing a simple melody as it is when listening to a professional orchestra performing a Beethoven symphony. The important thing is to share that aesthetic experience. It is part of what makes music and art special.

There are many ways to encourage exploration of and growth through aesthetic responsiveness. A common experience is a crucial starting point. Have the students listen to several pieces of music and, after listening attentively, ask them to describe how each one made them feel. It is often best to write their response down before starting a discussion. Then, ask them if they can explain why each piece of music made them feel the way they indicated. Younger students will likely provide simple, straightforward emotional responses (e.g., "It made me feel happy!"), while older students should be exploring why it affected the feelings that it did and using both musical concepts (e.g., "It made me feel happy because it was in a major key.) and non-musical associations (e.g., "It made me feel happy because it sounded like a circus and I like to go to the circus."). Through this kind of sharing, along with teacher insights and reading about how other people have responded to music, students can explore and come to a deeper understanding of their personal responses to music, other art forms, and possibly the world.

According to the objective, having an aesthetic experience, recognizing its value, and being able to grapple with discussing or sharing that experience are not enough. It is also important to promote and develop this part of the musical and artistic experience. Teachers and students must attempt to foster an appreciation for the arts and their ability to create meaning. The arts provide an opportunity to explore and express ideas and emotions through a unique view of life experiences. It is through the experience of music, or any art form, that people begin to transcend the mundane day-to-day experience and reach beyond to a richer life experience.

The objectives that deal with music include contexts for the music, concepts and skills involved in experiencing music, and the aesthetic and personal dimensions of music. Music does not exist in a vacuum. The context (e.g., historical or cultural) of a piece of music is very important. Students should know and be able to discuss the context of music through integration of subject matter. Music ought to be experienced in every way possible. Students must be given opportunities to develop basic performance skills as well as listening skills and vocabulary for responding to music. And, to pull all of these together, teachers and students should develop their aesthetic awareness and help others to do the same. While music and the musical experience can be complex, it is important to remember these basic ideas. In the end, it is not whether someone is a professional musician or an avid listener, but that they know the wonders of music and the arts.

Drama

Drama and theatre activities offer learners opportunities to experience an art form in many different ways. Whether studying a play, mounting a production, attending a performance, or engaging in creative drama in the classroom, drama helps students to learn about themselves and their world, develop social skills, strengthen both their verbal and nonverbal communication skills, creatively problem-solve, analyze, and collaborate. Some of the benefits inherent in this instructional methodology include developing concentration skills, analyzing content, demonstrating artistic discipline, improving listening, learning to apply research, communicating information, and making and justifying artistic choices. These are important to a student's educational growth, regardless of that individual's future career. Students who have a chance to learn about and through drama are motivated; their imaginations are engaged, and their work is often quite focused.

More specific aesthetic benefits also are acquired. By participating in these activities, students learn about dramatic process and product. They acquire knowledge of theatre artists and their responsibilities. They engage in making artistic choices and learn about the personal discipline that the arts demand. Furthermore, students develop personal aesthetics that are based on informed judgments. They develop insight into cultures and communities, and better understand how this art form is manifest in both their artistic and their everyday lives.

Drama means "to do, act." Drama/theatre is an experiential way to connect to content. Students are engaged physically, mentally, and emotionally. In today's classroom, infusing these techniques into the curriculum allows for hands-on learning that is meaningful and lasting. Young people can learn not only about drama/theatre but also through the art form if it is partnered with another subject. Using these techniques helps children to understand both artistic and paired subject content.

Drama offers multiple approaches to gaining knowledge. Whether a student's preferred learning style is visual, verbal, nonverbal, aural, or tactile/kinesthetic, infusing lessons with drama/theatre expands ways of knowing, especially because of the variety of activities available. Multiple approaches to knowledge acquisition and retention help to insure that all children learn. It should be no surprise, then, that in addition to students who regularly achieve in their studies, even those who generally are less successful may thrive in classrooms where drama/theatre is a regular part of their learning environment. Teaching and learning through and with dramatic art is a unique and effective approach to instruction at all educational levels and with students of varying degrees of academic achievement.

At one end of the drama/theatre spectrum is creative drama. In this format, process is more important than product; the benefit to the participant is paramount. Creative drama is frequently used in classrooms because it is informal drama that can work in any setting and with any number of children. Scenery, costumes, and/or props are not required. These activities move from teacher-centered to student-centered, from shorter to longer activities and sessions, from unison play to individual play, and from simple beginning activities to more complex story work. Participants need little, if any, previous experience with this approach

Fast Facts

Drama and theatre activities benefit students' educational growth, regardless of their future career.

to curriculum. Once they are introduced to this pedagogy, however, both their interests and their skills will grow.

Here are definitions for the many types of activities that are components of creative drama.

Beginning Activities: These are warm-up activities such as name games, chants, listening games, and other simple exercises designed to relax and motivate participants.

Games: These are more challenging than beginning activities and often focus upon developing players' concentration, imagination, and teamwork skills. Frequently, they are played with students seated or standing in a circle.

Sequence Games: The teacher takes a story or similar material and divides it into particular events or scenes, placing each on an index card. These are randomly distributed to players. When a student recognizes his/her cue being performed, that student goes next. Index cards should have the cue at the top and the new action at the bottom, preferably in a different font or color. The teacher should keep a master list, in order, of cues. This helps students if the correct sequence is interrupted or lost.

Pantomime: Players use their bodies to communicate rather than their voices. Pantomime sentences and stories, creative movement exercises, and miming games are common examples.

Improvisations: These are spontaneously created performances based upon at least two of the following: who (characters), what (conflict), where (setting), when (time), and how (specifics of interpretation). Performed either in pantomime or with dialogue, improvisations should not be planned or rehearsed. Interesting episodes that emerge may be further developed through story creation. Role-playing improvisations deal with problem solving. Students are exposed to differing points of view by replaying and switching roles. Role-playing should not be confused with playing in-role, which is when the teacher enters the dramatization as a character.

Stories: A number of activities can be based upon stories and can range from simple to complex. In the former category, for example, are _noisy stories_. These are simple stories that players help to tell by making sounds or saying words associated with characters. _Story creation_ activities require that players develop stories, and these activities can be stimulated by various items, including props, titles, students' own writing, or true events. _Open-ended stories_ are those from which students build stories given only a beginning and then share their creations either orally, in writing, or through performance. *Story dramatization* is the most complex informal dramatic activity, as it utilizes players' previously developed skills in service to playing stories.

Several types of activities bridge the gap between creative drama and theatre for youth. These include theatre-in-education (TIE), readers' theatre, and puppetry. Each can be integrated into classroom practice.

Theatre-in-Education (TIE): Originating in Britain, Theatre-in-Education is performed by actor-teachers and students. Using material based upon curriculum or social issues, players assume roles and, through these, explore and problem-solve. TIE's structure is flexible and its focus is educational.

Puppetry: Puppets can range from simple paper bag or sock creations to elaborately constructed marionettes. Puppets can be used for creative drama and theatre activities. Likewise, puppet stages can be as simple as a desktop or table, or they can be intricately constructed with artistically designed settings and theatrical trappings.

Readers Theatre: Called Theatre of the Imagination, Readers Theatre offers performance opportunities without elaborate staging. Traditionally, this type of performance has players sitting on stools, using onstage and/or offstage focus, and employing notebooks or music stands to hold scripts. A narrator may be used and readers may or may not play multiple roles. This type of performance is wedded to literature. A common misconception, however, is that this is simply expressive reading. To truly impact an audience, Readers Theatre must be more than that. Rich characterization, suggested movement, and clear interpretation of the literature are required. In their minds' eyes, audience members complete the stage pictures suggested by the interpreters.

Children's theatre is product-oriented and audience-centered. This theatre for young people can be performed by and for children, by adults for youth, or with a combined cast of adults and young people. In addition, actors can be either amateurs or professionals. Here, dialogue is memorized, the number of characters in the play determines the cast size, and scenery and costumes are generally expected production elements.

Educators may take their students to see plays or they may wish to stage plays in their classrooms or other school facilities. In addition to the familiar format, plays for young people can also be done as participation plays and as story theatre. These last two are especially adaptable to educational venues.

Traditional Theatre: In this most commonly used form of theatre, performers and audience are separate entities. Actors use character and story to communicate and the audience responds with feedback (e.g., laughing, applauding). Typically, actors perform on a stage and are supported by others who contribute the technical elements of theatre.

Participation Theatre: Children are given opportunities to use their voices and bodies within the context of the play. They might be asked for their ideas, invited to join the actors, or given chances to contribute to the play in meaningful ways.

Story Theatre: In this format, actors can function as both characters and narrators, sometimes commenting upon their own actions in role. They can play one role or multiple parts. Scenery, if used, is minimal and costume pieces can suggest a character. Story theatre is classroom friendly and closely linked to literature.

Young people benefit from exposure to theatre, whether as participant or audience member. Opportunities abound for developing vocal skills, vocabulary, imagination, understanding of dramatic structure and types of conflict, physical skills, and empathy. Theatre offers innovative instructional options.

Theatre is not a new art form; it emerged in ancient Greece as a part of religious celebrations. The fact that theatre has evolved over centuries is a testament to its nature; it is both experimental and transitional, allowing innovative elements to be absorbed into the mainstream while continuing to look for new artistic inventions. This is not its only dichotomy. Theatre is a profession for some and an avocation for others. It is a communal and a collective art form. Regardless of its structure, theatre engages through both visual and auditory stimulation. And because it uses live actors performing for an audience that is "in the moment" with them, it can be repeated but it will never be exactly the same.

Using drama in the classroom may result in a lively educational environment. Teachers should welcome the energetic chatter and movement indicating students who are learning. They should also recognize that, in this type of experience, there might not be one correct answer or interpretation. Part of the joy and challenge of using drama in the classroom is that it pushes students to think creatively and independently. If teachers view themselves as co-explorers in this process, the journey they take with their students is both productive and fun!

Dance

It has been said, "to dance is human." How true! Dance is one of the most human of endeavors. Throughout history, dance has been rich with meaning and passion. It expresses the depths of humanness across all cultures. Dance may be looked at as a social activity, a performing art, and a creative pursuit.

Dance as a Mirror of Culture

As far back into ancient times as written records or artwork exist, we have evidence that all cultures danced. From the earliest artwork to that of today, the dancing figure is the artistic subject of many cultures. When we consider why people draw, paint, or sculpt, we learn that they portray what is important to them, or what their community or culture values. Dance is important enough to be represented in the art of most cultures from antiquity to today.

Cultural Values

When a culture values strength and power, their dance will show it. When a culture values the community over the individual, it is clear in the dance. When a culture values order and hierarchy in social structure, the dance will give evidence of the same structure. With an observant eye, one can learn a great deal about a culture by studying its dances. This section speaks to many dance-evident cultural values such as gender roles, sexuality, concepts of beauty and aesthetics, community solidarity, and creativity.

Religion

Most cultural dances are historically connected to religion. All over the world we can observe dances of devotion and worship of the deities where movements might include bowing in reverence, lifting arms to the heavens, and gestures of receiving of divine benefits. We can observe dances that tell stories of the power and conquests of deities (e.g., Egyptian, Greek, Indian, Japanese). These movements may include a wide, strong stance with fisted hands and stamping feet. It is also common to see the important stories of the gods told through dance and mime.

We can observe dances that appeal to the gods for survival. For hunting success (e.g., Native American, Inuit) movements may include pantomime of the animal and hunter and the inevitable killing of the animal. For fertile fields and lavish harvest (e.g., Hebrew, Egyptian, European) movements may include pantomime of the planting, tending, and harvesting, as well as lifting or expanding actions that suggest crop growth. For victory in war (e.g., Chinese, Roman, African) movements may include use of swords, spears, or shields and the miming of conflict and victory. In most cultures the power of the dance to cause the gods' positive response is unquestioned.

We can observe dances that ask for divine blessings on life events. For the birth of a child (e.g., African, Polynesian) the movements may include childbearing actions, cradling and "offering" the child up to the deity, and crawling, walking, and running to indicate growth of the child. For initiation into adulthood (e.g., Native American, African) the movements may include shows of strength and manhood for the male and swaying and nurturing gestures for the female. For marriage (in most cultures) movements are jubilant, reflect traditional gender roles for men and women, and may include movements that suggest sexuality and fertility. For funerals (e.g., Egyptian, Cambodian, Zimbabwean), movements may reenact the life story of the deceased and may include grieving as well as celebration of an afterlife. For many cultures, dance is the primary connection between people and their gods.

> **Dance expresses the depths of humanness across all cultures.**
>
> **Fast Facts**

Gender Roles

How should a man move? How should a woman move? Each culture answers these questions in dance. Most often the rules are unwritten, but they are clear nonetheless. In the dances of the Polynesian culture of the Cook Islands, for example, men keep a pulsing rhythm in their bodies by taking a wide stance and pumping knees open and closed. Their movements are always strong and powerful. The women stand with feet together and sway softly from side to side with undulating hips and rippling arms. In their dances, the man and woman never touch. In fact, they often dance in separate gender groups. In the ballroom dancing of European and American cultures, the man leads the woman by holding her and guiding her. She follows his lead. They move in perfect synchrony and reflect the western cultural ideal of a flawless heterosexual union (led by the man) that is effortless and perfect. Each culture defines gender-specific movements and speaks volumes about the roles of men and women through its dance.

Beauty and Aesthetics

All cultures define beauty in their own way. Dances clearly reflect that ideal (aesthetic) of beauty. Some African dances, for example, feature plump and fleshy women dancers who embody health, fertility, the earth, and beauty to their people. In the European traditional form of ballet, however, the skeletal ballerina is spotlighted to reflect the fragile, ethereal, romantic ideal of female beauty. Another contrast can be made between the traditional court dances of Bali and American Modern dance. In Bali, the court dances have existed for centuries. Dancers train for many years to perform with great serenity, balance, and symmetry. They embody the ideal beauty of Balinese culture. In contemporary America, modern dance can express the very different aesthetic of a driving, off-balance asymmetry. Each image mirrors a cultural definition of what is beautiful. We can all discover many different kinds of beauty through experiencing the dances of various cultures.

Dance as a Social Activity

Social dance has a relatively short history in the human race. Dance has always drawn people together as communicants in a common religion and as celebrants of community events in the context of religion. However, the practice of dance for the primary purpose of gathering people together to enjoy each other's company is only centuries old, rather than millennia-old. When we look at the history of social dance we can clearly see changes in social structure and accepted behavior through changes in the dances.

Folk Dances around the World

Folk dances are cultural dances that have remained quite stable for a long period of time. The music has remained constant and the movements have changed little over the years. Folk dances usually reflect the national traditions of various cultures. They evoke pride in people's traditions and culture by keeping alive the dances of their ancestors. Dancers swell with pride as they perform the dances of their forebears with others that share their heritage. Folk dances are usually about the group, not the specific dancer or couple. Folk dance is a solid connection to the past and a vehicle for "belonging." When one dances a dance, one belongs to the group that has danced that dance through the ages. For some cultures that are being absorbed into western society and swallowed by global culture, such as the Inuits of northern Canada, languages are gradually lost, traditional crafts are lost and ancient religion is lost, but the dances are the last to go. People cling to their dances as the last remnant of a shared past. For the Punjab Indians who immigrated to England in the past century, the dances of their Indian culture are so important to their understanding of their cultural heritage that all children study the dances and the people perform them at social gatherings. People dance their own culture's folk dances to understand who they are and where they came from. It is also valuable to learn the folk dances of other cultures. When we dance the dances of others, we learn about them and gain respect for them by "dancing in their shoes."

Social Dances of Western Cultures

Social dances of western cultures are usually about the couple and heterosexual courtship. In contrast with folk dance, social dances usually change over time. Through several centuries in Europe and America, changes in social dance have created a fascinating mirror of changing social attitudes toward courtship and gender. When the waltz emerged in full force on the European scene in the nineteenth century, it was soundly condemned as scandalous because the couple was for the first time dancing face to face in an embrace. However, the man continued to lead the dance and the woman followed. Each new social dance has met with similar resistance as the changes in social attitudes toward gender and sexuality have initiated new ways of moving. Embraces become closer, sexual movements become more suggestive, and clothing becomes more revealing as times and social attitudes change.

It is possible to clearly track changes in the social attitude in America by looking at the social dances of various times. The Lindy Hop of the late 1920s and 1930s is a good example. The earliest swing dance, the Lindy Hop emerged from the heart of the African-American culture of Harlem. African-Americans rightly viewed it as their dance. Its popularity grew and the mainstream white culture was fascinated. White Americans began to flock to Harlem to learn the Lindy Hop. In this time of great separation between the races, the Lindy Hop forged new connections between people of different skin color. Social strictures began to marginally break down.

Another example of the power of social dance to reflect changing social attitudes is the Twist. During the 1960s in America, the Twist emerged and took the social dance scene by storm. Its impact was felt in the fact that the couple did not have to synchronize their movements. In fact, the dancers no longer had to touch each other. Each one danced alone. This dance reflects an important social change in 1960s America when women's liberation and the civil rights movements announced that each person had equal rights regardless of gender or race. The Twist was a revolutionary dance that allowed the individual to pursue her/his own movement. Neither dancer leads or follows. What a mirror of society!

Dance as a Performing Art

Dance has played another role in history, the role of performing art. In various cultures elite groups of people are designated as dancers/performers. Their occupation is to dance before audiences. There are several examples of performing styles, old and new, among various cultures.

In Japan, Kabuki emerged as a performing art from a long history in the streets. Traditionally, men play all women's roles in elaborate makeup and costume. Highly controlled, stylized movements and lavish costumes represent favorite stories and characters. The theatre art is studied for a lifetime and the popularity of top Kabuki actors/dancers can equal the level of movie stars in Japan.

In India, the Bharata Natyam is a centuries-old dance rooted in the Hindu religion. A solo female dancer who is highly trained in this intricate form of storytelling performs the Bharata Natyam. The dancer utilizes the entire body, but especially the hands and eyes, in a very colorful and expressive dance.

From South Africa comes a style of dance called Gumboots. Out of the dark and silent gold-mines and the oppressive lives of the slave laborers emerges a style of dance performed by groups of men wearing miners' gumboots. The dancers leap, turn, and stamp their boots in well-grounded group formations. Their rhythmic and exuberant dance tells of solidarity within adversity and of the workers' amazing endurance.

Finally, out of Irish step-dancing traditions and American innovation comes the Riverdance phenomenon. In this vertically lifted, stylized Irish dancing, the dancers hold their arms tightly at their sides while making quick explosive movements of the legs. They balance mainly on their toes while creating lightning-fast tap rhythms with their hard-soled shoes in kaleidoscopic group patterns.

In Europe and America, the primary performance styles of dance are ballet, modern, jazz, and tap dance.

Ballet, a stylized form in which the body is elongated and extended into space, emerges from the royal courts of Renaissance Europe. Female dancers, or ballerinas, study for years to be able to dance "en pointe," on the tips of their toes. The romantic ballet literally elevates the ballerina to an otherworldly figure unhampered by gravity. Ballet has a long history as an elite form of dance that contains elements of the affectations of royalty. Modern forms of ballet, however, have stretched the limits of the traditional form to include many more movement possibilities.

Modern dance emerged around the turn of the twentieth century, primarily in America, as a reaction against the style restrictions of ballet. It is a "freer" form of dance in which the dancer explores and creates dance with very few stylistic limits. Modern, and now postmodern, dancers and choreographers use many existing movement styles and combine them in innovative ways to create new forms.

Jazz and tap dance emerged in America from a similar source. They both meld the dance styles of Europe, Africa, and various other cultures. Both grow from the fertile cross-cultural ground of nineteenth and twentieth century America to create new dance blends and hybrids. Jazz dance is a performing style that also borrows from American social dance and uses contemporary music, physical power, body-part isolations, and gravity to create strong and rhythmic dances. Tap dance uses metal taps attached to the toes and heels of dance shoes to create intricate and complex rhythms. These four western performing styles have greatly influenced each other throughout the twentieth and into the twenty-first centuries. Choreographers and dancers borrow from each other, style lines become blurred, and new blends between styles are common and exciting. Performing forms are constantly changing through time, but each has a cherished tradition.

It is important for teachers to expose students to many kinds of dance and for students to make cultural connections. Dance is also fun and a good form of exercise. The next section discusses its use in the classroom.

Dance as a Creative Pursuit

The more we use creative movement in the classroom, the greater the learning potential. As students create, they learn about the world, about others, and about themselves.

The Body as the Medium

Dance is an art that requires only the human body, standard equipment for all children. No pen, paintbrush, or musical instrument is needed. As children explore the basics of movement (body, space, time, and relationship), they gain the movement vocabulary to express themselves more and more eloquently. Mastery of the body as a creative medium should be a primary goal in dance education.

Dance Content

Usually, dances are about something. They often have identifiable content. Most dances create meaning in some form, even when quite abstract. When a human being creates a dance, he or she may be expressing such diverse ideas as: community, literary conflict, properties of magnets, regular or irregular rhythms, mathematical patterns, or visual design. A dancer/choreographer may be exploring feelings such as: alienation, comfort, precision, smooth or bumpy flow, anger, or peace. A choreographer may also be sharing experiences through dance by telling a story or by creating an environment that arises from their life experience. Students are encouraged to create meaning in dance by expressing ideas, exploring feelings, or sharing experiences learn a great deal about themselves while developing their creative problem-solving skills.

Dance in the Classroom and across the Curriculum

Why isn't there more dancing in the schools? General classroom teachers may feel inadequate to teach dance but maybe they define dance too narrowly as merely patterns of intricate steps. Dance in the elementary schools should be about creative movement. Any sensitive teacher can guide students through creative movement that builds upon classroom learning.

For example, in language arts, students can learn spelling and vocabulary words by groups spelling words with their bodies or acting out the meaning of the word. They can *embody* the concept of opposites, for example, by exploring (alone or with a partner) heavy/light, near/far, curved/angular, or symmetrical/asymmetrical. Students can also dance the character or mime the story they are studying.

Movement and math also share much ground. Creative movement studies can use repetition and rhythm to count in multiples or can use partner body sculptures to reflect symmetry and asymmetry, for example.

Science studies can include exploration of gravity, creating a group machine, demonstrating the flow of electrical currents and circuits, or moving within the properties of various types of clouds.

Social studies supply many rich ideas for creative movement, too. Some movement ideas include drawing a map of the classroom and creating a movement "journey" or exploring various occupations, transportation forms, or types of communities through creative movement. Folk dances are always a powerful means to experience other cultures.

Summary

Dance is a powerful force in human life that can express and teach about others, our world, and our selves. Dance is a mirror of culture, cultural values, religion, gender roles, and concepts of beauty. Dance is a social activity that draws people together into belonging and expresses community through folk dance and social dance. Dance is a performing art in many cultures, reflecting cultural ideals through choreography and performance. And finally, dance is a creative pursuit that uses creative problem solving to transform body movement into meaning: expressing ideas, exploring feelings, and sharing experiences. Dance is a powerful teaching tool that can bridge the disciplines of the curriculum.

Health and Physical Education

The health and physical education review section offers a perspective on the importance of maintaining a healthy mind and body as well as demonstrating how the two work in conjunction. This section includes discussions of cardiovascular fitness, nutrition, team sports, and the role of athletics. Preparing your mind through study will leave you in great shape to succeed on test day.

Movement and Physical Fitness

Understand principles, concepts, and practices related to movement and physical fitness and the role of physical activity in promoting students' personal and social development.

For example:
- Demonstrate understanding of fundamental motor, body control, and perceptual awareness skills and appropriate movement activities to promote the physical development of all students.
- Apply knowledge of basic principles and concepts of physical fitness (e.g., frequency, intensity, duration of training), the components of fitness (e.g., cardiovascular endurance, flexibility, muscular strength, body composition), and practices and activities that promote lifelong fitness and stress reduction.
- Recognize skill progressions, safety practices, equipment, strategies, rules, and appropriate behaviors for individual, group, and team activities and sports.
- Analyze how physical education activities can promote the development of personal, social, and workplace skills (e.g., responsibility, leadership, team building, perseverance, confidence, cooperation, fairness).

- Demonstrate knowledge of the interactions between physical, emotional, and social well-being and the importance of movement and fitness experiences in establishing productive, lifelong habits and behaviors.
- Apply knowledge of considerations and procedures in selecting and using various activities, instructional resources, and technologies to promote students' physical development and wellness.

Principles of Cardiovascular Fitness

Cardiovascular fitness, or aerobic capacity, is composed of four basic components: strength and power; endurance; movement speed and flexibility; and agility. Training is required to develop consistent aerobic capacity, and training is composed of several principles. To begin, a warm-up is essential. An effective warm-up will increase body temperature and blood flow, and it will guard against strains and tears to muscles, tendons, and ligaments. A good warm-up consists of stretching exercises, calisthenics, walking, and slow jogging. Although children have trouble understanding the importance of warm-up, they should get into the habit of doing it, because it will be particularly important as they grow older.

While exercising, a student must be aware of his or her body's adaptations to the demands imposed by training. Some of these adaptations are improved heart function and circulation, improved respiratory function, and improved strength and endurance. All of these lead to improved vigor and vitality. In order to effect these adaptations, the students must exert themselves to a far greater degree than their normal daily activities. This exertion is referred to as **overload**. Despite what this term suggests, it does not imply that children should work beyond healthy limits. However, it does imply that they must push themselves in order to see results. The rate of improvement and adaptation is directly related to the frequency, intensity, and duration of training.

In addition to regular training, you must gear your students' training toward those adaptations that are important to them. This is known as **specificity**. Performance improves when the training is specific to the activity being performed. That is, certain activities will have more effect on cardiovascular health than on overall muscle tone and appearance, and vice versa. Therefore, you should always try to maintain a balance in the exercise you assign.

The body thrives on activity, and therefore the axiom "use it or lose it" certainly holds true. Lack of activity can cause many problems, including flabby muscles, a weak heart, poor circulation, shortness of breath, obesity, and a degenerative weakening of the skeletal system.

Finally, a good program of exercise always ends with a cooling-off period. Very much like the warm-up, and just as essential, the same low-impact exercises used during a warm-up may be used to cool off after a period of intense exertion. Without cooling off, blood will pool and slow the removal of waste products. With this basic introduction in mind, let's look at some more specific forms of exercise and the positive effects they have on the body.

Aerobic Exercise

Aerobic exercise involves both muscle contraction and movement of the body. Aerobic exercise requires large amounts of oxygen and, when done regularly, will condition the cardiovascular system. Some aerobic exercises are especially suited to developing aerobic training benefits, with a minimum of skill and time involved. Examples of good aerobic activities are walking, running, swimming, rope skipping, and bicycling. These activities are especially good in the development of fitness because all of them can be done alone and with a minimum of special equipment. In order to be considered true aerobic conditioning, an activity must require a great deal of oxygen, must be continuous and rhythmic, must exercise major muscle groups and burn fat as an energy source, and must last for at least 20 minutes at an individual's target heart rate. You may determine the target heart rate by subtracting 80% of your age from 220 for adolescents; healthy younger children do not need to be restricted to an arbitrary limit on heart rate during exercise.

Interval training is also a good way to develop fitness. This type of exercise involves several different aerobic activities performed at intervals to create one exercise session. If a student learns about interval training, she will be better able to create her own fitness program.

Low-Impact Aerobics

For some people, low-impact aerobics may have some advantages over traditional, or high-impact, aerobics. Because low-impact aerobic exercise is easier to perform, it is an option for all ages and levels of fitness. It is easier to monitor heart rate, and there is less warm-up and cool-down required. Because one foot is on the ground at all times, there is less chance of injury. In all other respects, such as duration and frequency, low-impact aerobic exercise is identical to high-impact.

Anatomy and Physiology

Anatomy describes the structure, position, and size of various organs. Because our bones adapt to fill a specific need, exercise is of great benefit to the skeletal system. Bones that anchor strong muscles thicken to withstand the stress. Weight-bearing bones can develop heavy mineral deposits while supporting the body. Because joints help provide flexibility and ease of movement, it is important to know how each joint moves. Types of joints are ball and socket (shoulder and hip), hinge (knee), pivot (head of the spine), gliding (carpal and tarsal bones), angular (wrist and ankle joints), partially moveable (vertebrae), and immovable (bones of the adult cranium).

Muscles are the active movers in the body. In order to teach any physical education activity properly, the functions and physiology of the muscles must be understood. Since muscles move by shortening, or contracting, proper form should be taught so the student can get the most out of an activity. It is also important to know the location of each muscle. This knowledge will help in teaching proper form while doing all physical education activities. Understanding the concept of antagonistic muscles, along with the related information concerning flexors and extensors, is also vital to the physical educator. Imagine trying to teach the proper form of throwing a ball if you do not understand the mechanics involved. Knowledge of anatomy and physiology is also necessary to teach proper techniques used in calisthenics as well as in all physical activities. Some physical education class standbys are frequently done improperly or done when the exercise itself can cause harm. Examples of these are squat thrusts, straight-leg sit-ups, straight-leg toe touches, straight-leg push-ups for girls, and double leg lifts.

Sports and Games

Individual, dual, and team sports all have a prominent place in a successful physical education curriculum. Since one of the attributes of a quality physical education program is its carryover value, it is easy to justify the inclusion of these activities in a curriculum. Learning the rules and keeping score supplies a framework for goals and for learning how to deal with both victory and defeat. Here are examples of some sports and games that are useful to achieve the aforementioned goals:

Team Sports

- Volleyball—six players, two out of three games. Winner scores 25 points with a margin of 2.

- Basketball—five players. Most points at the end of the game wins.

- Softball—9 or 10 players. Most runs at the end of seven innings wins.

- Field hockey—11 players. Most goals wins.

- Soccer—11 players. Most goals wins.

- Flag football—9 or 11 players (can be modified to fit ability and size of the class). Six points for a touchdown, one or two for a point after, and two for a safety.

Dual Sports

- Tennis—Either doubles or singles. Four "points"—15, 30, 40, and game. Tie at forty—deuce. Winner must win by a margin of two. Remember, *love* means zero points in tennis.

- Badminton—Either doubles or singles. 15 points (doubles) or 21 (singles) by a margin of 2.

- Table tennis—Either doubles or singles. 21 points by a margin of 2.

- Shuffleboard—Either singles or doubles. 50, 75, or 100 points, determined by participants before the game begins.

Individual Sports

- Swimming—Very good for cardiovascular conditioning and can be done almost anywhere there is water.

- Track and field—Scoring varies with event.

- Bowling—Scoring is unique; good math skills are encouraged.

- Weight training—No scoring involved, but the benefits are many. Muscles are toned and strengthened through the use of weight training. Either weight machines or free weights can be used. It is important for students to learn the proper techniques and principles of weight training so they can reap the benefits while avoiding injury. When weight training, participants must consider the concept of muscular balance—this is equal strength in opposing muscle groups. All opposing groups (antagonistic muscles), i.e., triceps and biceps, hamstrings and quadriceps, need to be equal or body parts may become improperly aligned. The responsibility of the physical educator is to teach accurate information about the human body as well as teach ways to prevent injury and achieve efficiency in movement. Understanding that abdominal strength is important to lower back strength can help students create an exercise program to help avoid back injuries.

- Gymnastics—Includes tumbling. Excellent activity for developing coordination and grace. Also requires strength, which is developed by the activities done. This training can begin at a very early age with tumbling activities and progress to gymnastics.

- Golf—A fantastic carryover activity that can be taught on campus, at the golf course, or both. Requires coordination, concentration, and depth perception.

- Rhythmics—Includes ball gymnastics and other activities that may require music. Rhythmics can be taught in early elementary physical education, enabling students to develop music appreciation as well as spatial awareness.

- Dance—Can be done either individually or with a partner. Dance is especially good at developing spatial awareness and the ability to follow instructions. Dance instruction should begin in elementary school. Basic steps are walk and/or skip and are suitable to teach to first and second graders. Skip, slide, and/or run are suitable for second and third graders. The more difficult step-hop can be taught to grades 3 through 6. The ability to dance can also aid in the development of social skills and teamwork. The instructor must be careful not to teach too many steps before the dance is tried with the music. Most students enjoy dance in spite of themselves.

Adaptive Physical Education

Public Law 94-142 provides the legal definition for the term "handicapped children." It includes children who have been evaluated as being mentally impaired, deaf, speech impaired, visually handicapped, emotionally disturbed, orthopedically impaired, multi-handicapped, having learning disabilities, or having other health impairments (anemia, arthritis, etc.). PL 94-142 states that these children need special education and services. The challenge in teaching physical education to handicapped children is tailoring activities to fit each child. For example, blind or partially sighted students can participate in weight lifting, dance, and some gymnastic and tumbling activities. These students can also participate in some other activities with modifications. A beeper ball can be used for softball; a beeper can be used for archery. If a beeper is not available for archery, the teacher can put the student in position and assist in aiming. Many games and activities can be modified for the handicapped. Sometimes all it takes is a little ingenuity to change activities so that handicapped students can enjoy participating.

There are many students who are only temporarily disabled who will benefit from adaptive physical education. Examples of temporary disabilities are pregnancy, broken bones, and recovery from surgery and disease.

Movement Education

Movement education is the process by which a child is helped to develop competency in movement. It has been defined as "learning to move and moving to learn." Movement competency requires the student to manage his or her body. This body management is necessary to develop both basic and specialized activities. Basic skills are needed by the child for broad areas of activity that are related to daily living and child's play. Specialized skills are required to perform sports and have very clear techniques. Basic skills must be mastered before the child can develop specialized ones. The child controls his movement during nonlocomotor (stationary) activities, in movements across the floor or field, through space, and when suspended on an apparatus. To obtain good body management skills is to acquire, expand, and integrate elements of motor control. This is done through wide experiences in movement, based on a creative and exploratory approach. It is important that children not only manage the body with ease of movement but also realize that good posture and body mechanics are important parts of their movement patterns.

Perceptual motor competency is another consideration in body management. Perceptual motor concepts that are relevant to physical education include those that give attention to balance, coordination, lateral movement, directional movement, awareness of space, and knowledge of one's own body. Basic skills can be divided into three categories: locomotor, nonlocomotor, and manipulative skills. A movement pattern might include skills from each category.

Locomotor skills involve moving the body from place to place: walking, running, skipping, leaping, galloping, and sliding. Skills that move the body upward, such as jumping or hopping, are also locomotor skills.

Nonlocomotor skills are done in place or with very little spatial movement. Examples of nonlocomotor skills are bending and stretching, pushing and pulling, raising and lowering, twisting and turning, and shaking and bouncing.

Manipulative skills are skills used when the child handles a play object. Most manipulative skills involve using the hands and the feet, but other parts of the body may be used as well. Hand-eye and foot-eye coordination are improved with manipulative objects. Throwing, batting, kicking, and catching are important skills to be developed using balls and beanbags. Starting a child at a low level of challenge and progressing to a more difficult activity is an effective method for teaching manipulative activities. Most activities begin with individual practice and later move to partner activities. Partners should be of similar ability. When teaching throwing and catching, the teacher should emphasize skill performance, principles of opposition, weight transfer, eye focus, and follow-through. Some attention should be given to targets when throwing because students need to be able to catch and throw to different levels. Reaching is a "point-to-point" arm movement that is very common in our daily activities. In fact, reaching and grasping are typically used together to serve a number of purposes, such as eating, drinking, dressing, or cooking. The reaching/grasping task requires an "eye-hand" coordination and control of movement timing for a successful attempt.

Specialized skills are related to various sports and other physical education activities such as dance, tumbling, gymnastics, and specific games. To teach a specialized skill, the instructor must use explanation, demonstration, and drill. Demonstration can be done by other students, provided the teacher monitors the demonstration and gives cues for proper form. Drills are excellent to teach specific skills but can become tedious unless they are done in a creative manner. Using game simulations to practice skills is an effective method to maintain interest during a practice session.

Teachers must always remember to use feedback when teaching a skill or activity. Positive feedback is much more conducive to skill learning than negative feedback. Feedback means correcting with suggestions to improve. If a student continually hits the ball into the net while playing tennis, he or she is aware that something is not right. The teacher should indicate what the problem is and tell the student how to succeed in getting the ball over the net.

Movement education enables the child to make choices of activity and the method they wish to employ. Teachers can structure learning situations so the child can be challenged to develop his or her own means of movement. The child becomes the center of learning and is encouraged to be creative in carrying out the movement experience. In this method of teaching, the child is encouraged to be creative and progress according to her abilities. The teacher is not the center of learning, but suggests and stimulates the learning environment. Student-centered learning works especially well when there is a wide disparity of motor abilities. If the teacher sets standards that are too high for the less talented students, they may become discouraged and not try to perform.

Basic movement education attempts to develop the children's awareness not only of what they are doing but also how they are doing it. Each child is encouraged to succeed in his or her own way according to his or her own capacity. If children succeed at developing basic skills in elementary school, they will have a much better chance at acquiring the specialized skills required for all sports activities.

Psychological and Social Aspects of Physical Education

Physical education is a very important part of a student's elementary school education. It is not only an opportunity to "blow off steam," but it is also an arena of social interaction. One psychological aspect of physical education is the enhancement of self-esteem. Often students who have limited success in other classes can "shine" in physical education. This does not happen automatically; it is up to the teacher to create situations that enable students to gain self-esteem.

Teachers must also be careful not to damage self-esteem. An example of a potentially damaging situation occurs during the exercise of choosing members of a team. Teachers should not have captains choose the teams in front of the whole class. Nothing is more demeaning than to be the last person chosen. A better method is for the teacher to select the captains (this is also a very good way to separate the superstars: have the six best athletes be the captains). The captains then go to the sidelines and pick the teams from a class list. The teacher can then post or read the team lists after mixing up the order chosen so that no one knows who were the first and last picked.

From a developmental perspective, research suggests that children's participation in exercise or sports results in a number of long-term benefits, including the improvement of self-esteem, or self-confidence for social interactions; the development of sport leadership and sportsmanship; and motivation for participating in lifetime physical activities.

Health and Safety

Understand principles and practices related to personal, family, and community health and safety and ways to provide students with knowledge and skills that will help them make sound health-related decisions.

For example:

- Apply knowledge of basic principles of nutrition and the effects of food choices on health, and the benefits of good hygiene, adequate sleep and rest, and regular physical activity.
- Demonstrate knowledge of principles and techniques of conflict resolution and its relationship to health and well being.
- Apply knowledge of principles and strategies for accident prevention and risk reduction (e.g., making healthy choices by applying communication, self-monitoring, self-control, decision-making, and safety skills).
- Demonstrate understanding of factors that affect personal, interpersonal, family, and community health (e.g., pollution, cost of health care), and the implications and consequences of health risks for individuals and society.
- Recognize the roles of various health care providers, agencies, and organizations; sources of information about children's and family services; and techniques and criteria for evaluating the reliability and validity of health information and resources.
- Apply knowledge of how to select and use various activities, instructional resources, and technologies to promote students' development of skills that contribute to health and safety.

Benefits of Diet and Exercise

One of the primary reasons for teaching physical education is to instill a willingness to exercise. To that end, it is important to understand the benefits of participating in a lifelong program of exercise and physical fitness.

Fortunately, it is not difficult to find justification for exercising and maintaining a consistently high level of fitness. The benefits of a consistent program of diet and exercise are many. Improved cardiac output, improved maximum oxygen intake, and improvement of the blood's ability to carry oxygen are just a few. Exercise also lowers the risk of heart disease by strengthening the heart muscle, lowering pulse and blood pressure, and lowering the concentration of fat in both the body and the blood. It can also improve appearance, increase range of motion, and lessen the risk of back problems associated with weak bones and osteoporosis.

Good Nutrition

Along with exercise, a knowledge of and participation in a healthy lifestyle are vital to good health and longevity. Good nutrition, vitamins, elimination of risk factors, and strategies to control weight are all part of a healthy lifestyle.

Complex carbohydrates should constitute at least half the diet. This is important because these nutrients are the primary and most efficient source of energy. Examples of complex carbohydrates are vegetables, fruits, high-fiber breads, and cereals. Fiber in the diet is very important because it promotes digestion, reduces constipation, and has been shown to help reduce the risk of colon cancer. Another benefit of complex carbohydrates is that they are high in water content, which is vital to the functioning of the entire body.

Proteins should constitute about one-fifth of the diet. Protein builds and repairs the body. Sources of protein are beans, peas, lentils, peanuts, and other pod plants. Another source is red meat, which unfortunately contains a great deal of saturated fat.

There are two categories of fat: unsaturated, which is found in vegetables, and saturated, which comes from animals or vegetables. Cocoa butter, palm oil, and coconut oil are saturated fats that come from vegetables. Unsaturated vegetable fats are preferable to saturated fats because they appear to offset the rise in blood pressure that accompanies too much saturated fat. These fats may also lower cholesterol and help with weight loss. Whole milk products contain saturated fat, but the calcium found in them is vital to health. For this reason, most fat-limiting diets suggest the use of skim milk and low-fat cheese.

Research indicates a link between high-fat diets and many types of cancer. Diets high in saturated fats are also dangerous because fats cause the body to produce too much low-density lipoprotein in the system. Cholesterol, a substance found only in animals, is of two different kinds: LDL (low-density lipoproteins) and HDL (high-density lipoproteins). Some cholesterol is essential in order for the body to function properly. It is vital to the brain and is an important component in the creation of certain hormones. LDLs raise the probability of heart disease by encouraging the buildup of plaque in the arteries. HDLs do just the opposite. LDL can be controlled through proper diet, and HDL cholesterol levels can be raised by exercise. The body produces cholesterol in the liver. Excess cholesterol found in the blood of so many people usually comes from cholesterol in their diet rather than from internal production. Triglycerides are another form of fat found in the blood. It is important to monitor them because high triglycerides seem to be inversely proportional to HDLs.

Vitamins and Minerals

Vitamins are essential to good health. One must be careful, however, not to take too much of certain vitamins. Fat soluble vitamins—A, D, E, and K—will be stored in the body, and excessive amounts will cause some dangerous side effects. The remaining vitamins are water soluble and are generally excreted through the urinary system and the skin when taken in excess. A brief synopsis of the vitamins and minerals needed by the body follows:

- Vitamin A: Needed for normal vision, prevention of night blindness, healthy skin, resistance to disease, and tissue growth and repair. Found in spinach, carrots, broccoli and other dark green or yellow orange fruits and vegetables; also found in liver and plums.

- Vitamin D: Promotes absorption of calcium and phosphorus, and needed for normal growth of healthy bones, teeth, and nails. Formed by the action of the sun on the skin. Also found in halibut liver oil, herring, cod liver oil, mackerel, salmon, and tuna, and is added to many milk products.

- Vitamin E: Protects cell membranes; seems to improve elasticity in blood vessels; also may prevent formation of blood clots and protect red blood cells from damage by oxidation. Found in wheat germ oil, sunflower seeds, raw wheat germ, almonds, pecans, peanut oil, and cod liver oil.

- Thiamin/B_1: Needed for functioning of nerves, muscle growth, and fertility and for production of energy, appetite, and digestion. Found in pork, legumes, nuts, enriched and fortified whole grains, and liver.

- Riboflavin/B_2: Aids in the production of red blood cells, good vision, healthy skin and mouth tissue, and production of energy. Found in lean meat, dairy products, liver, eggs, enriched and fortified whole grains, and green leafy vegetables.

- Niacin/B_3: Promotes energy production, appetite, healthy digestive and nervous system, and healthy skin.

- Pyridoxine/B_6: Promotes red blood cell formation and growth. Found in liver, beans, pork, fish, legumes, enriched and fortified whole grains, and green leafy vegetables.

- Vitamin B_{12}: Promotes healthy nerve tissue, energy production, utilization of folic acid; also aids in the formation of healthy red blood cells. Found in dairy products, liver, meat, poultry, fish, and eggs.

- Vitamin C: Promotes healing and growth, resists infection, increases iron absorption, and aids in bone and tooth formation/repair. Found in citrus fruits, cantaloupe, potatoes, strawberries, tomatoes, and green vegetables.

- Sodium: Maintains normal water balance inside and outside cells; is a factor in blood pressure regulation and electrolyte and chemical balance. Found in salt, processed foods, bread, and bakery products.

- Potassium: Prevents muscle weakness and cramping; important for normal heart rhythm and electrolyte balance in the blood. Found in citrus fruits, bananas, leafy green vegetables, potatoes, and tomatoes.

- Zinc: Maintains taste, appetite, healthy skin, and wound healing. Found in lean meat, liver, milk, fish, poultry, whole grain cereals, and shellfish.

- Iron: Needed for red blood cell formation, oxygen transport to the cells; prevents nutritional anemia. Found in liver, lean meats, dried beans, peas, eggs, dark green leafy vegetables, and whole grain cereals.

- Calcium: Promotes strong bones, teeth, nails, muscle tone; prevents osteoporosis and muscle cramping; helps the nerves function and the heart beat. Found in milk, yogurt, and other dairy products, and dark leafy vegetables.

- Phosphorus: Regulates blood chemistry and internal processes; helps build strong bones and teeth. Found in meat, fish, poultry, and dairy products.

- Magnesium: Energy production, normal heart rhythm, nerve/muscle function; prevents muscle cramps. Found in dried beans, nuts, whole grains, bananas, and leafy green vegetables.

Weight Control Strategies

Statistics show that Americans get fatter every year. Even though countless books and magazine articles are written on the subject of weight control, often the classroom is the only place a student gets reliable information about diet. For example, it is an unfortunate reality that fat people do not live as long, on average, as thin ones. Being overweight has been isolated as a risk factor in various cancers, heart disease, gall bladder problems, and kidney disease. Chronic diseases such as diabetes and high blood pressure are also aggravated by, or caused by, being overweight.

Conversely, a great many problems are presented by being underweight. Our society often places too much value on losing weight, especially for women. Ideal weight as well as a good body-fat ratio is the goal when losing weight. Exercise is the key to a good body-fat ratio. Exercise helps to keep the ratio down, thus improving cholesterol levels, and helps in preventing heart disease.

In order to lose weight, calories burned must exceed calories taken in. No matter what kind of diet is tried, this principle applies. There is no easy way to maintain a healthy weight. Here again, the key is exercise. If calorie intake is restricted too much, the body goes into starvation mode and operates by burning fewer calories. Just a 250-calorie drop per day combined with a 250-calorie burn will result in a loss of one pound a week. Crash diets, which bring about rapid weight loss, are not only unhealthy but also ineffective. Slower weight loss is more lasting. Aerobic exercise is the key to successful weight loss. Exercise speeds up metabolism and causes the body to burn calories. Timing of exercise will improve the benefits. Exercise before meals speeds up metabolism and has been shown to suppress appetite. Losing and maintaining weight is not easy. Through education, people will be better able to realize that losing weight is hard work and is a constant battle.

Another aspect of health concerns awareness and avoidance of the health risks that are present in our everyday lives. Some risk factors include being overweight, smoking, using drugs, having unprotected sex, and stress. Students should learn the consequences of using drugs, both legal and illegal, and they should learn at least one of the several ways to reduce stress that are commonly used in most elementary schools. Education is the key to minimizing the presence of these risk factors. Unfortunately, because of the presence of peer pressure and the lack of parental control, the effect of education is sometimes not enough.

Family Health

The role of the family in health education deserves special consideration. The "family" includes people who provide unconditional love, understanding, long-term commitment, and encouragement. Variations in family living patterns in our society include, for example, nuclear and extended families, single-parent families, and blended families. Children from all types of families deserve equal consideration and respect; they should get it at least in the classroom, because they often do not in the larger society.

Community Health

The health of students and their families depends not only on individual and family decisions, but on the factors involving the wider society. One of these factors is advertising, which often encourages children to make unhealthy decisions. Students as young as kindergarten and first grade can learn how to recognize advertisements (e.g., for candy or sugar-laden cereal) that might lead them to unhealthy behavior, and by third or fourth grade, they should be able to demonstrate that they are able to make health-related decisions regarding advertisements in various media.

In addition, any studies of the physical environment—in science, social studies, or other subjects—should be related to health whenever possible. Examples include the effects of pollution on health, occupational-related disease (e.g., "black lung" disease and the effects of chemicals on soldiers), and the differences in health care options available to people in different parts of the world and in different economic circumstances.

Differentiation between communicable and noncommunicable disease can be taught at the youngest grade levels. Very young children should learn to wash their hands frequently, for instance. Older children should be able to explain the transmission and prevention of communicable disease, and all children should learn which diseases cannot be transmitted through casual contact.

ICTS

Illinois Certification Testing System
Elementary/Middle Grades

Practice Test

This test is also on CD-ROM in our special interactive ICTS TestWare®. It is highly recommended that you first take this exam on computer. You will then have the additional study features and benefits of enforced timed conditions and instant scoring. See page xii for guidance on how to get the most out of our ICTS book and software.

Answer Sheet

1. Ⓐ Ⓑ Ⓒ Ⓓ	33. Ⓐ Ⓑ Ⓒ Ⓓ	65. Ⓐ Ⓑ Ⓒ Ⓓ	97. Ⓐ Ⓑ Ⓒ Ⓓ
2. Ⓐ Ⓑ Ⓒ Ⓓ	34. Ⓐ Ⓑ Ⓒ Ⓓ	66. Ⓐ Ⓑ Ⓒ Ⓓ	98. Ⓐ Ⓑ Ⓒ Ⓓ
3. Ⓐ Ⓑ Ⓒ Ⓓ	35. Ⓐ Ⓑ Ⓒ Ⓓ	67. Ⓐ Ⓑ Ⓒ Ⓓ	99. Ⓐ Ⓑ Ⓒ Ⓓ
4. Ⓐ Ⓑ Ⓒ Ⓓ	36. Ⓐ Ⓑ Ⓒ Ⓓ	68. Ⓐ Ⓑ Ⓒ Ⓓ	100. Ⓐ Ⓑ Ⓒ Ⓓ
5. Ⓐ Ⓑ Ⓒ Ⓓ	37. Ⓐ Ⓑ Ⓒ Ⓓ	69. Ⓐ Ⓑ Ⓒ Ⓓ	101. Ⓐ Ⓑ Ⓒ Ⓓ
6. Ⓐ Ⓑ Ⓒ Ⓓ	38. Ⓐ Ⓑ Ⓒ Ⓓ	70. Ⓐ Ⓑ Ⓒ Ⓓ	102. Ⓐ Ⓑ Ⓒ Ⓓ
7. Ⓐ Ⓑ Ⓒ Ⓓ	39. Ⓐ Ⓑ Ⓒ Ⓓ	71. Ⓐ Ⓑ Ⓒ Ⓓ	103. Ⓐ Ⓑ Ⓒ Ⓓ
8. Ⓐ Ⓑ Ⓒ Ⓓ	40. Ⓐ Ⓑ Ⓒ Ⓓ	72. Ⓐ Ⓑ Ⓒ Ⓓ	104. Ⓐ Ⓑ Ⓒ Ⓓ
9. Ⓐ Ⓑ Ⓒ Ⓓ	41. Ⓐ Ⓑ Ⓒ Ⓓ	73. Ⓐ Ⓑ Ⓒ Ⓓ	105. Ⓐ Ⓑ Ⓒ Ⓓ
10. Ⓐ Ⓑ Ⓒ Ⓓ	42. Ⓐ Ⓑ Ⓒ Ⓓ	74. Ⓐ Ⓑ Ⓒ Ⓓ	106. Ⓐ Ⓑ Ⓒ Ⓓ
11. Ⓐ Ⓑ Ⓒ Ⓓ	43. Ⓐ Ⓑ Ⓒ Ⓓ	75. Ⓐ Ⓑ Ⓒ Ⓓ	107. Ⓐ Ⓑ Ⓒ Ⓓ
12. Ⓐ Ⓑ Ⓒ Ⓓ	44. Ⓐ Ⓑ Ⓒ Ⓓ	76. Ⓐ Ⓑ Ⓒ Ⓓ	108. Ⓐ Ⓑ Ⓒ Ⓓ
13. Ⓐ Ⓑ Ⓒ Ⓓ	45. Ⓐ Ⓑ Ⓒ Ⓓ	77. Ⓐ Ⓑ Ⓒ Ⓓ	109. Ⓐ Ⓑ Ⓒ Ⓓ
14. Ⓐ Ⓑ Ⓒ Ⓓ	46. Ⓐ Ⓑ Ⓒ Ⓓ	78. Ⓐ Ⓑ Ⓒ Ⓓ	110. Ⓐ Ⓑ Ⓒ Ⓓ
15. Ⓐ Ⓑ Ⓒ Ⓓ	47. Ⓐ Ⓑ Ⓒ Ⓓ	79. Ⓐ Ⓑ Ⓒ Ⓓ	111. Ⓐ Ⓑ Ⓒ Ⓓ
16. Ⓐ Ⓑ Ⓒ Ⓓ	48. Ⓐ Ⓑ Ⓒ Ⓓ	80. Ⓐ Ⓑ Ⓒ Ⓓ	112. Ⓐ Ⓑ Ⓒ Ⓓ
17. Ⓐ Ⓑ Ⓒ Ⓓ	49. Ⓐ Ⓑ Ⓒ Ⓓ	81. Ⓐ Ⓑ Ⓒ Ⓓ	113. Ⓐ Ⓑ Ⓒ Ⓓ
18. Ⓐ Ⓑ Ⓒ Ⓓ	50. Ⓐ Ⓑ Ⓒ Ⓓ	82. Ⓐ Ⓑ Ⓒ Ⓓ	114. Ⓐ Ⓑ Ⓒ Ⓓ
19. Ⓐ Ⓑ Ⓒ Ⓓ	51. Ⓐ Ⓑ Ⓒ Ⓓ	83. Ⓐ Ⓑ Ⓒ Ⓓ	115. Ⓐ Ⓑ Ⓒ Ⓓ
20. Ⓐ Ⓑ Ⓒ Ⓓ	52. Ⓐ Ⓑ Ⓒ Ⓓ	84. Ⓐ Ⓑ Ⓒ Ⓓ	116. Ⓐ Ⓑ Ⓒ Ⓓ
21. Ⓐ Ⓑ Ⓒ Ⓓ	53. Ⓐ Ⓑ Ⓒ Ⓓ	85. Ⓐ Ⓑ Ⓒ Ⓓ	117. Ⓐ Ⓑ Ⓒ Ⓓ
22. Ⓐ Ⓑ Ⓒ Ⓓ	54. Ⓐ Ⓑ Ⓒ Ⓓ	86. Ⓐ Ⓑ Ⓒ Ⓓ	118. Ⓐ Ⓑ Ⓒ Ⓓ
23. Ⓐ Ⓑ Ⓒ Ⓓ	55. Ⓐ Ⓑ Ⓒ Ⓓ	87. Ⓐ Ⓑ Ⓒ Ⓓ	119. Ⓐ Ⓑ Ⓒ Ⓓ
24. Ⓐ Ⓑ Ⓒ Ⓓ	56. Ⓐ Ⓑ Ⓒ Ⓓ	88. Ⓐ Ⓑ Ⓒ Ⓓ	120. Ⓐ Ⓑ Ⓒ Ⓓ
25. Ⓐ Ⓑ Ⓒ Ⓓ	57. Ⓐ Ⓑ Ⓒ Ⓓ	89. Ⓐ Ⓑ Ⓒ Ⓓ	121. Ⓐ Ⓑ Ⓒ Ⓓ
26. Ⓐ Ⓑ Ⓒ Ⓓ	58. Ⓐ Ⓑ Ⓒ Ⓓ	90. Ⓐ Ⓑ Ⓒ Ⓓ	122. Ⓐ Ⓑ Ⓒ Ⓓ
27. Ⓐ Ⓑ Ⓒ Ⓓ	59. Ⓐ Ⓑ Ⓒ Ⓓ	91. Ⓐ Ⓑ Ⓒ Ⓓ	123. Ⓐ Ⓑ Ⓒ Ⓓ
28. Ⓐ Ⓑ Ⓒ Ⓓ	60. Ⓐ Ⓑ Ⓒ Ⓓ	92. Ⓐ Ⓑ Ⓒ Ⓓ	124. Ⓐ Ⓑ Ⓒ Ⓓ
29. Ⓐ Ⓑ Ⓒ Ⓓ	61. Ⓐ Ⓑ Ⓒ Ⓓ	93. Ⓐ Ⓑ Ⓒ Ⓓ	125. Ⓐ Ⓑ Ⓒ Ⓓ
30. Ⓐ Ⓑ Ⓒ Ⓓ	62. Ⓐ Ⓑ Ⓒ Ⓓ	94. Ⓐ Ⓑ Ⓒ Ⓓ	
31. Ⓐ Ⓑ Ⓒ Ⓓ	63. Ⓐ Ⓑ Ⓒ Ⓓ	95. Ⓐ Ⓑ Ⓒ Ⓓ	
32. Ⓐ Ⓑ Ⓒ Ⓓ	64. Ⓐ Ⓑ Ⓒ Ⓓ	96. Ⓐ Ⓑ Ⓒ Ⓓ	

Practice Test: Elementary/Middle Grades

Time: 5 hours

In this section, you will find examples of test questions similar to those you are likely to encounter on the ICTS.

DIRECTIONS: Choose the word that best fills the blank.

1. When reading, the semantic cueing system refers to _____.

    A. the meaning system of language

    B. the structural system of language

    C. the letter-sound relationships in written language

    D. the social and cultural aspects of language

2. When reading, the syntactical cueing system refers to _____.

    A. the meaning system of language

    B. the structural system of language

    C. the letter-sound relationships in written language

    D. the social and cultural aspects of language

3. When reading, the phonological cueing system refers to_____.

    A. the meaning system of language

    B. the structural system of language

    C. the letter-sound relationships in written language

    D. the social and cultural aspects of language

4.   When reading, the pragmatic cueing system refers to _____.

    A.   the meaning system of language

    B.   the structural system of language

    C.   the letter-sound relationships in written language

    D.   the social and cultural aspects of language

5.   Literacy is a person's ability to _____.

    A.   compute using technology

    B.   read and write

    C.   encode and be pragmatic

    D.   comprehend and engage

DIRECTIONS: Use the following graph to answer questions 6 and 7.

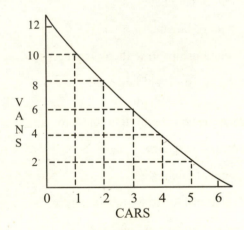

Figure 1   Production Possibilities Curve

Figure 1 represents an economy that produces vehicles. The economy represented by Figure 1 is presently producing 12 vans and zero cars.

6.   The opportunity cost of increasing the production of cars from zero units to two units is the loss of production of _____ of vans.

    A.   one unit

    B.   two units

    C.   three units

    D.   four units

7. This is an example of _____ opportunity costs per unit for cars.

    A. constant

    B. increasing

    C. decreasing

    D. zero

8. The United States Constitution defines the powers of the United States Congress and the states. The U.S. Constitution reserves powers to the states in the 10th Amendment, while Article I, Section 8 of the U.S. Constitution delegates powers to the federal government. Some powers are shared concurrently between the states and federal government. Which of the following powers are concurrent powers?

    > I. Lay and collect taxes
    > II. Regulate commerce
    > III. Establish post offices
    > IV. Borrow money

    A. I and II only

    B. II and III only

    C. III and IV only

    D. I and IV only

9. The United States has a two-party system while several European governments have a multiparty system. Which of the following statements is true about political parties in the United States but not true about political parties in multiparty European governments?

    A. Political parties form coalitions in order to advance their policy initiatives through Congress.

    B. Single member district voting patterns clearly identify candidates for seats in political offices.

    C. Parties provide candidates for office and organize campaigns to get the candidate elected.

    D. Political parties are linked to religious, regional, or social class groupings.

10. The Pacific Northwest receives the greatest annual precipitation in the United States. Which of the following statements best identifies the reason that this occurs?

    A. The jet stream moving south from Canada is responsible for pushing storms through the region.

    B. The region's mountains along the coast cause air masses to rise and cool, thereby reducing their moisture-carrying capacity.

    C. Numerous storms originating in Asia build in intensity as they move across the Pacific Ocean and then dump their precipitation upon reaching land.

    D. The ocean breezes push moisture-laden clouds and fog into the coastal region, producing humid, moist conditions that result in precipitation.

11. Six employees at a circuit board factory—strangers to each other—are chosen to compose a new work team. So that the workers might get to know each other better, they are asked to arrange short, one-on-one introductory meetings with each other. If every worker meets individually with each of the other team members, how many one-on-one meetings will there be?

   A. 12

   B. 36

   C. 15

   D. 18

12. The distance from Tami's house to Ken's house is 3 miles. The distance from Ken's house to The Soda Depot is 2 miles. Which of the following statements are true?

   I. The greatest possible distance between Tami's house and The Soda Depot is five miles.
   II. The greatest possible distance between Tami's house and The Soda Depot is six miles.
   III. The shortest possible distance between Tami's house and The Soda Depot is one mile.
   IV. The shortest possible distance between Tami's house and The Soda Depot is two miles.

   A. I and III only

   B. I and IV only

   C. II and III only

   D. II and IV only

13. Use the figure to answer the question that follows.

   Which inequality describes the allowable speeds indicated by the speed limit sign?

   ```
   75 MPH
   MAXIMUM

   40 MPH
   MINIMUM
   ```

   A. $75 \leq x \leq 40$

   B. $75 < x > 40$

   C. $40 \leq x \leq 75$

   D. $40 < x > 75$

14. Which types of graphs or charts would be appropriate for displaying the following information?

Favorite lunch foods of 40 surveyed 6th graders

Pizza	18
Chicken Nuggets	12
Macaroni and Cheese	4
Tacos	4
Hamburgers	2

    I. bar graph
   II. circle (pie) chart
  III. scatter plot
  IV. broken-line graph

A. I and II only

B. III and IV only

C. I and III only

D. II and IV only

15. Which of the following illustrates The Distributive Property?

A. Multiplying 23 by 16 gives the same product as multiplying 16 by 23.

B. 65, 70, and 12 can be added together in any order; the sum will always be the same.

C. The sum of 102 and 9 is the same as the sum of 9 and 102.

D. The product of 3 and 42 is the same as the sum of the products 3×2 and 3×40.

16. You have stepped into an art museum and are drawn to a painting you know nothing about. In order to appreciate the painting, it is helpful to

    I. know all of the details of the artist's intentions and motivations.
   II. study the clues in the artwork for potential meaning.
  III. determine the cultural significance of every visual clue in the painting.
  IV. consider the art elements and principles in the work of art.

A. I and II only

B. I and III only

C. II and IV only

D. III and IV only

17. Which one of the following statements is most true regarding the materials of visual art?

A. Industrial innovations in art making materials have improved art in the past 150 years.

B. The use of uncommon materials in art making has improved art in the past 150 years.

C. The use of unusual materials in art making has changed the standards by which we view art.

D. Industrial innovations in art-making materials have had little influence on visual art.

18. Which of the following is an important reason why music should be included in every child's daily classroom activities?

    A. The imagination, creativity, and aesthetic awareness of a child can be developed through music for more creative living in our mechanized society.

    B. Students need an opportunity to stay current with today's popular music culture.

    C. Making and listening to music is part of our cultural experience and provides opportunities for personal aesthetic growth.

    D. Participating in creatively planned musical activities helps build a child's self-esteem and understanding of others.

19. Pitch is the relative _____ of a musical sound.

    A. duration, or length

    B. loudness or softness

    C. highness or lowness

    D. rhythm

20. This pyramid represents the pattern of progression from simple to complex activities in creative drama. Using the base of the pyramid for the simplest activities and the tip for the most complex, which of the following patterns correctly represents this progression?

    A. Story dramatization, story creation, improvisation, pantomime, beginning activities.

    B. Improvisation, pantomime, beginning activities, story dramatization, story creation.

    C. Beginning activities, improvisation, pantomime, story dramatization, story creation.

    D. Beginning activities, pantomime, improvisation, story creation, story dramatization.

21. If a teacher is interested in improving the comprehension skills of students, that teacher should
    I.   teach students to decode well.
    II. allow time during the day to read and reread selections.
    III. discuss the selections after reading to clarify meaning and make connections.
    IV. tell jokes.

    A. I and II only

    B. I, II, and IV

    C. I, II, and III

    D. All of the above

BESSIE

I began my days as a cow. Well, a calf, to be more precise. I was born to the world a soft tawny color, with liquid brown eyes and soft, floppy ears that begged to be touched. My days were simple. I spent all my time in the company of other bovine females, most especially my mother. She was a prized breeder, my mother; as a result it was my misfortune to be weaned earlier than most other calves.

Only hours after my weaning, a miraculous event changed the course of my life. Princess Georgette happened to be riding by on her shaggy little pony, alongside her nanny, when she heard my lows of despair and turned.

"Whatever could be making that pitiful noise?" she asked aloud.

One of the farmers called out to her, "'Tis only a wee calf, Highness. She'll not be at it long, I assure you."

"I shall see the creature at once," she ordered, pulling her pony up against the rail and dismounting.

At this point, I had moved hopefully toward the commotion, and, as I inched my tender nose out of the barn to investigate, I came face-to-face with the oddest-looking creature I had seen so far in my somewhat short existence. She had outrageous red curls rioting all over her head, and tumbling down over her shoulders. The thing I noticed most, though, was her hopelessly freckled nose, which, at that moment, was uncomfortably close to my own. So close, in fact, that I decided to remedy my discomfort, and did so by lowing rather loudly in her petulant little face. To my astonishment, she giggled with delight at my rudeness, and reached out to stroke my furry forehead. I found myself nuzzling up to her small chest. "Oh Nan, I must have it. Such a funny furry thing must be kept in my garden where I might entertain myself endlessly with it."

So that is how I became a member of the royal household.

My days fell into an odd sort of routine. I spent my mornings cropping on the lawns and shrubs until Georgette would appear, luring me into the hedge ways with a handful of cresses nipped from the kitchen. As soon as I got close enough and started to nibble, she would shriek, and startle me into a canter, at which she would chase me into the hedges until I was so thoroughly lost, I would have to low helplessly until Georgette found me.

Tragically, calves do not stay calves forever. As the seasons passed, her interest in our games began to wane. The gardeners had, at this time, gotten very tired of working around me as I lumbered through the hedges. They communicated up through the chain of command, straight to the king himself, their wish to be rid of me. He dismissed the problem with an order to have me put down.

Georgette pouted at this and stamped her foot, but her father would not budge an inch. "Now, don't get missish with me, Georgette. I've given the order, and I'll see it done as I've dictated whether you like it or not."

Georgette, during this speech, had become thoughtful. After a long pause, she proposed: "Well, if I must see my Bessie put down as you've said, mightn't I get a handbag and boots out of her at least?"

"Very well," sighed her father.

For my part, it was a stroke of luck that this conversation had taken place just on the other side of the hedge where I had been, only moments before, contently munching on the last bit of clover to be found this season. Naturally, I took exception to being discussed in such a candid manner. In fact, I could not believe my furry, floppy ears. I felt myself slipping into a sort of self-pity, and walked away. When I passed the westernmost gate, it occurred to me that I might not have to face my doom. This door, that was normally latched and guarded, stood open. I was out that gate and on the lane nearby in an instant.

I wandered aimlessly for hours, when I abruptly came upon a little clearing. A stream ran through it, past the coziest of tiny cottages. I trotted straight over to the stream and began drinking in long draughts. After several moments of such behavior, I became aware of another presence nearby. It was a small, old man, leaning toward me in a strange sort of furry robe, and balancing himself on the most incredibly gnarled staff, and holding a silver bucket that steamed and hissed, yet smelled overwhelmingly delicious.

"Hello," he said in a pleasant tone. "I'm happy you have finally arrived. I read it in *The Book*. Would you care to drink from my bucket?" he asked. . . .

22.   This is the beginning of a story. To what genre does it belong?

    A.   poetry

    B.   historical fiction

    C.   nonfiction

    D.   fantasy

23.   What do you think will happen next?

    A.   Bessie will go to a barn.

    B.   Bessie will catch frogs.

    C.   Bessie will run away.

    D.   Bessie will drink the potion, and turn into a brown-eyed girl.

24.   How did you know what might happen next?

    A.   I watch *Friends* often. [The nanny never wanted the princess to have a pet cow in the first place.]

    B.   Magical things often happen in stories that begin with a princess.

    C.   I read about dysfunctional families often.

    D.   The princess will have a new handbag and boots.

25.   How should this sort of story be introduced to children?

    A.   Complete a K-W-L to activate prior knowledge about fairy tales.

    B.   Ask the children to look up vocabulary words in a dictionary.

    C.   Read the children a nonfiction book about dairy farming.

    D.   Show a video about talking to strangers.

DIRECTIONS: Use the information below to answer the three questions that follow.

An experiment is planned to test the effect of microwave radiation on the success of seed germination. One hundred corn seeds will be divided into four sets of twenty-five each. Seeds in Group 1 will be microwaved for one minute, seeds in Group 2 for two minutes, and seeds in Group 3 for ten minutes. Seeds in Group 4 will not be placed in the microwave. Each group of seeds will be soaked overnight and placed between the folds of water-saturated newspaper.

26. When purchasing the seeds at the store no single package contained enough seeds for the entire project, most contain about thirty seeds per package. Which of the following is an acceptable approach for testing the hypotheses?

    I.   Purchase one packet from each of four different brands of seed, one packet for each test group.
    II.   Purchase one packet from each of four different brands of seed and divide the seeds from each packet equally among the four test groups.
    III.   Purchase four packets of the same brand, one packet for each test group.
    IV.   Purchase four packets of the same brand, and divide the seeds from each packet equally among the four test groups.

A. I and II only

B. II and IV only

C. III and IV only

D. IV only

27. During the measurement of seed and root length it is noted that many of the roots are not growing straight. Efforts to manually straighten the roots for measurement are only minimally successful as the roots are fragile and susceptible to breakage. Which of the following approaches is consistent with the stated hypothesis?

A. At the end of the experiment, straighten the roots and measure them.

B. Use a string as a flexible measuring instrument for curved roots.

C. Record the mass instead of length as an indicator of growth.

D. Record only the number of seeds that have sprouted, regardless of length.

28. In presenting the results of this experiment which of the following could be used to present the data to confirm or refute the hypothesis?

> I. A single bar graph with one bar for each test group indicating the number of days until the first seed sprouts.
> II. A pie chart for each test group showing the percent of seeds in that group that sprouted.
> III. A line graph plotting the total number of sprouted seeds from all test groups vs. time (experiment day).
> IV. A line graph plotting the number of germinated seeds vs. the minutes of time exposed to the microwave.

  A. I only

  B. II only

  C. II and IV only

  D. III and IV only

29. A hot-air balloon rises when propane burners in the basket are used to heat the air inside the balloon. Which of the following statements correctly identifies the explanation for this phenomenon?

  A. Heated gas molecules move faster inside the balloon, their force striking the inside causes the balloon to rise.

  B. Hot gas molecules are themselves larger than cool gas molecules, resulting in the expansion of the gas.

  C. The amount of empty space between gas molecules increases as the temperature of the gas increases, resulting in the expansion of the gas.

  D. The combustion of propane releases product gases that are lighter than air which are trapped in the balloon causing it to rise.

30. A marble and a feather are both released at the same time inside a tube that is held at very low pressure (a near vacuum). Which of the following correctly links the observation to explanation?

  A. The marble falls faster because it is heavier.

  B. The marble falls faster because it has less air resistance.

  C. Both fall at the same rate because there is no air resistance in a vacuum.

  D. Both fall at the same rate because the forces of gravity are different in a vacuum.

31. Which of the following descriptions best describes the western, Pacific region of Canada comprising British Columbia and the Yukon?

   A. The area contains many uninhabitable areas, including a mix of arid desert-like terrain and rugged mountain ranges that hinder rail and car transportation, resulting in minimal population settlement.

   B. The area contains arid deserts and vast grasslands that are ideal for cattle farming and oil production.

   C. The area contains the vast majority of Canada's natural resources and the majority of Canada's population.

   D. The area contains fifty percent of Canada's population, resulting in seventy percent of Canada's manufacturing.

DIRECTIONS: Read the following passage and answer the question that follows:

The Police believed that Dollree Mapp was hiding a person suspected in a crime. The police went to her home in Cleveland, Ohio, knocked, and requested entry. Mapp refused. After more officers arrived on the scene, police forced their way into Mapp's house. During the police search of the house they found pornographic books, pictures, and photographs. They arrested Mapp and charged her with violating an Ohio law against possession of pornographic materials. Mapp and her attorney appealed the case to the Supreme Court of Ohio. The Ohio Supreme Court ruled in favor of the police. Mapp's case was then appealed to the Supreme Court of the United States. Mapp and her attorney asked the Supreme Court to determine whether or not evidence obtained through a search that violated the Fourth Amendment was admissible in state courts. The U.S. Supreme Court, in the case *Mapp v. Ohio*, ruled that evidence obtained in a search that violates the Fourth Amendment is not admissible. The majority opinion states, "Our decision, founded on reason and truth, gives to the individual no more than that which the Constitution guarantees him, to the police officer no less than that to which honest law enforcement is entitled, and, to the courts, that judicial integrity so necessary in the true administration of justice."

32. The excerpt above best illustrates which of the following features of judicial proceedings in the United States?

   A. due process of law

   B. a fair and speedy trial

   C. judicial review

   D. the exclusionary rule

33. Which of the following statements are true about economic activity in Illinois?

> I. Illinois ranks in about the middle of the fifty states in terms of dollars generated by manufacturing.
> II. Federal environmental laws passed in the twentieth century had a devastating effect on the Illinois coal industry.
> III. Corn, soybeans, and wheat have about an equal share of cultivated land in Illinois.
> IV. Although manufacturing employs a significant number of people around the state, most manufacturing in Illinois is in the Chicago area.

A. I and II only

B. I and III only

C. II and III only

D. II and IV only

34. Which of the following statements best defines the role of the World Trade Organization (WTO)?

A. It resolves trade disputes and attempts to formulate policy to open world markets to free trade through monetary policy and regulation of corruption.

B. It is an advocate for human rights and democracy by regulating child labor and providing economic aid to poor countries.

C. It establishes alliances to regulate disputes and polices ethnic intimidation.

D. It regulates trade within the United States in order to eliminate monopolistic trade practices.

35. The drought of the 1930s that spanned from Texas to North Dakota was caused by

> I. overgrazing overuse of farmland.
> II. natural phenomena, such as below-average rainfall and wind erosion.
> III. environmental factors, such as changes in the jet stream.
> IV. the lack of government subsidies for new irrigation technology.

A. I and II only

B. II and III only

C. I and III only

D. II and IV only

36. What does it mean that multiplication and division are *inverse operations*?

    A. Multiplication is commutative, whereas division is not. For example: 4×2 gives the same product as 2×4, but $4 \div 2$ is not the same as $2 \div 4$.

    B. Whether multiplying or dividing a value by 1, the value remains the same. For example, 9×1 equals 9; $9 \div 1$ also equals 9.

    C. When performing complex calculations involving several operations, all multiplication must be completed before completing any division, such as in $8 \div 2 \times 4 + 7 - 1$.

    D. The operations "undo" each other. For example, multiplying 11 by 3 gives 33. Dividing 33 by 3 then takes you back to 11.

37. One day, 31 students were absent from Pierce Middle School. If that represents about 5.5% of the students, what is the population of the school?

    A. 177

    B. 517

    C. 564

    D. 171

38. Which of the following are equivalent to 0.5%?
    I.   One-half of one percent
    II.   5%
    III. 1/200
    IV.   0.05

    A. I and III only

    B. I and IV only

    C. II and III only

    D. II and IV only

39. The primary and most efficient energy source of the body comes from

    A. proteins.   C. complex carbohydrates.

    B. fats.   D. simple sugars.

40. Which of the following is a locomotor skill?

    A. bouncing   C. throwing

    B. catching   D. leaping

41. Which is NOT a principle of aerobic conditioning?

    A. requires oxygen

    B. continuous and rhythmic

    C. burns protein for energy

    D. uses major muscle groups

42. Dr. Kenneth Goodman developed the notion of miscue analysis. This is a system for examining how a child's oral reading of a passage varies from _____.

    A. singing the same passage

    B. encoding the passage from a dictation

    C. the printed text

    D. diagrams of the sentences

43. If you were going to ask the children to finish the story on page 311 as a writing activity, what would you do next?

    A. Have them complete a worksheet about the vocabulary words.

    B. Ask them to diagram the first sentence.

    C. Ask them to form small groups, and talk about what might happen next.

    D. Have them complete a Venn diagram about Bessie and a real cow.

44. Which of the following describes best practice in writing instruction?

    A. Instruct students in writing, and give them time to write.

    B. Have students complete worksheets about writing.

    C. Have students copy famous speeches. [Have the students, in groups, convert the story into a script, and perform it in a reader's theatre format.]

    D. Have the children create a mural of the story so far, and label all of the characters.

45. Each month the teacher kept track of the number of books as well as the genre of the books the students read during free-reading time in school. Here is the graph constructed from the data from September and May of the same year. This teacher completed a unit on fairy tales in April. What conclusions could be reached?

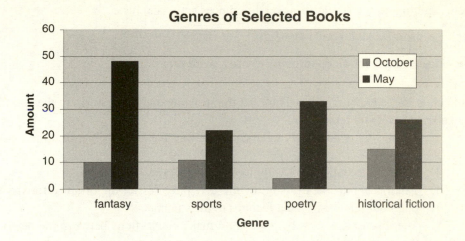

I. These children are reading more titles during free reading time.
II. Completing a fairy tale unit created interest in the fantasy genre.
III. These children need to complete more worksheets.
IV. These children are participating in an Accelerated Reader Program.

A. I, II, and III

B. All of the above

C. None of the above

D. I and II

46. Listening is a process students used to extract meaning out of oral speech. Activities teachers can engage in to assist students in becoming more effective listeners include:

I. clearly setting a purpose for listening.
II. allow children to relax by chewing gum during listening.
III. asking questions about the selection.
IV. encouraging students to forge links between the new information and knowledge already in place.

A. I and II

B. II, III, and IV

C. I, III, and IV

D. All of the above

47. Why should children be taught to use graphic organizers as a method of organizing data during an inquiry?

    A.   It discourages the practice of copying paragraphs out of the source book.

    B.   It helps children to see similarities and differences across sources.

    C.   Graphic organizers look good to parents.

    D.   It provides the students an opportunity to use a word processor.

48. Why should children be encouraged to figure out the structure and the features of the text they are attempting to comprehend and remember?

    I.   It helps the students to understand the way the author organized the material to be presented.
    II. It helps the students to really look at the features of the text.
    III. Talking about the structure of the text provides an opportunity for the teacher to point out the most salient features to the students.
    IV. The discussions may help the child make connections between the new material in the chapter and what is already known about the topic.

    A.   I and III

    B.   II and IV

    C.   I and IV

    D.   All of the above

49. Which equation could be used to answer the following question?

    Together, a pen and a pencil cost $2.59 (ignoring tax). The pen cost $1.79 more than the pencil. What was the cost of the pencil?

    A. $x = (2.59 - 1.79) \times 2$

    B. $2.59 = x - 1.79$

    C. $2.59 = x + (x + 1.79)$

    D. $x = 2.59 - 1.79$

50. Use the figure to answer the question that follows.

Which of the following situations might the graph illustrate?
 I. The varying speed of an experienced runner over the course of a 26-mile race.
 II. The number of households a census taker still has to visit over the course of a week.
 III. The value of a savings account over time, assuming steady growth.
 IV. The changing height of a sunflower over several months.

A. I and II only

B. III and IV only

C. II, III, and IV only

D. I, III, and IV only

51. Which line on the chart best matches the resources with the historical question that is being asked?

Line	Historical Research Question	Source of Information
1	How many people were living in Boston, MA, during the time of the American Revolution?	Historical atlas
2	What role did Fort Mackinaw fulfill during the American Revolution?	Encyclopedia article
3	How did the average temperatures and snowfall during the winter of 1775–1776 compare with previous winters?	Historical almanac
4	When was the first U.S. treaty signed and what were the terms of the treaty?	Government publication

A. line 1

B. line 2

C. line 3

D. line 4

DIRECTIONS: Use the passages below, adapted from Herodotus's *Histories*, to answer the two questions that follow:

Passage A: I think, too, that those Egyptians who dwell below the lake of Moiris and especially in that region which is called the Delta, if that land continues to grow in height according to this proportion and to increase similarly in extent, will suffer for all remaining time, from the Nile not overflowing their land, that same thing which they themselves said that the Hellenes would at some time suffer: for hearing that the whole land of the Hellenes has rain and is not watered by rivers as theirs is, they said that the Hellenes would at some time be disappointed of a great hope and would suffer the ills of famine. This saying means that if the god shall not send them rain, but shall allow drought to prevail for a long time, the Hellenes will be destroyed by hunger; for they have in fact no other supply of water to save them except from Zeus alone. This has been rightly said by the Egyptians with reference to the Hellenes: but now let me tell how matters are with the Egyptians themselves in their turn.

Passage B: If, in accordance with what I before said, their land below Memphis (for this is that which is increasing) shall continue to increase in height according to the same proportion as in the past time, assuredly those Egyptians who dwell here will suffer famine, if their land shall not have rain nor the river be able to go over their fields. It is certain however that now they gather in fruit from the earth with less labour than any other men and also with less than the other Egyptians; for they have no labour in breaking up furrows with a plough nor in hoeing nor in any other of those labours which other men have about a crop; but when the river has come up of itself and watered their fields and after watering has left them again, then each man sows his own field and turns into it swine, and when he has trodden the seed into the ground by means of the swine, after that he waits for the harvest, and when he has threshed the corn by means of the swine, then he gathers it in.

52. Which of the following best states the main issues being discussed in the above passages?

    A. Ancient Egyptians were so dependent upon the Nile River that one's location determined one's prosperity.

    B. The Nile River was so important to the prosperity of ancient Egyptians that it determined where many Egyptians settled.

    C. Egyptians who depend upon the Nile River for irrigation will not suffer from famine as those who depend upon rain.

    D. Egyptians settling in the Delta were dependent upon religion because irrigation from rain was more unpredictable than the Nile.

53. Herodotus, in passage A, could best support assertions made in the passage by presenting which of the following types of evidence?

    A. Data showing the productivity of Egyptian farmers in both the Delta and Memphis regions.

    B. Data showing the average rainfall in the Delta as compared to average rainfall in Memphis.

    C. Data showing the cycle of flooding along the Nile as compared to the cycles of rainfall in the Delta.

    D. Data showing the wealth of Egyptians in the Delta as compared to the wealth of Egyptians in Memphis.

54. Light is refracted when it passes across a boundary between media with different densities. This can occur between solids, liquids, gases, or even due to differences within the same phase. The longer wavelengths of light are refracted less than the shorter wavelengths. Which of the following correctly places the colors of the visible spectrum in order from lowest extent of refraction to highest?

    A. Blue/Violet – Green – Orange – Yellow – Red

    B. Blue/Violet – Green – Yellow – Orange – Red

    C. Red – Yellow – Green – Orange – Blue/Violet

    D. Red – Orange – Yellow – Green – Blue/Violet

55. Around the time of World War II the chemical industry developed several new classes of insecticide that were instrumental in protecting our soldiers from pest-borne diseases common to the tropic regions they were fighting in. These same insecticides found widespread use at home to increase production of many agricultural crops by reducing the damage from insects like cotton weevils and grasshoppers. While farmers continued to use the same levels of insecticide, over time it was found that the insect population was increasing. Identify the best explanation for this observation:

    A. Insecticides, like most chemicals, lose their potency when stored.

    B. The insect population was increasing to reach the carrying capacity of a given ecosystem.

    C. The initial doses of pesticide were too low to effectively kill the insects.

    D. Insects with a tolerance to insecticide survived the initial doses and lived to produce insecticide resistant offspring.

56. Under the right conditions of temperature and pressure any type of rock can be transformed into another type of rock in a process called the Rock Cycle. Which of the following processes is not a part of the Rock Cycle?

    A. the drifting and encroachment of sand at the edge of a desert

    B. the melting of rock beneath the surface to form magma

    C. the erosion of sedimentary rocks to form sand

    D. the eruption of a cinder cone volcano

57. Dance can be a mirror of culture. Which of the following is not an illustration of this statement?

   A.   Women in the Cook Islands dance with their feet together and sway while the men take a wide stance and flap their knees.

   B.   Movement basics include body, space, time, and relationship.

   C.   In Africa, the birth of a child is an occasion for a dance that asks for divine blessings.

   D.   The court dancers of Bali study for many years to achieve the balance, beauty, and serenity of their dance.

Use the image below to answer the two questions that follow.

Student work by Sara Goodrich

58. As seen in the figure, the technique of gluing imagery to a two-dimensional surface is referred to as

   A.   montage.

   B.   frottage.

   C.   collage.

   D.   assemblage.

59. In the above image, the chair is the focal point of the drawing. Why?

    A. It is large, frontal, and drawn in high contrast.

    B. It is highly simplified and minimally detailed.

    C. It is asymmetrically balanced in the drawing.

    D. It is drawn in three-point perspective.

60. Mr. Nelson's class has just returned from seeing a children's theatre production at a nearby university. Now, Mr. Nelson plans to ask his students to discuss what they have seen. In preparation for this, he plans to model the types of responses desired. Which of the following should he use as examples?

    I. I liked the play.
    II. I liked the play because the characters reminded me of people I know.
    III. I liked the play because the theatre was big.
    IV. I liked the play because sometimes the story was funny and sometimes it was sad.

    A. I only

    B. II and IV

    C. I and III

    D. IV only

61. Which of the following would be considered a primary source in researching the factors that influenced U.S. involvement in the Korean War?

    I. The personal correspondence of a military man stationed with the 5th Regimental Combat Team (RCT) in Korea.
    II. A biography of Harry S. Truman by David McCullough, published in 1993.
    III. A journal article about the beginning of the Korean War by a noted scholar.
    IV. An interview with Secretary of Defense George Marshall.

    A. I and II only

    B. II and IV only

    C. II and III only

    D. I and IV only

62. Which of the following was *not* a major Native American tribe that resided in Illinois before the 1700s?

    A. the Ojibwe

    B. the Miami

    C. the Mississippian

    D. the Kaskaskia

63. Which of the following best describes a major difference between a state government and the federal government?

    A. State governments have more responsibility for public education than the federal government.

    B. State governments are more dependent upon the personal income tax for revenue than the federal government.

    C. State governments are more dependent upon the system of checks and balances than the federal government.

    D. State governments are subject to term limits, where as federal government representatives serve unlimited terms.

64. Which of the following were major causes of the Great Depression?
    I. Hoarding money greatly reduced the money supply, resulting in higher prices on consumer goods.
    II. The gold standard limited the amount of money in supply, reducing money circulation, and causing a drop in prices and wages.
    III. Smoot-Hawley Tariff increased tariffs, which resulted in increased prices for consumer goods.
    IV. The stock market crash reduced the value of companies, causing them to raise prices of consumer goods.

    A. I and II only

    B. II and III only

    C. III and IV only

    D. I, II, and III

Read the passage below; then answer the four questions that follow.

The issue of adult literacy has finally received recognition as a major social problem. Unfortunately, the issue is usually presented in the media as a "women's interest issue." Numerous governors' wives and even Laura Bush have publicly expressed concern about literacy. As well-meaning as the politicians' wives may be, it is more important that the politicians themselves recognize the seriousness of the problem and support increased funding for literacy programs.

Literacy education programs need to be directed at two different groups of people with very different needs. The first group is composed of people who have very limited reading and writing skills. These people are complete illiterates. A second group is composed of people who can read and write but whose skills are not sufficient to meet their needs. This second group is called *functionally illiterate*. Successful literacy programs must meet the needs of both groups.

Instructors in literacy programs have three main responsibilities. First, the educational needs of the illiterates and functional illiterates must be met. Second, the instructors must approach the participants in the program with empathy, not sympathy. Third, all participants must experience success in the program and must perceive their efforts as worthwhile.

65. What is the difference between illiteracy and functional illiteracy?

     A.   There is no difference.

     B.   A functional illiterate is enrolled in a literacy education program but an illiterate is not.

     C.   An illiterate cannot read or write, a functional illiterate can read and write but not at a very high skill level.

     D.   There are more illiterates than functional illiterates in the United States today.

66. What does "women's interest issue" mean in the passage?

     A.   The issue is only interesting to women.

     B.   Many politicians' wives have expressed concern over the issue.

     C.   Women illiterates outnumber male illiterates.

     D.   Politicians interested in illiteracy often have their wives give speeches on the topic.

67. According to the passage, which of the following is NOT a characteristic of successful literacy programs?

     A.   Participants should receive free transportation.

     B.   Participants should experience success in the program.

     C.   Instructors must have empathy, not sympathy.

     D.   Programs must meet the educational needs of illiterates.

68. What is the author's opinion of the funding for literacy programs?

     A.   Too much

     B.   Too little

     C.   About right

     D.   Too much for illiterates and not enough for functional illiterates

69. Use the figure to answer the question that follows.

What is the approximate area of the shaded region, given that:

   a.   the radius of the circle is 6 units

   b.   the square inscribes the circle?

A.   106 square units

B.   31 square units

C.   77 square units

D.   125 square units

70. How many lines of symmetry do all non-square rectangles have?

A.   0

B.   2

C.   4

D.   8

71. Use the figure to answer the question that follows.

The figure above is a sketch of a ramp. Given that the two ramp supports (DB and EC) are perpendicular to the ground, and the dimensions of the various parts are as noted, what is the approximate distance from point B to point C?

A.   4.7 feet

B.   4.5 feet

C.   4.3 feet

D.   4.1 feet

72. Bemus School is conducting a lottery to raise funds for new band uniforms. Exactly 1000 tickets will be printed and sold. Only one ticket stub will be drawn from a drum to determine the single winner of a big-screen television. All tickets have equal chances of winning. The first 700 tickets are sold to 700 different individuals. The remaining 300 tickets are sold to Mr. Greenfield.

Given the information above, which of the following statements are true?

    I.   It is impossible to tell in advance who will win.

    II.   Mr. Greenfield will probably win.

    III.   Someone other than Mr. Greenfield will probably win.

    IV.   The likelihood that Mr. Greenfield will win is the same as the likelihood that someone else will win.

A.   I and II only

B.   I and III only

C.   II and IV only

D.   III and IV only

73. Which of the following tenets of the Atomic Theory is not correct:

A.   Elements comprise extremely small particles called atoms.

B.   All atoms of a given element are identical, having the same size, mass, and chemical properties.

C.   The atoms of one element are different from the atoms of all other elements.

D.   Compounds are comprised of more than one atom from one or more element.

> DIRECTIONS: The following two questions are based upon this excerpt from Jules Verne's 1870 work *From the Earth to the Moon and Round the Moon* pp. 39–40 (Dodd, Mead & Company 1962), where plans are made to construct a cannon 900 feet long to shoot a projectile to the Moon.

The problem before us is how to communicate an initial force of 12,000 yards per second to a shell of 108 inches in diameter, weighing 20,000 pounds. Now when a projectile is launched into space, what happens to it? It is acted upon by three independent forces: the resistance of the air, the attraction of the earth, and the force of impulsion with which it is endowed. Let us examine these three forces. The resistance of the air is of little importance. The atmosphere of the earth does not exceed forty miles. Now, with the given rapidity, the projectile will have traversed this in five seconds, and the period is too brief for the resistance of the medium to be regarded otherwise than as insignificant. Proceeding, then, to the attraction of the earth, that is, the weight of the shell, we know that this weight will diminish in the inverse ratio of the square of the distance. When a body is left to itself falls to the surface of the earth, it falls five feet in the first second: and if the same body were removed 257,542 miles farther off, in other words, to the distance of the moon, its fall would be reduced to about half a line in the first second.

74. Propelling such a large projectile requires a massive force. The "initial force of 12,000 yards per second" is really a reference to the projectile's initial speed. The calculation of force required to move an object with a mass of 20,000 pounds from rest to a speed of 12,000 yards per second in a time span of 0.05 seconds is reflected in which of the following:

    A. $20,000 \times 12,000 / 0.05$

    B. $20,000 \times 12,000 \times 0.05$

    C. $(20,000 \times 9.8) / (20,000 \times 0.05)$

    D. $(20,000 / 9.8) \times (12,000 / 0.05)$

75. The acceleration due to gravity is generally accepted as 9.8 m/sec^2 for objects near the Earth's surface, and the Earth's radius is approximately 4,000 miles. Given that the proposed projectile weighs 20,000 lbs at the surface, what would be the approximate mass at a distance of 8,000 miles from the surface of the Earth?

    A. 20,000 lbs / 2

    B. 20,000 lbs / 4

    C. 20,000 lbs / 8

    D. 20,000 lbs / 16

76. The atmospheres of the Moon and other planets were studied using telescopes and spectrophotometers long before the deployment of interplanetary space probes. In these studies scientists studied the spectral patterns of sunlight that passed through the atmosphere of distant objects to learn what elements make up those atmospheres. Which of the following explains the source of the black-line spectral patterns?

   A.   When an element is excited, it gives off light in a characteristic spectral pattern.

   B.   When light strikes an object, some wavelengths of light are absorbed by the surface and others are reflected to give the object its color.

   C.   When light passes through a gas, light is absorbed at wavelengths characteristic of the elements in the gas.

   D.   The black lines are the spectra of ultraviolet light, which is called black light because it cannot be seen with human eyes.

77. We may be told to "gargle with saltwater" when we suffer from a sore throat. Which of the following phenomena would be used to explain this advice?

   A.   lowering of vapor pressure

   B.   increasing osmotic pressure

   C.   increasing boiling point

   D.   decreasing freezing point

78. In announcing the Emancipation Proclamation, Lincoln's immediate purpose was to

   A.   free black slaves in all of the slave states.

   B.   free black slaves in only the border slave states that had remained loyal to the Union.

   C.   let the Southern states know that whether or not they chose to secede from the Union, slavery would not be tolerated by his administration once he took office.

   D.   rally Northern morale by giving the war a higher moral purpose than just preserving the Union.

79. In its decision in the case of *Dred Scott v. Sanford*, the U.S. Supreme Court held that

   A.   separate facilities for different races were inherently unequal and therefore unconstitutional.

   B.   no black slave could be a citizen of the United States.

   C.   separate but equal facilities for different races were constitutional.

   D.   Affirmative Action programs were acceptable only when it could be proven that specific previous cases of discrimination had occurred within the institution or business in question.

80. Thomas Paine's pamphlet *Common Sense* was significant in that it

    A.   emotionally aroused thousands of colonists to the abuses of British rule, the oppressiveness of the monarchy, and the advantages of colonial independence.

    B.   rallied American spirit during the bleak winter of 1776, when it appeared that Washington's forces, freezing and starving at Valley Forge, had no hope of surviving the winter, much less defeating the British.

    C.   called for a strong central government to rule the newly independent American states and foresaw the difficulties inherent within the Articles of Confederation.

    D.   asserted to its British readers that they could not beat the American colonists militarily unless they could isolate New England from the rest of the American colonies.

81. In order to achieve lasting weight loss, students should

    A.   enter a commercial diet program.

    B.   combine permanent dietary changes with exercise.

    C.   cut calories to below 100 per day.

    D.   exercise for two hours a day.

82. Which of the following vitamins is not fat soluble?

    A.   Vitamin D   C.   Vitamin E

    B.   Vitamin C   D.   Vitamin K

83. Of the following, which test does NOT measure muscular strength and endurance in children?

    A.   Pull-ups   C.   Grip strength test

    B.   Flexed arm hang   D.   Sit-and-reach test

84. Dance can reflect the religion of a culture by
    I.   offering adoration and worship to the deity.
    II.   appealing to the deity for survival in war.
    III.   asking the deity for success in the hunt.
    IV.   miming the actions of planting and harvesting crops.

    A.   I and II only

    B.   I and III only

    C.   II, III, and IV only

    D.   I, II, III, and IV

85. Which of the following do the dances of Waltz, Lindy Hop, and Twist have in common?

    A. They became popular in the nineteenth century.

    B. They are forms of "swing" dance.

    C. They reflect changes in social attitudes of their time.

    D. They are danced by couples touching each other.

86. Identify the incorrect statement from the following:

    A. Heredity is the study of how traits are passed from parent to offspring.

    B. The chemical molecule that carries an organism's genetic makeup is called DNA.

    C. Sections of the DNA molecule that determine specific traits are called chromosomes.

    D. The genetic makeup of an organism is altered through bioengineering.

87. Which of the following sources of energy is nonrenewable?

    A. hydrogen-cell

    B. geothermal

    C. nuclear

    D. hydroelectric

88. To move a heavy book across a tabletop at a constant speed, a person must continually exert a force on the book. This force is primarily used to overcome which of the following forces?

    A. The force of gravity

    B. The force of air resistance

    C. The force of friction

    D. The weight of the book

89. Which of the following best explains why the boiling point of water is reduced and cooking times are increased at high altitudes?

    A. At high altitudes there is greater atmospheric pressure than at sea level.

    B. At high altitudes there is less oxygen than at sea level.

    C. At high altitudes the vapor pressure of water is reduced because of the reduced atmospheric pressure.

    D. At high altitudes water boils at a lower temperature because of the reduced atmospheric pressure.

The fourth-grade students in Mrs. Alvarez's class are studying Native Americans. Mrs. Alvarez wants to strengthen her students' ability to work independently. She also wants to provide opportunities for the students to use a variety of print and media resources during this unit of study. Mrs. Alvarez plans to begin the unit by leading the class in a brainstorming session to formulate questions to guide their research about Native Americans.

90. Which of the following criteria should guide Mrs. Alvarez as she leads the initial brainstorming session?

    A.   The questions should emphasize the factual content presented in the available print materials.

    B.   The questions should emphasize higher order thinking skills, such as comparison, analysis, and evaluation.

    C.   The questions should reflect the interest of the students.

    D.   The questions should include all of the fourth-grade objectives for this unit.

91. Mrs. Alvarez has collected a variety of print and media resources for the students to use in their research. Which of the following will probably be the best way to motivate students to research the questions they have prepared?

    A.   The teacher should assign two to three questions to each student so that all the questions are covered.

    B.   The teacher should allow individual students to select the questions they would like to research.

    C.   The teacher should select three key questions and assign them to all the students.

    D.   The teacher should assign one topic to each student, then provide the students with additional information.

Mrs. Gitler teaches 26 third graders in a large inner city school. About one-third of her students participate in the ESL program at the school. Mrs. Gitler suspects that some of the students' parents are unable to read or write in English. Four of the students receive services from the learning resource teacher. At the beginning of the year, none of the students read above 2.0 grade level, and some of the students did not know all the letters of the alphabet.

92. Which of the following describes the instructional strategy that is most likely to improve the reading levels of Mrs. Gitler's students?

    A.   An intensive phonics program that includes drill and practice work on basic sight words.

    B.   An emergent literacy program emphasizing pattern books and journal writing using invented spelling.

    C.   An instructional program that closely follows the third-grade basal reader.

    D.   All the students should participate in the school's ESL program and receive services from the learning resource center.

93. Mrs. Gitler is selecting books for the classroom library. In addition to student interest, which of the following would be the most important considerations?

   A.   The books should have a reading level that matches the students' independent reading ability. .

   B.   All books should have a reading level that is challenging to the students.

   C.   The books should include separate word lists for student practice.

   D.   A classroom library is not appropriate for students at such a low reading level.

94. Matt earned the following scores on his first six weekly mathematics tests: 91%, 89%, 82%, 95%, 86%, and 79%.

   He had hoped for an average (mean) of 90% at this point, which would just barely give him an A– in math class on his first report card. How many more total percentage points should Matt have earned over the course of those six weeks to qualify for an A–?

   A.   87

   B.   3

   C.   90

   D.   18

95. Ms. Williams plans to buy carpeting for her living room floor. The room is a rectangle measuring 14 feet by 20 feet. She wants no carpet seams on her floor, even if that means that some carpeting will go to waste. The carpeting she wants comes in 16-foot-wide rolls. What is the minimum amount of carpeting that will have to be wasted if Ms. Williams insists upon her no-seams requirement?

   A.   40 square feet

   B.   60 square feet

   C.   80 square feet

   D.   100 square feet

96. Use the figure to answer the question that follows.

   Consider this sequence of calculator keystrokes:

   That sequence would be useful for finding which of the following values?

   A.   The total distance an automobile travels if it covers 182 miles one day, but only 1.03 and 1.04 miles over the next two days.

   B.   The amount of money in a savings account after the original deposit of $182 earns 3% and then 4% simple annual interest over two years.

   C.   The total distance an automobile travels if it covers 182 miles one day, 103 miles the next day, and 104 miles the third day.

   D.   The amount of money in a savings account after the original deposit of $182 grows by $1.03 and $1.04 in interest over two days.

97. The Silk Road did not connect to which of the following countries?

    A. China

    B. Greece

    C. Iran

    D. India

98. The characteristics of fascism include all of the following EXCEPT:

    A. democracy.

    B. totalitarianism.

    C. romanticism.

    D. militarism.

99. The industrial economy of the nineteenth century was based upon all of the following EXCEPT:

    A. the availability of raw materials.

    B. an equitable distribution of profits among those involved in production.

    C. the availability of capital.

    D   a distribution system to market finished products.

100. The term "Trail of Tears" refers to

    A. the Mormon migration from Nauvoo, Illinois, to what is now Utah.

    B. the forced migration of the Cherokee tribe from the southern Appalachians to what is now Oklahoma.

    C. the westward migration along the Oregon Trail.

    D. the migration into Kentucky along the Wilderness Road.

101. When a member of the House of Representatives helps a citizen from his or her district receive federal aid to which that citizen is entitled, the representative's action is referred to as

    A. casework.

    B. pork barrel legislation.

    C. lobbying.

    D. logrolling.

102. Which of the following types of pollution or atmospheric phenomena are correctly matched with their underlying causes?

    I. global warming – carbon dioxide and methane
    II. acid rain – sulfur dioxide and nitrogen dioxide
    III. ozone depletion – chlorofluorocarbons and sunlight
    IV. aurora borealis – solar flares and magnetism

A. I and II only

B. II and III only

C. I and IV only

D. I, II, III, and IV

103. Which of the following characteristics of a sound wave is associated with its pitch?

    I. Amplitude
    II. Frequency
    III. Wavelength
    IV. Speed

A. I only

B. II only

C. II and III only

D. IV only

104. Which of the following statements correctly describes each group of vertebrates?

    I. Amphibians are cold-blooded, spending part of their life cycle in water and part on land.
    II. Reptiles are generally warm-blooded, having scales that cover their skin.
    III. Fish are cold-blooded, breathing with gills, and covered by scales.
    IV. Mammals are warm-blooded with milk glands and hair.

A. I and IV only

B. I, III, and IV only

C. IV only

D. I, II, III, and IV

105. The floor of a rectangular room is to be covered in two different types of material. The total cost of covering the entire room is $136.00. The cost of covering the inner rectangle is $80.00. The cost of covering the shaded area is $56.00.

We wish to determine the cost of material per square foot used to cover the shaded area. What information given below is unnecessary for this computation?

     I.   The total cost of covering the entire room.
    II.   The cost of covering the inner rectangle
   III.   The cost of covering the shaded area.

A.   I only

B.   II only

C.   I and II

D.   I and III

106. The distribution of a high school chorus is depicted in the graph below. There is a total of 132 students in the chorus.

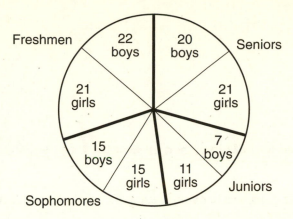

Which of the following expressions represents the percentage of freshman and sophomore girls in the chorus?

A. $\dfrac{21+15}{132} \times 100$

B. $\dfrac{21+15}{132} + 100$

C. $\dfrac{21+15}{132}$

D. $\dfrac{21+15}{100} \times 132$

107. Which of the following is NOT a characteristic of cholesterol?

A. Cholesterol plays a role in the function of the brain.

B. Cholesterol is a component in the creation of certain hormones.

C. Cholesterol is produced in the liver.

D. Excess cholesterol found in the blood of many people usually comes from internal production.

108. A table tennis game is scored to

A. 15 points.

B. 15 points, with a margin of two.

C. 21 points, with a margin of two.

D. 21 points.

109. To complete an effective aerobic workout, exercise should be performed at an individual's target heart rate for a minimum of

   A.   15 minutes.

   B.   20 minutes.

   C.   30 minutes.

   D.   45 minutes.

> **Read the statement below; then answer the three questions that follow.**

Mr. Drake is a first-grade teacher who is using the whole-language method while teaching about animals.

110. Before reading a story to the students, Mr. Drake tells the students what he is expecting them to learn from reading the story. What is his reason for doing this?

   A.   The students should know why the instructor chose this text over any other.

   B.   It is important for teachers to share personal ideas with their students in order to foster an environment of confidence and understanding.

   C.   Mr. Drake wants to verify that all students are on-task before he begins the story.

   D.   Mr. Drake is modeling a vital pre-reading skill in order to teach it to the young readers.

111. Mr. Drake has a heterogeneously grouped reading class. He has the students in groups of two—one skilled reader and one remedial reader—reading selected stories to one another. The students read the story and question each other until they feel that they both understand the story. By planning the lesson this way, Mr. Drake has

   A.   set a goal for his students.

   B.   condensed the number of observations necessary, thereby creating more time for class instruction.

   C.   made it possible for another teacher to utilize the limited materials.

   D.   utilized the students' strengths and weaknesses to maximize time, materials, and the learning environment.

112. Before reading a story about a veterinary hospital, Mr. Drake constructs a semantic map of related words and terms using the students' input. What is his main intention for doing this?

    A. To demonstrate a meaningful relationship between the concepts of the story and the prior knowledge of the students

    B. To serve as a visual means of learning

    C. To determine the level of understanding the students will have at the conclusion of the topic being covered

    D. To model proper writing using whole words

113. Examine the elementary school student's work below. Analyze what the error pattern is that the student is making. If the student worked the problem 88 plus 39, what incorrect answer would the student give (assuming the use of the error pattern exhibited below)?

74	35	67	56
+56	+92	+18	+97
1,210	127	715	1,413

    A. 127

    B. 131

    C. 51

    D. 1,117

114. The needle on the dial points most nearly to which reading?

    A. 108

    B. 128

    C. 114

    D. 117

115. How many ten thousands are there in one million?

    A.   100

    B.   10

    C.   1,000

    D.   10,000

116. An owner of twin Siamese cats knows the following data:

        I.   Cost of a can of cat food

        II.   Volume of a can of cat food

        III. Number of cans of cat food eaten each day by one cat

        IV.   The weight of the cat food in one can

    Which of the data above can be used to determine the cost of cat food for 7 days for the 2 cats?

    A.   I and II only.

    B.   I and III only.

    C.   I and IV only.

    D.   III and IV only.

117. Which of the learners indicated would be capable of conserving information; that is, information will be recognized as being the same even though its context changes?

    A.   Nursery school and kindergarten children

    B.   First and second grade children

    C.   Third and fourth grade children

    D.   Fifth and sixth grade children

118. Harmony results when a melody is accompanied by
        I.   a rhythm instrument.
        II.   a guitar.
        III. another instrument or singer playing or singing the melody.
        IV.   another instrument playing chords.

    A.   I and II only

    B.   I and III only

    C.   II and III only

    D.   IV only

119. Read this nursery rhyme, and then choose the letter that contains the words that would occur on the beat.

Little boy blue come blow your horn,

The sheep's in the meadow, the cow's in the corn.

Where is the boy who looks after the sheep,

He's under the haystack fast asleep.

A. Lit, boy, come, your, the, in, dow, cow's, corn. Where, the, who, ter, sheep, under, hay, a.

B. Lit, blue, blow, horn, sheep's, mea, cow's, corn. Where, boy, aft, sheep, un, hay, fast, sleep.

C. Lit, blow, sheep's, cow's. Where, aft, under, fast.

D. Little, The. Where, He's.

120. Reading and then dramatizing a story, using that story as the basis of a puppet play, scripting that story and performing it in the classroom, and then attending a performance of that story done as a play by a theatre company illustrates which of the following concepts?

A. Teachers should work with material until they find the correct way to use it with students.

B. There are multiple ways to express and interpret the same material.

C. Plays are more interesting than classroom dramatizations.

D. Students learn less as audience members than as participants in drama activities.

121. Which of the following observations explains the geologic instability surrounding the Pacific Ocean known as the "Ring of Fire"?

A. Similarities in rock formations and continental coastlines suggest that the Earth's continents were once one landmass.

B. The Earth's plates collide at convergent margins, separate at divergent margins, and move laterally at transform-fault boundaries.

C. Earthquakes produce waves that travel through the Earth in all directions.

D. Volcanoes form when lava accumulates and hardens.

122. The Earth's Moon is

A. generally closer to the Sun than it is to the Earth.

B. generally closer to the Earth than to the Sun.

C. generally equidistant between the Earth and Sun.

D. closer to the Earth during part of the year, and closer to the Sun for the rest of the year.

123. Which of the following statements is not true?

    A. Infectious diseases are caused by viruses, bacteria, or protists.

    B. Cancers and hereditary diseases can be infectious.

    C. Environmental hazards can cause disease.

    D. The immune system protects the body from disease.

124. One advantage of using interactive videodisk technology is that students have the opportunity to actually observe demonstrations of how such phenomena as sound waves work. Teaching students by allowing them to see the natural phenomenon of sound waves taking place instead of merely offering complex theoretical descriptions of sound waves is most important for students at what stage of development?

    A. Piaget's sensorimotor stage

    B. Piaget's concrete operational stage

    C. Piaget's formal operational stage

    D. Piaget's interpersonal concordance stage

125. Which of the following choices correctly lists the first three state capitals of Illinois?

    A. Vandalia, LaSalle, Springfield

    B. Vandalia, Fort Dearborn, Kaskaskia

    C. Kaskaskia, Marion, Vandalia

    D. Kaskaskia, Vandalia, Springfield

ICTS

Illinois Certification Testing System
Elementary/Middle Grades

Practice Test Answers

Answer Key

1. (A)	33. (A)	65. (C)	97. (B)
2. (B)	34. (A)	66. (B)	98. (A)
3. (C)	35. (A)	67. (A)	99. (B)
4. (D)	36. (D)	68. (B)	100. (B)
5. (B)	37. (C)	69. (B)	101. (A)
6. (D)	38. (A)	70. (B)	102. (D)
7. (A)	39. (C)	71. (A)	103. (C)
8. (D)	40. (D)	72. (B)	104. (B)
9. (B)	41. (C)	73. (B)	105. (C)
10. (B)	42. (C)	74. (A)	106. (A)
11. (C)	43. (C)	75. (B)	107. (D)
12. (A)	44. (A)	76. (C)	108. (C)
13. (C)	45. (D)	77. (B)	109. (B)
14. (A)	46. (C)	78. (D)	110. (D)
15. (D)	47. (B)	79. (B)	111. (D)
16. (C)	48. (D)	80. (A)	112. (A)
17. (C)	49. (C)	81. (B)	113. (D)
18. (C)	50. (B)	82. (B)	114. (D)
19. (C)	51. (C)	83. (D)	115. (A)
20. (D)	52. (C)	84. (D)	116. (B)
21. (C)	53. (D)	85. (C)	117. (D)
22. (D)	54. (D)	86. (C)	118. (D)
23. (D)	55. (D)	87. (C)	119. (B)
24. (B)	56. (A)	88. (C)	120. (B)
25. (A)	57. (B)	89. (D)	121. (B)
26. (B)	58. (C)	90. (C)	122. (B)
27. (D)	59. (A)	91. (B)	123. (B)
28. (C)	60. (B)	92. (B)	124. (B)
29. (C)	61. (D)	93. (A)	125. (D)
30. (C)	62. (A)	94. (D)	
31. (A)	63. (A)	95. (A)	
32. (D)	64. (B)	96. (B)	

Detailed Explanations of Answers

1. **A**

   Semantic cueing involves using the meaning of the text and the context to figure out an unknown word. The genre of the selection, the illustrations, the reader's knowledge of the topic of the selection, and the context of the written words can provide semantic cues as the reader tries to unlock an unknown word.

2. **B**

   Syntactic cueing involves using the reader's grammatical knowledge of spoken and written language to figure out the significance of an unknown word in a text.

3. **C**

   Phonological cueing involves using the knowledge of matching written symbols with their sounds. This cueing strategy has limitations: it can be used effectively only for words where the letter patterns are known by the reader. The reader must also know how to analyze an unknown word.

4. **D**

   The pragmatic cueing system involves using the understanding that people use language differently in different contexts. This knowledge may help a reader to correctly interpret a text.

5. **B**

   The most basic definition of literacy is the ability to read and write.

6. **D**

If you look at the intersection of the production of 0 cars (that is, the y axis) with the production possibilities curve, you can see that the production of 0 cars allows for the production of 12 vans. The straight line drawn upward from 2 on the x axis (that is, the production of 2 cars) intersects the production possibilities curve at 8 on the y (van axis). Thus, the loss of production is 12 – 8 = 4 vans.

7. **A**

Scarcity necessitates choice. Consuming or producing one commodity or service means consuming or producing less of another commodity or service. The opportunity cost of using scarce resources of one commodity or service instead of another is graphically represented as a production possibility curve.

8. **D**

Both state and federal government have the power to lay and collect taxes and to borrow money. Article I, Section 8 of the Constitution establishes the powers of Congress, whereas the 10th Amendment to the Constitution (the last amendment within the Bill of Rights) sets forth the principle of reserved powers to state governments. Reading state constitutions will show that states also possess the power to lay and collect taxes.

9. **B**

Multiparty systems use an electoral system based upon proportional representation. Therefore, each party gets legislative seats in proportion to the votes it receives. In the United States the candidate who receives a plurality of the votes is declared the winner.

10. **B**

The region's mountain ranges are the main reason for both the high precipitation and varied climate.

11. **C**

There are several methods available to determine the answer. Making a sketch is a classic approach to mathematical problem solving, which is helpful here. You could draw six x's, representing the six workers:

Then you could connect each x with all other x's, counting the number of connecting lines as they were added. The connecting lines represent individual meetings.

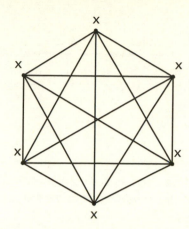

In the figure, there are 15 connecting lines, so there were 15 meetings. (You need to be sure to count the outermost lines forming the hexagon.)

Here's another approach: Worker number 1 must have had five meetings. Once she completed her fifth meeting she was done with her meetings and could be considered out of the picture for the moment. Worker number 2 also had five meetings, but you shouldn't count the one he had with worker number 1; it's already accounted for in the first worker's tally of five meetings. So worker number 2 had only **four more** new meetings. Worker number 3 had five meetings, but you shouldn't count the first two; she had only **three more** new meetings. Continuing the pattern for all six workers, you see that you need to add together 5, 4, 3, 2, and 1 meetings. This again gives the correct answer of 15 meetings.

12. **A**

Drawing a sketch with dots marking the possible locations of the two houses and The Soda Depot is a good idea. You can start with dots for the two houses, using inches for miles:

If you then draw a dot representing The Soda Depot two miles (inches) to the right of Ken's house, as in the figure that follows, you see that the greatest possible distance between Tami's house and The Soda Depot is five miles.

If you draw *The Soda Depot* dot to the left of Ken's house, as in the figure below, you see that *The Soda Depot could be as close as one mile to Tami's house, but no closer. Only statements I and III, then, are true.*

1 miles   2 miles

Tami's   Soda   Ken's
house   depot   house

13. **C**

Each combined inequality can be seen as the combination of two single inequalities. Inequality A, for instance, can be seen as the combination of the following two single inequalities:

$75 \leq x$

and

$x \leq 40.$

The meaning of a single inequality is often made clearer if you transpose the statement, placing the variable on the left. That is:

$75 \leq x$

means the same thing as

$x \geq 75.$

So, combined inequality A says that **x** *(the speeds that vehicles may drive at) is greater than or equal to 75 mph* **and** *less than or equal to 40 mph.*

You can separate combined inequalities B and D into individual inequalities in the same way:

Combined inequality B, $75 < x > 40$, *means the same as*

$x > 75$

and

$x > 40.$

That means that drivers have to drive **faster** *than 75 mph! That doesn't match what the sign says. Combined inequality D,* $40 < x > 75$ *means the same as*

$x > 40$

and

$x > 75.$

That's the same as combined inequality B.

The correct answer is C, 40 ≤ x ≤ 75, because that combined inequality means the same as

$x \geq 40$

and

$x \leq 75.$

That is, vehicles can travel at or faster than 40 mph, but no faster than 75 mph.

14. A

A bar graph works well here. The height of each of five bars would be determined by the number of votes for each lunch food.

A circle or pie chart could also be used. The 18 votes for pizza give the fraction 18/40, so pizza would be assigned 45% of the area of a circle chart, or 162°. The same approach would tell us the appropriate size of each lunch food's slice of the pie chart.

A scatter plot illustrates the relationship between sets of data. A broken-line graph generally illustrates change over time. Neither is appropriate for illustrating the given data.

15. D

In simple notation form, The Distributive Property is as follows:

$a(b + c) = (a \times b) + (a \times c)$

*This means that when multiplying, you may have some computational options. Consider answer D. The Distributive Property allows us to break 42 down into the convenient addends 2 and 40. You can then **separately** multiply each addend by 3. Thus, 3 × 2 equals 6, and 3 × 40 equals 120. We can then (courtesy of The Distributive Property) add those products together to get 126. Only answer D above is illustrative of The Distributive Property.*

16. C

Choice C, statements II and IV, is correct. You would want to (a) study the clues in the artwork for potential meaning and (b) consider the art elements and principles in the work of art. The more you know about the context in which the artist worked, the more you can appreciate the work itself. Not everything will be immediately evident, so you will want to assume the role of detective.

17. C

Choice C is the correct answer. The use of uncommon materials has dramatically changed the criteria by which one assesses visual art.

18. C

This question is focused on the large-scale objectives as stated in the Illinois standards. Therefore, it is important to look for the answer that best reflects the objectives. Answer C is the best answer because it covers all three of the objectives in at least a minimal way. Answer A is a good answer and the second best answer because it deals with several of the objectives, but the focus on creativity keeps it from being the best answer. Answers B and D are not good answers because they do not deal with the objectives.

19. C

This question focuses on a specific but very basic musical concept, pitch. Answer C is the best answer and the only correct answer. Answer A refers indirectly to the basic concept of rhythm. This relates to answer D, which is totally wrong because it is another concept and not a descriptor of the concept of pitch. Answer B is wrong because it refers directly to the basic concept of dynamics.

20. D

In creative drama, activities build upon one another and establishing a foundation of skill building activities is the norm. Beginning activities are warm-ups. These are used to introduce a session and to help players become comfortable with one another. Pantomime activities are next, as these help children to develop nonverbal communication abilities and to clearly express ideas without speaking. Without these experiences, players too often rely only upon voice for sharing ideas and for characterization. As improvisations can be done with or without speaking, they follow pantomimes. When students incorporate dialogue into their improvisations, they have a better understanding of how an actor uses voice and body as artistic tools. Improvisations also help students learn to think quickly and creatively. Story creation is next. There are multiple ways of creating stories. These can be done using unison or individual play and in pantomime or with dialogue. The result can be simple or complex stories. In order to successfully engage in story creation, students should understand characterization and plot. They should be experienced at using imagination and ensemble play. Story dramatization is the most complex creative drama activity, as it incorporates skills developed at lower levels. Here, players engage in individual rather than unison play. Story dramatizations are often student-directed activities based upon original stories or stories from literature. These require an investment of time if believable characterizations are to result. Engaging in story dramatizations encourages an understanding of both drama and literature. If one were to construct a hierarchy of creative drama activities, story dramatization would be at the top.

21. C

Teaching effective comprehension is a process that takes time and practice. It seems obvious that a student cannot comprehend a text if the text cannot be decoded. It also seems obvious that, if you want students to get better at reading, they need time to read. Students also need time and input, usually in the form of conversation, to make connections between what is read and what is already known.

22. D

Many of the classic stories for children exist in the realm of fancy because of the timeless quality of such tales. Fantasy allows children to explore places and events that have never taken place, and will never take place, yet somehow contain messages that we can discuss, savor, and learn from. Faith Ringgold, an author of books for children has stated, "One of the things you can do so well with children is to blend fantasy and reality. Kids are ready for it; they don't have to have everything lined up and real. It's not that they don't know it's not real, they just don't care."

23. **D**

Well, you've read books that begin with a spoiled princess before; doesn't it seem probable to you that Bessie will do just that?

24. **B**

If this answer isn't obvious to you, you need to read more stories that begin with an issue and a princess in place. Please consider some of the following titles: **The Paper Bag Princess** by Robert Munsch; **The Frog Prince, Continued** by Jon Scieszka; **Princess Furball** by Charlotte Huck; and **Sleeping Ugly** by Jane Yolan.

25. **A**

A K-W-L isn't just for content area lessons. Some children come to think of fairy tales as "babyish" or "girlish." This kind of discussion, laced with little chunks of stories being read aloud, helps children to recognize how delightful and charming this genre can be. It also helps them to figure out the rules of the genre, which improves their reading and writing.

26. **B**

The experiment requires a control of all variables other than the one identified in the hypothesis—exposure to microwave radiation. Seeds from different suppliers may be different; for example, one brand may be treated with a fungicide or a different fungicide. While it is likely that item III might be acceptable, without confirming that all packages are from the same year and production run, the four packages may be significantly different from each other. The best solution is to randomly divide the available seeds equally between the four test groups. Item II allows the experiment to also compare the germination rates between the different brands, but only if the seeds from each packet are isolated within each test group, and the number of seeds large enough to create a statistically significant sample.

27. **D**

The hypothesis is to evaluate seed germination as a function of microwave irradiation. Recording the overall growth or length of the seed root, while interesting, is not the stated hypothesis. Item C would be a good approach if the hypothesis were to relate seed growth to some variable, as it would more accurately reflect the growth of thicker or multiple roots in a way that root length might not measure.

28. **C**

Item I will not reflect the success of seed germination overall, one seed in a given sample may germinate early. Reporting the time until the last seed germinates would also not be useful. Item

III combines the number of all the sprouted seeds, losing the differentiation of the test groups. Items II and IV maintain the distinction between test groups and indicate the overall success rate of the germination.

29. C

The gas molecules themselves do not expand in size when heated, but the spaces between them increases as the molecules move faster. The expanding hot air leaves the balloon body through the opening at the bottom. With less air in the balloon casing, the balloon is lighter. The combustion products of propane are carbon dioxide (molar mass 44 g/mol), which is heavier than air, and water (molar mass 18 g/mol), which is lighter.

30. C

The upward force of air resistance partially counteracts the force of gravity when a feather falls in air. In a vacuum, or near vacuum, this force is dramatically reduced for the feather and both objects will fall at the same rate. The effect can be modeled without a vacuum pump by comparing the falling of two papers, one crumpled to reduce air resistance and the other flat.

31. A

The western, or Pacific, coast of Canada is known as the Cordillera region. It receives an exceptional amount of rain and includes some of the tallest and oldest trees in Canada, similar to northern California. The area is full of rugged mountains with high plateaus and desert-like areas. For more information on Canada's regions visit http://www.members.shaw.ca/kcic1/geographic.html.

32. D

Due process is the legal concept that every citizen is entitled to equal treatment under the law. The excerpt illustrates one aspect of due process, the exclusionary rule. The exclusionary rule is applied when evidence is seized in violation of due process. So the most correct answer is the exclusionary rule.

33. A

Statements III and IV are wrong. Illinois consistently ranks in the top five states in the United States with respect to dollars generated by manufacturing. (It also ranks in the top five in agriculture.) Corn and soybeans each occupy about 40 percent of cultivated land in Illinois, whereas there is relatively little wheat grown in Illinois. (Illinois ranks second in the United States in the production of both corn and soybeans.) Statement IV is true: the East St. Louis area, Decatur, Bloomington, the Quad Cities, Rockford, and Peoria (among others) have manufacturing that is significant to their local economies, but the Chicago area still does the bulk of Illinois manufacturing. Statement II is also true: Illinois' coal is the soft bituminous variety, which is no longer suitable for use because it gives off too many emissions when burned, and strip mining is much less economically feasible than it was before laws were passed that required strip mining companies to reclaim the land.

34. **A**

The main purpose of the WTO is to open world markets to all countries to promote economic development and to regulate the economic affairs between member states.

35. **A**

Overgrazing, overuse, and a lack of rainfall caused the drought of the 1930s.

36. **D**

It's true that multiplication is commutative and division isn't, but that's not relevant to them being inverse operations. Answer A doesn't address the property of being inverse.

Answer B also contains a true statement, but again, the statement is not about inverse operations.

Answer C gives a false statement. In the example shown in answer C, the order of operations tells you to compute 8 ÷ 2 first, before any multiplication.

As noted in answer D, the inverseness of two operations indeed depends upon their ability to undo each other.

37. **C**

*One way to arrive at the answer is to set up a proportion, with one corner labeled **x**:*

$$\frac{31}{x} = \frac{5.5}{100}$$

To complete the proportion (and to find the answer), we can cross-multiply 31 and 100, giving 3100, which we then divide by 5.5, giving approximately 564.

38. **A**

*The value 0.5 is equivalent to $\frac{5}{10}$ or $\frac{1}{2}$. That means that 0.5 **percent** (which is one way to read the original numeral) is the same as one-half of one percent, so answer I is correct.*

One-half of one percent can't be the same as five percent, so answer II cannot be correct.

*$\frac{1}{200}$ is equivalent to 0.5%. Here's why: One percent is equivalent to $\frac{1}{100}$ or 0.01. **Half** of one percent, (0.5%, as noted above) is therefore $\frac{1}{200}$, so answer III is correct.*

39. **C**

Complex carbohydrates are the most efficient energy source for the body. While other choices provide some energy, they are not nearly as efficient as complex carbohydrates.

40. **D**

Leaping is the only locomotor skill listed. Bouncing (A), catching (B), and throwing (C) are manipulative movements.

41. **C**

A, B, and D are principles of aerobic conditioning. C is not.

42. **C**

Miscue analysis is designed to assess the strategies that children use in their reading. Goodman was interested in the processes occurring during reading, and he believed that any departure from the written text could provide a picture of the underlying cognitive processes. Readers' miscues include substitutions of the written word with another, additions, omissions, and alterations to the word sequence.

43. **C**

This is the next step in the writing process.

44. **A**

There is a direct relationship between what is taught in school and what is learned in school. Also, if you want children to improve in writing, they need time to write.

45. **D**

This teacher is doing a good thing by collecting data and displaying the data. I hope this teacher also shared the findings with the children, their parents, and anybody else who would look at it. Look how successful the literacy program is!

46. **C**

Clearly setting a purpose for listening, asking questions about the selection, and encouraging students to forge links between the new information and knowledge already in place are all supported by research as effective strategies.

47. **B**

Asking children to complete a graphic organizer as they research an issue helps them keep organized, helps them see connections, and helps them pull together what they can then use in some interesting and meaningful way.

48. **D**

Children learn more from a text if the teacher helps them figure out how the book was put together. It makes the text more understandable. It also helps them to read the text critically, as part of the conversation can address the issue of what is missing in the text.

49. **C**

*The **total price** of the two items in the original problem is given as $2.59, hinting that equation B or C may be correct. (In both cases, $2.59 is shown as **the sum of** two values.)*

*Examine the right side of equation C: You note that one value is $1.79 higher than the other. That is, in equation C, **x** could stand for the price of the pencil, and (**x** + 1.79) could stand for the price of the more expensive pen. Hence, equation C is the right one. None of the others fit the information given.*

50. **B**

*One way to approach the problem is to examine each scenario for reasonableness. Regardless of a runner's mile-by-mile pace in a marathon, the runner continually increases the distance covered, and the graph will always move upward, so situation I doesn't go with the graph in problem 10. The number of households a census taker has left to visit **decreases** with each visit, so situation II doesn't fit either.*

*Both situations III and IV are examples of **steady growth**, so both match the graph. Answer B is therefore correct.*

51. **C**

Historical almanacs contain yearly data of certain events, including the time at sunrise and sunset along with weather-related data and statistics. Historical atlases contain a collection of historical maps. These maps may or may not include population data. Historical population data may best be found in government publications on the census. An encyclopedia article would contain a factual summary of the colonial period and the American Revolution, but may not include an analysis of the role of Fort Mackinaw during the American Revolution, as encyclopedias attempt to give overviews rather than interpretations or analysis. A secondary source on Michigan during the colonial period may better address this question. Information on when the first treaty was signed and the terms of the treaty would most likely appear in a history book or government publication.

52. **C**

The Nile River's flooding was more predictable than rainfall in Greece was.

53. **D**

Data showing productivity will directly measure the prosperity and viability of farming in an area.

54. **D**

Red light is refracted less, having a longer wavelength. This is the basis for our observation of a red sunrise or red sunset as light passes through more of the atmosphere than at midday. The high number of particles in a polluted or particulate laden atmosphere leads to intense red sunsets as the more refractive blue wavelengths are refracted away from view. Differences in refraction are also the basis of TV commercials for sunglasses with yellow lenses that improve the clarity of vision. As light from an object passes through the lens of the eye, the blue wavelengths are refracted more and may be focused before reaching the retina while the longer wavelengths are focused on the retina. Multiple images within the eye leads to the perception of a blurred image. Yellow glasses that filter out the blue wavelengths eliminate one image and give the perception of sharper, clearer vision for the wearer.

55. **D**

Early doses of pesticide were strong enough to kill most of the insects, only a few survived who, perhaps because of some genetic trait, had a slightly higher tolerance to the poison. When these pesticide tolerant insects reproduced they passed the tolerance to their offspring. Higher doses of pesticide are initially effective, but again a few individuals survive with tolerance to that new level. Control of pest populations generally requires access to a variety of pesticides that work through different mechanisms, and which are applied in such a way as to minimize buildup of tolerance in the insect population.

56. **A**

The physical movement and accumulation of sand is not part of the rock cycle, because no transformation of rock type is involved.

57. **B**

The statement "Movement basics include body, space, time, and relationship" is the correct answer because this describes only the dimensions of dance movement; in no way does it speak to how dance reflects the culture of which it is part.

58. **C**

Choice C is the correct answer. This is collage.

59. **A**

It is large, frontal, and drawn in high contrast.

60. **B**

In offering criticism of the play, students should give opinions that not only reveal how they feel about what they saw but also the reasons for their opinions. In other words, they should be able to support their judgments based upon their personal aesthetic. Both II and IV are supported opinions that show an appreciation for the theatrical elements of character and plot. These also reveal connections to the viewer's emotions and life experiences. Choice I is an unsupported opinion and is, therefore, incorrect. III is a response to the theatre building in which the play was presented rather than a response to the play, and it is the latter that Mr. Nelson wants his students to give.

61. **D**

Both the personal correspondence of a military man stationed with the 5th RCT in Korea and an interview with Secretary of Defense George Marshall are primary sources, as they involve correspondence or testimony from individuals who were actually involved with the Korean War.

62. **A**

Although a few Ojibwe came to northern Illinois in the late 1700s, they were to the north and east of Illinois before 1700. The Miami, although a predominantly Indiana tribe, did have some groups in northern Illinois beginning from about 1650. The Kaskaskia were a member of the Illinois Confederacy (Illini), and the Mississippians were the mound builders who came to Illinois in about 500 CE.

63. **A**

The responsibility for public education belongs to the state governments. The federal government has often passed legislation to regulate and provide funds for public education, but the main responsibility for establishing and regulating education resides with the state governments.

64. **B**

A limited money supply and rising prices were major causes of the Great Depression. The money supply was most affected by the Gold Standard and the Smoot-Hawley Tariff further affected consumer prices.

65. **C**

Choice C is correct because this is the definition of illiterate and functional illiterate stated in paragraph two. Choice A cannot be correct because the passage clearly distinguishes between illiterates and functional illiterates. Choice B is not correct because the definition stated is not related to participation in a program. The relative number of illiterates and functional illiterates is not discussed, so choice D is incorrect.

66. **B**

Choice B is correct because the passage begins by stating that many politicians' wives have expressed interest in literacy. Choice A is incorrect because the author of the passage does not suggest that only women are interested. Choice C is incorrect because the passage does not discuss the number of male or female illiterates. Choice D is incorrect because there is no discussion in the passage of politicians' wives giving speeches.

67. **A**

This question must be answered using the process of elimination. You are asked to select a statement that names a possible program component which is not characteristic of successful literacy programs. Choice A is correct because choices B, C, and D are specifically mentioned in the passage.

68. **B**

Choice B is correct because the author specifically states that politicians should support increased funding for literacy programs. Choices A and C are incorrect because the author states that funding should be increased. There is no discussion of funding for different programs, so choice D is incorrect.

69. **B**

First, it is helpful to view the shaded area as **the area of the square minus the area of the circle.** *With that in mind, you simply need to find the area of each simple figure, and then subtract one from the other.*

You know that the radius of the circle is 6 units in length. That tells you that the diameter of the circle is 12 units. Because the circle is inscribed in the square (meaning that the circle fits inside of the square touching in as many places as possible), you see that the sides of the square are each 12 units in length. Knowing that, you compute that the area of the square is 144 square units (12 × 12).

Using the formula for finding the area of a circle (πr^2), and using 3.14 for π, you get approximately 113 square units. (3.14 × 6 × 6). Then, you subtract 113 (the area of the circle) from 144 (the area of the square) for the answer of 31.

70. **B**

If you can fold a two-dimensional figure so that one side exactly matches or folds onto the other side, the fold line is a line of symmetry. The figure below is a non-square rectangle with its two lines of symmetry shown.

One might think that lines drawn from opposite corners are lines of symmetry, but they're not. The two halves would be the same size and shape, but wouldn't fold onto each other.

Note that the question asked about non-square rectangles. Squares (which **are** *rectangles) have* **four** *lines of symmetry.*

71. **A**

To answer the question, you must recognize that triangles ADB and AEC are similar triangles, meaning that they have the same shape. That means that the corresponding angles of the two triangles are the same, or congruent, and that corresponding sides of the two triangles are proportional. Given that, you can set up the following proportion, where **x** is the distance from point A to point C:

$$\frac{3}{7} = \frac{5}{x}$$

Solving the proportion by cross-multiplication, you see that the length of segment AC is about 11.7. Knowing that the length of segment AB is 7 feet, you subtract to find the length of BC (11.7 – 7 = 4.7).

72. **B**

Statement I is true because the winner **could be** Mr. Greenfield and it **could be** someone else. Statement II is not true, even though Mr. Greenfield bought many more tickets than any other individual. He still has a block of only 300; there are 700 ticket stubs in the drum that aren't his. This tells us that statement III is true.

Finally, statement IV is false. Don't confuse the true statement "all **tickets** have an equal chance of winning" with the false statement that "all **persons** have an equal chance of winning."

73. **B**

Not all atoms of an element are identical in mass, which is primarily the sum of the protons and neutrons. Isotopes, atoms with the same atomic number and thus the same element, vary only in the number of neutrons. The atomic masses listed on the periodic table represent the weighted average of the naturally occurring isotopes for each element. For example, most carbon atoms have a mass of 12 atomic mass units (amu), less than 1% have a mass of 14 amu. The average atomic mass of carbon is thus 12.011 amu.

74. **A**

Force is equal to mass multiplied by acceleration (F = ma). The force needed is the product of the objects mass (20,000 lbs) and the acceleration. Acceleration is the change in speed per unit of time. The projectile's acceleration is thus (12,000 yards/second – 0 yards/second) / 0.05 seconds).

75. **B**

The force of gravity is inversely proportional to the square of the distance; thus, doubling the distance reduces the gravitational force by a factor of 4. The mass reduction for this object at the top of the atmosphere, just forty miles above the surface, would be insignificant. However, experience tells us that objects are "weightless" in the space shuttle. This apparent weightlessness is a result of a balance between the forward motion of the shuttle and the gravitational attraction of the Earth. Both the shuttle and the objects in it are moving forward together at a high rate of speed, and falling together under the force of gravity. They are "weightless" only relative to each other. Were the shuttle to cease forward motion it would fall directly and precipitously to Earth under the unrelenting force of gravity.

76. C

Black line spectra are formed when the continuous spectra of the Sun passes through the atmosphere. The elements in the atmosphere absorb wavelengths of light characteristic of their spectra (these are the same wavelengths given off when the element is excited, for example the red color of a Neon light). By examining the line spectral gaps scientists can deduce the elements that make up the distant atmosphere. Item A is true, but it explains the source of a line spectrum. Item B is true, and it explains why a blue shirt is blue when placed under a white or blue light source. Recall that a blue shirt under a red light source will appear black because there are no blue wavelengths to be reflected. Item D is a partial truth, black lights do give off ultraviolet light that the human eye cannot see.

77. B

Salt is a strong electrolyte that completely dissociates in solution. When this solution is in contact with a semi-permeable membrane, like the inflamed cells in the throat, water moves across the membrane from the side with lowest solute concentration to the side of higher solute concentration. In the case of the sore throat, water from inside the inflamed cells moves out toward the higher concentration salt water and the throat cells shrink due to the loss of water. All the items listed are colligative properties that, like osmotic pressure, are a function of the number, but not the nature, of particles in solution.

78. D

Lincoln's immediate purpose in announcing the Emancipation Proclamation was to rally flagging Northern morale. Lincoln waited until after a major Union victory, at Antietam in 1862, so he couldn't be accused of making the announcement as an act of desperation. He recognized that the costs of the war had reached a point where preserving the Union would not be a powerful enough reason to motivate many Northerners to continue the war. Framing the war as a war against slavery would have mobilized powerful abolitionist forces in the North and perhaps create an atmosphere of a "holy crusade" rather than one of using war to resolve a political conflict.

While the Emancipation Proclamation had the announced purpose of freeing the slaves, Lincoln himself indirectly stated that freeing the slaves was a means to a greater end, preserving the Union. In a statement released before the Emancipation Proclamation, Lincoln asserted, "If I could save the Union without freeing any slave I would do it, and if I could save it by freeing all the slaves I would do it. . . What I do about slavery, and the colored race, I do because I believe it helps to save the Union."

79. B

In the 1857 case **Dred Scott v. Sanford,** the Supreme Court held that no black slave could be a citizen of the United States. It was in the 1954 case **Brown v. Topeka Board of Education** that *the court held separate facilities for the races to be unconstitutional (choice A). The reverse—choice C—was the court's holding in the 1896 case* **Plessy v. Ferguson.** *Affirmative action (choice D) was limited in the 1970s and 1980s.*

80. **A**

Thomas Paine wrote several pamphlets before and during the American Revolution. **Common Sense** *was the most significant because it carefully documented abuses of the British parliamentary system of government, particularly in its treatment of the American colonies. Paine portrayed a brutish monarchy interested only in itself and pointedly argued how independence would improve the colonies' long-term situation. His argument was directed at the common man, and it struck a chord unlike anything previously written in the colonies. Its publication in 1774 was perfect in reaching the public at just the moment that their questions and concerns regarding British rule were peaking. The answers provided in Paine's essays were pivotal in the subsequent behavior of many colonists who, until that time, had been unsure of what they believed regarding independence and British rule.*

Answer B is incorrect. Paine wrote another essay called **American Crisis** *during the winter of 1776. This essay, not* **Common Sense,** *helped rally American spirits during that long, demoralizing winter. Answers C and D are also incorrect. Paine wrote to an American, not a British audience. He also wrote* **Common Sense** *well before American independence was achieved.*

81. **B**

Permanent dietary changes and exercise are the only way to produce lasting weight loss. Commercial diets (A) do not always include a program of exercise, but rather concentrate on diet. Radically reducing calorie intake (C) will cause the body to go into starvation mode and slow down digestion to conserve energy. Two hours of daily exercise (D) is not very practical and without controlling calorie intake, it would be ineffective.

82. **B**

Vitamin C is water soluble—the remaining choices are fat soluble.

83. **D**

The grip strength test (C), pull-ups (for boys) (A), and flexed arm hang (for girls) (B), are all tests to measure muscular strength and endurance. The sit and reach test measures flexibility.

84. **D**

The correct choice is D, statements I, II, III, and IV. Dance can reflect the religion of a culture in many ways on account of its deep historical roots in religious tradition.

85. **C**

The Waltz, Lindy Hop, and the Twist each reflect changes in social attitudes of their time.

86. **C**

Genes are the sections of the DNA molecule that determine specific traits.

87. **C**

Nuclear energy is nonrenewable. Nuclear energy has potential advantages in providing large quantities of energy from a small amount of source material, but once the process of radioactive decay is nonreversible.

88. **C**

The force of friction between the book and the table is the primary force that must be overcome to move the book. An experiment to study these frictional forces could keep all other variables (size and weight of the book, speed of travel) constant while measuring the force needed to move the book using a spring scale. Different experiments could change the surface of the book by covering the book with wax paper, construction paper, or sandpaper.

89. **D**

A liquid will boil when its vapor pressure, which depends on temperature, is equal to the atmospheric pressure above the liquid. At high altitudes the atmospheric pressure is lower, thus water will boil at a lower temperature. The boiling point of water is only 100°C at 1 atmosphere pressure (760 torr). In Leadville, Colorado, elevation 10,150, when the atmospheric pressure may be as low as 430 torr, the boiling point of water may be 89°C. The lower temperature increases cooking times.

90. **C**

The use of instructional strategies that make learning relevant to individual student interests is a powerful motivating force that facilitates learning and independent thinking. Choices A and B are both important factors to consider during a brainstorming session of this type, but both of these factors should influence the teacher only after the student interests have been included. Choice D indicates a misunderstanding of the situation described. The students are setting the objectives for the unit as they brainstorm questions.

91. **B**

Choice is an important element in motivating students to learn. Answer A is contradictory to the stated purpose of the activity. The students proposed the questions, so covering all the questions should not be a problem. Choice C is incorrect because the students have chosen what they consider to be key questions; the teacher should select different or additional key questions. Choice D is a possibility, but only if there is a specific reason why all the students should not research all the questions.

92. **B**

The best way to teach children to read, regardless of grade level, is to use a program of emergent literacy that includes pattern books and journal writing with invented spelling. Choice A is incorrect because, although an intensive phonics program that includes drill and practice seatwork on basic sight words may be effective with some students, it is not the most effective way to teach all students to read. Choice D is incorrect because an ESL program is intended to provide assistance to only those students who are learning English as a second language. Additionally, the learning resource teacher should provide assistance to only those students who have been identified as having a learning disability that qualifies them to receive services.

93. **A**

By selecting books for the classroom library that match students' independent reading abilities, the teacher is recognizing that students must improve their reading ability by beginning at their own level and progressing to more difficult materials. Choice B is incorrect because books that are challenging will most likely be frustrating to at least some of the students. Choice C is incorrect because the presence or absence of separate word lists should not be a determining factor in selecting books for a classroom library. Choice D is incorrect because all children need access to a classroom library regardless of their reading abilities.

94. **D**

It is helpful to compute Matt's current average. Adding up his scores, you get 522. Dividing that by 6 (the number of scores), you find that his average is 87%. Similarly, you can multiply 90 by 6 to compute the number of total points it would take to have an average of 90 (90 × 6 = 540). Matt only earned 522 points, so he was 18 shy of the A–.

95. **A**

The only way carpet from a 16-foot-wide roll will cover Ms. Williams' floor without seams is if she buys 20 feet of it. She can then trim the 16-foot width to 14 feet so that it fits her floor. Buying 20 feet of a 16-foot-wide roll means that she will have to buy 320 square feet. Her living room has an area of only 280 square feet (14 feet × 20 feet), so she'll be wasting 40 square feet (320 – 280), but no more.

96. **B**

The keystrokes indicate multiplication, and only answer B involves multiplication. Multiplication is hidden within the concept of interest. One way to compute a new savings account balance after interest has been earned is to multiply the original balance by (1 + the rate of interest). In this case, that's first 1.03, then 1.04. The keystrokes match that multiplication.

97. **B**

The Silk Road was a transcontinental trade route that branched out over a vast area, including A, western China; C, northern Iran; D, northern India; and eventually the Sahara.

98. **A**

Democracy is the correct response because it is the antithesis of the authoritarianism of fascism. Indeed, the totalitarian, romantic, militaristic, and nationalistic characteristics were, in large part, a reaction against the perceived inadequacies of democracy.

99. **B**

The industrial economy of the nineteenth century was not based upon an equitable distribution of profits among all those who were involved in production. Marxists and other critics of capitalism condemned the creed of capitalists and the abhorrent conditions of the industrial proletariat. Raw materials, a constant labor supply, capital, and an expanding marketplace were critical elements in the development of the industrial economy.

100. **B**

The term "Trail of Tears" is used to describe the relocation of the Cherokee tribe from the southern Appalachians to what is now Oklahoma. The migration of Mormons from Nauvoo, Illinois, to the Great Salt Lake in Utah, the westward movements along the Oregon Trail, and, much earlier, the Wilderness Road, all took place and could at times be as unpleasant as the Cherokees' trek. They were, however, more voluntary than the Cherokee migration and therefore did not earn such sad titles as the "Trail of Tears."

101. **A**

A is the best answer, since the term "casework" is used by political scientists to describe the activities of congressmen on behalf of individual constituents. These activities might include helping an elderly person secure social security benefits, or helping a veteran obtain medical services. Most casework is actually done by congressional staff and may take as much as a third of the staff's time. Congressmen supply this type of assistance for the good public relations it provides. Answer B fails because pork barrel legislation is rarely if ever intended to help individual citizens. Pork barrel legislation authorizes federal spending for special projects, such as airports, roads, or dams, in the home state or district of a congressman. It is meant to help the entire district or state. Also, there is no legal entitlement on the part of a citizen to a pork barrel project, such as there is with social security benefits. C is not the answer because lobbying is an activity directed towards congressmen, not one done by congressmen. A lobbyist attempts to get congressmen to support legislation that will benefit the group that the lobbyist represents. Logrolling, D, is incorrect, because it does not refer to a congressional service for constituents. It refers instead to the congressional practice of trading votes on different bills. Congressman A will vote for Congressman B's pork barrel project and in return B will vote for A's pork barrel project.

102. **D**

All are correctly matched.

103. **C**

The frequency of a wave is associated with pitch. Middle C has a frequency of 440 cycles per second. However, wavelength and frequency are directly related by the relationship $\nu = c\,/\,\lambda$ where ν (nu) is the frequency, c is the speed of sound, and λ (lambda) is wavelength.

104. **B**

Reptiles are not generally warm-blooded; all other statements are correct.

105. **C**

The total area of the larger rectangle is

base × height = 12 × 9 = 108 sq. ft.

Therefore, the area of the shaded portion surrounding the inner rectangle is

108 sq. ft. – 80 sq. ft. = 28 sq. ft.

If the total cost of material used to cover the shaded area is $56 and we have 28 sq. ft., the cost per square foot is $\frac{\$56}{28 \text{ sq. ft.}}$ = $2.00 per square foot.

Answers A, B, and D are incorrect. Neither I nor II is necessary to determine the cost per square foot of the shaded area. D is incorrect because III is needed to determine the cost per sq foot.

106. **A**

In order to solve this problem we must first add the number of freshman girls to the number of sophomore girls (21 + 15). In order to find the percentage we divide this sum by the total number of students in the chorus and multiply by 100.

$$\frac{21+15}{132} \times 100 = \% \text{ of freshman and sophomore girls in chorus}$$

Answer B is incorrect; in order to find the percentage we need to multiply the fraction by 100, not divide by 100. Answers C and D are incorrect because the number of freshman and sophomore girls must be divided by the total number of students in the chorus. We then multiply by 100 to get the percent.

107. **D**

Excess cholesterol found in the blood typically comes from cholesterol in a diet rather than internal production. Cholesterol, which is produced in the liver (C), plays a vital role in brain function (A) and is important for creating certain hormones (B).

108. **C**

Table tennis is scored to 21 and must be won by a margin of two points. In doubles play for badminton, the winner must score 15 points (A). Singles badminton is also scored to 21 points with a margin of two points needed for victory.

109. **B**

Exercising cardiovascularly for a minimum of 20 minutes per session, as part of an exercise program, will lead to effective physical results with a proper nutritional diet. Forty-five minutes (D) is an effective time period when performing a weight-lifting exercise session.

110. **D**

Comprehension is shown when the reader questions his or her intent for reading. For example, one may be reading a story to find out what terrible things may befall the main character. The rationale for choosing a book may be an interesting bit of information (A), but it is not a major topic of discussion with the students. Sharing personal information (B) creates a certain bond, but this is not directly relevant to the question. It is also important that all students are on-task before the beginning of a lesson (C), but this is a smaller part of the skill modeled in response D.

111. **D**

When a mixed-level pair read together, the remedial student receives instruction and the skilled student receives reinforcement. It uses alternative teaching resources, the students themselves, to enhance the learning environment. A certain goal, comprehension, has been set (A), but this is not the most likely outcome. The teacher will need to observe fewer groups (B), but it is unlikely that this will change the time needed to work with all groups as long as quality is to be maintained. Although reading in pairs, each student should have a book, and it would be impractical to permit another teacher to utilize the books while one teacher is using them (C).

112. **A**

By mapping out previous knowledge, information already known can be transferred to support new information. Although words on the board are visual (B), this is not the underlying motive. Semantic mapping done at the beginning of a story tests how much prior knowledge the students have about the topic at the outset (C). This does model proper use of words (D), but this is not the main intent of the exercise.

113. **D**

You should note that the student is failing to carry in both the ones and tens places. 56 + 97 is being treated as 5 + 9 and 6 + 7. The two answers are then combined for a total of 1413.

Choice A is the standard answer. It is eliminated, since there is no error pattern. Choice C exhibits switching from addition to subtraction (9 – 8 = 1) and (8 – 3 = 5). Also, the child subtracts the top number from the bottom one on the first step. In choice B the child subtracts 8 from 9, and also 3 from 8, and then adds to the 8 in the tens place. Only choice D illustrates the pattern of recording the sum and not carrying. The correct answer is D.

114. **D**

You should first count the number of spaces on the dial. There are 10 spaces. Five spaces equals 90 units, and 90 divided by 5 is 18 units. Each space is worth 18 units. The needle points to about halfway between the marks numbered 6 and 7. Thus, one half of 18, plus 6 times 18, is 117. Choice D is the correct reading.

115. A

You know that ten thousand contains 4 zeros, or 10^4 in place value. One million contains 10^6, or six zeros. You may divide out 10,000 into one million, but that is the laborious way to solve this. Choice A is correct.

116. B

You are challenged to analyze which data you would need to calculate the cost of feeding 2 cats for 7 days. If you calculate the cost for one cat for 7 days, then double the answer, you will have an approximate cost for 2 cats. The total cost for one cat is the cost of a can of food, times the number of cans of food eaten each day by one cat, times 7 days.

117. D

This question deals with the idea of conserving information, which is one of the concepts dealt with in the discussion of the first objective—to "understand historical, cultural, and societal contexts for the visual and performing arts (art, music, drama/theatre, dance)." In order to employ teaching techniques effectively, it is important to understand when a child is ready for that technique. Most children are not able to conserve information until fifth or sixth grade. So, answer D is correct. Since some children will begin conserving information earlier, answer C could be considered partially correct, but is certainly not the best answer.

118. D

This question focuses on a basic musical concept, "harmony." Harmony is the performance of two or more different pitches simultaneously. Therefore, when looking at the answers provided, it is good to begin by eliminating answers that have nothing to do with pitch. A rhythm instrument is a non-pitched instrument in almost all cases, so choice I is not pitch-related and that means that answers A and B are eliminated because they both include choice I. Since two or more different pitches must be performed simultaneously to have harmony, choice III can also be eliminated because there are two performers, but not two different pitches. That eliminates answer C and leaves answer D as the best and correct answer.

119. B

Through this question, a person will demonstrate their understanding of the difference between the concept of steady beat and the concept of rhythm. Answers B and C are both good answers, but the best answer is B because each of the syllables listed falls on a strong pulse (i.e., the beat) when spoken or sung. Answer C is made up of words that fall on the beat, but highlights larger segments encompassing multiple beats. Answer D highlights the beginnings of lines with no regard for the beat and answer A has no regard for the beat at all.

120. B

One of the virtues of using drama/theatre with young people is that it challenges them to think independently and creatively. Often, there is not one right answer or interpretation. Using the same material in a variety of ways offers the following advantages: (1) Information is presented through multiple channels, thereby increasing opportunities for knowing; (2) Using different types of dramatic activities broadens both the appeal of and the learning opportunities inherent in the material; (3) Multiple formats increase opportunities to engage students and to address their learning styles; (4) Students can see that there are various ways of creating meaning and expressing ideas. Answer A is incorrect because there may not be only one correct way to use material. As the rationale for the correct answer implies, exploring content is one way to move students beyond the obvious and encourage them to use higher-level thinking skills. Answer C is incorrect because it requires a value judgment based upon personal preference; it is not grounded in fact. Likewise, D is incorrect because it reflects a value judgment that is without substance. Some students may learn more by directly participating in activities; some may learn more by watching a performance. Both creative drama activities and theatre performances are educationally sound undertakings.

121. B

Expansion occurring on the ocean floor along the Mid-Atlantic ridge presses creates pressure around the edges of the Pacific Plate creating geologic instability where the Pacific Plate collides with the continental plates on all sides.

122. B

The Moon is much closer to the Earth than to any other planet or the Sun.

123. B

Diseases caused by viruses, bacteria, or protists that invade the body are called infectious diseases. These disease-causing organisms are collectively referred to as germs. Cancers and hereditary diseases are not infectious.

124. B

Children operating at the concrete operating stage greatly benefit from direct observation. Infants operate at the sensorimotor stage; observing a demonstration of how sound waves work would be of no use to infants (A). While students operating at the formal operational level would greatly benefit from direct observation of sound waves in addition to complex theoretical descriptions, the direct observation is absolutely essential to the understanding of the concrete thinker (C). There is no Piagetial interpersonal concordance stage. Interpersonal concordance is a stage of moral development described by Lawrence Kohlberg (D).

125. D

Kaskaskia (1818–20), Vandalia (1820–39), and Springfield are the only three capitals Illinois has had.

Index

K

Keywords, 220
Kilogram, 235
Kilometer, 235

L

Language
    cueing systems, 207–208
    mastery of, 207
    social and cultural restraints on, 208
Language arts and literacy (Basic Skills
        Test), 33–78
    adjectives and adverbs, 68–72
    capitalization, 53–54
    grammar and usage, testing objectives,
        34
    modifiers, misplaced and dangling, 38–39
    parallelism, 37–38
    pronouns, 54–61
    punctuation, 42–53
    purpose of, 33
    questions, 36–37
    reading passages, 35–36
    run-on/fused sentences, 40–41
    sentence fragments, 40
    sentence structure, 37–42
    subordination, coordination, and
        predication, 41–42
    test format, 33
    test-taking strategies, 33
    transitions and coherence, 74–78
    verbs, 61–68
    writing, testing objectives, 33, 34–35
    word choice, 72–74
Language arts and literacy (Elementary/
        Middle Grades Review), 207–222
    genre, 214–217
    listening and speaking processes, 221–
        222
    reading competence, development of,
        208–210
    reading comprehension, 212–214
    research skills and strategies, 219–221
    vocabulary building, 210–212
    writing process, 217–219

Learning to Read: The Great Debate, 208
Letter groups, 211
Life science, teaching of
    cells, 244
    classification, 245
    ecology, 246–247
    evolution, 245–246
    heredity, 245
    testing objectives, 244
Light, 252
Line graphs, 26–27, 92, 96
Listening and speaking skills, 221–222, 280
Liter, 235
Literacy, defined, 208
Literal comprehension, 212
Locomotor skills, 298
Low-impact aerobics, 294

M

Main idea questions, 19–20
Manipulative skills, 298
Mass, 248
Mathematical operations, order of, 94
Mathematical reasoning processes, 240–
    241
Mathematics (Basic Skills Test)
    basic number skills, 92–95
    data analysis, 95–100
    geometric figures, problems involving,
        109–111
    notation symbols, 94
    one- and two-variable equations, solving,
        106–107
    operations with algebraic expressions,
        107–108
    reasoning skills, application of, 111–113
    test-taking objectives, 91–92
    two-dimensional graphing, 100–105
    word problems, 95, 107
Mathematics (Elementary/Middle Grades
    Review)
    algebraic concepts and methods, 233–
        235
    conversions, 230
    geometry, 236–239